Documents in World History

VOLUME 2

SAINT IGNATIUS COLLEGE PREPARATORY

JOHN STIEGELER

2001 - 37th Avenue
San Francisco, California 94116

Tel. (415) 731-7500
Fax (415) 731-2227

DOCUMENTS IN WORLD HISTORY

Volume 2

The Modern Centuries: From 1500 to the Present

SECOND EDITION

Peter N. Stearns
George Mason University

Stephen S. Gosch
University of Wisconsin, Eau Claire

Erwin P. Grieshaber
Mankato State University

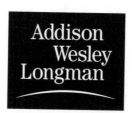

An imprint of Addison Wesley Longman, Inc.

New York • Reading, Massachusetts • Menlo Park, California • Harlow, England
Don Mills, Ontario • Sydney • Mexico City • Madrid • Amsterdam

Editor-in-Chief: Priscilla McGeehon

Development Editor: Joy Hilgendorf

Executive Marketing Manager: Sue Westmoreland

Supplements Editor: Joy Hilgendorf

Full Service Production Manager: Mark Naccarelli

Project Coordination and Text Design: Nesbitt Graphics, Inc.

Electronic Page Makeup: Nesbitt Graphics, Inc.

Cover Design Manager: Nancy Danahy

Cover Designer: Silvers Design

Cover: Painted cotton cloth costume worn by Senufo Poro society masquerader. Werner/Forman/Art Resource, NY

Art Studio: Mapping Specialists Limited

Photo Researcher: Photosearch, Inc.

Senior Print Buyer: Hugh Crawford

Printer and Binder: The Maple Vail Book Manufacturing Group

Cover Printer: Coral Graphics

Library of Congress Cataloging-in-Publication Data

Stearns, Peter N.
    Documents in world history / Peter N. Stearns, Stephen S. Gosch,
Erwin P. Grieshaber, — 2nd ed.
      p. cm.
    Contents: v. 1. The great traditions, from ancient times to 1500 —
v. 2. Modern centuries, from 1500 to the present.
    ISBN 0-321-03856-8 (pbk. : v. 1). — ISBN 0-321-03857-6 (pbk. : v. 2)
    1. World history—Sources. I. Gosch, Stephen S. (Stephen
Spencer), 1941–   . II. Grieshaber, Erwin P. (Erwin Peter), 1943–   .
III. Title.
D5.D623   1999
909—DC21   99-25704
                                      CIP

Please visit our website at http://www.awlonline.com

ISBN 0-321-03857-6

5678910-MA-0201

Contents

Geographical Contents:
The Major Societies

China and Japan

Latin America

Sub-Saharan Africa

Topical Contents

Preface

This volume focuses on the major currents in the development of the modern world—not just the American or Western world, but the wider world in which we live today. It deals with the interaction between established civilizations and new forces of change, many of them springing from intensifications of international commerce and the results of industrialization, and with the impact of change on loyalties and beliefs, on social institutions and the conditions of various groups such as workers and women, and on the activities and the organization of the state.

The book examines the formation of the modern world not through an overview or through scholarly interpretation, but by presenting primary sources—that is, documents written at the time. Such an approach is inherently selective, leaving many important developments out; and it is meant to be combined with some kind of textbook coverage. But primary source documents do convey elements of the flavor and tensions of history in the making that cannot be captured by a progression of names, dates, and main events or trends. The book presents what people—great and ordinary—expressed in various societies in the modern periods, and it challenges the reader to distill the meaning of these expressions.

The various documents offered illustrate characteristic features of key civilizations in the major modern stages of world history from about 1500 c.e. to the present. These documents were not written for posterity; some were not even intended for a wide audience at the time. They are collected here to plumb the depths of history and raise issues of understanding and interpretation that can enliven and enrich the study of world history.

The book covers several key facets of the human experience, again in various times and places. It deals with the organization and functions of the state. It treats philosophy and religion and, at points, literature and science. It explores contacts among civilizations, particularly the diverse impacts of Western imperialism and international commercial expansion and heightened cultural interchange in recent centuries. It also deals with families and women and with issues of social structure.

The book's organization facilitates relating it to a core textbook. Major civilizations—East Asia, the West, India, the Middle East, Eastern Europe, Africa, and Latin America—are represented with several readings. Thus a course can trace elements of change and continuity within each civilization. The readings are divided into three modern periods: 1500 to 1750, during which the rise of the West and diverse reactions to the rise formed a central thread in world history; 1750 to 1914, a century dominated by new patterns of manufacturing, new international technologies for transportation and communication, and new cultural forces such as nationalism; and the twentieth century, during which Western influence continued strong but the other major civilizations also began to find their own distinctive modern voices.

The goal of the book is not, however, maximum coverage. Many interesting and significant documents are left out, of necessity. Readings have been chosen that illustrate important features of an area or period, that raise challenging problems of interpretation, and that—at least in many cases—express some charm and human drama. The readings also invite comparisons across cultures and over time. Chapter introductions not only identify the readings but also raise some issues that can be explored. Study Questions at the end of each chapter further facilitate an understanding of issues.

This book was prepared by three world history teachers at work in several kinds of institutions. It is meant, correspondingly, to serve the needs of different kinds of students. It is motivated by two common purposes: first, a strong belief that some perspective on the world is both desirable and possible as a key element in contemporary American education; and second, that an understanding of world history can be greatly enhanced by exposure not just to an overall factual and interpretive framework but also to the kinds of challenges and insights raised by primary materials, written not by scholars but by people actually living out the diverse and changing patterns we are grappling to understand.

Dealing with primary sources is not an easy task. Precisely because the materials are not written with American college students in mind, they require some thought. They must be related to other elements we know about a particular society; they must be given meaning; and they must be evaluated more carefully than a secondary account or textbook designed deliberately to pinpoint what should be learned. By the same token, however, gaining ease with the meaning of primary sources is a skill that carries well beyond a survey history course, into all sorts of research endeavors. Gaining such skill in the context of the civilizations that compose the world goes some distance toward understanding how our world has become what it is—which is, in essence, the central purpose of history.

Thanks go to the reviewers of this edition. They are Professor Jolane Culhane, Western New Mexico University; Professor Susan Hult, Houston Community College Central; Professor Gary Land, Andrews University; Mary Lauranne Lifka, Lewis University; Professor William Rodner, Tidewater Community College; Professor Arthur Schmidt, Temple University; Professor Marvin Slind, Washington State University; and Professor Andrew Zimmerman, University of California–San Diego.

Peter N. Stearns

Documents in World History

History

VOLUME 2

Introduction

The past five centuries have been a busy time in world history. Many Americans, accustomed to a culture that emphasizes change, believe that the modern age has witnessed more fundamental shifts, coming at a more rapid pace, than any other time in the human past. Although the notion of accelerating change may be somewhat exaggerated, it is true that relationships among major areas of the world (including the gradual integration of the Americas into a wide network), basic technologies, belief systems, forms of government, and even fundamental ingredients of daily life such as the relationship between men and women have changed mightily, not only in the United States and Western civilization but in every major society in the world. This volume, with selected documents on a number of significant areas of change, conveys something of the flavor of the modern world in transition.

The need to study modern world history becomes increasingly apparent. Although the twentieth century was hailed as the "American century," it is obvious that given the United States' claim to some world leadership, it must interact with various other societies, and in part on their terms. As a power with worldwide military responsibilities or aspirations, the United States maintains increasingly close diplomatic contacts with all the inhabited continents. Economically, American reliance on exports and imports—once a minor footnote to the nation's industrial vigor—grows greater every year. Cultural influences from abroad are significant. Even though the United States remains a leading exporter of consumer fads and styles, we can see among the American people European cultural standards and popular fashion and musical imports from Britain joined by interest in various offshoots of Buddhism or a fascination with Japan's gifts at social coordination. Even the composition of the United States' population reflects growing worldwide contacts. The United States is now experiencing its highest rates of immigration ever, with new arrivals from Latin America and various parts of Asia joining earlier immigrant groups from Europe and Africa.

Enmeshed in this world, shaping it but also shaped by it, United States citizens need to know something of how that world has been formed and what major historical forces created its diversities and contacts. We need to know, in sum, something about world history. Study of our own past—that is, United States history—or even the larger history of Western civilization from which many American institutions and values spring, now risks being unduly narrow, though worthy and interesting. This is why the study of world history is receiving renewed attention.

The need to know leading themes in world history thus involves the need to understand why, because of earlier tradition, Chinese and Japanese governments are today more effective in regulating personal behaviors such as birthrates than are governments in other parts of Asia, such as India. East Asian traditions never posited the boundary line between state and society that other cultures (including our own in the United States) take for granted, and the contemporary version of this special tradition has produced fascinating results. Tradition combined with more recent changes, including bitter experience with Western intrusions, helps explain why many countries in the Islamic world are demonstrating strong opposition to lifestyles and economic forms that many modern Westerners assume to be normal. Our world, obviously, is shaped by the past; we can best understand changes we are experiencing when we compare them with past changes. And so, on an interdependent globe, a grasp of world history becomes an intellectual necessity.

A danger exists, however, in stressing the need to study world history too piously. It is true that growing global interdependence and communication make knowledge of past world patterns increasingly useful as the basis for interpreting policy options open to the United States or American businesses—or simply for grasping the daily headlines in more than a superficial manner. But the mission of a world history course does not rest entirely on the desire to create a more informed and mature citizenry. It can also rest on the intrinsic interest and the analytical challenge world history offers.

The modern centuries in particular involve a growing drama of confrontation between deeply rooted, highly valued, and often successful cultural forms and some common forces of change. Over the past 500 years, all the major civilizations have encountered growing pressures from new ideas and institutions, often initially generated in Europe or the United States—and often brute force and commercial exploitation from the West as well. During the past century (and in some cases longer) these same civilizations have tried to take into account the new technologies springing from industrialization; new ways of thinking shaped by modern science and belief systems such as nationalism and socialism; the need to reshape government functions and the contacts between government and citizens; pressures to redefine the family to allow for children's formal education, new roles for women, and often a reduction in traditional birthrates. The modern drama, played out in different specific ways depending on region, has involved combining some of the common, worldwide pressures with retention of vital continuities from the past.

The varieties of response have been considerable, because the variety of past cultures is great and because the modern centuries have seen a number of distinctly new experiences through, for example, differences in the timing and form of Western intrusions. Some societies—often after experimenting with other responses—copied Western technologies and organizations sufficiently to industrialize while embellishing revealing deviations from "Western" standards as well. Other societies have faced greater problems in matching the West's industrial might. Some—such as Latin America—partially merged with cultural styles initially developed in the West; others have tried to remain aloof from Western art or popular culture. Some societies have widely embraced new belief systems, whereas in others—such as the Islamic Middle East—pressures to retain older religious values have maintained great force. The point is clear: No civilization in the modern world has been able to stand pat, and all have responded to challenge in some similar ways—using nationalism, for example, or extending formal systems of education. At the same time, overall responses have been extremely varied, because of continuities from diverse pasts and diverse modern experiences. Defining the tension between common directions of change and the variety that still distinguishes the major civilizations forms one of the major analytical tasks of modern world history.

The examples of both change and variety are endless. Not only general features of key civilizations or periods but also major events, such as the British efforts to import opium into China and the belated ending of the slave trade from Africa, compel attention. Historical events worldwide illustrate ways that different societies interacted and the range of evil and good of which humans have proved capable. Modern world history, in sum, can be interesting, even enjoyable—that is, unless the human panorama offers no appeal. It has grown unfashionable in American education to emphasize joy in learning, lest a subject seem frivolous or irrelevant to careers and earning power. But the fact is that world history, like many but not all other academic subjects, offers potential for pleasure as well as support for an informed citizenry.

World history is also challenging. Putting the case mildly, much has happened in the history of the world; and although some developments remain unknown for want of records, the amount that we do know is astounding—and steadily expanding. No person can master the whole; and in presenting a manageable course in world history, selectivity is certainly essential. Fortunately, there is considerable agreement on certain developments that are significant to a study of world history. The student must gain, for example, some sense of the special political characteristics of Chinese civilization; or of the new world economy that Western Europe organized, to its benefit, after about 1500; or of the ways major technological changes developed, spread, and had an impact on leading societies at various points in time, including the Industrial Revolution and even the more recent innovations in information technology. The list of history basics, of course, is not uniform, and it can change with new interests and new data. The condition of women, for example, as it varied from one civilization to the next and changed over time, has become a staple of up-to-date world history teaching in ways that could not have been imagined 20 years ago. Despite changes in the list, though, the idea of approaching world history in terms of basics—key civilizations, key points of change, key factors such as technology and family—begins the process of making the vast menu of data digestible.

In practice, however, the teaching of world history has sometimes obscured the focus on basics with a stream-of-narrative textbook approach. The abundance of facts and their importance and/or interest can produce a way of teaching world history so bent on leaving nothing out (though in fact much must be omitted even in the most ponderous tome) that little besides frenzied memorization takes place. Yet world history, though it must convey knowledge, must also stimulate thought—about why different patterns developed in various civilizations, about what impact new contacts between civilizations had, about how our present world relates to the past.

One way to stimulate thought—and to give some sense of the spice of particular currents or episodes in world history—is to provide access to original sources.

Volume II of *Documents in World History,* obviously, is intended to facilitate world history teaching that includes but transcends a purely textbook-survey approach.

The readings in this volume are designed to illustrate several features of various civilizations at crucial points in modern world history through direct evidence. Thus the readings convey, through direct statements, some sense of how Gandhi defined Indian nationalism and its relation to the West, or what a number of twentieth-century social revolutionaries said were their goals. Because the documents were written for specific themes and audiences, they invariably require some effort of interpretation. The writers, by trying to persuade others of their beliefs or reporting what they saw at the time, did not focus on distilling the essence of a religion, a political movement, or a list of government functions for early-twenty-first-century students of world history. The reader must provide such distillation, aided by the brief introduction given in each chapter before the selections, as well as the Study Questions at the end of chapters, designed to stimulate thoughtful discussion. Analytical thinking is also encouraged and challenged by recurrent comparisons across space and time. Thus documents dealing with social or family structure in China can be compared with documents on the same subject for the Middle East, and a picture of China's isolation 500 years ago begs for juxtaposition with descriptions of twentieth-century Chinese world contacts to see what changed and what persists. Another example, in Chapter 22, explicitly organizes comparison of documents around the theme of mass education.

The documents presented are not randomly chosen; and it will help, in using them, if the principles of organization are made clear—for these principles correspond to some of the selection-for-manageability essential in studying world history. The hope is, of course, that the documents reflect particularly interesting insights; they were selected in part because they are lively as well as significant. They were *not* selected to maximize factual coverage. This is a difficult goal even in a text, and it becomes almost impossible in a collection of readings. In our choices of materials we wanted to present passages of some substance (rather than snippets) and depth (rather than just a law or two, a real discussion of how government worked). By the same token the materials leave out vastly more possibilities than they embrace, even in the realm of "famous" documents such as treaties and constitutions. The book is thus intended to stimulate, but it is decidedly not intended to pepper the carcass of world history with as much buckshot as possible.

Eschewing coverage as a goal, we follow certain general principles around which an approach to world history can be organized. Quite simply, these principles involve place, time, and topic. By choosing readings—which may or may not be important documents in themselves—that illustrate important societies in distinctive periods of time and in significant facets of the human experience, the book offers a collection of telling insights that usually complement and challenge the survey approach. Knowing the principles of selection, in turn, facilitates relating the readings to each other and to a more general understanding of world history.

First is the principle of major civilizations in organizing choice of place. The readings focus on seven parts of the world that have produced durable civilizations still in existence, at least in part. They do not simply focus on the West in a world context. East Asia embraces China and a surrounding zone that came under partial Chinese influence—most notably Japan. India, which comprises the second area, had considerable influence in other parts of southern Asia, although we do not offer readings on Southeast Asia directly. The Middle East and North Africa, where civilization was first born, form a third society to be addressed at various points in time, from the glories of the Ottoman Empire that unified much of the region in the fifteenth century to the obvious troubles and divisions of the late twentieth century. Sub-Saharan Africa, a vast region with great diversity, is the fourth case. Europe—although ultimately sharing some common values through Christianity and a recollection of the glories of Greece and Rome—had developed before the fifteenth century two partially distinct civilizations, one in the West and the other in the East (centered on Russia). East-West divisions in Europe did not remain constant over the modern centuries, but some demarcation has persisted. Western civilization also spread beyond Europe's borders to the United States, Canada, Australia, and New Zealand. Finally, civilization developed independently in the Americas and then mingled American Indian influences with those of Spain and Portugal to form Latin American civilization, the newest on the world's roster. The seven civilizations represented in the readings are not sacrosanct: They do not embrace all the world's cultures, past or present. They overlap at points, as in the case of Western and Eastern European patterns, and they contain some marked internal divisions, such as between China and Japan in East Asia. But these civilizations do provide some geographic coherence for the study of world history, and they are all represented repeatedly in the selections that follow.

Separate civilizations, even when compared, are only one of the geographic or cultural bases for world history. The second basis is contact among different societies, as a result of migration, invasion and war, trade, deliberate borrowing, or missionary intrusion. Documents on the nature and results of significant contacts complement those focused on major civilization characteristics.

Time is the second organizing principle. World history falls into a number of distinct, if rather general, time periods. Prehistory—before the rise of agriculture and the development of civilization—stretches for hundreds of thousands of years, with divisions according to the evolution of the species and the major stages in early technology. Early civilizations formed around river valleys in Asia and North Africa starting more than 5000 years ago. Then between 1000 B.C.E. and 500 C.E. larger civilizations told hold—in China and India and around the Mediterranean, establishing some of the modern world's leading intellectual and political traditions. A final traditional period took shape after the fall of the classical civilizations. Between 500 and about 1500 C.E., major world religions developed further, particularly through the spread of Buddhism, Christianity, and Islam. Essentially new civilizations were launched in Western and Eastern Europe, in sub-Saharan Africa, and in parts of the Americas; and distinct extensions of the older civilizations developed in places like Japan. Again, basic traditions were set that continue to be influential today.

Many readers of this collection will already have covered the traditional periods of world history. Volume 1 of *Documents in World History*, a companion reader organized in ways similar to this volume, offers source materials on important features of the traditional world and its major civilizations, describing the great religions, durable political patterns, and aspects of social structure and family life. Such features should be compared with developments after 1500 C.E., to obtain a full sense of the interplay between the continuity of civilizations' traditions and the general forces shaping the modern world.

Volume 2 focuses on three basic modern periods that took shape after 1500 C.E. During the first period, which began to form around 1500 and extended to the mid-eighteenth century, the rise of the West and Western sponsorship of a new world economy provided a clear central theme for world history against which other, separate civilizations reacted to produce their own balance between continuity and change. Other major forces included the capacity to form new empires—the territorial agglomerations developed by the Ottomans, Russians, and Mughals—and the diverse impacts of contact with the Americas. Specific patterns varied. Russia, for example, reached out for selective contacts with Western Europe, while East Asia opted for a policy of splendid isolation. The West itself was undergoing a fascinating series of changes that produced new political and intellectual forms. Latin America became defined, under heavy Western influence; and Africa and India encountered different degrees of Western impact. In retrospect, these early modern centuries were a time of transition, with a growing Western role but very diverse reactions, all complicated by the fact that the West itself was changing its geographical shape.

The second modern period in world history opened in the middle of the eighteenth century and extended until about 1914. After 1750, Western influence intensified, becoming more literally international; and during the nineteenth century, Western controls—through imperialism—extended over new sections of the world. The only societies that remained fully independent were those that struggled frantically to change, notably Russia and Japan. And the West itself underwent the Industrial Revolution, which heightened its economic advantage over the rest of the world while ushering in radically new technological, social, and cultural forms. Western influence was furthered by the expansion of frontier societies in North America and in Australia and New Zealand, heavily influenced by European settlers, institutions, and cultures. Yet, even amid the undeniable Western preponderance and the resultant international contacts, situations continued to vary widely. Different societies reacted to change distinctively, depending in part on prior values. New forces, such as nationalism, promoted significant political and cultural adjustments while also invigorating diverse traditions.

The third chronological section of this book is reserved for the twentieth century. In part this simply reflects the fact that twentieth-century developments such as the Russian Revolution and feminism are particularly important today because of their proximity. Readings on the twentieth century allow analysis of what has changed and what persists in the world's major societies. But the twentieth century also serves as the beginning of a new period in world history, marked by the relative decline of the West, the development of radically new forms of warfare, and the extension of at least partial industrialization and urbanization to most portions of the world. The twentieth century is not only, then, close to us by definition; it also seems to harbor an unusual number of fundamental changes in world history. These transitions—and the various efforts to resist them in the name of older values, ranging from Islamic purity to yearnings for Western supremacy—provide some of the overriding themes for the selections in the final group of readings.

Placing stress on the twentieth century is not always characteristic of courses in world history, which often focus on the fascinating passages of the world in earlier periods of time. And the claim that the twentieth century is ushering in a new period of world history—based on a heightened pace of change in various parts of the world and the decline of at least certain forms of Western predominance—should be tested, not simply accepted on faith. Using the selections dealing with the most recent century, readers can question the proposition that change is taking new forms in the world at large and compare twentieth-century developments with those that occurred earlier in the modern era. Beginning in the past several decades, are most civilizations becoming comfortable enough with patterns pioneered in the West to produce their own statements of change and not simply react to Western intrusion? However this question is answered (and the answer may vary from case to case), this book's provision of a full section on the twentieth century is meant to encourage making a connection between our time and the past, seeing how older values echo in a modern age, as well as gaining insight into some of the newer issues of world history.

The time factor in this volume can be summarized as follows. By around 1500 several new themes in world history had begun to take shape, including the rise of a more dynamic Western civilization and the development of more intricate economic contacts around the world, now comprised of the Americas as well as Afro-Eurasia. After 1750, the spread of more advanced technologies, population growth in many societies, and challenges to traditional belief systems and governmental forms heightened the complexity of change. All three of the major periods—1500 to 1750, 1750 to 1914, and the twentieth century—must be seen through the seven major civilizations, in each of which the central modern drama of change shaping but also shaped by past values took its own particular form—from China's attempt to develop a political regime suitable for modern economic growth to Islamic or Soviet attempts to build modern societies free of the trappings of Western consumerism or family instability to attempts by the West itself to come to terms with its new position in the world.

The third principle by which to organize world history is topical. In dealing with the major modern periods and the leading civilizations, the readings in this book reflect an attempt to convey the four features of any human society: its political, economic, cultural, and social expressions. Added to the categories of place (the seven civilizations) and time (the three major modern periods), this topical categorization can facilitate any comparisons among past and present periods. Every society must develop some governmental structure and political values. It must generate a culture, that is, a system of beliefs and artistic expressions that help explain how the world works. Among these, religion is often a linchpin of a society's culture, but science and art play crucial roles as well. Many civilizations have seen tensions among various cultural expressions, which can be a source of creativity. Economic relationships—the nature of agriculture, the level of technology and openness to technological change, the position of merchants—form a third feature of a civilization. And finally, social groupings and hierarchies and family institutions—including gender relations—organize human relationships and provide for the training of children. Until recently, world history focused primarily on the political and cultural side of the major societies, with some bows to technology and trade. More recently, the explosion of social history, with its inquiry into popular as well as elite cultures and into families and social structure, has broadened world history concerns. Readings in this book provide a sense of all four aspects of the leading civilizations—political, economic, cultural, and social—and a feeling for how they changed under the impact of new beliefs, new international contacts, and the growth of industrial cities.

The effort to present lively documents that illuminate several time periods, different cultural traditions, and various features of the way societies function must, again, be evocative. This book is not intended to teach everything one should know about the evolution of Western families, Chinese attempts to change without becoming "Western," or the development of the modern world economy. It aims, rather, at providing the flavor of such topics, a sense of how people at the time lived and perceived them, and some understanding of the issues involved in interpreting and comparing diverse documents from the past. The collection is meant to help readers themselves breathe life into world history and grasp some of the ways that people, both great and ordinary, have lived, suffered, and created in various parts of the world at various times in the rich human past.

SECTION ONE

The Early Modern Period, Centuries of Dramatic Change: 1500–1750

Western Europe's emergence as an increasingly important actor on the world stage by 1500 depended on several developments: new technologies, in part gained by previous contacts with Asia (such as explosive powder and the compass); acute international trade problems and fear of Muslim power, which prompted Europeans to seek new routes to Asia and also sources of gold that would give them greater bargaining power; and changes within European society itself, including greater rivalries among monarchs. New international positions continued the process of change within Europe, helping to promote new attitudes to science. Western Europe's power at the same time affected other societies, particularly of course in the Americas, which were now open to growing European control. Elsewhere, the impact of Western gains, higher levels of international trade, and the foodstuffs available from the Americas had diverse results, ranging from altered commercial patterns in Africa, to deliberate imitation from Russia, to deliberate isolation in East Asia. Other developments shaped the early modern centuries as well, including the formation of vigorous new empires (the Ottoman and the Mughal) in the Middle East and India, both of which extended Muslim power. Renewed political strength in China was another vital Asian development, as European influence and new global trading patterns had only selective impact on the largest continent during the early modern centuries.

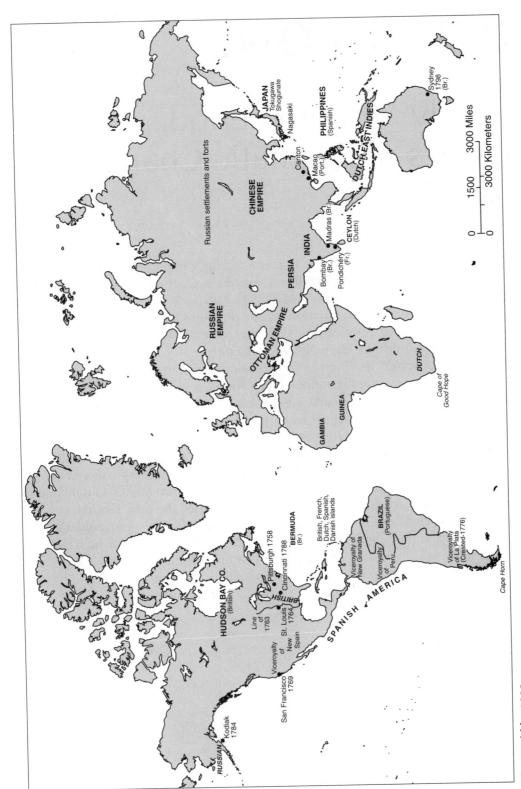

The World by 1800

RUSSIAN EMPIRE

Russian settlements and forts

JAPAN
Tokugawa
Shogunate
Nagasaki

**CHINESE
EMPIRE**

PHILIPPINES
(Spanish)

DUTCH EAST INDIES

Canton
Macao
(Port.)

INDIA
Madras (Br.)
CEYLON
(Dutch)
Bombay
(Br.)
Pondichéry
(Fr.)

PERSIA

OTTOMAN EMPIRE

GAMBIA

GUINEA

DUTCH

Cape of
Good Hope

Sydney
1798
(Br.)

3000 Miles
3000 Kilometers
1500
0
0
1500
3000

Kodiak
1784
RUSSIAN

San Francisco
1769
Viceroyalty
of
New Spain

St. Louis
1764

Line
of
1763

HUDSON BAY CO.
(British)

Pittsburgh 1758
Cincinnati 1788
BRITISH

BERMUDA
(Br.)

British, French,
Dutch, Spanish,
Danish Islands

Viceroyalty
of New Granada

Viceroyalty
of
Peru

SPANISH AMERICA

BRAZIL
(Portuguese)

Viceroyalty
of La Plata
(Created–1776)

Cape Horn

1

New Tensions in the Western Political Tradition: Absolutism and Parliament

A leading historian-sociologist, Charles Tilly, has recently argued that one of the few great changes in early modern Western history was the strengthening of the state under national monarchs. Without question, many European governments in the seventeenth century completed the tasks of seizing basic political powers from the feudal nobility, developing a strong bureaucracy, and expanding the functions of the central government. New or revived ideals of government power accompanied this shift. In the first selection, Bishop Bossuet expounds the doctrine of a strong king— essential to keep order among unruly subjects, father to his people, owed all respect and obedience. The result, Bossuet argued, would be far from arbitrary rule and would work to the greater benefit of the subjects—but there was no question about who was in command. Bossuet was writing in the period of Louis XIV, the model for the absolute monarch not only in France but across Europe.

Older ideals of limited government did not die, however. They revived in seventeenth-century England at the same time that France was constructing its newly absolute monarchy. Civil war led to the execution of one king; then renewed unrest, in 1688, brought a strong statement of the rights of the parliament and of individual liberties, as King James II was forced to flee, replaced by a Dutch ruler, William of Orange. The so called "Glorious Revolution" brought an unprecedented statement on the limits of royal power, as England moved from feudal practices toward parliamentary monarchy.

The diverse changes in the Western political tradition proved durable. Government functions expanded, though less in England than elsewhere until the twentieth

Selection 1 from J. B. Bossuet, *Politique Tirée des Propres Paroles de l'Ecriture Sainte* (1870), translated by L. Pearce Williams, published in Brian Tierney, Donald Kagan, and L. Pearce Williams, eds., *Great Issues in Western Civilization*, Vol. I (New York: Random House, Inc., 1967), pp. 659–663. Copyright © 1967 by Random House, Inc. Reprinted by permission. Selection 2 from E. P. Cheyney, *Readings in English History* (New York: Ginn and Company, 1922), pp. 545–547.

century. Even when kings were toppled, the state continued to wield new powers— as in revolutionary France after 1789. But the idea of limiting government through individual rights and controlling it through elected bodies remained an important Western emphasis, later copied in some other parts of the world. Some historians have argued that it was the flexibility of the Western political tradition, in contrast, say, to the purer Russian or Chinese emphasis on the state, that has fostered the development and, at times, the distinctive vigor of Western society.

The two selections invite comparison. Were those who sought to limit the state in times of unrest—as in seventeen-century England—talking the same language, or did goals and methods shift? How did the constitutional parliamentary ideal differ from the absolutist standards of Bossuet? Has the West managed successfully to reconcile its two modern political traditions?

1. ABSOLUTISM: BISHOP BOSSUET'S THEORY OF DIVINE-RIGHT MONARCHY

Justice has no other support than authority and the subordination of powers.

It is this order which restrains license. When everyone does what he wishes and has only his own desires to regulate him, everything ends up in confusion. . . .

By means of government each individual becomes stronger.

The reason is that each is helped. All the forces of the nations concur in one and the sovereign magistrate has the right to reunite them. . . .

Thus the sovereign magistrate has in his hand all the forces of the nation which submits itself to obedience to him. . . .

Thus, an individual is not troubled by oppression and violence because he has an invincible defender in the person of the prince and is stronger by far than all those who attempt to oppress him.

The sovereign magistrate's own interest is to preserve by force all the individuals of a nation because if any other force than his own prevails among the people his authority and his life is in peril. . . .

The law is sacred and inviolable.

In order to understand perfectly the nature of the law it is necessary to note that all those who have spoken well on it have regarded it in its origin as a pact and a solemn treaty by which men agree together under the authority of princes to that which is necessary to form their society.

This is not say that the authority of the laws depends on the consent and acquiescence of the people; but only that the prince who, moreover by his very station has no other interest than that of the public good, is helped by the sagest heads in the nation and leans upon the experience of centuries gone by. . . .

Everybody thus begins with monarchy and almost everybody has retained it as being the most natural state.

We have also seen that it has its foundation and its model in the rule of the father, that is to say in nature itself.

All men are born subjects: and paternal authority which accustoms them to obey, accustoms them at the same time to have only one chief.

Monarchical government is the best.

If it is the most natural, it is consequently the most durable and from that it follows also the strongest.

It is also the most opposed to divisiveness, which is the worst evil of states, and the most certain cause of their ruin. . . . "Every kingdom divided against itself is brought to desolation; and every city or house divided against itself shall not stand."

We have seen that Our Lord in this sentence has followed the natural progress of government and seems to have wished to show to realms and to cities the same means of uniting themselves that nature has established in families.

Thus, it is natural that when families wish to unite to form a body of State, they will almost automatically coalesce into the government that is proper to them.

When states are formed there is the impulse to union and there is never more union than under a single leader. Also there is never greater strength because everything works in harmony. . . .

Royal authority is paternal and its proper character is goodness.

After what has been said, this truth has no need of proof.

We have seen that kings take the place of God, who is the true father of the human species. We have also seen that the first idea of power which exists among men is that of the paternal power; and that kings are modeled on fathers.

Everybody is also in accord, that the obedience which is owned to the public power can be found in the ten commandments only in the precept which obliges him to honor his parents.

Thus it follows from this that the name of king is a name for father and that goodness is the most natural character of kings. . . .

The prince must provide for the needs of the people.

It is a royal right to provide for the needs of the people. He who undertakes it at the expense of the prince undertakes royalty: this is why it has been established. The obligation to care for the people is the foundation of all the rights that sovereigns have over their subjects.

This is why, in time of great need, the people have the right to have recourse to its prince. . . .

2. THE ENGLISH BILL OF RIGHTS, 1689

Whereas the said late King James II having abdicated the government, and the throne being thereby vacant, his Highness the prince of Orange (whom it hath pleased Almighty God to make the glorious instrument of delivering this kingdom from popery and arbitrary power) did (by the advice of the lords spiritual and temporal, and diverse principal persons of the Commons [parliament]) caused letters to be written to the lords spiritual and temporal, being Protestants . . . to meet and sit at Westminster upon the two and twentieth day of January, in this year 1689, in order to such an establishment as that their religion, laws, and liberties might not again be in danger of being subverted; upon which letters elections have been accordingly made.

And thereupon the said lords spiritual and temporal and Commons, pursuant to their respective letters and elections, being now assembled in a full and free representation of this nation, taking into the most serious consideration the best means for attaining the ends aforesaid, do in the first place (as their ancestors in like case have usually done), for the vindication and assertion of their ancient rights and liberties, declare:

1. That the pretended power of suspending laws, or the execution of laws, by regal authority, without consent of parliament is illegal.
2. That the pretended power of dispensing with the laws, or the execution of law by regal authority, as it hath been assumed and exercised of late, is illegal.
3. That the commission for erecting the late court of commissioners for ecclesiastical causes, and all other commissions and courts of like nature, are illegal and pernicious.
4. That levying money for or to use of the crown by pretense of prerogative, without grant of parliament, for longer time or in other manner than the same is or shall be granted, is illegal.
5. That it is the right of the subjects to petition the king, and all commitments and prosecutions for such petitioning are illegal.
6. That the raising or keeping a standing army within the kingdom in time of peace, unless it be with consent of parliament, is against law.
7. That the subjects which are Protestants may have arms for their defense suitable to their conditions, and as allowed by law.
8. That election of members of parliament ought to be free.
9. That the freedom of speech, and debates or proceedings in parliament, ought not to be impeached or questioned in any court or place out of parliament.
10. That excessive bail ought not to be required, nor excessive fines imposed, nor cruel and unusual punishments inflicted. . . .
13. And that for redress of all grievance and for the amending, strengthening, and preserving of the laws, parliament ought to be held frequently.

And they do claim, demand, and insist upon all and singular the premises, as their undoubted rights and liberties. . . .

STUDY QUESTIONS

1. How does Bossuet define the powers of monarchy? How does he argue that these powers are essential?
2. Why did this kind of monarchy become known as "absolute"?
3. What were the key features of the "parliamentary monarchy" established in principle in Great Britain during 1688 and 1689?
4. What general rights were accorded to all Englishmen by the Bill of Rights? What freedoms were not granted to all?
5. What were the key differences between absolute and parliamentary monarchies? What caused two such different patterns to emerge?

2

The Scientific Revolution and the Enlightenment: New Intellectual Standards in the West

From the fifteenth century through the eighteenth, intellectual life in the West went through a dizzying series of changes, some contradictory. Renaissance thinkers and artists challenged medieval styles and standards, urging a greater focus on humanity and things of this world. The Reformation, shortly on the heels of the Renaissance, argued for a return to religious authority, but it also shattered the unity of Western Christendom. Ultimately—as became clear by the later seventeenth century—the cutting edge of Western intellectual life was redefined away from religion and toward the growing authority of science. By science, in turn, Western intellectuals meant a set of rational operations, including both experiment and deductive reasoning, by which scientists could discover the clear-cut laws of nature. Religious authority was not directly attacked, but it was sidestepped in favor of a belief that humans could know what they needed to know by unaided reason. Knowledge itself could progress, rather than referring constantly to faith or tradition.

The following selections, by leading figures in the Scientific Revolution in the seventeenth century and its aftermath, the eighteenth-century Enlightenment, describe the new intellectual framework. Isaac Newton, whose great discoveries in physics and mathematics brought together more than a century of work on planetary motion and the laws of gravity, shows how science and religion could be combined—but obviously on the terms of science. John Locke, also a seventeenth-century Englishman, sketches new principles of knowledge wherein reason has the crucial role.

Locke, and Enlightenment figures after him, intended to apply rational principles and the idea of a harmonious, knowable nature to human society. Obviously, education had to change in order to develop the rational spark inherent in each

Selection 1 from Sir Isaac Newton, *Optics, or A Treatise of the Reflections, Refractions, Inflections and Colours of Light,* 4th ed. (London: 1730), p. 18. Selection 2 from John Locke, *An Essay Concerning Human Understanding* (Oxford: 1894), pp. 28, 37–38, 121–122, 387, 412–416, 420–421, 425–426. Selection 3 reprinted with permission of Macmillan Publishing Company. From Cesare Beccaria, *On Crimes and Punishments,* translated by Henry Paolucci, p. 67. Copyright © 1963 by Macmillan Publishing Company. Reprinted by permission of Prentice Hall/Pearson Education.

child. Human institutions, such as criminal punishments, long based on outmoded religion and tradition, could be rethought, again to make the best of the fundamental reason and goodness in each person. An Italian Enlightenment writer, Cesare Beccaria, took the lead here.

Science and the Enlightenment were not unchallenged in the Western world, but they did reshape previously dominant belief. Western intellectual life came to rest on assumptions radically different from those of a few centuries before. And there was more. The intellectual revolution reverberated in the wider culture of the West, as ordinary people picked up some of the same assumptions and began to challenge many traditions of popular culture. Finally, as the West spread its influence in the wider world, the baggage of the Age of Reason accompanied its journeys, challenging traditional cultures in Asia and Africa. Here, too, the intellectual revolution that started in the West is still working in the world, though with varied results.

1. NEWTON'S VIEW OF THE WORLD (1704)

All these things considered, it seems probable to me, that God in the beginning formed matter in solid, massy, hard, impenetrable, moveable particles [atoms], of such sizes and figures, and with such other properties, and in such proportion to space, as most conduced to the end for which he formed them; and that these primitive particles, being solids, are incomparably harder than any porous bodies compounded of them; even so very hard, as never to wear or break in pieces; no ordinary power being able to divide what God himself made one in the first creation. . . .

Now by the help of these principles, all material things seem to have been composed of the hard and solid particles above-mentioned, variously associated in the first creation by the counsel of an intelligent agent. For it became him who created them to set them in order. And if he did so, it's unphilosophical to seek for any other origin of the world or to pretend that it might arise out of a chaos by the mere laws of nature; though being once formed, it may continue by those laws for many ages.

2. JOHN LOCKE ON THE POWER OF REASON (1690)

I

It is an established opinion amongst some men, that there are in the understanding certain *innate principles;* some primary notions, characters, as it were stamped upon the mind of man; which the soul receives in its very first being, and brings into the world with it. It would be sufficient to convince unprejudiced readers of the falseness of this supposition, if I should only show (as I hope I shall in the following parts of this Discourse) how men, barely by the use of their natural faculties, may attain to all the knowledge they have, without the help of any innate impressions; and may arrive at certainty, without any such original notions or principles. . . .

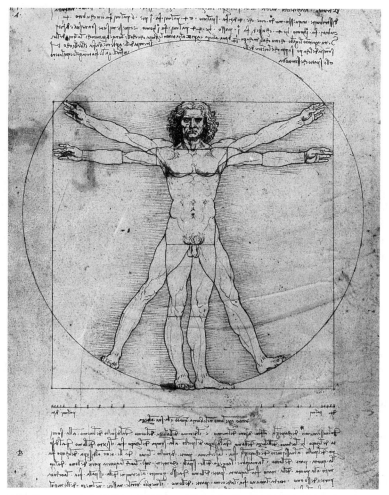

Renaissance Art Often Prefigured the Scientific Revolution.
Anatomical sketches by Leonardo da Vinci. (Alinari/Art Resource, NY.)

Let us then suppose the mind to be, as we say, white paper, void of all characters, without any ideas:—How comes it to be furnished? Whence comes it by that vast store which the busy and foundless fancy of man has painted on it with an almost endless variety? Whence has it all the *materials* of reason and knowledge? To this I answer, in one word, from EXPERIENCE. In that all our knowledge is founded; and from that it ultimately derives itself. Our observation employed either about external sensible objects, or about the internal operations of our minds perceived and reflected on by ourselves, is that which supplies our understandings with all the *materials* of thinking. These two are the fountains of knowledge, from whence all the ideas we have, or can naturally have, do spring. . . .

Sense and intuition reach but a very little way. The greatest part of our knowledge depends upon deductions and intermediate ideas: and in those cases where we are fain to substitute assent instead of knowledge, and take propositions for true, without being certain they are so, we have to find out, examine, and compare the grounds of their probability. In both these cases, the faculty which finds out the means, and rightly applies them, to discover certainty in the one, and probability in the other, is that which we call reason. . . .

II

Assent to supposed innate truths depends on having clear and distinct ideas of what their terms mean, and not on their innateness. A child knows not that three and four are equal to seven, till he comes to be able to count seven, and has got the name and idea of equality; and then, upon explaining those words, he presently assents to, or rather perceives the truth of that proposition. But neither does he then readily assent because it is an innate truth, nor was his assent wanting till then because he wanted the use of reason; but the truth of it appears to him as soon as he has settled in his mind the clear and distinct ideas that these names stand for.

III

Faith and Reason

By what has been said of reason, we may be able to make some guess at the distinction of things, into those that are according to, above, and contrary to reason. 1. *According to reason* are such propositions whose truth we can discover by examining and tracing those ideas we have from sensation and reflection; and by natural deduction find to be true or probable. 2. *Above reason* are such propositions whose truth or probability we cannot by reason derive from those principles. 3. *Contrary to reason* are such propositions as are inconsistent with or irreconcilable to our clear and distinct ideas. Thus the existence of one God is according to reason; the existence of more than one God, contrary to reason; the resurrection of the dead, above reason. . . .

From these things thus premised, I think we may come to lay down *the measures and boundaries between faith and reason:* the want whereof may possibly have been the cause, if not of great disorders, yet at least of great disputes, and perhaps mistakes in the world. For till it be resolved how far we are to be guided by reason, and how far by faith, we shall in vain dispute, and endeavour to convince one another in matters of religion. . . .

Reason, therefore, here, as contradistinguished to *faith,* I take to be the discovery of the certainty or probability of such propositions or truths, which the mind arrives at by deduction made from such ideas, which it has got by the use of its natural faculties: viz. by sensation or reflection.

Faith, on the other side, is the assent to any proposition, not thus made out by the deductions of reason, but upon the credit of the proposer, as coming from God, in some extraordinary way of communication. This way of discovering truths to men, we call *revelation.* . . .

But yet nothing, I think, can, under that title [revelation] shake or overrule plain knowledge; or rationally prevail with any man to admit it for true, in a direct contradiction to the clear evidence of his own understanding. . . . And therefore *no proposition can be received as divine revelation . . . if it be contradictory to our clear intuitive knowledge.* Because this would be to subvert the principles and foundations of all knowledge, evidence, and assent whatsoever: and there would be left no difference between truth and falsehood, no measures of credible and incredible in the world, if doubtful propositions shall take place before self-evident; and what we certainly know give way to what we may possibly be mistaken in. In propositions therefore contrary to the clear perception of the agreement or disagreement of any of our ideas, it will be in vain to urge them as matters of faith. They cannot move our assent under that or any other title whatsoever. For faith can never convince us of anything that contradicts our knowledge. . . .

Thus far the dominion of faith reaches, and that without any violence or hindrance to reason; which is not injured or disturbed, but assisted and improved by new discoveries of truth, coming from the eternal fountain of all knowledge. Whatever God hath revealed is certainly true; no doubt can be made of it. This is the proper object of faith: but whether it be a *divine* revelation or no, reason must judge; which can never permit the mind to reject a greater evidence to embrace what is less evident, nor allow it to entertain probability in opposition to knowledge and certainty. There can be no evidence that any traditional revelation is of divine origin, in the words we receive it, and in the sense we understand it, so clear and so certain as that of the principles of reason: and therefore *Nothing that is contrary to, and inconsistent with, the clear and self-evident dictates of reason, has a right to be urged or assented to as a matter of faith, wherein reason hath nothing to do.*

3. BECCARIA APPLIES RATIONALISM TO PUNISHMENT (1764)

A. Crimes and Punishments

To examine and distinguish all the different sorts of crimes and the manner of punishing them would not be our natural task, were it not that their nature, which varies with the different circumstances of times and places, would compel us to enter upon too vast and wearisome a mass of detail. But it will suffice to indicate the most general principles and the most pernicious and common errors, in order to undeceive no less those who, from a mistaken love of liberty, would introduce anarchy, than those who would be glad to reduce their fellow men to the uniform regularity of a convent.

What will be the penalty suitable for such and such crimes?

Is death a penalty really *useful and necessary* for the security and good order of society?

Are torture and torments *just,* and do they attain the *end* which the law aims at?

What is the best way of preventing crimes?

Are the same penalties equally useful in all times?

What influence have they on customs?

These problems deserve to be solved with such geometrical precision as shall suffice to prevail over the clouds of sophistication, over seductive eloquence, or timid doubt. Had I no other merit than that of having been the first to make clearer to Italy that which other nations have dared to write and are beginning to practise, I should deem myself fortunate; but if, in maintaining the rights of men and of invincible truth, I should contribute to rescue from the spasms and agonies of death any unfortunate victim of tyranny or ignorance, both so equally fatal, the blessings and tears of single innocent man in the transports of his joy would console me for the contempt of mankind. . . .

B. Torture

The torture of a criminal during the course of his trial is a cruelty consecrated by custom in most nations. It is used with an intent either to make him confess his crime, or to explain some contradictions into which he had been led during his examination, or discover his accomplices, or for some kind of metaphysical and incomprehensible purgation of infamy, or, finally, in order to discover other crimes of which he is not accused, but of which he may be guilty.

No man can be judged a criminal until he be found guilty; nor can society take from him the public protection until it has been proved that he has violated the conditions on which it was granted. What right, then, but that of power, can authorize the punishment of a citizen so long as there remains any doubt of his guilt? This dilemma is frequent. Either he is guilty, or not guilty. If guilty, he should only suffer the punishment ordained by the laws, and torture becomes useless, as his confession is unnecessary. If he be innocent his crime has not been proved. Besides, it is confounding all relations to expect a man should be both the accuser and accused; and that pain should be the test of truth, as if truth resided in the muscles and fibres of a wretch in torture. By this method the robust will escape, and the feeble be condemned.

STUDY QUESTIONS

1. How did Newton seek to reconcile the idea of a scientifically discoverable nature with Christianity? What was new about his approach?
2. How did Locke alter common Christian thinking about human nature? How would his ideas lead to growing emphasis on the importance of education?
3. Would Locke and Newton have agreed about the importance of religion?
4. How did Beccaria suggest a new approach to the punishment of criminals? Did his approach suggest the scientific and philosophical ideas earlier pioneered by people like Newton and Locke?
5. Were the Scientific Revolution and Enlightenment, in fact, revolutionary compared with earlier Western culture? Would their implications be radical in the context of most other major cultures in the early modern world?

Russian Society

3

Peter the Great Reforms Russia

Peter the Great ruled Russia as tsar from 1682 until 1725. A huge man, Peter pushed his government into many new directions. He brutally repressed protest, executing certain army mutineers personally. He moved vigorously in war, winning new territory in the Baltic region, where he located a new westward-looking capital he modestly called St. Petersburg. With its military success, Russia was on its way toward becoming a major European power; it was already a growing empire in Central Asia.

Peter was also eager to update Russia's administration and economy, which he saw as essential for military purposes and to establish Russian prestige and position in the wider European arena. His measures were both symbolic and real: he enforced Western-style dress on his boyars (the nobles) and required them to cut off their Mongol-style beards. He developed a major iron industry to serve as a basis for armaments production and to avoid Russian dependence on the West in this crucial sector.

The selections show a number of Peter's initiatives to reform Russia and bring it in line with Western patterns. In these reforms Peter sets up an administrative council to improve the direction of the state bureaucracy and expand its functions. He works to improve education, particularly of the nobility, and to facilitate manufacturing as well. These reforms, in sum, give a good picture of the directions in which the tsar was pushing his vast empire.

Peter's reforms also suggest important links with authoritarian political trends in Russia, including a willingness to regiment ordinary workers and peasants. While

All selections from Basil Dmytryshyn, *Imperial Russia: A Sourcebook, 1700–1917* (New York: Holt, Rinehart and Winston, Inc., 1967), pp. 14–16, 18–19, 21–22. Copyright © 1967 by Holt, Rinehart and Winston, Inc. Reprinted by permission. Duties of the Senate from *Polnoe Sobranie,* Vol. 4, No. 2321, p. 627 and No. 2330, p. 643. Compulsory Education from *Polnoe Sobranie,* Vol. 5, No. 2762, p. 78 and No. 2778, p. 86. Instructions to Students from *Pisma I Bumagi Imperatora Petra Velokogo* (Letters and Papers of Emperor Peter the Great) (St. Petersburg: 1887), Vol. 1, pp. 117–118. Right of Factories from *Polnoe Sobranie,* Vol. 6, No. 3711, pp. 311–312. Founding of the Academy from *Polnoe Sobranie,* Vol. 7, No. 4443. Reprinted by permission of Academic International Press.

other European rulers at this time, such as Louis XIV in France, were claiming new powers in the name of military goals, Peter seemed unusually free to order his nobility about and command their service. He was not interested in aspects of Western politics that stressed restraints on the monarch such as parliaments. Not surprisingly, then, Peter's vision of a Westernized Russia proved highly selective, as he found certain aspects of the Russian tradition eminently useful. Peter's reforms must be interpreted in terms of how much they changed, but also in terms of their confirmation of distinctive features of, the Russian state and society.

Peter the Great clearly illustrates a reform process from the top down. How do you think Russians at various levels would have reacted? From what you can judge by these documents, was Peter moving Russia in a useful direction?

1. DECREES ON THE DUTIES OF THE SENATE

This *ukaz* [decree] should be made known. We have decreed that during our absence administration of the country is to be [in the hands of] the Governing Senate [Peter then names its new members].

. . .

Each *gubernia* [region] is to send two officials to advise the Senate on judicial and legislative matters. . . .

In our absence the Senate is charged by this *ukaz* with the following:

1. To establish a just court, to deprive unjust judges of their offices and of all their property, and to administer the same treatment to all slanderers.
2. To supervise governmental expenditures throughout the country and cancel unnecessary and, above all, useless things.
3. To collect as much money as possible because money is the artery of war.
4. To recruit young noblemen for officer training, especially those who try to evade it; also to select about 1000 educated boyars for the same purpose.
5. To reform letters of exchange and keep these in one place.
6. To take inventory of goods leased to offices or *gubernias*.
7. To farm out the salt trade in an effort to receive some profit [for the state].
8. To organize a good company and assign to it the China trade.
9. To increase trade with Persia and by all possible means to attract in great numbers Armenians [to that trade]. To organize inspectors and inform them of their responsibilities.

2. DECREES ON COMPULSORY EDUCATION OF THE RUSSIAN NOBILITY (JANUARY 12 AND FEBRUARY 28, 1714)

Send to every *gubernia* [region] some persons from mathematical schools to teach the children of the nobility—except those of freeholders and government clerks—mathematics and geometry; as a penalty [for evasion] establish a rule that no one will be allowed to marry unless he learns these [subjects]. Inform all prelates to issue no marriage certificates to those who are ordered to go to schools. . . .

The Great Sovereign has decreed: in all *gubernias* children between the ages of ten and fifteen of the nobility, of government clerks, and of lesser officials, except those of freeholders, must be taught mathematics and some geometry. Toward that end, students should be sent from mathematical schools [as teachers], several into each *gubernia,* to prelates and to renowned monasteries to establish schools. During their instruction these teachers should be given food and financial remuneration of three *altyns* and two *dengas* per day from *gubernia* revenues set aside for that purpose by personal orders of His Imperial Majesty. No fees should be collected from students. When they have mastered the material, they should then be given certificates written in their own handwriting. When the students are released they ought to pay one ruble each for their training. Without these certificates they should not be allowed to marry nor receive marriage certificates.

3. AN INSTRUCTION TO RUSSIAN STUDENTS ABROAD STUDYING NAVIGATION

1. Learn [how to draw] plans and charts and how to use the compass and other naval indicators.
2. [Learn] how to navigate a vessel in battle as well as in a simple maneuver, and learn how to use all appropriate tools and instruments; namely, sails, ropes, and oars, and the like matters, on row boats and other vessels.
3. Discover as much as possible how to put ships to sea during a naval battle. Those who cannot succeed in this effort must diligently ascertain what action should be taken by the vessels that do and those that do not put to sea during such a situation [naval battle]. Obtain from [foreign] naval officers written statements, bearing their signatures and seals, of how adequately you [Russian students] are prepared for [naval] duties.
4. If, upon his return, anyone wishes to receive [from the Tsar] greater favors for himself, he should learn, in addition to the above enumerated instructions, how to construct those vessels aboard which he would like to demonstrate his skills.
5. Upon his return to Moscow, every [foreign-trained Russian] should bring with him at his own expense, for which he will later be reimbursed, at least two experienced masters of naval science. They [the returnees] will be assigned soldiers, one soldier per returnee, to teach them [what they have learned abroad]. And if they do not wish to accept soldiers they may teach their acquaintances or their own people. The treasury will pay for transportation and maintenance of soldiers. And if anyone other than soldiers learns [the art of navigation] the treasury will pay 100 rubles for the maintenance of every such individual. . . .

4. A DECREE ON THE RIGHT OF FACTORIES TO BUY VILLAGES (JANUARY 18, 1721)

Previous decrees have denied merchants the right to obtain villages. This prohibition was instituted because those people, outside their business, did not have any establishments that could be of any use to the state. Nowadays, thanks to Our decrees, as every one can see, many merchants have companies and many have succeeded in establishing new enterprises for the benefit of the state; namely: silver, copper, iron, coal and the like, as well as silk, linen, and woolen industries, many of which have begun operations. As a result, by this Our *ukaz* aimed at the increase of factories. We permit the nobility as well as merchants to freely purchase villages for these factories, with the sanction of the Mining and Manufacturing College, under one condition: that these villages be always integral parts of these factories. Consequently, neither the nobility nor merchants may sell or mortgage these villages without the factories . . . and should someone decide to sell these villages with the factories because of pressing needs, it must be done with the permission of the Mining and Manufacturing College. And whoever violates this procedure will have his possessions confiscated.

And should someone try to establish a small factory for the sake of appearance in order to purchase a village, such an enterpreneur should not be allowed to purchase anything. The Mining and Manufacturing College should adhere to this rule very strictly. Should such a thing happen, those responsible for it should be deprived of all their movable and immovable property.

5. A DECREE ON THE FOUNDING OF THE ACADEMY (JANUARY 28, 1724)

His Imperial Majesty decreed the establishment of an academy, wherein languages as well as other sciences and important arts could be taught, and where books could be translated. On January 22 [1724], during his stay in the Winter Palace, His Majesty approved the project for the Academy, and with his own hand signed a decree that stipulates that the Academy's budget of 24,912 rubles annually should come from revenues from custom dues and export-import license fees collecting in the following cities: Narva, Dorpat, Pernov and Arensburg. . . .

Usually two kinds of institutions are used in organizing arts and sciences. One is known as a University; the other as an Academy or society of arts and sciences.

1. A University is an association of learned individuals who teach the young people the development of such distinguished sciences as theology and jurisprudence (the legal skill), and medicine and philosophy. An Academy, on the other hand, is an association of learned and skilled people who not only know their subjects to the same degree [as their counterparts in the University] but who, in addition, improve and develop them through research and inventions. They have no obligation to teach others.

2. While the Academy consists of the same scientific disciplines and has the same members as the University, these two institutions, in other states, have no connection between themselves in training many other well-qualified people who could organize different societies. This is done to prevent interference into the activity of the Academy, whose sole task is to improve arts and sciences through theoretical research that would benefit professors as well as students of universities. Freed from the pressure of research, universities can concentrate on educating the young people.

3. Now that an institution aimed at the cultivation of arts and sciences is to be chartered in Russia, there is no need to follow the practice that is accepted in other states. It is essential to take into account the existing circumstances of this state [Russia], consider [the quality of Russian] teachers and students, and organize such an institution that would not only

immediately increase the glory of this [Russian] state through the development of sciences, but would also, through teaching and dissemination [of knowledge], benefit the people [of Russia] in the future.

4. These two aims will not be realized if the Academy of Sciences alone is chartered, because while the Academy may try to promote and disseminate arts and sciences, these will not spread among the people. The establishment of a university will do even less, simply because there are no elementary schools, gymnasia or seminaries [in Russia] where young people could learn the fundamentals before studying more advanced subjects [at the University] to make themselves useful. It is therefore inconceivable that under these circumstances a university would be of some value [to Russia].

5. Consequently what is needed most [in Russia] is the establishment of an institution that would consist of the most learned people, who, in turn, would be willing: (a) to promote and perfect the sciences while at the same time, wherever possible, be willing (b) to give public instruction to young people (if they feel the latter are qualified) and (c) instruct some people individually so that they in turn could train young people [of Russia] in the fundamental principles of all sciences.

STUDY QUESTIONS

1. What were the main purposes of Peter's reforms?
2. What relationship between tsar and nobility did the reforms suggest?
3. What kind of economy was Peter seeking to build? For what reasons?
4. How did Peter's moves relate to changes occurring in Western European politics and culture around 1700? What major trends did Peter ignore?
5. Did Peter's reforms make Russian society more or less like that of Western Europe at the time?

4

Suleiman the Lawgiver and Ottoman Military Power

In 1300 the Ottoman Turks were one of many groups of Muslim warriors living on the frontier of the Byzantine Empire in western Anatolia. As the power of the Byzantine emperors weakened, the Ottoman *gazis* (warriors fighting on behalf of Islam) began to conquer nearby regions. During the 1350s Turkish armies crossed the Dardenelles (or Hellespont), the narrow strait separating Anatolia from the Balkan Peninsula, and began to establish their power in southeast Europe. By 1400 the Ottomans controlled most of the Balkan Peninsula. The most dramatic victory of the Turks came in 1453. In the spring of that year they broke through the massive walls surrounding Constantinople—the capital of the Byzantine Empire and the center of Orthodox Christianity—and captured the city (now known as Istanbul). It had taken only 150 years for the former frontier *gazis* to establish one of the most powerful empires in the world.

Ottoman power continued to expand for about another century or so following the capture of Constantinople. For much of this period the Turkish state was led by Suleiman, the greatest of the Turkish sultans, who reigned from 1520 to 1556 and was known to his subjects as *Kanuni,* the "Lawgiver." Under Suleiman's leadership the Ottoman system of governance reached a high level of efficiency and the Ottoman army and navy continued to be formidable fighting forces.

Ottoman strength rested, in part, on a form of slavery. Christian children in the Balkans were regularly conscripted by the Turks, a practice known to the Turks as the *devshirme* (collection), and taken to Constantinople, where they were trained to be palace officials, governmental administrators, or members of the elite Janissary

From Halil Inalcik, *The Ottoman Empire: The Classical Age, 1300–1600,* translated by Norman Itzkowitz and Colin Imber (New Rochelle, N.Y.: Aristide D. Caratzas, 1989), p. 41; and *The Turkish Letters of Ogier Ghiselin de Busbecq,* translated by Edward Seymour Foster (Oxford: The Clarendon Press, 1968), pp. 67–68, 109–114, 135–137.

The New Mosque in Istanbul. It is one of the great Ottoman religious buildings. (Stephen S. Gosch.)

corps in the army. This distinctive way of "recruiting" effective administrators and soldiers was already flourishing when Suleiman came to power and continued to work well for a couple of generations after this death.

The following two selections provide us with clues to the reasons for the success of the Ottomans during the reign of Suleiman. In the first selection, which is an inscription from a citadel built by the Turks at Bender in the northern Balkans in 1538, Suleiman describes his power. The second selection is a series of excerpts from letters written by Ogier Ghiselin de Busbecq, the ambassador from the Holy Roman Empire to the Ottoman Empire from 1554 to 1562. During Busbecq's time as ambassador to Constantinople there was much concern among Europeans about the military power of the Ottomans. In 1529 the Turks had surrounded Vienna, the capital of the Holy Roman Empire, and nearly captured it. The memory of this near-disaster and the continuing military threat posed by the Turks form part of the subtext of Busbecq's letters.

1. SULEIMAN THE LAWGIVER DESCRIBES HIS POWER

I am God's slave and sultan of this world. By the grace of God I am head of Muhammad's community. God's might and Muhammad's miracles are my companions. I am Süleymân, in whose name the *hutbe* [sermon] is read in Mecca and Medina. In

Baghdad I am the shah, in Byzantine realms the Caesar, and in Egypt the sultan; who sends his fleets to the seas of Europe, the Maghrib and India. I am the sultan who took the crown and throne of Hungary and granted them to a humble slave. The voivoda Petru raised his head in revolt, but my horse's hoofs ground him into the dust, and I conquered the land of Moldavia.

2. FROM BUSBECQ'S LETTERS

A. *The Turkish Army (1560)*

The Sultan, when he sets out on a campaign, takes as many as 40,000 camels with him, and almost as many baggage-mules, most of whom, if his destination is Persia, are loaded with cereals of every kind, especially rice. Mules and camels are also employed to carry tents and arms and warlike machines and implements of every kind. The territories called Persia which are ruled by the Sophi, as we call him (the Turkish name being Kizilbash), are much less fertile that our country; and, further, it is the custom of the inhabitants, when their land is invaded, to lay waste and burn everything, and so force the enemy to retire through lack of food. The latter, therefore, are faced with serious peril, unless they bring an abundance of food with them. They are careful, however, to avoid touching the supplies which they carry with them as long as they are marching against their foes, but reserve them, as far as possible, for their return journey, when the moment for retirement comes and they are forced to retrace their steps through regions which the enemy has laid waste, or which the immense multitude of men and baggage animals has, as it were, scraped bare, like a swarm of locusts. It is only then that the Sultan's store of provisions is opened, and just enough food to sustain life is weighed out each day to the Janissaries and the other troops in attendance upon him. The other soldiers are badly off, if they have not provided food for their own use; most of them, having often experienced such difficulties during their campaigns—and this is particularly true of the cavalry—take a horse on a leading-rein loaded with many of the necessities of life. These include a small piece of canvas to use as a tent, which may protect them from the sun or a shower of rain, also some clothing and bedding and a private store of provisions, consisting of a leather sack or two of the finest flour, a small jar of butter, and some spices and salt; on these they support life when they are reduced to the extremes of hunger. They take a few spoonfuls of flour and place them in water, adding a little butter, and then flavour the mixture with salt and spices. This, when it is put on the fire, boils and swells up so as to fill a large bowl. They eat of it once or twice a day, according to the quantity, without any bread, unless they have with them some toasted bread or biscuit. They thus contrive to live on short rations for a month or even longer, if necessary. Some soldiers take with them a little sack full of beef dried and reduced to a powder, which they employ in the same manner as the flour, and which is of great benefit as a more solid form of nourishment. Sometimes, too, they have recourse to horseflesh; for in a great army a large number of horses necessarily dies, and any that die in good condition furnish a welcome meal to men who are starving. I may add that men whose horses have died, when the Sultan moves his camp, stand in a long row on the road by which he is to pass with their harness or saddles on their heads, as a sign that they have lost their horses, and implore his help to purchase others. The Sultan then assists them with whatever gift he thinks fit. . . .

I mentioned that baggage animals are employed on campaign to carry the arms and tents, which mainly belong to the Janissaries. The Turks take the utmost care to keep their soldiers in good health and protected from the inclemency of the weather; against the foe they must protect themselves, but their health is a matter for which the State must provide. Hence one sees the Turk better clothed than armed. He is particularly afraid of the cold, against which, even in the summer, he guards himself by wearing three garments, of which the innermost—call it shirt or what you will—is woven of coarse thread and provides much warmth. As a further protection against cold and rain tents are always carried, in which each man is given just enough space to lie down, so that one tent holds twenty-five or thirty Janissaries. The material for the garments to which I have referred is provided at the public expense. To prevent any disputes or suspicion of favour, it is distributed in the following manner. The soldiers are summoned by companies in the darkness to a place chosen for the purpose—the balloting station or whatever name you like to give it—where are laid out ready as many portions of cloth as there are soldiers in the company; they enter and take whatever chance offers them in the darkness, and they can only ascribe it to chance whether they get a good or a bad piece of cloth. For the same reason their pay is not counted out to them but weighed, so that no one can complain that he has received light or chipped coins. Also their pay is given them not on the day on which it falls due but on the day previous.

The armour which is carried is chiefly for the use of the household cavalry, for the Janissaries are lightly armed and do not usually fight at close quarters, but use muskets. When the enemy is at hand and a battle is expected, the armour is brought out, but it consists mostly of old pieces picked up in various battlefields, the spoil of former victories. These are distributed to the household cavalry, who are otherwise protected by only a light shield. You can image how badly the armour, thus hurriedly given out, fits its wearers. One man's breastplate is too small, another's helmet is too large, another's coat of mail is too heavy for him to bear. There is something wrong everywhere; but they bear it with equanimity and think that only a coward finds fault with his arms, and vow to distinguish themselves in the fight, whatever their equipment may be; such is the confidence inspired by repeated victories and constant experience of warfare. Hence also they do not hesitate to re-enlist a veteran infantryman in the cavalry, though he has never fought on horseback, since they are convinced that one who has warlike experience and long service will acquit himself well in any kind of fighting. . . .

B. Bows and Arrows and Other Matters (1560)

In many streets of Constantinople and at cross-roads there are shooting-grounds where not only boys and young men but even men of more advanced years congregate. An official is put in charge of the target and looks after it, watering the butt every day, since otherwise it would dry up and the arrows would not stick in it; for in the shooting-grounds they only use blunt arrows. The custodian of the target is always present and extracts the arrows from the earth, and after cleaning them throws them back to the archers. This entitles him to a fixed payment from every one, which provides him with a livelihood. The front of the target looks like a small door, which may perhaps have given rise to the proverb about 'shooting against the door,' which the Greeks applied to any one who altogether missed the target. For I believe that the Greeks formerly used the same kind of target, and that the Turks adopted it from them. I know, of course, that the use of the bow by the Turks is very ancient, but there is no reason why, when they came as conquerors to the Greek cities, they should not have continued the use of the target and butt which they found there. For no nation has shown less reluctance to adopt the useful inventions of others; for example, they have appropriated to their own use large and small cannons and many other of our discoveries. They have, however, never been able to bring themselves to print books and set up public clocks. They hold that their scriptures, that is, their sacred books, would no longer be scriptures if they were printed; and if they established public clocks, they think that the authority of their muezzins and their ancient rites would suffer diminution. In other matters they pay great respect to the time-honoured customs of foreign nations, even to the detriment of their own religious scruples. This, however, is only true of the lower classes. Every one knows how far they are from sympathizing with the rites of the Christian Church. The Greek priests, however, have a custom of, as it were, opening the closed sea by blessing the waters at a fixed date in the spring, before which the sailors do not readily entrust themselves to the waves. This ceremony the Turks do not altogether disregard. And so, when their preparations for a voyage have been made, they come to the Greeks and ask whether the waters have been blessed; and if they say that they have not been blessed, they put off the sailing, but, if they are told that the ceremony has been performed, they embark and set sail. . . .

There is one point about Turkish military manœuvres which I must not omit, namely, the old custom which goes back to the Parthians of pretending to flee on horseback and then shooting with their arms at the enemy when he rashly pursues. They practise the rapid execution of this device in the following manner. They fix a brazen ball on the top of a very high pole, or mast, erected on level ground, and urge their horses at full speed towards the mast; and then, when they have almost passed it, they suddenly turn round and, learning back, discharge an arrow at the ball, while the horse continues its course. By frequent practice they become able without any difficulty to hit their enemy unawares by shooting backwards as they fly. . . .

C. Christian Slaves (1555)

After remaining about a fortnight at Constantinople in order to regain my strength, I started on my journey to Vienna, the beginning of which may be said to have been ill omened. Just as we were leaving the city, we were met by wagon-loads of boys and girls who were being brought from Hungary to be sold in Constantinople. There is no commoner kind of merchandise than this in Turkey; and, just as on the roads out of Antwerp one meets loads of various kinds of goods, so from time to time we were met by gangs of wretched Christian slaves of every kind who were being led to horrible servitude. Youths and men of advanced years were driven along in herds or else were tied together with chains, as horses with us are taken to market, and trailed along in a long line. At the sight I could scarcely restrain my tears in pity for the wretched plight of the Christian population. . . .

STUDY QUESTIONS

1. In the inscription what does Suleiman reveal about his religious convictions? How does Suleiman describe the extent of his power?
2. According to Busbecq, in what ways did the Ottomans attempt to ensure the effectiveness of their army? In what ways did the Turkish army combine the use of new technologies with very old approaches to warfare?
3. What does Busbecq observe about the openness of the Turks to borrowing from other cultures? What technologies that were important to the Europeans did the Turks choose not to borrow? Why?
4. What is Busbecq's reaction to the *devshirme?*
5. Do you detect any bias in Busbecq's observations? Are there hints of exaggeration in Busbecq's letters? Why might he have wanted to overplay Ottoman military strength?
6. How did slavery in the Ottoman Empire compare with slavery in other parts of the world, for example, the Americas and Africa?
7. What are the advantages and disadvantages of using travelers' reports like that of Busbecq as sources of historical evidence?

5

Babur and the Establishment of Mughal Rule in India

In 1000 C.E. Muslim nomads from the region of present-day Afghanistan began to conduct raids against the predominantly Hindu princes and peasants of India. The nomads were soon able to establish their control over much of northern India, making Delhi their capital in 1206. For the next three centuries Islamic sultans in Delhi struggled, with intermittent success, against both rival Muslim and native Hindu military leaders to make their rule effective.

By 1500 the regime of the Delhi sultans was falling apart. A powerful new Muslim military leader of Turkish and Mongol descent, Babur (1483–1530), emerged on the arid plains northwest of India. In 1504 Babur captured Kabul and made this city his capital. From Kabul Babur carried out a series of raids on the Muslim and Hindu warlords of northern India, finally capturing Delhi in 1526.

Babur's seizure of Delhi was a major turning point in the history of India. Babur and his son and successor, Humayam (reigned 1530–1556), established a new system of rule known as the Mughal dynasty (1526–1858), which brought political unity to India for the first time since the fall of the Gupta dynasty a thousand years earlier. During the first half of the Mughal period, from the 1550s to the early 1700s, the new dynasty provided effective centralized rule to much of the Indian subcontinent. In addition, during the Mughal era many Hindus converted to Islam, a process which had begun under the Delhi sultans but now continued and accelerated. Although the great majority of the Indian peasantry remained Hindu, many urban dwellers, lower-caste Hindus, and residents of certain regions such as east Bengal voluntarily adopted the faith of the Mughal conquerors. Political and economic pressures exerted by the Mughal rulers, beginning with Babur, also led to conversions. As a result of the conversions to Islam, the religious map of India was significantly altered in ways that continue to shape the lives of south Asians today.

Babur was a fierce warrior, but he also loved Persian poetry and elaborate gardens. Although he seems to have spent much of his life on horseback, he nonetheless found the time to write a fascinating account of his own life. Babur's memoirs,

From *The Baburnama: Memoirs of Babur, Prince and Emperor*, translated, edited, and annotated by Wheeler M. Thackston. Translation copyright © 1996 by Smithsonian Institution. Used by permission of Oxford University Press, Inc., pp. 185, 323–327, 363, 415.

known as the *Baburnama*, are often remarkably revealing about personal matters and provide scholars with valuable information regarding state-building in sixteenth-century Asia. In the selections from the *Baburnama* we can follow Babur and his soldiers as they enter India for the first time in 1505, win the decisive battle at Panipat north of Delhi in 1526, and then begin the process of establishing their new regime.

First Incursion into Hindustan

In the month of Sha'ban [January 1505] when the sun was in the sign of Aquarius we rode out of Kabul for Hindustan. Stopping six times overnight on the Badam Chashma and Jagdalak road, we came to Adinapur. I had never seen a hot climate or any of Hindustan before. When we reached Nangarhar, a new world came into view—different plants, different trees, different animals and birds, different tribes and people, different manners and customs. It was astonishing, truly astonishing. . . .

. . .

Preparation for Battle [1526]

We marched from there, arrayed the right and left wings and center, and had a *dim* [a count of the soldiers]. We had fewer men than we had estimated. I ordered the whole army, in accordance with rank, to bring carts, which numbered about seven hundred altogether. Master Ali-Quli was told to tie them together with ox-harness ropes instead of chains, after the Anatolian manner, keeping a distance of six to seven large shields between every two carts. The matchlockmen could then stand behind the fortification to fire their guns. Five or six days were spent arranging it, and when it was ready I summoned to general council all the begs and great warriors who knew what they were talking about. We discussed the following: Panipat was a town with lots of suburbs and houses. The suburbs and houses would protect one side, but it was necessary to fortify our other sides with the carts and shields and to station matchlockmen and foot soldiers behind them. This having been decided, we marched, bivouacked, and then came to Panipat on Wednesday the last day of Jumada II [April 12].

To our right were the town and suburbs. Directly before us were the arranged shields. To the left and elsewhere were trenches and pylons. At every distance of an arrow shot, space was left for one hundred to 150 cavalrymen to emerge. Some of the soldiers were hesitant, but their trepidation was baseless, for only what God has decreed from all eternity will happen. They cannot be blamed, however, for being afraid, even if God was on their side. They had traveled for two or three months from their homeland, and had had to deal with an unfamiliar people whose language we did not know and who did not know ours. . . .

Sultan Ibrahim's army was estimated at one hundred thousand. He and his commanders were said to have nearly a thousand elephants. Moreover, he possessed the treasury left over from two generations of his fathers. The custom in Hindustan is to hire liege men for money before major battles. Such people are called *badhandi*. If Sultan Ibrahim had had a mind to, he could have hired one hundred thousand to two hundred thousand troops. Thank God he was able neither to satisfy his warriors nor to part with his treasury. How was he to please his men when

Babur Receiving Gifts on the Birth of His Eldest Son in 1507.
Mughal culture introduced new forms of portraiture to India; from
the Baburnama Gouache Mughal (Akbar period), ca. 1590.
(Victoria & Albert Museum/Art Resource, NY.)

his nature was so overwhelmingly dominated by miserliness? He himself was an in-
experienced young man who craved beyond all things the acquisition of money—
neither his oncoming nor his stand was calculated to have a good end, and neither
his march nor his fighting was energetic. . . .

The Battle of Panipat [1526]

On Friday the eighth of Rajab [April 20] news came at dawn from the scouts that
the enemy was coming in battle array. We put on our armor, armed ourselves, and
got to horse.

The enemy's troops appeared, headed toward the left wing. For this reason
Abdul-Aziz, who had been assigned to the reserve, was dispatched as reinforcement

to the left wing. Sultan Ibrahim's army could be seen nearby, coming quickly without stopping. However, as they came farther forward and our troops became visible to them, they broke the ranks they had maintained and, as though undecided whether to stand or proceed, were able to do neither.

The order was given for the men who had been assigned to the flank assault to circle around to the enemy's rear from left and right, shoot their arrows, and begin to fight, and for the right and left wings to advance and engage the enemy. The flank assaulters circled around and began to shoot. From the left wing Mahdi Khwaja had already reached the enemy; advancing upon him was a contingent with an elephant, but by shooting many arrows he drove them back.

Master Ali-Qulī got off a few good gunshots from in front of the center. Mustafa the artilleryman also fired some good shots from the mortars mounted on carts to the left of the center. Right wing, left, wing, center, and flank assault shot arrows into the enemy from all sides and fought in all seriousness. Once or twice the enemy tried halfhearted assaults in the direction of our right and left wings, but our men pushed them into their own center by shooting. The enemy's right and left flanks were so crowded into one spot that they were not able to go forward or to find a way to escape.

The sun was one lance high when battle was enjoined. The fighting continued until midday. At noon the enemy was overcome and vanquished to the delight of our friends. By God's grace and generosity such a difficult action was made easy for us, and such a numerous army was ground into the dust in half a day. Five or six thousand men were killed in one place near Ibrahim. All told, the dead of this battle were estimated at between fifteen and sixteen thousand. Later, when we came to Agra, we learned from reports by the people of Hindustan that forty to fifty thousand men had died in the battle. With the enemy defeated and felled, we proceeded. Along the way the men began to capture the fallen commanders and Afghans and bring them in. Droves of elephants were caught and presented by the elephant keepers. Thinking that Ibrahim may have escaped, we assigned Qīsïmtay Mirza, Baba Chuhra, and Böchkä's troops from the royal tabin to pursue him behind the enemy lines and move with all speed to Agra. Crossing through the midst of Ibrahim's camp, we inspected the tents and pavilions and then camped beside a still river. It was midafternoon when Tahir the Axman, Khalifa's brother-in-law, discovered Sultan Ibrahim's body amidst many corpses and brought in his head.

That very day we assigned Humayun Mirza, Khwaja Kalan, Muhammadi, Shah-Mansur Barlas, Yunus Ali, Abdullah, and Wali Khazin to proceed swiftly and unencumbered, get hold of Agra, and confiscate the treasury. We appointed Mahdi Khwaja, Muhammad-Sultan Mirza, Adil Sultan, Sultan-Junayd Barlas, and Qutlugh-Qadam to separate themselves from the baggage and ride fast, enter the Delhi fortress, and guard the treasuries. The next morning we proceeded for a league and then, for the sake of the horses, camped beside the Jumna.

Babur Enters Delhi

On Tuesday, after two bivouacs, I circumambulated Shaykh Nizam Awliya's tomb and camped beside the Jumna directly opposite Delhi. That evening I toured the Delhi fortress, where I spent the night; the next morning, Wednesday, I circumambulated Khwaja Qutbuddin's tomb and toured Sultan Ghiyasuddin Balban's and

Sultan Aluddin Khalji's tombs, buildings, and minaret, the Shamsi pool, the Khass pool, and Sultan Bahlul's and Sultan Iskandar's tombs and gardens. After the tour I returned to the camp, got on a boat, and drank spirits.

I made Wali Qizil the provost of Delhi; I made Dost the divan of the province of Delhi; and I had the treasuries there sealed and turned them over to them for safekeeping.

On Thursday we marched out and camped beside the Jumna directly opposite Tughluqabad.

On Friday we stayed in camp. Mawlana Mahmud, Shaykh Zayn, and some others went to perform the Friday prayer in Delhi and read the proclamation in my name. Having distributed some money to the poor and unfortunate, they returned to camp.

On Saturday the army proceeded by forced march toward Agra. I went for a tour of Tughluqabad and returned to camp.

On Friday the twenty-second of Rajab [May 4] we stopped in Sulayman Farmuli's quarters in the suburbs of Agra. Since this site was far from the fortress, we moved the next morning to Jalal Khan Jighat's palace. Humayun had gone on ahead, but the men inside the fortress made excuses to keep him out. When they noticed how unruly the people were, they maintained watch over the exit, afraid someone might pilfer the treasury, until we should get there. . . .

• • •

Ali-Quli Casts a Mortar

Master Ali-Quli was ordered to cast a large mortar to be used on Bayana and some of the other fortresses that had not yet entered our domain. When he had the smelting furnace and all the implements ready, he sent someone to inform me. On Monday the fifteenth of Muharram [October 22, 1526] we went to watch Master Ali-Quli cast the mortar. Around the place where it was to be cast he had constructed eight smelting furnaces and had already melted the metal. From the bottom of each furnace he had made a channel straight to the mortar mold. Just as we got there he was opening the holes in the furnaces. The molten metal was pouring like water into the mold, but after a while, before the mold was filled, one by one the streams of molten metal coming from the furnaces stopped. There was some flaw either in the furnace or in the metal. Master Ali-Quli went into a strange depression and was about to throw himself into the mold of molten bronze, but I soothed him, gave him a robe of honor, and got him out of his black mood. A day or two later, when the mold had cooled, they opened it, and Master Ali-Quli sent someone to announce with glee that the shaft was flawless. It was then easy to attach the powder chamber. He took out the shaft and assigned some men to fix it, and got to work connecting the chamber.

• • •

Post System Established Between Agra and Kabul

On Thursday the fourth of Rabi' II [December 17, 1528], it was decided that Chaqmaq Beg with Shahi Tamghachi as recorder should measure by cord the distance from Agra to Kabul. Every nine kos they were to raise a tower twelve yards high with a chardara on top. Every eighteen kos six post horses were to be kept, and maintenance for the post riders, grooms, and feed for the horses were to be assigned. It was ordered that if the place where the post horses were kept was a royal demesne, the above-mentioned items were to be taken care of therefrom. Otherwise, they were to make it the responsibility of the beg on whose estate it was. Chaqmaq and Shahi left Agra that same day. . . .

STUDY QUESTIONS

1. What was Babur's first reaction to India?
2. What measures did Babur take to prepare for the battle of Panipat?
3. How does Babur compare his army with that of Sultan Ibrahim?
4. How does Babur explain his victory at Panipat? In Babur's judgment which was more important, his own preparations for the battle or God's "grace and generosity"?
5. What measures did Babur take to consolidate his power and establish a new regime after his victory at Panipat?
6. What weapons seem to have been most important to Babur? Where did he obtain these weapons?
7. How does Babur's army compare with that of Suleiman the Lawgiver? (See Chapter 4.)
8. In what ways were the Ottoman and Mughal states similar and different in the sixteenth centuries?

6

Confucian Ideals in Ming China: A Set of Family Instructions

The ideas of Confucius, the great Chinese philosopher who was born in the sixth century B.C.E., have been enormously influential in China for the past 2000 years. During the Han dynasty (206 B.C.E.–220 C.E.) Confucian ideas were adopted as the official state ideology in China. Following the collapse of the Han dynasty, Confucianism lost influence to Daoism and to Buddhism, the latter a Chinese "import" from India. However, beginning in the ninth century Confucian ideas made a comeback in China, and they became increasingly important in succeeding centuries.

The conquest of China by the Mongols, who ruled China from 1279 to 1368, was something of a setback for Confucianism. But the restoration of native Chinese rule by the Ming emperors beginning in 1368 marked the beginning of another major period of Confucian renewal in China, a period which lasted, in some ways, into the twentieth century. (See Chapters 15, 32, and 33 on China in the nineteenth and twentieth centuries.) Chinese emperors during the Ming dynasty (1368–1644) and succeeding Ch'ing dynasty (1644–1912) gave strong support to Confucian ideals as a way of promoting social order.

In the selection that follows, dating from the late Ming period, Confucian ideals are vividly illustrated in a set of instructions for families compiled by the Miu lineage in Guandong province in southern China. Lineages, also known as clans or common-descent groups, were alliances of extended families who joined together for mutual support. The members of lineages met together regularly to celebrate the memory of their ancestors and to manage their common interests, which often included the joint ownership of land. Lineages were quite important in China from the Ming period onward, especially in the southern part of the country.

Work Hard at One of the Principal Occupations

1. To be filial to one's parents, to be loving to one's brothers, to be diligent and frugal—these are the first tenets of a person of good character. They must be thoroughly understood and faithfully carried out.

From *Chinese Civilization: A Sourcebook*, Second Edition by Patricia Buckley Ebrey, pp. 238–244. Copyright © 1993 by Patricia Buckley Ebrey. Reprinted with the permission of The Free Press, a Division of Simon & Schuster, Inc.

One's conscience should be followed like a strict teacher and insight should be sought through introspection. One should study the words and deeds of the ancients to find out their ultimate meanings. One should always remember the principles followed by the ancients, and should not become overwhelmed by current customs. For if one gives in to cruelty, pride, or extravagance, all virtues will be undermined, and nothing will be achieved.

Parents have special responsibilities. The *Book of Changes* says: "The members of a family have strict sovereigns." These "sovereigns" are the parents. Their position in a family is one of unique authority, and they should utilize their authority to dictate matters to maintain order, and to inspire respect, so that the members of the family will all be obedient. If the parents are lenient and indulgent, there will be many troubles which in turn will give rise to even more troubles. Who is to blame for all this? The elders in a family must demand discipline of themselves, following all rules and regulations to the letter, so that the younger members emulate their good behavior and exhort each other to abide by the teachings of the ancient sages. Only in this way can the family hope to last for generations. . . .

2. Those youngsters who have taken Confucian scholarship as their hereditary occupation should be sincere and hard-working, and try to achieve learning naturally while studying under a teacher. Confucianism is the only thing to follow if they wish to bring glory to their family. Those who know how to keep what they have but do not study are as useless as puppets made of clay or wood. Those who study, even if they do not succeed in the examinations, can hope to become teachers or to gain personal benefit. However, there are people who study not for learning's sake, but as a vulgar means of gaining profit. These people are better off doing nothing.

Youngsters who are incapable of concentrating on studying should devote themselves to farming; they should personally grasp the ploughs and eat the fruit of their own labor. In this way they will be able to support their families. If they fold their hands and do nothing, they will soon have to worry about hunger and cold. If, however, they realize that their forefathers also worked hard and that farming is a difficult way of life, they will not be inferior to anyone. In earlier dynasties, officials were all selected because they were filial sons, loving brothers, and diligent farmers. This was to set an example for all people to devote themselves to their professions, and to ensure that the officials were familiar with the hardships of the common people, thereby preventing them from exploiting the commoners for their own profit.

3. Farmers should personally attend to the inspection, measurement, and management of the fields, noting the soil as well as the terrain. The early harvest as well as the grain taxes and the labor service obligations should be carefully calculated. Anyone who indulges in indolence and entrusts these matters to others will not be able to distinguish one kind of crop from another and will certainly be cheated by others. I do not believe such a person could escape bankruptcy.

4. The usual occupations of the people are farming and commerce. If one tries by every possible means to make a great profit from these occupations, it usually leads to loss of capital. Therefore it is more profitable to put one's energy into farming the land; only when the fields are too far away to be tilled by oneself should they be leased to others. One should solicit advice from old farmers as to one's own capacity in farming.

Those who do not follow the usual occupations of farming or business should be taught a skill. Being an artisan is a good way of life and will also shelter a person from hunger and cold. All in all, it is important to remember that one should work hard when young, for when youth expires one can no longer achieve anything. Many people learn this lesson only after it is too late. We should guard against this mistake. . . .

6. Housewives should take full charge of the kitchen. They should make sure that the store of firewood is sufficient, so that even if it rains several days in succession, they will not be forced to use silver or rice to pay for firewood, thereby impoverishing the family. Housewives should also closely calculate the daily grocery expenses, and make sure there is no undue extravagance. Those who simply sit and wait to be fed not only are treating themselves like pigs and dogs, but also are leading their whole households to ruin. . . .

Observe the Rituals and Proprieties

1. Capping and wedding ceremonies should be carried out according to one's means. Funerals and burials, being important matters, should be more elaborate, but one should still be mindful of financial considerations. Any other petty formalities not found in the *Book of Rites* should be abolished.

2. Marriage arrangements should not be made final by the presenting of betrothal gifts until the boy and girl have both reached thirteen; otherwise, time might bring about changes which cause regrets.

3. For the seasonal sacrifices, the ancestral temple should be prepared in advance and the ceremonies performed at dawn in accordance with [Zhu Xi's] *Family Rituals* and our own ancestral temple regulations.

4. For burials one should make an effort to acquire solid and long-lasting objects to be placed in the coffin; but one need not worry as much about the tomb itself, which can be constructed according to one's means. The ancients entrusted their bodies to the hills and mountains, indifferent to whether their names would be remembered by posterity; their thinking was indeed profound.

5. Sacrifices at the graves should be made on Tomb Sweeping Day and at the Autumn Festival. Because the distances to different mountains vary, it is difficult to reach every grave on those days. Therefore, all branch families should be notified in advance of the order of priority: first, the founding father of our lineage; then ancestors earlier than great-great-grandfather; next, ancestors down to each person's grandfather. Established customs should be followed in deciding how much wine and meat should be used, how many different kinds of sacrificial offerings should be presented, and how much of the yearly budget should be spent on the sacrifices. All of these should be recorded in a special "sacrifice book" in order to set standards.

6. Not celebrating one's birthday has since ancient times been regarded as an exemplary virtue. An exception is the birthdays of those who are beyond their sixty-first year, which should be celebrated by their sons and grandsons drinking to their health. But under no circumstances should birthdays become pretexts for heavy drinking. If either of one's parents has died, it is an especially unfilial act to forget him or her and indulge in drinking and feasting. Furthermore, to drink until dead-drunk not only affects one's mind but also harms one's health. The numbers of people who have been ruined by drinking should serve as a warning.

7. On reaching five, a boy should be taught to recite the primers and not be allowed to show arrogance or laziness. On reaching six, a girl should be taught [Ban Zhao's] *Admonitions for Women* and not be allowed to venture out of her chamber. If children are frequently given snacks and playfully entertained, their nature will be spoiled and they will grow up to be unruly and bad. This can be prevented if caught at an early age.

8. When inviting guests to dinner, one should serve not more than five dishes or more than two soups. Wine and rice should also be served in the right proportion.

9. When attending a funeral service, one should bring only incense and paper money, never hand towels, fruit, or wine, and should stay for only one cup of tea.

10. Gifts presented to us on the occasion of ancestor worship are to be properly compensated for by cash. If the gift box contains a pig's head, the corresponding return would be one-tenth of a tael of silver; for two geese and wine it would be three-tenths of a tael; for a lamb and wine, half a tael; a pig and wine, one tael. In addition, two-hundredths of a tael should be placed in an envelope and presented as a token compensation for fruit and wine. Whether or not these are accepted, and whether or not another present is given in return, depends on the other party. For ceremonies held in our own village, each person should contribute two-hundredths of a tael of silver, and four people should share one table. Those who have contributed yet fail to attend the banquet will get their money back in the original envelope. This is to be stated in the village agreements and to be practiced by all.

Prohibit Extravagance

1. All our young people should wear cotton clothes and eat vegetables. Only on special occasions such as ancestor worship or dinner parties are they to be allowed to drink wine, eat meat, and temporarily put on new clothes. They are fortunate enough to be sheltered from hunger and cold; how dare they feel ashamed of their coarse clothing and coarse food! Also, they should do physical labor. As long as they are capable of carrying loads with their hands and on their backs, they have no need to hire servants. They are fortunate enough not to be ordered around by others; how dare they order other people around! They should learn to cherish every inch of cloth and every half-penny, thereby escaping poverty.

2. Among relatives, presents should not be exchanged more than twice a year, and the gifts should not cost more than one-tenth of a tael of silver. Relatives should agree to abide by the principle of frugality and refuse any gift exceeding this limit. This rule, however, does not include celebrations and funerals, for which custom should be followed. . . .

Exercise Restraint

1. Our young people should know their place and observe correct manners. They are not permitted to gamble, to fight, to engage in lawsuits, or to deal in salt privately. Such unlawful acts will only lead to their own downfall.

2. If land or property is not obtained by righteous means, descendants will not be able to enjoy it. When the ancients invented characters, they put gold next to two spears to mean "money," indicating that the danger of plunder or robbery is associated with it. If money is not accumulated by good means, it will disperse like overflowing water; how could it be put to any good? The result is misfortune for

oneself as well as for one's posterity. This is the meaning of the saying: "The way of Heaven detests fullness, and only the humble gain." Therefore, accumulation of great wealth inevitably leads to great loss. How true are the words of Laozi!

A person's fortune and rank are predestined. One can only do one's best according to propriety and one's own ability; the rest is up to Heaven. If one is easily contented, then a diet of vegetables and soups provides a lifetime of joy. If one does not know one's limitations and tries to accumulate wealth by immoral and dishonest means, how can one avoid disaster? To be able to support oneself through life and not leave one's sons and grandsons in hunger and cold is enough; why should one toil so much?

3. Pride is a dangerous trait. Those who pride themselves on wealth, rank, or learning are inviting evil consequences. Even if one's accomplishments are indeed unique, there is no need to press them on anyone else. "The way of Heaven detests fullness, and only the humble gain." I have seen the truth of this saying many times.

4. Taking concubines in order to beget heirs should be a last resort, for the sons of the legal wife and the sons of the concubine are never of one mind, causing innumerable conflicts between half brothers. If the parents are in the least partial, problems will multiply, creating misfortune in later generations. Since families have been ruined because of this, it should not be taken lightly.

5. Just as diseases are caused by what goes into one's mouth, misfortunes are caused by what comes out of one's mouth. Those who are immoderate in eating and unrestrained in speaking have no one else to blame for their own ruin.

6. Most men lack resolve and listen to what their women say. As a result, blood relatives become estranged and competitiveness, suspicion, and distance arise between them. Therefore, when a wife first comes into a family, it should be made clear to her that such things are prohibited. "Start teaching one's son when he is a baby; start teaching one's daughter-in-law when she first arrives." That is to say, preventive measures should be taken early.

7. "A family's fortune can be foretold from whether its members are early risers" is a maxim of our ancient sages. Everyone, male and female, should rise before dawn and should not go to bed until after the first drum. Never should they indulge themselves in a false sense of security and leisure, for such behavior will eventually lead them to poverty.

8. Young family members who deliberately violate family regulations should be taken to the family temple, have their offenses reported to the ancestors, and be severely punished. They should then be taught to improve themselves. Those who do not accept punishment or persist in their wrongdoings will bring harm to themselves.

9. As a preventive measure against the unpredictable, the gates should be closed at dusk, and no one should be allowed to go out. Even when there are visitors, dinner parties should end early, so that there will be no need for lighting lamps and candles. On very hot or very cold days, one should be especially considerate of the kitchen servants.

10. For generations this family has dwelt in the country, and everyone has had a set profession; therefore, our descendants should not be allowed to change their place of residence. After living in the city for three years, a person forgets everything about farming; after ten years, he does not even know his lineage. Extravagance and leisure transform people, and it is hard for anyone to remain unaf-

fected. I once remarked that the only legitimate excuse to live in a city temporarily is to flee from bandits.

11. The inner and outer rooms, halls, doorways, and furniture should be swept and dusted every morning at dawn. Dirty doorways and courtyards and haphazardly placed furniture are sure signs of a declining family. Therefore, a schedule should be followed for cleaning them, with no excuses allowed.

12. Those in charge of cooking and kitchen work should make sure that breakfast is served before nine o'clock in the morning and dinner before five o'clock in the afternoon. Every evening the iron wok and other utensils should be washed and put away, so that the next morning, after rising at dawn, one can expect tea and breakfast to be prepared immediately and served on time. In the kitchen no lamps are allowed in the morning or at night. This is not only to save the expense, but also to avoid harmful contamination of food. Although this is a small matter, it has a great effect on health. Furthermore, since all members of the family have their regular work to do, letting them toil all day without giving them meals at regular hours is no way to provide comfort and relief for them. If these rules are deliberately violated, the person in charge will be punished as an example to the rest.

13. On the tenth and twenty-fifth days of every month, all the members of this branch, from the honored aged members to the youngsters, should gather at dusk for a meeting. Each will give an account of what he has learned, by either calling attention to examples of good and evil, or encouraging diligence, or expounding his obligations, or pointing out tasks to be completed. Each member will take turns presenting his own opinions and listening attentively to others. He should examine himself in the matters being discussed and make efforts to improve himself. The purpose of these meetings is to encourage one another in virtue and to correct each other's mistakes.

The members of the family will take turns being the chairman of these meetings, according to schedule. If someone is unable to chair a meeting on a certain day, he should ask the next person in line to take his place. The chairman should provide tea, but never wine. The meetings may be canceled on days of ancestor worship, parties, or other such occasions, or if the weather is severe. Those who are absent from these meetings for no reason are only doing themselves harm.

There are no set rules for where the meeting should be held, but the place should be convenient for group discussions. The time of the meeting should always be early evening, for this is when people have free time. As a general precaution the meeting should never last until late at night.

14. Women from lower-class families who stop at our houses tend to gossip, create conflicts, peek into the kitchens, or induce our women to believe in prayer and fortune-telling, thereby cheating them out of their money and possessions. Consequently, one should question these women often and punish those who come for no reason, so as to put a stop to the traffic.

15. Blood relatives are as close as the branches of a tree, yet their relationships can still be differentiated according to importance and priority: Parents should be considered before brothers, and brothers should be considered before wives and children. Each person should fulfill his own duties and share with others profit and loss, joy and sorrow, life and death. In this way, the family will get along well and be blessed by Heaven. Should family members fight over property or end

up treating each other like enemies, then when death or misfortune strikes they will be of even less use than strangers. If our ancestors have consciousness, they will not tolerate these unprincipled descendants who are but animals in man's clothing. Heaven responds to human vices with punishments as surely as an echo follows a sound. I hope my sons and grandsons take my words seriously.

16. To get along with patrilinear relatives, fellow villagers, and relatives through marriage, one should be gentle in speech and mild in manners. When one is opposed by others, one may remonstrate with them; but when others fall short because of their limitations, one should be tolerant. If one's youngsters or servants get into fights with others, one should look into oneself to find the blame. It is better to be wronged than to wrong others. Those who take affront and become enraged, who conceal their own shortcomings and seek to defeat others, are courting immediate misfortune. Even if the other party is unbearably unreasonable, one should contemplate the fact that the ancient sages had to endure much more. If one remains tolerant and forgiving, one will be able to curb the other party's violence.

Preserve the Family Property

1. The houses, fields, and ponds that have been accumulated by the family should not be divided or sold. Violators of this rule will be severely admonished and barred from the ancestral temple. . . .

STUDY QUESTIONS

1. According to the *Miu Family Instructions,* what are the attributes of someone with "good character"?
2. What roles are prescribed in the *Family Instructions* for parents, young people, and women?
3. What procedures does the lineage have for enforcing these prescriptions?
4. What do we learn from the *Family Instructions* about the importance of ritual and ancestor worship in Chinese culture?
5. What do the *Family Instructions* reveal about the Chinese economy?
6. What can you infer about the likely age, sex, and social class of the author of the *Family Instructions?*
7. What are the strengths and weaknesses of Confucianism as a means of providing for social order?
8. In what ways would the values in the *Family Instructions* promote or discourage the development of a modern industrial society?
9. How did lineages in China resemble and differ from castes in India?
10. Are social hierarchies inevitable in large-scale societies?

7

Economy and Society in Latin America

On settling in the Americas, Spanish and Portuguese colonists created new economic systems that tied the New World to European capitalism. By the middle of the sixteenth century, Spaniards discovered large veins of silver north of Mexico City at Zacatecas and in the southern Andes at Potosí. As the great wealth of these discoveries became apparent, Spaniards shaped the other sectors of the American economy to support silver. Colonists formed large landed estates (*haciendas*) and textile mills (*obrajes*) to supply animals, food, and clothing to mining centers and to growing cities that served as administrative centers as well as commercial and transportation hubs. Although most of the silver was exported to Europe, either going into the king's treasury or paying for luxury goods, enough minted money stayed in the New World to monetize the economy. In this process money exchange replaced tribute as the means by which producers transferred goods to consumers. In Portuguese America a similar process took place, except that the product was sugar, not silver. Sugar plantations, particularly in northeastern Brazil, forged a direct economic link to Europe, spurred the development of ranches and farms, and monetized the economy. Despite boom and bust periods, the economic ties between Europe and America became stronger, and the monetary economy spread ever more widely.

The formation of haciendas, plantations, mills, and mines had dramatic social consequences. To solve their labor needs, Spaniards and Portuguese recruited native Americans and African blacks. The unequal exploitative relationship between European owner and colored worker, whether Indian, black, or mixed, became the chief characteristic of society. These two passages describing work in the silver mine at Potosí and in a textile mill in Puebla, Mexico, were written by a Carmelite monk who traveled throughout Spanish America between 1612 and 1620.

Selection 1 from "The Potosí Mine and Indian Forced Labor in Peru," in Antonio Vásquez de Espinosa, *Compendium and Description of the West Indies*, translated by C. U. Clark (Washington, D.C.: The Smithsonian Institution, 1942), pp. 623–625. Selection 2 from "A Mexican Textile Factory," in Espinosa, *Compendium*, pp. 133–134.

1. THE POTOSÍ MINE AND INDIAN LABOR IN PERU

Continuing to Describe the Magnificence of the Potosí Range; and of the Indians There under Forced Labor (Mita) in Its Operations.

1652. According to His Majesty's warrant, the mine owners on this massive range have a right to the mita of 13,300 Indians in the working and exploitation of the mines, both those which have been discovered, those now discovered, and those which shall be discovered. It is the duty of the Corregidor of Potosí to have them rounded up and to see that they come in from all the provinces between Cuzco over the whole of El Collao and as far as the frontiers of Tarija and Tomina; this Potosí Corregidor has power and authority over all the Corregidors in those provinces mentioned; for if they do not fill the Indian mita allotment assigned each one of them in accordance with the capacity of their provinces as indicated to them, he can send them, and does, salaried inspectors to report upon it, and when the remissness is great or remarkable, he can suspend them, notifying the Viceroy of the fact.

These Indians are sent out every year under a captain whom they choose in each village or tribe, for him to take them and oversee them for the year each has to serve; every year they have a new election, for as some go out, others come in. This works out very badly, with great losses and gaps in the quotas of Indians, the villages being depopulated; and this gives rise to great extortions and abuses on the part of the inspectors toward the poor Indians, ruining them and thus depriving the caciques and chief Indians of their property and carrying them off in chains because they do not fill out the mita assignment, which they cannot do, for the reasons given and for others which I do not bring forward.

1653. These 13,300 are divided up every 4 months into 3 mitas, each consisting of 4,433 Indians, to work in the mines on the range and in the 120 smelters in the Potosí and Tarapaya areas; it is a good league between the two. These mita Indians earn each day, or there is paid each one for his labor, 4 reals. Besides these there are others not under obligation, who are mingados or hire themselves out voluntarily: these each get from 12 to 16 reals, and some up to 24, according to their reputation of wielding the pick and knowing how to get the ore out. These mingados will be over 4,000 in number. They and the mita Indians go up every Monday morning to the locality of Guayna Potosí which is at the foot of the range; the Corregidor arrives with all the provincial captains or chiefs who have charge of the Indians assigned them, and he there checks off and reports to each mine and smelter owner the number of Indians assigned him for his mine or smelter; that keeps him busy till 1 p.m., by which time the Indians are already turned over to these mine and smelter owners.

After each has eaten his ration, they climb up the hill, each to his mine, and go in, staying there from that hour until Saturday evening without coming out of the mine; their wives bring them food, but they stay constantly underground, excavating and carrying out the ore from which they get the silver. They all have tallow candles, lighted day and night; that is the light they work with, for as they are underground, they have need of it all the time. The mere cost of these candles used in the mines on this range will amount every year to more than 300,000 pesos, even though tallow is cheap in that country, being abundant; but this is a very great expense, and it is almost incredible, how much is spent for candles in the operation of breaking down and getting out the ore.

These Indians have different functions in the handling of the silver ore; some break it up with bar or pick, and dig down in, following the vein in the mind; others bring it up; others up above keep separating the good and the poor in piles; others are occupied in taking it down from the range to the mills on herds of llamas; every day they bring up more than 8,000 of these native beasts of burden for this task. These teamsters who carry the metal do not belong to the mita, but are mingados—hired.

2. A MEXICAN TEXTILE FACTORY

Continuing the Description of the Features of This City and Diocese, and of Other Cities.

There are in this city [Puebla] large woolen mills in which they weave quantities of fine cloth, serge, and grogram, from which they make handsome profits, this being an important business in this country; and those who run these mills are still heathen (gentiles) in their Christianity. To keep their mills supplied with labor for the production of cloth and grograms they maintain individuals who are engaged and hired to ensnare poor innocents; seeing some Indian who is a stranger to the town, with some trickery or pretext, such as hiring him to carry something, like a porter, and paying him cash, they get him into the mill: once inside, they drop the deception, and the poor fellow never again gets outside that prison until he dies and they carry him out for burial. In this way they have gathered in and duped many married Indians with families, who have passed into oblivion here for 20 years, or longer, or their whole lives, without their wives and children knowing anything about them; for even if they want to get out, they cannot, thanks to the great watchfulness with which the doormen guard the exits. These Indians are occupied in carding, spinning, weaving, and the other operations of making cloth and grograms; and thus the owners make their profits by these unjust and unlawful means.

And although the Royal Council of the Indies, with the holy zeal which animates it for the service of God our Lord, of His Majesty, and of the Indians' welfare, has tried to remedy this evil with warrants and ordinances, which it constantly has sent and keeps sending, for the proper administration and the amelioration of this great hardship and enslavement of the Indians, and the Viceroy of New Spain appoints mill inspectors to visit them and remedy such matters, nevertheless, since most of those who set out on such commissions, aim rather at their own enrichment, however much it may weigh upon their consciences, than at the relief of the Indians, and since the mill owners pay them well, they leave the wretched Indians in the same slavery; and even if some of them are fired with holy zeal to remedy such abuses when they visit the mills, the mill owners keep places provided in the mills in which they hide the wretched Indians against their will, so that they do not see or find them, and the poor fellows cannot complain about their wrongs. This is the usual state of affairs in all the mills of this city and jurisdiction, and that of

Mexico City; the mill owners and those who have the mills under their supervision, do this without scruple, as if it were not a most serious mortal sin.

STUDY QUESTIONS

1. How were *mita* laborers recruited? Describe the difference between a *mingado* laborer and a *mita* laborer. What does this difference suggest about the formation of a new society in Peru?
2. How were the workers in *obrajes* recruited? What was the result of government intervention to improve workers' conditions?
3. How do the conditions described here compare with those of Russian serfs?

8

Political Styles in Latin America: Colonial Bureaucracy

The first governments in Latin America, after the overthrow of Indian states, were colonial administrations set up by Spain and Portugal. The selection in this chapter deals with important aspects of their political style. Many historians argue that the nature of colonial administration helped shape later political values and institutions in Latin America—even when colonial controls themselves were thrown off.

In theory, Spanish and Portuguese governmental systems concentrated power in the hands of their monarchs. Once a decision was made, it was supposedly executed by a hierarchy of officials descending from the king and his advisors in Europe to a vice-king, or viceroy, in the New World to local officials, or *corregidores*. Since local officials often lived far from centers of administration, they had the opportunity to exercise much freedom in the application of the law. But more than distance, the social and economic positions of local officials influenced the execution of their duties. Being often poor relatives of high churchmen or top governmental officials, they came to the New World to gain wealth and elevate their status. Furthermore, since the few lucrative jobs in mining and merchant activity were long ago occupied, and since manual labor, whether agricultural or artisan, was performed by the colored majority, Spanish newcomers sought government positions as a way of entering the economy in a favorable capacity. Few alternatives for upward mobility existed, a condition that remained endemic and persists today. Local officeholding became a means of enrichment.

Just as the owners of haciendas and mines exploited the labor of Indians and blacks, so the corregidores extorted money from Indian communities. They manipulated the tribute tax, which since 1650 was a head tax on adult male Indians paid in money. The selection describes the activities of a corregidor in the viceroyalty of Peru in the 1740s. The account was written by two agents of the king sent specifically to find corruption. Potential exaggeration on the part of the king's "spies" is lessened by the structure of the system. Since the corregidores had to pay a "surety bond" before collecting the money, they were forced to make up what they already had pledged. The system invited extortion.

From Don Jorge Juan and Don Antonio De Ulloa, *Discourse and Political Reflections on the Kingdom of Peru*, edited by John J. TePaske, translated by John J. TePaske and Bessie A. Clement (Norman, Okla.: University of Oklahoma Press, 1978), pp. 70–72. Copyright © 1978 by University of Oklahoma Press. Reprinted by permission.

Corregidores use many methods to enrich themselves at the expense of the Indians, and we shall start with the collection of tribute. In this matter they institute severe treatment, ignore justice, forget charity, and totally disregard the fear of God. Tribute is one revenue that corregidores count as profit or personal gain from their corregimiento. Clearly if they made collections honestly, they would not profit personally from the tribute, would do no harm to the Indians, and would not defraud the king; but all three result from their corrupt conduct. Their insatiable greed seeks nothing but its own satisfaction; overwhelmed by avarice, corregidores satisfy it by any means possible. They keep accounts in such a way that when they have completed their term in office and the accounts are examined as part of their *residencia* [judicial review after completion of office], they are absolved of all guilt simply by payment of a bribe to the judge making the investigation.

Tribute paid by the Indians to Your Majesty is a perquisite of the corregimientos. If corregidores initially find some reason for not assuming the obligation to collect tribute, they discover their own revenues are so small that they are obliged to do so in order to enjoy their full salaries and enrich themselves. Royal treasury officials of the corregimiento confer the right to collect tribute on corregidores after requiring payment of a surety bond as security for the money collected. Since bonds must be paid to these royal officials, they appoint functionaries satisfactory to them. While they have no obligation to name the corregidor, this is usually the case in order to avoid conflicts that might arise if someone else were named.

In the province of Quito [Ecuador] collections are made in two ways—one for the king's account and another for the corregidores'. Using the first method, the corregidor submits to the royal treasury officials an account of the total amount collected, checked against a census of the Indians in the corregimiento based on the baptismal and death records for each parish. Using the second method, royal officials auction off the right to collect tribute to the highest bidder. In this case the corregidor gets preference, if he wishes to take this privilege for the highest amount bid. Although an official account is drawn up, the Indians are told only whom they should pay. The corregidor is obligated to send to the royal treasury only the total amount of tribute bid. He is not required to give detailed accounts. In the province of Quito they began to use the first method at the order of the Viceroy of Peru, the Marqués de Villagarcía, as a result of our visit with him. This occurred because of the great amount of fraud perpetrated by the corregidores to the detriment of the royal treasury. Corregidores included in their accounts only the number of Indians they wished to mention, a group much smaller than those from whom they actually collected tribute. The remainder were listed as absent, disabled, or unable to pay. Another reason for the change in method was delay in payment to the royal treasury. Corregidores used tribute monies for their own trade and personal profit. Thus, besides the losses, the royal treasury suffered greatly from delays, so long in some instances that eight to ten years passed without closing the accounts. Ultimately, the new method was a way of protecting corregidores from the extortions of royal treasury officials, which often resulted in complete loss of the tribute.

STUDY QUESTIONS

1. By what mechanisms did the corregidor profit from his office?
2. What device did the king institute to detect fraud? How did the corregidor avoid censure and punishment?
3. What kind of political heritage is suggested by this report on Peru for later Latin American rulers and also for the ruled?

9

Baroque Culture in Latin America

The intellectual, cultural, and religious life of Latin America during its formative period was largely Iberian but contained important indigenous and African elements as well. Peninsular Iberians living in the New World, as well as their American-born descendants (creoles), copied forms from Spain and Portugal whether in architecture, poetry, or Catholic ritual. The varieties of Iberian regional practices gave way in America to one broadly adopted style that spread throughout the region. The best example of this is the grid plan for city planning. This chapter includes two different types of materials on evolving cultural and intellectual forms in early modern Latin America.

By the late seventeenth century, Spanish American intellectuals created their own Baroque style. No person was more influential in this effort than the Jeronymite nun Sister Juana Inez de la Cruz (1651–1695). Like other Baroque poets, she mastered the intricate rules of Baroque style and became adept at wordplay that often obscured meaning. But her cleverness failed to hide a troubled soul. In several poems she confronted problems encountered by women intellectuals in a male-dominated society. Born to an unmarried mother in a small village outside of Mexico City, she rebuked, in her poetry, the double standard in sexual relations. Attracted by experimentation to establish truth, she ridiculed the scholastics of the Catholic Church who manipulated biblical texts and the writings of Church fathers to prove anything they wished. Such views conflicted with her status as a woman and a nun. Having vowed obedience to the Church and her religious order, she became increasingly tormented by the jealousy and criticism of her superiors, male and female. Four years before she died, Sister Juana stopped writing, sold all her books to charity, and submitted totally to serving members of her order, many of whom had fallen ill during the pestilence of 1691. One of Sister Juana's poems directly exposed the arrogance and stupidity of men in their relations with women.

Selection 1 from Robert Graves, "Juana Inez de la Cruz" in *Encounter,* vol. 1, no. 3 (December, 1953) pp. 10–12. Selection 2 from Carlos de Siguenza y Góngora, *Glorias de Querétaro en la Nueva Congregación Eclesiastica de Maria Santisima de Guadalupe* (Mexico City, 1680, reprinted 1945); translated by Irving A. Leonard, in *Baroque Times in Old Mexico* (Ann Arbor: University of Michigan Press, 1959), pp. 125–128. Copyright © 1959 by the University of Michigan Press. Reprinted by permission of the University of Michigan Press.

Although Baroque culture in Mexico tormented independent thinkers such as Sister Juana, its popular side attracted ordinary people. Commoners could not write, but they could dress up. To make their contributions to religious celebrations, the Indians organized costume parades, or *máscaras*. As described by Carlos de Siguenza y Góngora in 1680, the natives of Querétaro, a grain-producing area north of Mexico City, dedicated their *máscara* to the Virgin of Guadalupe, for whom they had recently built a new church that was officially opened on the day of the parade. The description of the *máscara* shows that the Indians remembered their separate cultural inheritance. It also shows that by encouraging cultural mixture, the Spaniards provided a place for the Indians within society.

1. SELECTION OF SISTER JUANA INEZ DE LA CRUZ'S POETRY

Ah stupid men, unreasonable
    In blaming woman's nature,
Oblivious that your acts incite
    The very faults you censure.

If, of unparalleled desire,
    At her disdain you batter
With provocation of the flesh,
    What should her virtue matter?

Yet once you wear resistance down
    You reprimand her, showing
That what you diligently devised
    Was all her wanton doing.

With love you feign to be distraught
    (How gallant is your lying!
Like children, masked with coconuts.
    Their own selves terrifying).

And idiotically would seek
    In the same woman's carriage
A Thais for the sport of love,
    And a Lucrece for marriage.

What sight more comic than the man,
    All decent counsel loathing,
Who breathes upon a mirror's face
    Then mourns: "I can see nothing."

Whether rejected or indulged,
    You all have the same patter:
Complaining in the former case,
    But mocking in the latter.

No woman your esteem can earn,
    Though cautious and mistrustful;
You call her cruel, if denied,
    And if accepted, lustful.

Inconsequent and variable
    Your reason must be reckoned:
You charge the first girl with disdain;
    With lickerishness, the second.

How can the lady of your choice
    Temper her disposition,
When to be stubborn vexes you,
    But you detest submission?

So, what with all the rage and pain
    Caused by your greedy nature,
She would be wise who never loved
    And hastened her departure.

Let loved ones cage their liberties
    Like any captive bird; you
Will violate them none the less,
    Apostrophising virtue.

Which has the greater sin when burned
    By the same lawless fever:
She who is amorously deceived,
    Or he, the sly deceiver?

Or which deserves the sterner blame,
    Though each will be a sinner:
She who becomes a whore for pay,
    Or he who pays to win her?

Are you surrounded at your faults,
    Which could not well be direr?
Then love what you have made her be,
    Or, make as you desire her.

I warn you: trouble her no more,
    But earn the right to visit
Your righteous wrath on any jade
    Who might your lust solicit.

This arrogance of men in truth
    Comes armoured with all evil—
Sworn promise, please of urgency—
    O world, O flesh, O devil!

The Portuguese Baroque Style of Architecture Was Used Frequently in South America. It is seen here in San Francisco church in Salvador de Bahia, Brazil. (AP/Wide World Photos.)

2. VIRGIN OF GUADALUPE PARADE

If I could present this *máscara* to the ears as it delighted the eyes, I doubt not that I could achieve with my words what the Indians accomplished in it with their adornments. I shall do all that I can, though I know that I shall expose myself to the censure of incredulity. . . .

At three o'clock in the afternoon the masquerade in four sections started to make its appearance on the city streets. The first part was not especially noteworthy as it consisted of a disorganized band of wild Chichimeca Indians who swarmed about the thoroughfares garbed in the very minimum that decency allows. They had daubed their bodies with clay paints of many hues, and their disheveled hair was made even more unsightly by filthy feathers thrust into it in no particular pattern. Like imaginary satyrs and demoniacal furies they whooped, yelled, and howled, waved clubs, and flourished bows and arrows in such a realistic imitation of their warlike practices, that spectators were quite startled and terrified.

More enthusiastic applause greeted the second section, a company of infantrymen formed by one hundred and eight youths marching six abreast, each one bedecked in finest Spanish regalia, with bright-colored plumes fluttering from the crest of helmets and multihued ribbons streaming in the breeze from their shoulders. They presented a noble and inspiring appearance, but nothing amazed me quite as much as the superb precision and perfect rhythm with which they marched, with no other practice or training than that acquired in festive parades and on like occasions. Veterans could not have kept their ranks more evenly, or shown greater dexterity in firing and reloading, or manoeuvered their squads more expertly. . . . This indicates very clearly . . . that these American-born youths are not incapable of discipline should it be necessary to make professional soldiers of them. The rapidity and skill with which the company leader flourished his pike astonished everyone.

Next came four buglers, mounted on well-trained horses barely visible under scarlet trappings and silver trimmings. The clear, shrill notes of their instruments heralded the approach of the most important section of this brilliant *máscara*. This was the part representing the nobility and lords of the aboriginal aristocracy which, even though it was pagan and heathenish, must be reckoned as majestic and august inasmuch as it held sway over a vast northern empire in the New World. In taking part in these festivities it is quite unthinkable that these Indians should put on tableaux borrowed from an alien culture when they have such an abundance of themes and subjects for pageantry in the lives of their kings and emperors and in the annals of their history. So it was that, on this occasion, they appeared in the ancient garbs of their people as portrayed in their hieroglyphic paintings and as still preserved in tribal memory. All were dressed alike with an amazing array of adornments. . . .

Bringing up the rear of this colorful section was a figure representing the august person of the most valiant Emperor Charles V of Spain and the Holy Roman Empire, whose dominions extended from Germany in the north to the western hemisphere of America. He was arrayed in full armor, burnished black and engraved in gold. Like the Indian monarchs preceding him in the procession, he rode behind airy steeds that pranced with grace and stately rhythm as if fully aware of the sublime majesty of the ruler who held the reins. Indeed, these gallant horses, with the rhythmic swaying of plumes and the even gait of their hooves and the carriage gliding like Apollo's chariot across the heavens, made them seem so like Pegasus that onlookers burst into enthusiastic applause. In short, the elegance and splendor of the trappings harmonized completely with the august majesty of the figure represented.

Then came the triumphal float, lovelier than the starry firmament and its twinkling constellations. The base, supported by wheels, was six yards long, about half that width, and from the ground it was raised about a yard and a half. On this ample space rested the form of a large ship plowing through imitation waves of silver and bluish white gauze. The sides covering the underparts of the float bore complex designs of involuted spirals, ornate capitals, and decorative emblems, imbuing the whole with an aura of brilliance and splendor. From a large figurehead at the bow of the ship ribbons of scarlet taffeta fell away, intertwined so intricately with the harness traces that they actually seemed to be drawing the conveyance. Above the stern of the simulated vessel rose two exceedingly graceful arches, forming a throne, in the middle of which reposed a large, curved shell, supported from behind by a pair of Persian caryatids. Within it was an image of the Virgin of Guadalupe, and from her canopied throne descended a staircase with silken mats. Further embellishing this lovely ensemble were varicolored taffeta streamers, and a plethora of bouquets of many hues. Like an ambulant springtime, it appeared, dedicated to the immortal Queen of the heavenly paradise, and far exceeding in beauty the Hanging Gardens of Babylon which, in their time, were dedicated to Semiramis. At appropriate intervals stood six graceful angels, symbolizing some of the attributes of the most Holy Virgin. Kneeling on the first step of the throne was a lovely child garbed in the native raiment of the Indians, who thus represented the whole of America, particularly this northern part which, in pagan days, was known as Anahuac. One hand held a heart while the other supported an incensor diffusing perfumes and delicate aromas. All about this triumphal float the Indians were dancing one of the famous, royal *toncontines* of the ancient Mexicans. If their costomes in such ceremonial festivities were lavishly colorful in the days of their monarchs, how much more they would be on so auspicious an occasion as this one!

STUDY QUESTIONS

1. In what ways did Sister Juana challenge authority? What did her poetry reveal about a woman's place in colonial Latin American society? Compare Sister Juana with women in Asian and European classical societies, discussed in Volume 1. How did they respond when they challenged traditional authority?

2. Referring to the parade for the Virgin of Guadalupe, indicate the ways Indians remembered their pre-Columbian past. In what ways did the Indians incorporate Spanish beliefs and practices? How did public celebrations, such as the parade, shape a culture different from Indian tradition and European models?

3. How would such parades and all the celebrations of popular Christianity likely influence the laborers at the silver mine at Potosí or the textile mill at Puebla described in Chapter 8?

4. Given the various cultural currents in early modern Latin America, discuss the relationship between Latin America and Western European intellectual and religious life.

10

Global Contacts: Africa and the European Slave Trade

Many developments took place in sub-Saharan Africa from the fifteenth through the eighteenth centuries. Major regional kingdoms were established in several sectors. Bantu immigration to the south persisted, spreading agriculture. Conversions to Islam increased in the area below the Sahara, particularly in the eighteenth century, and European adventurers and traders made their first contacts with the vast African subcontinent.

Because many African societies lacked writing and instead expressed their values and history through art and oral traditions, many key political and cultural developments were not recorded during this period using conventional historical records. Documentation focuses on the European impact, which was not the only major current of the period; and it focuses on European, not African, perceptions. This poses unusual dangers for the student of early modern African history in terms of incompleteness and distortion.

The European arrival, however, was a major new ingredient in African history. Because most Europeans worked through local traders and set up only small outposts of their own, their cultural impact before 1800 was limited. Even their political impact was highly localized, except in a few regions such as the Dutch-held Cape region in the south. African rulers used European funds and armaments in their own political rivalries, and while Westerners were often on the stage, they did not yet write the script. Direct penetration into the interior was rare. But Europe's vast appetite for slaves, intended for use in the Americas, did have huge consequences for many regions, reducing population and economic vitality despite the collaboration of many African rulers and traders in the process.

The following three selections range from the fifteenth to the eighteenth century and suggest aspects of European-African interaction. They are taken from the east coast, where European activity was less intense than in parts of the west. Coastal settlements along the Indian Ocean already participated in an extensive trading network dominated by Arabs. The Islamic religion had won many adherents, and a written language, Swahili, developed by the eighteenth century.

The first document, written around 1520 in Arabic, offers an unusual opportunity to glimpse directly African reactions to the first Portuguese explorers, colored of course by the Muslim author's hostility to Christianity. The second document, drawn from the same region on the coast around the port city of Kilwa Kisiwani, is a characteristic slave-trade treaty drawn up between a French adventurer and the Sultan of Kilwa. Around the same period a French ship's captain in the slave trade offered a businessman's approach to human trade, in which the view of slaves as profit-and-loss commodities comes through clearly.

While the documents sketch European activities in the period, they also allow some evaluation of diverse African reactions and the reasons why some Africans believed they profited from Western ventures.

1. REACTIONS TO THE FIRST PORTUGUESE ARRIVALS IN EAST AFRICA (1520)

During al-Fudail's reign there came news from the land of Mozambique that men had come from the land of the Franks. They had three ships, and the name of their captain was al-Mirati [Dom Vasco da Gama]. After a few days there came word that the ships had passed Kilwa and had gone on to Mafia. The lord of Mafia rejoined, for they thought they [the Franks] were good and honest men. But those who knew the truth confirmed that they were corrupt and dishonest persons who had only come to spy out the land in order to seize it. And they determined to cut the anchors of their ships so that they should drift ashore and be wrecked by the Muslims. The Franks learnt of this and went on to Malindi. When the people of Malindi saw them, they knew they were bringers of war and corruption, and were troubled with very great fear. They gave them all they asked, water, food, firewood, and everything else. And the Franks asked for a pilot to guide them to India, and after that back to their own land—God curse it!

Then in the [next] year . . . there came al-Kabitan Bidharis [Dom Pedro Alvarez Cabral] with a fleet of ships. He asked the people of Kilwa to send water and firewood and desired that the sultan or his son should go on board to converse with him. The amir and the people of the land decided it best to send him an important citizen. So they sent Sayyid Luqman ibn al-Malik al-Adil. They dressed him in royal robes and sent him over.

Then they wanted water, and the Kilwa people drew it in a number of water-skins, and the porters carried it to the shore. Then they called out to the Portuguese to come ashore and take it. As they were coming, one of the principal slaves of the Amir Hajj Ibrahim, who was surnamed Hajj Kiteta, order the water carriers [of Kilwa] to carry the water away. So they did so. When the Christians disembarked on shore to fetch water, they saw neither much nor little water, but none at all. So they went back to their ships in anger. They set off again—God curse them!—to Malindi, and received everything they wanted in the way of water, firewood and food. When the Franks went to their own land, they left seven convert Christians at Malindi. They told the people that two should remain there, and four were to be sent to Gujarat to Sultan Mahmud and one to Kilwa. Then the Portuguese left, and the four men went to India and were circumcised and became Muslims.

2. A SLAVE-TRADE AGREEMENT (1776)

A copy of M. Morice's Treaty with the King of Kilwa written in Arabic on the reverse side, with two identical octagonal seals inscribed in white in Arabic. On the front was the translation in these terms:

We the King of Kilwa, Sultan Hasan son of Sultan Ibrahim son of Sultan Yusuf the Shirazi of Kilwa, give our word to M. Morice, a French national, that we will give him a thousand slaves annually at twenty *piastres* each and that he [M. Morice] shall give the King a present of two *piastres* for each slave. No other but he shall be allowed to trade for slaves, whether French, Dutch, Portuguese, &c., until he shall have received his slaves and has no wish for more. This contract is made for one hundred years between him and us. To guarantee our word we give him the fortress in which he may put as many cannon as he likes and his Flag. The French, the Moors and the King of Kilwa will henceforth be one. Those who attack one of us we shall both attack. Made under our signs and seals the 14th X. 1776 signed Morice.

And further down is written:

We the undersigned Captain and Officer of the ship *Abyssinie,* commissioned by M. Morice, certify to all whom it may concern that the present treaty was made in our presence at Kilwa on the 14th X. 1776 signed Pichard, Pigné,—Bririard.

3. REPORT OF A FRENCH SLAVE-TRADER (1784–1785)

The country is superb and pleasing once one has extricated oneself from the forests of half submerged trees called Mangroves. Judging from the ruins of stone-built houses, which can be seen not only on the island of Kilwa but also on the southern side of the pass, it appears that this was once a very important town and that it must have had a big trade; at Kilwa one can see the whole of a big mosque built in stone whose arches are very well constructed. Within the last three years a pagoda which stood at the southern extremity, and which was very curious looking, fell. Finally, this country produces millet, indigo, superb cotton, silkier even than the cotton produced on the Ile de Bourbon, sugar cane, gums in abundance, brown cowries of the second sort which are currency at Jiddah and in Dahomey, besides elephant ivory which is very common, as are elephants, and lastly negroes— superb specimens if they are selected with care. This selection we cannot make ourselves, being at the discretion of the traders, who are now aware of our needs and who know that it is absolutely essential for us to sail at a given season in order to round the Cape of Good Hope. In addition to competition amongst ourselves the expeditions have never been properly thought out and always left to chance, and so it happens that three or four ships find themselves in the same place and crowd each other out. This would not happen if there were a properly organized body and the expeditions were planned to fit in with the seasons and the quantity of cargo and the means of using up surplus also planned, since it is not the business of seamen to concern themselves with correspondence and administration. To my knowledge, the trading that has been done in this port for the last three years, without counting traders not personally known to me, is as follows:

La Pintade	Capt.		600	blacks	
La Victoire	"	La Touche	224	"	1st Voyage
Les bons amis	"	Beguet	336	"	
La Samaritaine	"	Herpin	254	"	
La Créolle	"	Crassons	176	"	
La Victoire	"	La Touche 3rd voyage 230 }	690	"	In his three voyages
[omitted]	"	Berton	233	"	
La Grande Victoire	"	Michel	289	"	
La Thémis	"	Bertau	450	"	
La Grande Victoire	"	Michel	289	"	
La Créolle	"	Crassons	211	"	
La Thémis 2nd voyage	"	Bertau	480	"	
La Gde. Victoire	"	Rouillard	250	"	
				"	
			4,193	"	

A total, to my knowledge, of 4,193, and certainly there must have been more in three years.

It is clear that if this number of captives, i.e. 4,193, who were traded for at least in this period of three years, cost forty *piastres* each, this represents a sum of 167,720 *piastres,* raised for the most part from [French colonies] or from France direct. It is therefore important not only to safeguard this trade but also to find a way of spending rather fewer *piastres,* which would be quite possible if one considers that the *piastres* which we give them for their captives do not remain long in their hands and that they almost immediately give them to the Moors and Arabs who provide them with their needs which are rice, millet, lambs, tunics, shirts, carpets, needles, swords, shoes, and silk materials for dresses and linings. The Arabs obtain most of these things from Surat, and why should we not get them direct from there ourselves? We should make the profit they make, and we should employ men and ships and we should keep a good number of our *piastres* which would remain in the Ile de France and in Bourbon; more certainly still, if privately owned ships from Europe or these islands could not go to the coast of Mozambique and if ships belonging to a private company sent out from Europe could participate in this trade only by means of *piastres* taken to Kilwa, it can be estimated how much we have paid into the hands of the Portuguese at Mozambique, Kerimba and . . . [omitted: Ibo] where they make us pay fifty or sixty *piastres* each for them. This does not include presents and tiresome vexations. What need is there to give our money to the Portuguese, when we have the means to operate among ourselves and when we can use our own industry and keep our money? I have heard for a long time talk of establishing a settlement or trading post in Madagascar. Truly, seeing the number of idle hands we have and the great number of poor and needy and foundlings in our almshouses it is surprising that we have not yet considered this plan, at least as far as that part of the island which we have most visited over a long period is concerned, and also, in certain ports which are particularly well situated, trading posts could be established without straining the resources of the state.

STUDY QUESTIONS

1. Why might African reactions to Europeans vary? What probable causes differentiated the 1520 Arabic account of 1520 from the King of Kilwa's response to European demands?
2. What were the dominant motives of the French slave trader? What problems did he report, and how did he suggest they be resolved? Based on this account, what were the main features of early European colonialism in Africa?
3. What do the documents suggest about the impact of the slave trade on Africa and Africans in the early modern period?

11

Global Contacts: The Columbian Exchange in the Early Modern Period

Disseminated most widely by Alfred Crosby in *The Columbian Exchange: Biological and Cultural Consequences of 1492* (Westport, Connecticut: Greenwood Publishing Company, 1972), the term *Columbian exchange* refers to the worldwide transfer of pathogens, plants, and animals, resulting from the expanded and intensified contacts among civilizations after 1492. To America, Europeans brought diseases (smallpox and measles), animals (cows, horses, sheep, and pigs), and plants (grapes, sugar, wheat, barley, and oats). From America, traders carried away not only precious metals but corn (maize), potatoes, and sweet potatoes. These transfers contributed significantly to the formation of new civilizations in the Americas and altered the civilizations of Europe, Asia, and Africa.

In the Americas smallpox and measles reduced the indigenous population of the Caribbean Islands to the vanishing point by 1540. In Central Mexico, the Indian population declined from about 18 million at the time of contact to approximately 1 million in 1605. Peru's native American population declined from 11 million to about 700,000 by the early eighteenth century. Throughout the Americas, the indigenous population declined by about 90 percent.

In place of people, European animals claimed the land. This was especially true where open grasslands were available. To cite one example, in the Mesquital

Selection 1 from Bernardino de Sahagún, *Florentine Codex: General History of the Things of New Spain*, 2nd ed., translated by Arthur J. O. Anderson and Charles E. Dibble (Santa Fe, N. Mex.: The School of American Research and The University of Utah, 1975), part 13, p. 83. Reprinted courtesy of the University of Utah Press. Selection 2 from Antonio Vázquez de Espinosa, *Description of the Indies* (ca. 1620) (originally published as *Compendium and Description of the West Indies* in 1942), translated by Charles Upson Clark, (Washington, D.C.: Smithsonian Institution Press, 1968), pp. 170–171, 173–174, 175, 190–191, 731–733. Selection 3 from John Locke, *Locke's Travels in France, 1675–1679 as Related in His Journals, Correspondence and Other Papers*, edited by John Lough (Cambridge: Cambridge University Press, 1953), p. 236. Selection 4A from remarks by Robert Boyle in *Royal Society, 1662. Miscellaneous Papers of the Council*, etc., 20 March; Selection 4B from the gardener of Robert Boyle to Robert Boyle, *Royal Society Letter Book* (1663), vol. 1, p. 83. The two quotes may be found in Redcliffe N. Salaman, *The History and Social Influence of the Potato* (Cambridge: Cambridge University Press, 1949), pp. 228 and 238, respectively. Selection 5 from Adam Smith, *An Inquiry into the Nature and Causes of the Wealth of Nations*, edited by Edwin Caanan (New York: Random House, 1937) pp. 160–161. Selection 6 from *Studies on the Population of China* by Ping-Ti Ho (Cambridge, MA: Harvard University Press), pp. 142–143, 146–147, 149–151. Copyright © 1959 by the President and Fellows of Harvard College. Reprinted by permission of the publishers.

Valley north of Mexico City, sheep increased from 39,000 in 1539 to 4.4 million in 1589. As the number of sheep increased, the former corn-producing valley became scrub land. In other zones, now virtually empty of Indian farmers because of population loss, new crops of wheat, barley, and sugar became predominant.

In Europe and Asia, maize and potatoes, more than any other products from America, affected civilization. Maize and potatoes became the food for the poor and, in both areas, contributed to population increases. Between 1650 and 1750, the population of Europe, including Asiatic Russia, increased from 103 million to 144 million; and the population of Asia, excluding Russia, increased from 327 million to 475 million. As one of many factors, the new crops bore a direct relationship to the population rise. Maize and potatoes increased the total food supply because they allowed previously uncultivated land to be used, including fallow land.

The first selection describes a smallpox epidemic in the Aztec capital of Tenochtitlán, just months prior to the Spanish siege in August 1521. Written originally in Nahuatl (the Aztec language) in 1555 by native informants, the document was translated into Spanish in 1577 by Bernardino de Sahagún, a member of the Franciscan order. The selections on the spread of European plants and animals in Mexico and Chile were written in 1620 by a Carmelite friar, Antonio Vázquez de Espinosa. He not only identified the plants and animals but also described the native Americans' adjustments to their spread. The remaining selections show the importance of American products in Europe and Asia.

In addition to the impact of plants and animals on the development of society, the selections also reveal the differences among Latin American, Chinese, and European civilizations. It is hardly a coincidence that churchmen wrote compilations on plants and animals in colonial Latin America and that leaders of Europe's Scientific Revolution and Enlightenment were interested in maize and potatoes. Robert Boyle (1627–1691) discovered Boyle's law (the relationship between pressure and the volume of a gas). The treatises of John Locke (1632–1704) on religious toleration, human understanding, and education constituted an important part of the English Enlightenment. Adam Smith (1723–1790) was the foremost economist of Europe in the late eighteenth century. In contrast, the sources of information on maize and potatoes in China were local histories describing local problems. These authors, in emphasizing different aspects of raising animals and cultivating crops, revealed distinctive features in their respective civilizations.

1. DISEASE IN MEXICO

Twenty-ninth Chapter, in which it is told how there came a plague, of which the natives died. Its name was smallpox. It was at the time that the Spaniards set forth from Mexico.

But before the Spaniards had risen against us, first there came to be prevalent a great sickness, a plague. It was in Tepeilhuitl that it originated, that there spread over the people a great destruction of men. Some it indeed covered [with pustules]; they were spread everywhere, on one's face, on one's head, on one's breast, etc. There was indeed perishing; many indeed died of it. No longer could they walk; they only lay in their abodes, in their beds. No longer could they move, no longer could they bestir themselves, no longer could they raise themselves, no longer could they stretch themselves out on their sides, no longer could they stretch themselves out face down, no longer could they stretch themselves out on their backs. And when they bestirred themselves, much did they cry out. There was much perishing. Like a covering, covering-like, were the pustules. Indeed many people died of them, and many just died of hunger. There was death from hunger; there was no one to take care of another; there was no one to attend to another.

And on some, each pustule was placed on them only far apart; they did not cause much suffering, neither did many die of them. And many people were harmed by them on their faces; their faces were roughened. Of some, the eyes were injured; they were blinded.

At this time this plague prevailed indeed sixty days—sixty day-signs—when it ended, when it diminished; when it was realized, when there was reviving, the plague was already going toward Chalco.

2. EUROPEAN PLANTS AND ANIMALS IN MEXICO AND CHILE

Mexico: Mexico City

Of Other Features of the Archdiocese of Mexico, and of the Fruit Growing There.

481. In the provinces of this district of the Archdiocese of Mexico described in the preceding chapters, there are over 250 Indian villages, with many cities among them; 100 [of them] are county seats (cabezas de partido). In these, and on over 6,000 establishments—corn and wheat farms, sugar plantations, cattle, sheep, and hog ranches—there are over 500,000 Indians paying tribute, and more than 150 convents of the Dominican, Franciscan, and Augustinian orders, and many curacies under priests, not to speak of the [many] Spanish towns in the district of the Archiodicese, and especially all the silver-mining towns, which are Spanish settlements.

483. The city of Mexico is luxuriously provided with fruit, both of Spanish and native varieties: they all yield abundantly. There are excellent olive groves from which they gather quantities of eating olives. Grapes are brought in from Querétaro, and there are a few vines in the city, as well as peaches large and small, pippins, quinces, pomegranates, oranges, limes, grapefruit, citrons, and lemons; the gardens produce in abundance all varieties of Spanish garden stuff and vegetables; the lake provides delicious fish of different sorts, and the streams, bobos, which is an excellent fish, and others.

Mexico: Michoacán

The province has varieties of climate—cold, hot, and springlike—and famous valleys and meadowlands, with streams of crystal-clear water running through them; hot baths very beneficial for invalids; fertile fields which yield abundance of corn, wheat, and other cereals, both native and Spanish; there is plenty of pastureland, and in consequence large cattle ranches with constantly increasing product; sheep from Castile, from whose wool they weave in the mills fine and coarse woolen cloth, blankets, sombreros, etc.; they raise also many hogs.

At these villages they get two abundant harvests of wheat and corn each year, one in the rainy season and the other by irrigation; from them they supply many cities and towns in New Galicia, and San Luís de Potosí.

491. In the northern part of this diocese, along their frontier with the Indian tribe of the Chichimecas, they gather wild cochineal, very fine when worked up; there are large cattle, sheep, and hog ranches: they raise excellent horses and mules.

Mexico: Michoacán

499. The town of La Concepción de Celaya was founded by the Viceroy Don Martin Enríquez in the year 1570 on the Zacatecas King's Highway to New Galicia and New Vizcaya, as a frontier post against the Chichimeca Indians. It has a spring-like climate and fertile fields with wealth of pastureland, for which reason there are large cattle, sheep, and hog ranches, with good mules and horses; they harvest abundance of corn, wheat, and other cereals, (Marg.: for which there are large irrigation ditches); they raise many kinds of native fruit and all the Spanish ones. The town will contain 400 Spanish residents, with a parish church, Franciscan, Augustinian, and Barefoot Carmelite convents, with other hospitals, churches, and shrines; there are many Indian villages in the district. In this region there are other Spanish settlements with many farms full of cattle, [which I do not enumerate because it would be almost impossible]. Celaya belongs to the Marqués de Villamayor.

Mexico: New Viscaya

536. The Diocese and State of New Vizcaya begins at the mines of Fresnillo, 12 leagues distant from Zacatecas; there will be 100 Spanish residents here, with a Franciscan convent; it has rich silver mines and veins. Twelve leagues farther on, as one travels toward Guadiana, like the mines of Los Plateros and Sombrerete and others, with rich silver veins and ore beds, and some establishments in which they smelt the metal. All this country has a good climate and is provided with plenty of supplies, for it is very fertile; they raise quantities of wheat, corn, and other cereals, with abundance of native and Spanish fruit and grapes, and much cattle, sheep, swine, mules, and horses.

Chile: City of Santiago

In the district of the city of Santiago there are 48 small Indian villages, assigned to 30 encomenderos. In the 48 villages in the year 1614 when they were inspected by Licentiate Machado, Justice of that Circuit Court, there were 2,345 Indians, 331 old people, etc. Tribute payers in the villages were 696; the others were away, some out on their work, others in the service of their encomenderos. In these villages of the district of this city and Diocese, and on the farms, there are 23 curacies, 21 administered by clerics and 2 by friars.

1934. At the above date there were 72 Indian men and 85 Indian women (?) slaves captured in the war after the slavery proclamation. There were likewise 501 Huarpes Indians from the Province of Cuyo residing in the country, of those who had come in for their mita, and 225 from Peru and Tucumán. There were likewise 481 of the Beliches tribe from these villages, who were artisans: Carpenters, 124; tanners, 100; tailors, 33; shoemakers, 81; silk weavers, 3; ropemakers for rigging, 2; masons, 30; blacksmiths, 7; water-jar makers, 19; stonecutters, 6; house painters, 4; they all lived and resided in the outer wards of the city of Santiago; the artisans alone numbered 409.

Round about the city there were 102 chacras, of wheat, corn, chickpeas, lentils, kidney beans, and other cereals and vegetables; there were some carts (carretas) which brought wood into the city and transported merchandise from the port and did all else necessary in the city service. In the city and on the chacras and ranches there are 41 tanneries in which every year they tan over 30,000 pieces of cordovan leather, and some hides for soles. On the river bank and on the chacras and ranches of the district there are 39 gristmills for wheat, and 3 woolen mills in which they work up and turn out every year over 14,000 varas of coarse cloth and grograms and more than 500 blankets.

Chapter IV
Continuing the Description of the Preceding Subject.

1935. Besides the above there were 354 farms—cattle ranches, corn, wheat, and other cereals; on them there were some Beliches Indians and 2,162 Yanaconas—part of them from the upcountry cities abandoned because of the rebellion of the Indians in that Kingdom, and others from elsewhere. These Indians are civilized (Ladinos); because their villages and natural surroundings are uncongenial, or because they are escaping from troubles they might have at home, or because they are wanderers, they bring themselves to enter the Spaniards' service. They are assigned (repartidos) to these farms, with their wives and children, 4, 6, or more to each, just as they would naturally settle: normally they live there and cultivate their own gardens and fields for their necessities, in addition to what the masters they serve give them in clothing, cash, or food.

On the majority of the farms there are superintendents (mayor-domos), Spanish soldiers or mestizos, the sons of Spaniards and Indian women, or mulattoes or free Negroes. These keep track of the figures for the sowing and the harvest, and see that the people work and do all else necessary. On all the farms and ranches in the Indies, of any importance, they are to be found and have excellent salaries, according to the size of the establishment. In this Kingdom most are paid one-fourth of the products of the soil and of the stock bred; some are paid less, for there is every sort of system.

1936. In this Kingdom there are very large rivers, swollen in winter with water from the rains and in summer from the great freshets from the snow melting under the sun up on the Cordillera Nevada. These all run from E. to W., to the Pacific; with them they irrigate their property and fields. They are utilized for a distance of about 40 leagues, in which irrigation produces large amounts of wheat, corn, barley chickpeas, lentils, peas (porotos), and other cereals and vegetables, which yield abundantly; they raise a few potatoes. The fanega of wheat is usually worth 8 reals; they normally ship large amounts to Lima when they need it there, and it is also taken for His Majesty's camp and army, for the soldiers' sustenance.

There are quantities of vineyards around Santiago and on the farms; every year they get more than 200,000 jugs of wine from them; that was the figure in the year 1614, when they made the inspection of that Kingdom. In the 3 preceding years they had planted 498,500 vines, and many more have been set out since then; the land is very fertile and the vine grows thick, strong, and sturdy; they treat it with gypsum and ferment (cocido) as is done in many places. It is all consumed within the country; some is taken for His Majesty's army to the city of La Concepción.

1937. The residents of Santiago possessed in the district of the city 39,250 cattle, the yearly increase of which was 13,500; quantities are slaughtered every year for tallow; they raise oxen for plowing and for their carts. Every young steer is worth 4 8-real pesos; an ox broken to work, 8; when a herd is sold, it is at the rate of 12 reals a head. There were on the ranches in the district 4,278 mares, and their annual increase, 1,200; each is worth 4 reals. Riding horses are worth from 16 to 20 8-real pesos; sumpter horses, 8 to 10; choice fine steeds, from 100 to 200 pesos.

They had in the district 323,956 goats, whose annual increase was 94,764; they slaughter quantities of gelded males and of females, and get over 2,500 quintals of tallow from them annually, worth 13 8-real pesos a quintal, and 25,100 pieces of cordovan leather, which they ship to Callao for Lima, since it is the best in the Kingdom. Before tanning, each sells for 16 reals; tanning each piece comes to 3½ reals. There were 623,825 sheep, whose annual increase was 223,944; they slaughter great numbers of them and get on the average 7,650 quintals of tallow from them every year. The usual price of a sheep is 2 reals, and a dressed mutton (carnero) the same, and in the city, 4. They are large, fat, and very good.

3. JOHN LOCKE ON MAIZE IN FRANCE

"MOND. SEPT. 12 from Petit Niort to Blay 6 (leagues). The country between Xantes & Blay is a mixture of corne, wine, wood, meadow, champaine inclosure, wall nuts & chestnuts, but that which I observd particularly in it was plots of Maize in severall parts, which the country people call bled d'Espagne, &, as they told me, serves poor people for bred. That which makes them sow it, is not only the great increase, but the convenience also which the blade & green about the stalke yeilds them, it being good nourishment for their cattle."

4. POTATOES IN IRELAND AND ENGLAND

A. Robert Boyle on Potatoes in Ireland (1662)

[H]e knew that in a time of famine in Ireland, there were kept from starving, thousands of poor people by potatoes; and that this root would make good bread, mixed with wheaten meale; that it will yield good drink too, but of no long duration; that it feeds poultry and other animals well; that any refuse will keep them from frost; that the very stalks of them thrown into the ground, will produce good roots; that the planning of them doth not hinder poor people from other employment.

B. Robert Boyle's Gardener (1663)

I have according to your desire sent a box of Potato rootes; my care hath been to make choice of such, that are fit to set without cutting; for many, that have not small ones enough, are constrained to cut the great ones; but I doe not approve of that husbandry, neither do I make use of it, because when they are cut, the wormes doe feed on them, and so devouring the substance, the branch groweth the weaker, and the roote small: the ground which they thrive best in is a light sandy soyle, where ferns or briars do naturally grow. Their nature is not to grow fruitful in a rich soyle because they will spring forth many branches, and so encumber the ground, that they will have but small roots. You may cause them to be set a foot apart or something better, whole as they are, and there will be great encrease, and the branch will bring forth fruit which we call the Potato-apple, they are very good to pickle for winter and sallets, and also to preserve; I have tasted of many sorts of fruit, and have not eaten the like of that, they are to be gathered in September, before the first frost doth take them. If you are minded to have great store of small rootes which are fittest to set, you may cause them to lay down the branches; in the month before named, and cover them with earth three or four inches thick, and the branch of every joint will bring forth small rootes in so great number that the increase of one yard of ground will set twenty the next season, and it must be the care of the gardner to cover the ground where the rootes are with fearns or straw, halfe a foote thick and better at the beginning of the winter, otherwise the frost will destroy the rootes; and as they have occasion to dig out the great rootes, they may uncover the ground, and leave the small ones in the earth, and cover them as before and preserve the seed.

Now the season to dig the ground is April or May, but I hold it best the latter end of April, and when they dig the ground let them pick out as many as they can find small and great, and yet there will be enough for the next crop left; let the covering which they are covered withall be burried in the ground, and that is all the improvement that I doe bestow. I could speak in praise of the roote, what a good and profitable thing it is, and might be to a commonwealth, could it be generally experienced; as the inhabitants of your towne can manifest the truth of it, but I will be silent in speaking in the praise of them, knowing you are not ignorant of it.

5. ADAM SMITH ON POTATOES

[A]n acre of potatoes will still produce . . . three times the quanity [of food] produced by the acre of wheat . . . [and] is cultivated with less expence than an acre of wheat; the fallow, which generally precedes the sowing of wheat, more than compensating the hoeing and other extraordinary culture which is always given to potatoes. Should this root ever become in any part of Europe, like rice is in some rice countries, the common and favourite vegetable food of the people, so as to occupy the same proportion of the lands in tillage which wheat and other sorts of grain for human food do at present, the same quanity of cultivated land would maintain a much greater number of people, and the labourers being generally fed with potatoes, a greater surplus would remain after replacing all the stock and maintaining all the labour employed in cultivation. A greater share of this surplus too would belong to the landlord. Population would increase, and rents would rise much beyond what they are at present. . . .

It is difficult to preserve potatoes through the year, and impossible to store them like corn [refers to traditional grain crops such as wheat, oats and barley; corn does not refer to maize] for two or three years together. The fear of not being able to sell them before they rot, discourages their cultivation, and is perhaps, the chief obstacle to their ever becoming in any great country, like bread, the principal vegetable food of all the different ranks of the people.

6. AMERICAN CROPS IN CHINA

Szechwan

[1814 history of San-t'ai county referring to immigrants and new products, which were identified as maize and sweet potatoes.]

Our soil is not poor and our people are not lazy. The innumerable immigrants have brought with them every conceivable food plant or product, all of which have been extensively propagated here. Many things that were unknown in the past are now our staple products. Our locality is so full of life and vigor that prosperity surpasses that of any previous period.

West-Central Kiangsi, Bordering Hunan (Yangtze Highlands)

[1760 edition of history of Yüan-chou prefecture.]

Formerly this prefecture abounded in idle land. On account of rapid population increase more land was cultivated but it was still confined to level areas. Since the influx of immigrants from Fukien and Kwangtung, their men and womenfolk have systematically cultivated high hills and even steep mountains.

[1873 local history of Kiangsi.]

The leading crop of hills and mountains is maize . . . which provides half a year's food for the mountain dwellers. . . . In general maize is grown on the sunny side of the hills, sweet potatoes on the shady side.

[1745 testimony of resident of Wu-ning county in Kiangsi.]

The shack people usually dig the mountain soil five or six inches deep. The loosened soil at first yielded ten times as large a crop (as when shallow planting was practiced). But from time to time there were torrential rains which washed down the soil and choked rivers and streams. After consecutive planting for more than ten years none of the fertile topsoil was left and the soil was utterly exhausted. Now in such places . . . mountains are reduced to bare rocks. Unless land is rested for several decades there is no hope of renewed cultivation.

Han River Drainge Area (Tributary of Yangtze)

[1864 edition of the history of I-ch'ang prefecture.]

Maize . . . had originally been grown only in Szechwan. Since our area became a prefecture (in 1735), the natives have opened up mountains and grown maize to an ever increasing extent until now it is grown everywhere.

[1866 edition of Fang-hsien prefecture.]

After several consecutive bumper crops from 1752 on, maize has become the mountain farmers' very source of sustenance and has been grown by every household.

[1866 edition of Fang-hsien prefecture (introduction of "Irish" potato after 1800).]

The Irish potato is mostly grown in the southwestern mountains. In the level area in the vicinity of the walled city rice is usually grown. In the comparatively shallow hills and mountains maize predominates. In the lofty mountains where maize cannot be successfully grown the only source of food is the Irish potato. . . . Some local people of means buy Irish potatoes, which are ground into flour, and occasionally make a fortune of it.

[1837–1838 testimony of Lin Tse-Hsü, governor-general of Hupei and Hunan.]

Formerly the bed of the Hsiang River (a tributary of the Han River which runs through southwestern Honan and Northern Hupei) was several tens of feet deep. Ever since the systematic deforestation consequent upon maize growing the topsoil has been washed down by torrential rains and silted up (the Hsiang River). Between Han-yang (where the Han River joins the Yangtze) and Hsiang-yang (the junction of the Hsiang and Han rivers) the further upstream one goes, the shallower the river bed becomes. Small wonder that from 1821 to the present there has hardly been a single year in which the Hsiang river did not flood.

STUDY QUESTIONS

1. Description of smallpox epidemic in Tenochtitlán: What statements in the document indicate that community cohesiveness broke down as a result of the disease? What are the military implications of such a breakdown?
2. Spread of animals and plants in Mexico and Chile: Identify the plants and animals introduced from Europe. Review numbers of animals compared with people. Indians who survived the epidemics were forced to adjust to new conditions. How did they adjust? What jobs did they perform? How were the jobs related to the new plants and animals? Who controlled the conditions under which they worked? What are the implications for social relations?
3. American crops in France, England, and Ireland: Who were Locke, Boyle, and Smith? In what way did they represent Western civilization? Why were they optimistic about cultivation of maize and potatoes? What were the advantages of cultivating these crops?
4. American crops in China: What types of sources were used to describe the cultivation of maize and potatoes in China? Who were the cultivators of maize and potatoes? In what kind of terrain did they cultivate these crops? What was the environmental result?
5. How do these reports reflect differences in civilizations? What was the result of the Columbian exchange on population in the Americas? On population in Europe and China? Why might Chinese commentators be less enthusiastic than Europeans about American crops?

SECTION TWO

The Long Nineteenth Century: 1750–1914

The framework for world history from the late eighteenth to the early twentieth centuries was increasingly shaped by growing European power. This power was based on previous gains in international trade and key colonies planted in India, Indonesia, and elsewhere. It was increased by European population growth and by a more explicit imperialist spirit, eager to seek new gains and conquests in the wider world. And it was greatly furthered by Europe's growing industrial strength. Industrialization, beginning in the late eighteenth century, generated new goods to sell, new modes of international transportation that facilitated wider market contacts, and new and more lethal weaponry that enhanced Europe's military advantage. Yet the long nineteenth century was by no means shaped by European activities alone. Most societies could resist European penetration to at least some degree, and several undertook active reform programs designed to enhance independence and the preservation of important values. Latin America freed itself from direct European control early in the nineteenth century, although its economic subordination in many ways intensified. The development of new institutions and social patterns in the United States, Canada, and Australia, although they reflected Western European strength, added another important source of complexity to modern world history. Finally, the emergence of various kinds of nationalisms and other cultural responses, in many otherwise different societies, reflected the capacity to define distinctive identities combined with the pressing need to innovate. By 1900 reform developments, independence movements, and nationalism were beginning to limit Western European hegemony, although the full reaction would begin to take shape only after 1914.

12

Work and Workers in the Industrial Revolution

The Industrial Revolution was one of the great changes in Western and ultimately world history. Taking shape toward the end of the eighteenth century in Great Britain, industrialization dominated the nineteenth century in Western Europe and North America. Based on radically new technologies, including the use of fossil fuels for power, industrialization revolutionized the production and transportation of goods. It sustained rapid population growth in the West and created growing material abundance as well. This industrialization transformed a social structure once based on the land into divisions based on urban wealth and property. It fostered large organizations and a growing state capable of using new technologies of communication and marshaling large amounts of capital and large numbers of goods and people. It challenged family life by taking work out of the home and redefining the roles of many women and children. It was, in sum, as basic a change in human history as had occurred since the advent of settled agriculture.

One of the many areas altered by industrialization was the nature of work, particularly for those people who labored in the proliferating mines and factories. Some features of industrialization benefited work: machines could lighten labor; factories could provide social stimulation; and some jobs that demanded new technical expertise became unusually interesting. But many workers found industrial working conditions a strain because they challenged a number of traditional values and habits. Certainly, changes in work provide one way of measuring the human impact of the vast industrialization process—some would say, of measuring human degradation.

The selections focus on three aspects of industrial work during the nineteenth century. The first document comes from a parliamentary inquiry on child labor, con-

Selection 1 from *British Sessional Papers, 1831–1832*, House of Commons, Vol. XV, pp. 17–19. Selection 2 from *The Archives du Haut Rhin* IM123C1, translated by Peter N. Stearns. Selection 3 from Adolf Levenstein, *Aus Der Tief, Arbeiterbriefe*, translated by Gabriela Wettbert (Berlin: 1905), pp. 48, 57, 60.

ducted in Britain in the early 1830s and ultimately the source of laws restricting children's work. Child labor was not in fact new, so one question to ask is what aspects of the factory system made it seem newly shocking. A second, related feature of industrial work—and one that persisted far longer than child labor—was the attempt to bring new discipline to the labor force. In the second document, shop rules—in this case, from a French factory in the late 1840s—did battle with a number of customary impulses in an effort to make work more predictable, less casual. Finally, new working conditions provoked direct comment by workers through protest and individual statements. The comment offered in the third document, by an unusually sensitive German miner around 1900—among other things, an ardent socialist—is not typical, but it does express some widely shared grievances. All three documents suggest the tensions that changes in work could bring. A basic feature of Western life in the nineteenth century, this strain spread with industrialization to other societies later on. How could workers modify or adapt to new work habits? How might changes in work affect other aspects of their lives, in the family, politics, or culture?

1. BRITISH CHILD LABOR INQUIRY (1831–1832)

Mr. Abraham Whitehead

431. What is your business?—A clothier.

432. Where do you reside?—At Scholes, near Holmfirth.

433. Is not that in the centre of very considerable woollen mills? Yes, for a space of three or four miles; I live nearly in the centre of thirty or forty woollen mills. . . .

436. Are there children and young persons of both sexes employed in these mills?—Yes.

437. At how early an age are children employed?—The youngest age at which children are employed is never under five, but some are employed between five and six in woollen mills at piecing.

438. How early have you observed these young children going to their work, speaking for the present in the summer time?—In the summer time I have frequently seen them going to work between five and six in the morning, and I know the general practice is for them to go as early to all the mills. . . .

439. How late in the evening have you seen them at work, or remarked them returning to their homes?—I have seen them at work in the summer season between nine and ten in the evening; they continue to work as long as they can see, and they can see to work in these mills as long as you could see to read. . . .

441. You say that on your own personal knowledge?—I live near to parents who have been sending their children to mills for a great number of years, and I know positively that these children are every morning in the winter seasons called out of bed between five and six, and in some instances between four and five.

442. Your business as a clothier has often led you into these mills?—Frequently. . . .

· · ·

460. What has been the treatment which you have observed that these children received at the mills, to keep them attentive for so many hours at such early ages?—They are generally cruelly treated; so cruelly treated, that they dare not hardly for their lives be too late at their work in a morning. . . . My heart has been ready to bleed for them when I have seen them so fatigued, for they appear in such a state of apathy and insensibility as really not to know whether they are doing their work or not. . . .

461. Do they frequently fall into errors and mistakes in piecing when thus fatigued?—Yes; the errors they make when thus fatigued are, that instead of placing the cording in this way [describing it], they are apt to place them obliquely, and that causes a flying, which makes bad yarn; and when the billy-spinner sees that, he takes his strap or the billy-roller, and says, "Damn thee, close it, little devil, close it," and they smite the child with the strap or the billy-roller. . . .

510. You say that the morals of the children are very bad when confined in these mills; what do you consider to be the situation of children who have nothing to do, and are running about such towns as Leeds, with no employment to keep them out of mischief?—Children that are not employed in mills are generally more moral and better behaved than children who are employed in mills.

511. Those in perfect idleness are better behaved than those that are employed?—That is not a common thing; they either employ them in some kind of business at home, or send them to school.

512. Are there no day-schools to which these factory children go?—They have no opportunity of going to school when they are thus employed at the mill.

2. RULES FOR WORKERS IN THE FACTORY OF BENCK AND CO. IN BÜHL, ALSACE (1842)

Article 1. Every worker who accepts employment in any work-site is obligated to read these rules and to submit to them. No one should be unfamiliar with them. If the rules are violated in any work-site, the offenders must pay fines according to the disorder or damage they have caused.

Art. 2. All workers without exception are obligated, after they have worked in the factory for fourteen days, to give a month's notice when they wish to quit. This provision can be waived only for important reasons.

Art. 3. The work day will consist of twelve hours, without counting rest periods. Children under twelve are excepted; they have to work only eight hours a day.

Art. 4. The bell denotes the hours of entry and departure in the factory when it first rings. At the second ring every worker should be at his work. At quitting time the bell will also be sounded when each worker should clean his workplace and his machine (if he has one). It is forbidden under penalty of fines to abandon the workplace before the bell indicates that the work-site is closed.

Art. 5. It is forbidden to smoke tobacco inside the factory. Whoever violates this prohibition is subjected to a heavy fine and can be dismissed. It is also forbidden under penalty of fines to bring beer or brandy into the factory. Any worker who comes to the factory drunk will be sent away and fined.

Art. 6. The porter, whoever he may be, is forbidden to admit anyone after the workday begins. If someone asks for a worker he will make him wait and have the worker called. All workers are forbidden to bring anyone into the factory and the porter is forbidden to admit anyone. The porter is also forbidden to let any workers in or out without the foreman's permission during the hours of work.

Art. 7. Any worker who misses a day without the Director's permission must pay a fine of two francs. The fine is doubled for a second offense. Any worker who is absent several times is dismissed, and if he is a weaver he is not paid for any piece he may have begun unless he can prove he missed work because of illness and should therefore be paid for work he has already done.

Art. 8. All workers in the factory are obligated to be members of the Sickness Fund, to pay their dues, and conduct themselves according to its statutes.

Art. 9. The foreman and the porter are empowered to retain any worker leaving the factory and to search him, as often as the interests of the Director may require. It is also recommended to the foreman to close the work-site himself, give the key to the porter, and to allow no worker inside during meal periods.

Art. 10. Workers should only go in and out of doors where a porter resides, else they will be fined, brought under suspicion, and dismissed. They cannot refuse to surrender any of their belongings at work, for which they will be reimbursed according to the valuation of the Director and the foreman. Workers are also ordered to be obedient to the foreman, who is fully empowered by the Director. Any disobedience will be punished by fines according to the importance of the case. Any offender is responsible for the consequences of his action. It is also forbidden for any worker to seek work in any of the company's work-sites other than the one in which he is employed; anyone encountered in another work-site will be punished.

Art. 11. Every worker is personally responsible for the objects entrusted to him. Any object that cannot be produced at the first request must be paid for. Weavers are obligated to pay careful attention to their cloth when they dry it. They will be fined and held responsible for any damage.

Art. 12. In return for the protection and care which all workers can expect from the Director, they pledge to him loyalty and attachment. They promise immediately to call to his attention anything that threatens good order or the Director's interests. Workers are also put on notice that any unfortunate who commits a theft, however small it may be, will be taken to court and abandoned to his fate.

3. MAX LOTZ, A GERMAN MINER, DESCRIBES HIS WORK (ca. 1900)

A trembling of the pupils forms in the eyes of many miners. At first it is not noticeable but it gradually becomes stronger. Where this eye ailment reaches a certain stage the stricken person becomes unable to work in the pit any longer. The stricken man becomes unsure of his grip, he often misses the desired object by one foot. He has particular difficulties in directing his glance upward. If he fixes but barely on an object his eyes begin to tremble immediately. But this calamity only appears in the mine or in artificial light. Above ground and in daylight it is never present. I know a laborer working quite close to me who takes a quart of liquor daily into the shaft. As soon as the trembling begins he takes a sip and the pupil becomes calm for a short while—so he states. Thus one can become a habitual drunk, too.

But this is not all. Almost all miners are anemic. I do not know what causes this pathological diminution of blood corpuscles in miners, whether this results from a general lack of protein in the blood. I suppose that it is caused mainly by the long, daily stay in bad air combined with the absence of sun or day light. I reason that if one places a potted plant in a warm but dark cellar for a long time it will grow significantly more pale and sickly than her beautifully scenting sisters in the rose-colored sunlight. It must be like this for the drudges down there. Anemia renders the miner characteristically pale. . . .

Let's go, shouted Prüfer, who had already picked up a shovel. Four more wagons have to fall. It is almost 12:30 [p.m.] now. All right, I agreed, and we swung the shovels.

Away it goes, commanded Bittner when the wagons were fully loaded. Jump to it, there is plenty of coal. Well, if I were a pickman, mumbled the chief pickman then I'd have myself a drink. And he breathed heavily behind the wagon.

Let's set up the planking until Rheinhold comes back so that things don't look so scruffy, I said to Bittner even though we would rather have stretched out on the pile of coal because we were so tired.

He replied: I don't care, but first I want to wring out my trousers. And standing there naked he started to squeeze the water from the garment. I followed his example. When we had finished, it looked around us as though a bucket full of water had been spilled. I do not exaggerate. In other locations where it was warmer yet, the workers were forced to undergo this procedure several times during their working hours. But let us remain here.

We put our undergarments back on and did not pay attention to the unpleasant feeling which we had doing so. We placed the wooden planks and cleared aside the debris in order to establish good working conditions for the other third which usually did not do the same for us—because they were too fatigued.

The work is becoming increasingly mechanical. No more incentive, no more haste, we muddle along wearily, we are worn out and mindless. There was sufficient coal, Rheinhold could come at any time. My forehead burned like fire. As a consequence of the anemia from which I suffer I occasionally experience a slight dizzy spell. Bittner does not know about it. But in my head it rages and paralyzes me beyond control or without my being able to think. When it becomes unbearable I stop my slow, phlegmatic and energyless working. I then sit on the side wall of the mountain in order to slurp the last remaining coffee. . . .

This is a brief description of one shift in the pit. And this torture, this inhuman haste repeats itself day after day [so] that the various states of exhaustion express themselves mildly or very pronouncedly in the physical state of the individuals. And that is not all; the spirit, too, the conscience of the individual degenerates. And one drudge, grown vacuous through his work, is put beside another one, and another one and finally this "modern" circle has closed in on the entire working force. And he who says that primarily the professional group of the miners is the rudest, least educated and spiritually lowest class of men does not lie. Of course, there are exceptions here, too. But these exceptions are supposed to validate the rule according to a simple type of logic. In any event, it truly takes spiritual magnitude to occupy still oneself with belletristic, scientific and thought-provoking materials after a completed shift. When I come home in that condition I still have to cope with other necessary heavy work around the house. And finally there only re-mains the evening hours for the writing tasks which I deem noble.

STUDY QUESTIONS

1. What features of child labor seemed newly objectionable in the context of fac-tory industry?
2. What were the main goals of factory work rules? What problems did they ad-dress? What innovations did they particularly suggest, compared with more tra-ditional work patterns?
3. What does Max Lotz see as the primary problems of mine work? Were work conditions getting better or worse by 1900, in highly industrialized societies like Germany? Why might some workers disagree with Lotz's assessment?
4. Do problems of work in nineteenth-century Europe suggest that industrializa-tion deteriorated the quality of human life? What other factors need to be taken into account? How did workers and others deal with the issues identified in these documents?

13

The Expansion of Frontier Societies

One of the crucial developments in nineteenth-century world history involved developments in relatively new nations like the United States and Australia, where expanding frontiers created space for massive immigration and economic growth. These new nations, which also included New Zealand and Canada, shared several characteristics. They contained aboriginal populations, such as Native Americans, which were steadily pushed back by the combined forces of disease, military force, and seizures of property. Expanding frontiers (facilitated by rapid railroad development) created conditions for extensive farming and stock-raising, which in turn—particularly after further developments in shipping, around 1870—provided massive grain and meat exports to European markets; mining resources added to this export thrust. New immigrants flocked to the frontier societies, although they filled cities as well as farmlands and mining territories; most of them came from Europe. Finally, European, particularly British, institutions and cultural values were extensively imported.

The result was a set of societies closely tied to Western European civilization, but also colored by distinctive racial combinations, frontiers, and export economics. There were, of course, important differences among these new societies. The United States was larger than the others in population, and it industrialized more quickly, which added to its world power. It also had the distinctive experience and then legacy of extensive slavery. Finally, it had won independence through military action, whereas the other societies evolved toward increasingly autonomous political expression within the British Empire; Australia, for example, gained independence within the British Commonwealth only in 1900. But all the societies were marked by their combination of frontier and Western European characteristics. They all moved relatively quickly to leadership in the development of democratic political reforms, including, by 1900, pressure to provide voting rights for women. They all gained growing economic importance and potential military-diplomatic importance in world affairs during the nineteenth century, in trends that would continue through the twentieth century as well.

Selection 1 from *Twenty Years on the Pacific Slope: Letters of Henry Eno from California and Nevada, 1848–1871*, edited by E. Turentine Jackson (New Haven: Yale University Press, 1965), pp. 97–99. Selection 2 from *Discourses of Brigham Young*, edited by John A. Widtsoe (Salt Lake City: Deseret Book Co., 1925), pp. 738–741. Selection 3 from David Fitzpatrick, *Oceans of Consolation: Personal Accounts of Irish Migration to Australia* (Ithaca: Cornell University Press, 1994). Reprinted by permission of the Public Record Office of Northern Ireland.

The selections offer personal reactions to the nineteenth-century frontier, all by people of European origin. In the first document, Henry Eno talks about prospects and prospecting in Nevada, as he writes to his brother William on August 21, 1869. Eno was one of many pioneers bent on gaining wealth in the Western territories. Miners were first to arrive, moving back east from California when the California gold rush of 1849 subsided. In Nevada, prospectors like Eno looked for gold but more often found silver; 1869 was the height of Nevada's fame as a mining territory.

In the second document, also from the American West, Brigham Young, leader of the movement of the Latter-day Saints (Mormons) to Utah in 1847, writes of the gains he saw in his new home. The Latter-day Saints had launched their religious movement in upstate New York, claiming divine inspiration for a new Christian community; encountering persecution in several places, they finally settled in Utah, where their community took deep roots.

The third document comes from a Protestant Irish immigrant to Australia. John McCance came from County Down in 1853, with his wife and family, settling in the goldfields of the province of Victoria. He came after the first big gold rushes and never managed to become wealthy, although he earned enough to support his family. Here he writes in 1858 to an Irish former neighbor, William Orr, a wealthier man, whom McCance had charged with looking after his elderly parents.

1. A NEVADA SILVER MINER, HENRY ENO (1869)

Dear Brother:

Yours of the 11th August was received yesterday. Have now been here since 3rd of July. I came here expecting to find a rich mineral country, also to find much such a population as California had in 1849 and 1850. The great mineral wealth of eastern Nevada has not been exaggerated. In fact I did not expect to find so rich or so many silver mines. There is not so much wild reckless extravagance among the people of the towns and the miners as in the early days of California. There are not as many homicides according to the numbers, but there is perhaps more highway robberies committed. We have here, as twenty years ago, numbers too lazy to work but not too lazy to steal, and some too proud to work and not afraid to steal. The laws of Nevada license gambling, and here at Hamilton, in Treasure City, and Shermantown are some ten or twelve licensed gambling tables. The next session of the legislature may perhaps license highway robbery.

There are two banking establishments, two express offices. Wells Fargo and Union Express, some ten or twelve assay offices, and a small army of lawyers. The District Court has been in session ever since I arrived. A trial often occupies ten or twelve days. A very few lawyers are doing well. From what I can discover I believe that lawyers depend more upon perjury and subornation of perjury than upon principles of law or precedents. Experts in mining do a thriving business as witnesses.

There are, I judge, nearly 200 paying mines within four miles square. There ought to be a dozen more quartz mills erected and would find full employment. The price of crushing and working ores is too high for low grade ores. The common price is $30 per ton. Under ordinary circumstances free ores yielding $15 per ton can be worked at a fair profit. There are very many mining districts within 80 and 100 miles that are now attracting attention of miners and capitalists. The merchants of Chicago are turning their attention to this silver country and will enter into competition with San Francisco, and I should not be surprised if they succeed in establishing and building up a heavy business and a profitable one. The money market in California as well as in Nevada is very stringent. There is much financial distress. Very many men reputed to be worth their many thousands last spring are now reputed worthless. But in no country that I have ever seen (not even in California) do I believe that well-directed industry and judiciously invested capital would meet with richer rewards.

It will never be considered a good grain country, but as a pastoral country it is unquestionably a good one. Millions of sheep can be kept here and without cutting hay for winter. It is also a good dairy country. There is a great scarcity of water, it is true, but artesian wells can supply it. It is also a healthy country: no fever and ague. At this high elevation, persons of weak lungs are subject to pneumonia, but a little care will prevent it. It is *no money,* not *pneumonia,* that I am troubled about and am afraid it will become chronic.

I went out a few days ago with a young fellow on a prospecting trip, about four or five miles from here. Went over as rough a country as I ever traveled over. Stiping Mountain is but a molehill compared with ours. On our return, struck a silver lode. Brought home some specimens and had them assayed. Sent you the assay, so that you may see how we manage here. Intend to prospect it further.

Have made up my mind to go to Iowa and St. Louis, if I can possibly raise the means, the forepart of October and return in the spring. I made the acquaintance of Judge G. C. Bates of Chicago who was here a short time since. I formerly knew him in Sacramento. He tells me I can make money by lecturing, advises me to make my debut at Chicago, and that he will introduce me. And also at Detroit. Am now busily engaged in preparing several lectures, but I labor under many disadvantages. Still hope to overcome them. If I can but put my foot on the lower round of fortune's ladder and grasp with my hand another, I have faith to believe I can yet climb it.

Was pleased to hear about your farming operations. Reapers, mowing machines, gang plows, and the threshers have found their way to the Pacific Coast. Between Elko and Hamilton there are several mowing machines at work. Almost all the wheat of California is harvested by machines. Last year a Mr. Mitchell on the San Joaquin plains raised 14,000 acres of wheat, and that year Bidwell of the Sacramento Valley, candidate for governor last year, raised 27,000 acres of wheat. Last year, in June I was in San Francisco. A farmer living near Sacramento River told me that he had 1,500 acres of wheat which would yield on an average, 30 bushels to the acre. He said he could harvest it, thrash it, put in sacks and store it in a warehouse in San Francisco within a fortnight's time. There have been fifty-six harvesting machines employed this year on the Salinas Plains. I crossed them in 1850, and there was not a furrow turned.

Our markets here are well supplied with everything man wants to sustain life and some of the luxuries. Flour, $8 per hundredweight; beef and mutton, 15 to 20 cents per lb.; sugar, 3 lbs. for $1; bacon, 40 cents per lb.; applies, peaches, apricots, nectarines, and grapes from California in abundance, all about 25 cents per lb.; potatoes, 10 cents per lb.; beans the same; and rice, 12½ cents a bucket; $7 a day for a horse-ride—I find it cheaper to go afoot for wood, $6 per cord. Rents all the way from $40 to $400 per month for one or two rooms. Plenty of good air but of rather light quality, nothing.

I think you would like a trip to wild country and to the more civilized portion of California. It would give materials for thought and reflection and would in all probability enable you to enjoy with a greater zest the comforts of a quiet home. As for me, I feel as if I had no country and no home, but try to make the best of wherever I am.

2. THE MORMONS OF UTAH'S BRIGHAM YOUNG (1847)

Seven years ago tomorrow, about 11 o'clock, I crossed the Mississippi River with my brethren for this place, not knowing, at the time, whither we were going, but firmly believing that the Lord had in reserve for us a good place in the mountains, and that He would lead us directly to it. . . .

The most of the people called Latter-day Saints have been taken from the rural and manufacturing districts of this and the old countries, and they belonged to the poorest of the poor. Many of them, I may say the great majority, never had anything around them to make life very desirable; they have been acquainted with poverty and wretchedness, hence it cannot be expected that they should manifest that refinement and culture prevalent among the rich. Many and many a man here, who is now able to ride in his wagon and perhaps in his carriage, for years before he started for Zion never saw daylight. His days were spent in the coal mines, and his daily toil would commence before light in the morning and continue until after dark at night.

Now, what can be expected from a community, so many of whose members have been brought up like this, or, if not just like this, still under circumstances of poverty and privation? Certainly not what we might expect from those reared under more favorable circumstances. But I will tell you what we have in our mind's eye with regard to these very people and what we are trying to make of them.

We take the poorest we can find on earth who will receive the truth, and we are trying to make ladies and gentlemen of them. We are trying to educate them, to school their children, and to so train them that they may be able to gather around them the comforts of life that they may pass their lives as the human family should do—that their days, weeks, and months may be pleasant to them. We prove that this is our design, for the result, to some extent, is already before us.

Talk about these rich valleys, why there is not another people on the earth that could have come here and lived. We prayed over the land and dedicated it and the water, air, and everything pertaining to them unto the Lord; and the smiles of Heaven rested on the land, and it become productive and today yields us the best of grain, fruit, and vegetables.

There never has been a land, from the Days of Adam until now, that has been blessed more than this land has been blessed by our Father in Heaven; and it will still be blessed more and more, if we are faithful and humble and thankful to God for the wheat and the corn, the oats, the fruit, the vegetables, the cattle, and everything He bestows upon us, and try to use them for the building up of His kingdom on the earth. . . .

When water is brought to the termination of the canal, which we can accomplish in a few days, I presume that the reservoirs on the line of the work and those portions which are excavated in full will contain water enough to allow the people to irrigate when necessary and thus do away with the practice of watering only two hours a week on a city lot, and much of that to be done in the night. And that is not all, for by the time the water is fairly on a lot it is taken to the next person whose right it is to use it. And lots which have had thousands of dollars expended on them, and which would yield more than a thousand dollars' worth of fruit and vegetables, could they be properly irrigated, are only allowed a small stream of water for two hours once a week, and at the same time an adjoining lot planted with corn, the hills six feet apart and one stalk in a hill, comparatively speaking, the balance of the ground being covered with weeds, is allotted the same time and amount of water as the one on which the fruit trees and other choice vegetation are worth thousands of dollars. . . .

Until the Latter-day Saints came here, not a person among all the mountaineers and those who had traveled here, so far as we could learn, believed that an ear of corn would ripen in these valleys. We know that corn and wheat produce abundantly here, and we know that we have an excellent region wherein to raise cattle, horses, and every other kind of domestic animal that we need. . . .

3. AN IMMIGRANT MINER IN AUSTRALIA: JOHN McCANCE (1858)

Chewton Forest Creek
June 7th/58.

Dear Sir

(a) I would wish to write a few more lines to you but realy I scarcely do Know what to write to you as there is very little new here that I do Know or remember as this does leave us in our useual health Praise the Lord for His continued merceys to us as we are very unworthy of the least of His notice yet still He spares our very unworthy lives and bestows on us a good measure of hea[l]th and strength and a good many of His bountys and we trust that this will find you all as a family in good health also and now what shall I say.

(b) If I was to till you of our own township how it is growing as if it were by m[a]gic and also our market town Castlemaine you would not feel much interest in them. But realy they astonish me. As to our digging there is little new but likely I will send you a newspaper which will give you all the information of these Things. I sent you one by the last mail of the 15th may. I hope you may have got it. Our great railway is now all the talk but is not begun yet. It was to have begun on the first of June but oweing to the severe illness of a great ireish man a Mr Duffy it is put off till the tenth of June. There is a great many goldmining compenys starting up about this place I beleive five or six some of them so large as 2000 shares. It is causing work to get more plenty for those who is willing to work for wages and if our great railway was started I think there need not be many idle. But I think that wages will never be high again as there is still a goodly number waiting in hops of the same perhaps more Than will work when they get the chance. But now what shall I say more.

(c) I wish I could Know what you would wish to Know but I will begin with our season. This is now the month of June and our white frosts are now set in. I have washed my face in icey water this last week. We have it nearly one eighth of an inch thick betimes but allways followed by a most beautifull day. We have a good deal of our garden seed sowen and above the ground such as the frost will not Kill. That is onions leeks parsnips carrotts lettuces cress Redish parsley celery and peas which are fit for stakeing at this time. Cabbage curley Kale culiflowers and all such like I have had sowen and all grew very well even the seeds which I kindly received from you. But alas this blight with which we are sorly perplexed pays no respect to seeds or where they come from. As soon as the plant gets its second or third leaf the blight lays hold on them and in spite of all our care it has Killed the most of them but still I have preserved a few of all sorts yet espeicly the curley Kale. I have also a little of all the flower seeds sowen which you sent but the are not up yet. But I intend to protect them from the frost by means of a square of calico and four posts which will furle up every morning and spread out every eve[*n*]ing.

(d) Now sir supose I would turn to nature a little but realy I scarsley dare as I am no naturlist. But perhaps you might wonder what sort of things we may have here and I think I have hinted at our trublesome things. Our venomous Reptiles are very numerous. We have a great variety of birds more than I could now inform you of and some of most beautifull plumbage. If you would give me a hint of your desire to hear of them I would take a list of them. We have some very nice butterflys of almos every hue except white as I have never saw a white one yet. I have seen no bees as yet either tame or wild although I beleive that there is some in this colney [*colony*]. Our bat is the very same as the are with you. They fly about very thick every eveining. Our swallow is much the same also. They remain with us all winter but there is more in summer. Now I must tell you that we have lots of mice here although I think they are not natives and we have plenty of rats in severl places although I have not seen any on the diggings as yet. They have plenty in Castlemaine and they are awefull numerious in Melbourne a perfect plague. They are not natives either but indeed I could scarcely tell you what is natives. I have seen the Kangaroo and the opossum the Kangaroorat about the size of a rabbit. The native cat is a prety thing. It is not so large as our cat is all spotted like a laopord withe spots about the size of buttons. I have never saw a native dog but I beleive they are very pretty alaso rather like a fox. Now I have told you what I have seen & must refer you to natural history for the others. I have never seen a hare but there [*are*] plenty of tame Rabbits and I belive there is some wild ones which has been let loose. I have never seen either pheasent or patridge. We have plenty of Quales and native pidgeons. But perhaps this will wearie you but what shall I say next.

(e) I would ask you a very important Questin and that is as I Know that my father is not very plenty of ready Change if you would be so Kind (as I cannot doubt your Kindness) as to give him a half or whole Quire of letter paper ink pens &c. and every letter that he would bring in to you if you would back it and stamp it that is with postage stamps. By so doeing you would certinly very much oblidge me and it may be that I may get an oppertunity of some one returning home by which I may recomepence you. If not sooner I shall have a chance when Thomas Brooks des go and if I do not get any I shall not forget to pay you with intresst.

(f) Now as I have named T. B. I must tell you that he is in good health and I have heard good accounts of his hole by Mrs John McMillin who is up with us at this time to stop a week or so. Thomas still lives with them. John Regan is in good health also and works in the same hole with Thomas. Mrs Boyce and all her family are well also. I suppose you will have heard that her doughter Eliza is got married since they came. Hamilton lives up here now close to our garden fence. James McMillin still works at the work with me as I still work at the companys work yet but we have had no word from Nathaniel yet. Thomas & Alexander are still out in the bush at stations. I have never had the chance of seeing any aquentance of yous and may be I never shall unless they make themselves Known to me.

(g) I still hold the Boomarang yet. I have just been showing it to Mrs McMillin and another young woman a Mrs McAnally from Bellfast who is up with her. She would wish that you would let her father & Mother Know that they are all well also but there is nothing new with them. They are still working at thair deep hole also that is Mrs John McMillin.

(h) Now I do not Know what news to ask of you but you may let me Know of any deaths that may occour in the old neighbourhood with any perticular news that you may think right. When you write you may direct to myself John McCance Chewton forest Creek by Castlemaine Victoria Australia. So I conclude with your friend & wellwisher

John McCance

STUDY QUESTIONS

1. What criteria does Eno use to evaluate Nevada? How do his criteria compare with those of Brigham Young?
2. What is Brigham Young's religious interpretation of the Mormon settlement in Utah? How does he combine his faith with insistence on human effort? How was Mormon Utah different from Nevada, as a result of religion?
3. What pulled McCance to Australia? How did he assess the frontier?
4. How do McCance and Eno suggest possible failures on the frontier?
5. What does "civilization" mean to former Europeans on the frontiers?
6. Did people of European origin on the frontiers feel that the frontier had changed them? Were immigrants, like McCance, more or less likely than simple migrants to feel the results of a new environment?
7. What kinds of values for the building societies of Australia and the United States do these documents suggest? How do they compare?

Russia

14

Russian Peasants: Serfdom and Emancipation

More than most Eurasian societies, Russia long remained a land of small cities with limited manufacturing. Not only a majority but a vast majority of its people were peasants well into the nineteenth century. Numbers alone, however, do not account for the omnipresence of peasant issues in Russian history. From a once-held position of substantial freedom and control of village lands, Russian peasants had been subjected to increasingly rigorous serfdom—by the state or by noble landlords—from the fifteenth century onward. Their trend thus reversed that of Western Europe, where serfdom on the whole became lighter over time. The Russian economy relied on agricultural exports forced from peasant labor on the large estates; and Russian politics and society, which traded noble control over their peasants for docility to the Russian tsar, relied heavily on the subjection of the serfs.

Yet the peasants' condition created increasingly visible problems. It violated standards of justice felt keenly by many Russians, including those open to Western ideas during the eighteenth and nineteenth centuries. Serfs rioted frequently, for peasants were quite aware of their own servitude. Furthermore, tight control of peasant labor limited Russia's economic flexibility, making it hard to recruit urban labor and, at least in the eyes of some observers, reducing productivity on the land as well. Finally, prodded by its loss in the Crimean War, the Russian government took the step of emancipation, ending serfdom while trying to preserve the noble-

Selection 1 from Alexander Radishchev, *A Journey from St. Petersburg to Moscow* (Cambridge, Mass.: Harvard University Press, 1958), pp. 158–160. Copyright © 1958 by the President and Fellows of Harvard College. Reprinted by Permission. Selection 2 from Basil Dmytryshyn, *Imperial Russia: A Sourcebook, 1700–1917* (New York: Holt, Rinehart and Winston, Inc., 1967), pp. 221–223, 225. Copyright © 1967 by Holt, Rinehart and Winston, Inc. Reprinted by permission. Manifesto from *Polnoe Sobranie Zakonov Russkoi Imperii* (Complete Collection of the Laws of the Russian Empire), 2nd series, Vol. 36, No. 36,490, pp. 130–134.

dominated social hierarchy. This move redefined the peasant question but did not remove it.

The following selections stem from two sources. The first document is an account by an early Russian intellectual, Alexander Radishchev (1749–1802), who wrote about the peasants' condition in a book, *A Journey from St. Petersburg to Moscow* (1790), repressed by the government until 1905. His account reveals peasants' suffering and reactions and also the reformist zeal of a segment of the educated upper class. The second document presents excerpts from the emancipation decree of 1861. They reveal how a new tsar, Alexander II, tried to juggle reform interests with noble resistance. The document invites appraisal in terms of how much was changed, and why peasants were so widely disappointed with the results.

1. RADISHCHEV'S JOURNEY (1790)

I suppose it is all the same to you whether I traveled in winter or in summer. Maybe both in winter and in summer. It is not unusual for travelers to set out in sleighs and to return in carriages. The corduroy road tortured my body; I climbed out of the carriage and went on foot. While I had been lying back in the carriage, my thoughts had turned to the immeasurable vastness of the world. By spiritually leaving the earth I thought I might more easily bear the jolting of the carriage. But spiritual exercises do not always distract us from our physical selves; and so, to save my body, I got out and walked. A few steps from the road I saw a peasant ploughing a field. The weather was hot. I looked at my watch. It was twenty minutes before one. I had set out on Saturday. It was now Sunday. The ploughing peasant, of course, belonged to a landed proprietor, who would not let him pay a commutation tax [*obrok*]. The peasant was ploughing very carefully. The field, of course, was not part of his master's land. He turned the plough with astonishing ease.

"God help you," I said, walking up to the ploughman, who, without stopping, was finishing the furrow he had started. "God help you," I repeated.

"Thank you, sir," the ploughman said to me, shaking the earth off the ploughshare and transferring it to a new furrow.

"You must be a Dissenter, since you plough on a Sunday."

"No, sir, I make the true sign of the cross," he said, showing me the three fingers together. "And God is merciful and does not bid us starve to death, so long as we have strength and a family."

"Have you no time to work during the week, then, and can you not have any rest on Sundays, in the hottest part of the day, at that?"

"In a week, sir, there are six days, and we go six times a week to work on the master's fields; in the evening, if the weather is good, we haul to the master's house the hay that is left in the woods; and on holidays the women and girls go walking in the woods, looking for mushrooms and berries. God grant," he continued, making the sign of the cross, "that it rains this evening. If you have peasants of your own, sir, they are praying to God for the same thing."

"My friend, I have no peasants, and so nobody curses me. Do you have a large family?"

"Three sons and three daughters. The eldest is nine years old."

"But how do you manage to get food enough, if you have only the holidays free?"

"Not only the holidays: the nights are ours, too. If a fellow isn't lazy, he won't starve to death. You see, one horse is resting; and when this one gets tired, I'll take the other; so the work gets done."

"Do you work the same way for your master?"

"No, Sir, it would be a sin to work the same way. On his fields there are a hundred hands for one mouth, while I have two for seven mouths: you can figure it out for yourself. No matter how hard you work for the master, no one will thank you for it. The master will not pay our head tax; but, though he doesn't pay it, he doesn't demand one sheep, one hen, or any linen or butter the less. The peasants are much better off where the landlord lets them pay a commutation tax without the interference of the steward. It is true that sometimes even good masters take more than three rubles a man; but even that's better than having to work on the master's fields. Nowadays it's getting to be the custom to let villages to tenants, as they call it. But we call it putting our heads in a noose. A landless tenant skins us peasants alive; even the best ones don't leave us any time for ourselves. In the winter he won't let us do any carting of goods and won't let us go into town to work; all our work has to be for him, because he pays our head tax. It is an invention of the Devil to turn your peasants over to work for a stranger. You can make a complaint against a bad steward, but to whom can you complain against a bad tenant?"

"My friend, you are mistaken; the laws forbid them to torture people."

"Torture? That's true; but all the same, sir, you would not want to be in my hide." Meanwhile the ploughman hitched up the other horse to the plough and bade me goodbye as he began a new furrow.

The words of this peasant awakened in me a multitude of thoughts. I thought especially of the inequality of treatment within the peasant class. I compared the crown peasants with the manorial peasants. They both live in villages; but the former pay a fixed sum, while the latter must be prepared to pay whatever their master demands. The former are judged by their equals; the latter are dead to the law, except, perhaps, in criminal cases. A member of society becomes known to the government protecting him, only when he breaks the social bonds, when he becomes a criminal! This thought made my blood boil.

Tremble, cruelhearted landlord! on the brow of each of your peasants I see your condemnation written.

2. THE EMANCIPATION MANIFESTO (1861)

By the Grace of God We, Alexander II, Emperor and Autocrat of All Russia, King of Poland, Grand Duke of Finland, etc., make known to all Our faithful subjects:

Called by Divine Providence and by the sacred right of inheritance to the throne of Our Russian ancestors, We vowed in Our heart to respond to the mission which is entrusted to Us and to surround with Our affection and Our Imperial solicitude all Our faithful subjects of every rank and condition, from the soldier who nobly defends the country to the humble artisan who works in industry; from the career official of the state to the plowman who tills the soil.

Examining the condition of classes and professions comprising the state, We became convinced that the present state legislation favors the upper and middle classes, defines their obligations, rights, and privileges, but does not equally favor the serfs, so designated because in part from old laws and in part from custom they have been hereditarily subjected to the authority of landowners, who in turn were obligated to provide for their well being. Rights of nobles have been hitherto very broad and legally ill defined, because they stem from tradition, custom, and the good will of the noblemen. In most cases this has led to the establishment of good patriarchal relations based on the sincere, just concern and benevolence on the part of the nobles, and on affectionate submission on the part of the peasants. Because of the decline of the simplicity of morals, because of an increase in the diversity of relations, because of the weakening of the direct paternal attitude of nobles toward the peasants, and because noble rights fell sometimes into the hands of people exclusively concerned with their personal interests, good relations weakened. The way was opened for an arbitrariness burdensome for the peasants and detrimental to their welfare, causing them to be indifferent to the improvement of their own existence.

These facts had already attracted the attention of Our predecessors of glorious memory, and they had adopted measures aimed at improving the conditions of the peasants; but these measures were ineffective, partly because they depended on the free, generous action of nobles, and partly because they affected only some localities, by virtue of special circumstances or as an experiment. Thus Alexander I issued a decree on free agriculturists, and the late Emperor Nicholas, Our beloved father, promulgated one dealing with the serfs. In the Western *gubernias,* inventory regulations determine the peasant land allotments and their obligations. But decrees on free agriculturists and serfs have been carried out on a limited scale only.

We thus became convinced that the problem of improving the condition of serfs was a sacred inheritance bequeathed to Us by Our predecessors, a mission which, in the course of events, Divine Providence has called upon Us to fulfill.

We have begun this task by expressing Our confidence toward the Russian nobility, which has proven on so many occasions its devotion to the Throne, and its readiness to make sacrifices for the welfare of the country.

We have left to the nobles themselves, in accordance with their own wishes, the task of preparing proposals for the new organization of peasant life—proposals that would limit their rights over the peasants, and the realization of which would inflict on them [the nobles] some material losses. Our confidence was justified. Through members of the *gubernia* committees, who had the trust of the nobles' associations, the nobility voluntarily renounced its right to own serfs. These committees, after collecting the necessary data, have formulated proposals on a new arrangement for serfs and their relationship with the nobles.

These proposals were diverse, because of the nature of the problem. They have been compared, collated, systematized, rectified and finalized in the main committee instituted for that purpose; and these new arrangements dealing with the peasants and domestics of the nobility have been examined in the Governing Council.

Having invoked Divine assistance, We have resolved to execute this task.

On the basis of the above mentioned new arrangements, the serfs will receive in time the full rights of free rural inhabitants.

The nobles, while retaining their property rights on all the lands belonging to them, grant the peasants perpetual use of their domicile in return for a specified obligation; and, to assure their livelihood as well as to guarantee fulfillment of their obligations toward the government, [the nobles] grant them a portion of arable land fixed by the said arrangements, as well as other property.

While enjoying these land allotments, the peasants are obliged, in return, to fulfill obligations to the noblemen fixed by the same arrangements. In this state, which is temporary, the peasants are temporarily bound.

At the same time, they are granted the right to purchase the domicile, and, with the consent of the nobles, they may acquire in full ownership the arable lands and other properties which are allotted them for permanent use. Following such acquisition of full ownership of land, the peasants will be freed from their obligations to the nobles for the land thus purchased and will become free peasant landowners. . . .

We leave it to the nobles to reach a friendly understanding with the peasants and to reach agreements on the extent of the land allotment and the obligations stemming from it, observing, at the same time, the established rules to guarantee the inviolability of such agreements. . . .

What legally belongs to nobles cannot be taken away from them without adequate compensation, or through their voluntary concession; it would be contrary to all justice to use the land of the nobles without assuming responsibility for it.

And now We confidently expect that the freed serfs, on the eve of a new future which is opening to them, will appreciate and recognize the considerable sacrifices which the nobility has made on their behalf.

STUDY QUESTIONS

1. What are Radishchev's main arguments against serfdom? Where did he derive his criteria for judgment? What kind of society does he find preferable to Russia's?

2. Was the emancipation of the serfs a radical move? Why did it provoke renewed discontent among the peasants? How did the arguments and implementation relate to earlier critiques by Westernizers like Radishchev?

3. What does the emancipation document suggest about the flexibility of Russia's authoritarian political structure?

4. Do these two documents provide clues as to why Russia encountered less social protest than Western Europe did during the first half of the nineteenth century, but more fundamental protest movements by the century's end?

Asia

15

China and the West:
Opium and "Self-Strengthening"

During most of the Ming dynasty (1368–1644) and during the first half of the Ch'ing dynasty (1644–1912) Chinese emperors presided over an orderly and prosperous society. Jesuit missionaries to the Ch'ing court, who had little success in winning converts, nonetheless sent letters to their colleagues in Europe that were highly positive about what they observed in China. Leaders of the European Enlightenment such as Voltaire (1694–1778), basing their views on the Jesuit reports, praised the Chinese political system for its stability and reasonableness.

Around 1800, however, much began to go wrong in China. By this date the Chinese population, which had been growing rapidly for the past three centuries, began to press hard against the available food supply. In the past the Chinese had been among the world's most innovative people with regard to technology, but, for reasons that are poorly understood, this was no longer the case. In consequence, living standards in China, which scholars think were roughly comparable to those in Europe up to 1800, began to decline. In addition, Chinese emperors in the nineteenth century were less competent than those who had reigned during the first half of the Ch'ing period.

The emperors' problems were exacerbated by the actions of the British East India Company and other Western traders who began to ship huge quantities of opium to China around 1800. Attempts by the Chinese authorities to halt the trade in opium (which was grown in British-controlled Bengal) proved ineffective; addiction to the drug began to spread. In response, the Ch'ing court dispatched one of its most highly regarded officials, Lin Tse-hsu, to Canton in 1839 to find a remedy. It was in these circumstances that Lin addressed his famous letter to Queen Victoria

From *China's Response to the West: A Documentary Survey, 1839–1923*, edited by Ssu-Yu Teng and John King Fairbank (Cambridge, MA: Harvard University Press), pp. 24–26, 51–54. Copyright 1952 and renewed 1980 by Alfred A. Knopf Inc. Reprinted by permission of the publisher.

(1837–1901), an excerpt from which appears in the first selection. Lin also had a large quantity of the drug seized and publicly destroyed. The British responded by attacking Canton and several other Chinese ports. Overwhelmed, the Chinese surrendered in 1842. By the terms of the subsequent Treaty of Nanking the Chinese were forced to open several ports to trade, to cede the island of Hong Kong, and to make other significant concessions to the British (which were soon extended to other Western governments). For the West, the door to China was now open. For the Chinese, the downward slide now accelerated.

The humiliating outcome of the Opium War was a great shock to China's Confucian scholars. During the rest of the nineteenth century and beyond they wrestled with the fundamental issue posed by the war with the British: What should be done in the face of the huge disparity in wealth and power that had developed between China and the West? Feng Kuei-fen (1809–1874) was one of the first Chinese thinkers to address this issue. In the second selection excerpts are presented from two of Feng's essays which were written around 1860.

1. LIN TSE-HSU'S LETTER TO QUEEN VICTORIA (1839)

A communication: magnificently our great Emperor soothes and pacifies China and the foreign countries, regarding all with the same kindness. If there is profit, then he shares it with the peoples of the world; if there is harm, then he removes it on behalf of the world. This is because he takes the mind of heaven and earth as his mind.

The kings of your honorable country by a tradition handed down from generation to generation have always been noted for their politeness and submissiveness. We have read your successive tributary memorials saying, "In general our countrymen who go to trade in China have always received His Majesty the Emperor's gracious treatment and equal justice," and so on. Privately we are delighted with the way in which the honorable rulers of your country deeply understand the grand principles and are grateful for the Celestial grace. For this reason the Celestial Court in soothing those from afar has redoubled its polite and kind treatment. The profit from trade has been enjoyed by them continuously for two hundred years. This is the source from which your country has become known for its wealth.

But after a long period of commercial intercourse, there appear among the crowd of barbarians both good persons and bad, unevenly. Consequently there are those who smuggle opium to seduce the Chinese people and so cause the spread of the poison to all provinces. Such persons who only care to profit themselves, and disregard their harm to others, are not tolerated by the laws of heaven and are unanimously hated by human beings. His Majesty the Emperor, upon hearing of this, is in a towering rage. . . . He has especially sent me, his commissioner, to come to Kwangtung, and together with the governor-general and governor jointly to investigate and settle this matter.

All those people in China who sell opium or smoke opium should receive the death penalty. If we trace the crime of those barbarians who through the years have been selling opium, then the deep harm they have wrought and the great profit they have usurped should fundamentally justify their execution according to law. We take into consideration, however, the fact that the various barbarians have still known how to repent their crimes and return to their allegiance to us by taking the

20,183 chests of opium from their storeships and petitioning us, through their consular officer [superintendent of trade], Elliot, to receive it. It has been entirely destroyed and this has been faithfully reported to the Throne in several memorials by this commissioner and his colleagues.

Fortunately we have received a specially extended favor from His Majesty the Emperor, who considers that for those who voluntarily surrender there are still some circumstances to palliate their crime, and so for the time being he has magnanimously excused them from punishment. But as for those who again violate the opium prohibition, it is difficult for the law to pardon them repeatedly. Having established new regulations, we presume that the ruler of your honorable country, who takes delight in our culture and whose disposition is inclined towards us, must be able to instruct the various barbarians to observe the law with care. It is only necessary to explain to them the advantages and disadvantages and then they will know that the legal code of the Celestial Court must be absolutely obeyed with awe.

We find that your country is sixty or seventy thousand *li* [three *li* make one mile, ordinarily] from China. Yet there are barbarian ships that strive to come here for trade for the purpose of making a great profit. The wealth of China is used to profit the barbarians. That is to say, the great profit made by barbarians is all taken from the rightful share of China. By what right do they then in return use the poisonous drug to injure the Chinese people? Even though the barbarians may not necessarily intend to do us harm, yet in coveting profit to an extreme, they have no regard for injuring others. Let us ask, where is your conscience? I have heard that the smoking of opium is very strictly forbidden by your country; that is because the harm caused by opium is clearly understood. Since it is not permitted to do harm to your own country, then even less should you let it be passed on to the harm of other countries—how much less to China! Of all that China exports to foreign countries, there is not a single thing which is not beneficial to people: they are of benefit when eaten, or of benefit when used, or of benefit when resold: all are beneficial. Is there a single article from China which has done any harm to foreign countries? Take tea and rhubarb, for example; the foreign countries cannot get along for a single day without them. If China cuts off these benefits with no sympathy for those who are to suffer, then what can the barbarians rely upon to keep themselves alive? Moreover the woolens, camlets, and longells [i.e., textiles] of foreign countries cannot be woven unless they obtain Chinese silk. If China, again, cuts off this beneficial export, what profit can the barbarians expect to make? As for other foodstuffs, beginning with candy, ginger, cinnamon, and so forth, and articles for use, beginning with silk, satin, chinaware, and so on, all the things that must be had by foreign countries are innumerable. On the other hand, articles coming from the outside to China can only be used as toys. We can take them or get along without them. Since they are not needed by China, what difficulty would there be if we closed the frontier and stopped the trade? Nevertheless our Celestial Court lets tea, silk, and other goods be shipped without limit and circulated everywhere without begrudging it in the slightest. This is for no other reason but to share the benefit with the people of the whole world. . . .

Suppose there were people from another country who carried opium for sale to England and seduced your people into buying and smoking it; certainly your honorable ruler would deeply hate it and be bitterly aroused. We have heard heretofore that your honorable ruler is kind and benevolent. Naturally you would not wish to give unto others what you yourself do not want. We have also heard that the ships coming to Canton have all had regulations promulgated and given to them in which it is stated that it is not permitted to carry contraband goods. This indicates that the administrative orders of your honorable rule have been originally strict and clear. Only because the trading ships are numerous, heretofore perhaps they have not been examined with care. Now after this communication has been dispatched and you have clearly understood the strictness of the prohibitory laws of the Celestial Court, certainly you will not let your subjects dare again to violate the law. . . .

2. TWO ESSAYS BY FENG KUEI-FEN (ca. 1860)

A. On the Adoption of Western Knowledge

The world today is not to be compared with that of the Three Dynasties (of ancient China). . . . Now the globe is ninety-thousand *li* around, and every spot may be reached by ships or wheeled vehicles . . . According to what is listed on the maps by the Westerners, there are not less than one hundred countries. From these one hundred countries, only the books of Italy, at the end of the Ming dynasty, and now those of England have been translated into Chinese, altogether several tens of books. Those which expound the doctrine of Jesus are generally vulgar, not worth mentioning. Apart from these, Western books on mathematics, mechanics, optics, light, chemistry, and other subjects contain the best principles of the natural sciences. In the books on geography, the mountains, river, strategic points, customs, and native products of the hundred countries are fully listed. Most of this information is beyond the reach of our people. . . .

If today we wish to select and use Western knowledge, we should establish official translation offices at Canton and Shanghai. Brilliant students up to fifteen years of age should be selected from those areas to live and study in these schools on double rations. Westerners should be invited to teach them the spoken and written languages of the various nations, and famous Chinese teachers should also be engaged to teach them classics, history, and other subjects. At the same time they should learn mathematics. (Note: All Western knowledge is derived from mathematics. Every Westerner of ten years of age or more studies mathematics. If we now wish to adopt Western knowledge, naturally we cannot but learn mathematics. . . .)

After three years all students who can recite with ease the books of the various nations should be permitted to become licentiates; and if there are some precocious ones who are able to make changes or improvements which can be put into practice, they should be recommended by the superintendent of trade to be imperially granted a *chü-jen* degree as a reward. As we have said before, there are many brilliant people in China; there must be some who can learn from the barbarians and surpass them. . . .

If we let Chinese ethics and famous [Confucian] teachings serve as an original foundation, and let them be supplemented by the methods used by the various nations for the attainment of prosperity and strength, would it not be the best of all procedures?

Moreover, during the last twenty years since the opening of trade, a great many of the foreign chiefs have learned our written and spoken language, and the best of them can even read our classics and histories. They are generally able to speak on our dynastic regulations and government administration, on our geography and the state of the populace. On the other hand, our officers from generals down, in regard to foreign countries are completely uninformed. In comparison, should we not feel ashamed? . . .

If my proposal is carried out, there will necessarily be many Chinese who learn their written and spoken languages; and when there are many such people, there will certainly emerge from among them some upright and honest gentlemen who thoroughly understand the fundamentals of administration, and who would then get hold of the essential guiding principles for the control of foreigners. . . .

B. On the Manufacture of Foreign Weapons

The most unparalleled anger which has ever existed since the creation of heaven and earth is exciting all who are conscious in their minds and have spirit in their blood; their hats are raised by their hair standing on end. This is because the largest country on the globe today, with a vast area of 10,000 *li*, is yet controlled by small barbarians. . . . According to a general geography by an Englishman, the territory of our China is eight times larger than that of Russia, ten times that of America, one hundred times that of France, and two hundred times that of England. . . . Yet now we are shamefully humiliated by these four nations in the recent treaties— not because our climate, soil, or resources are inferior to theirs, but because our people are really inferior. . . . Why are they small and yet strong? Why are we large and yet weak? We must try to discover some means to become their equal, and that also depends upon human effort. Regarding the present situation there are several major points: in making use of the ability of our manpower, with no one neglected, we are inferior to the barbarians; in securing the benefit of the soil, with nothing wasted, we are inferior to the barbarians; in maintaining a close relationship between the ruler and the people, with no barrier between them, we are inferior to the barbarians; and in the necessary accord of word with deed, we are also inferior to the barbarians. The way to correct these four points lies with ourselves, for they can be changed at once if only our Emperor would set the general policy right. There is no need for outside help in these matters. [Here Feng goes on to point out that the only help China needs from the West is in modern arms, and claims that in recent contests with Western troops the Chinese army has not been inferior in physical qualities, nor even sometimes in morale, but always in arms.]

What we then have to learn from the barbarians is only the one thing, solid ships and effective guns. . . .

Funds should be assigned to establish a shipyard and arsenal in each trading port. Several barbarians should be invited and Chinese who are good in using their minds should be summoned to receive their instructions so that they may in turn teach many artisans. When a piece of work is finished and is indistinguishable from that made by the barbarians, the maker should be given a *chü-jen* degree as a reward, and be permitted to participate in the metropolitan examination on an equal footing with other scholars. Those whose products are superior to the barbarian manufacture should be granted a *chin-shih* degree as a reward, and be permitted to participate in the palace examinations on the same basis as others. The workers should be double-paid so as to prevent them from quitting.

Our nation has emphasized the civil service examinations, which have preoccupied people's minds for a long time. Wise and intelligent scholars have exhausted their time and energy in such useless things as the eight-legged essays [highly stylized essays for the civil service examination, divided into eight paragraphs], examination papers, and formal calligraphy. . . . Now let us order one-half of them to apply themselves to the pursuit of manufacturing weapons and instruments and imitating foreign crafts. . . . The intelligence and wisdom of the Chinese are necessarily superior to those of the various barbarians, only formerly we have not made use of them. When the Emperor above likes something, those below him will pursue it even further, like the moving of grass in the wind or the response of an echo. There ought to be some people of extraordinary intelligence who can have new ideas and improve on Western methods. At first they may learn and pattern after the foreigners; then they may compare and try to be their equal; and finally they may go ahead and surpass them—the way to make ourselves strong actually lies in this. . . .

Two years ago the Western barbarians suddenly entered the Japanese capital to seek trade relations, which were permitted. Before long the Japanese were able to send some ten steamships of their own over the western ocean to pay return visits to the various countries. They made many requests for treaties which were also granted by these countries, who understood Japan's intentions. Japan is a tiny country and still knows how to exert her energy to become strong. Should we, as a large country, alone accept defilement and insult throughout all time? . . . We are just now in an interval of peaceful and harmonious relations. This is probably an opportunity given by heaven for us to strengthen ourselves. If we do not at this point quickly rise to this opportunity but passively receive the destiny of heaven, our subsequent regret will come too late. . . . If we live in the present day and speak of rejecting the barbarians, we should raise the question as to what instruments we can reject them with. . . .

Some suggest purchasing ships and hiring foreign people, but the answer is that this is quite impossible. If we can manufacture, can repair, and can use them, then they are our weapons. If we cannot manufacture, nor repair, nor use them, then they are still the weapons of others. When these weapons are in the hands of others and are used for grain transportation, then one day they can make us starve; and if they are used for salt transportation, one day they can deprive us of salt. . . . Eventually we must consider manufacturing, repairing, and using weapons by ourselves. . . . Only thus will we be able to pacify the empire; only thus can we play a leading role on the globe; and only thus shall we restore our original strength, and redeem ourselves from former humiliations.

STUDY QUESTIONS

1. What are the main points that Commissioner Lin makes in objecting to the opium trade?
2. In Lin's view, who is responsible for the opium traffic? How should it be ended?
3. What does Lin's letter suggest about how Chinese leaders viewed China's place in the world? What seems to be the attitude of the Chinese government toward trade and diplomatic relations with the West?

4. In Feng Kuei-fen's first essay, what does he think is most valuable and least valuable about Western knowledge?

5. What reforms does Feng propose so that China can benefit from Western knowledge?

6. In Feng's second essay, what does he see as the four weaknesses of China compared with the West?

7. How does Feng propose to end the disparity between China and the West?

8. Who is more loyal to the Confucian ideas illustrated in Chapter 6, Lin or Feng? How do you explain the differences?

9. Compare the responses to the rise of European power in China, India, the Ottoman Empire, Japan, and Latin America. (See Chapters 16, 17, and 20, and the Fukuzawa excerpt in Chapter 22; see also the earlier Russian response in Chapter 3.)

16

Language, Religion, and National Identity in India

During the eighteenth century the authority of the Mughal emperors in India declined sharply. Princely states and regional kingdoms emerged in various parts of the Indian subcontinent, steadily eroding the power of the emperors in Delhi. In 1739 the Shah of Iran invaded India, pillaged the capital, and made off with the Peacock Throne, the symbol of Mughal rule. As the position of the Mughal regime weakened, India became vulnerable to new invasions from the sea.

From 1498 onward the Portuguese, Dutch, French, and English sent maritime expeditions to India with the goal of profiting from trade. In the end, the British won out over their rivals. Beginning in the 1750s the British East India Company pursued a two-pronged strategy of conquering Indian territory and allying with Indian princes. By the 1810s the British were dominant over much of the subcontinent (although Mughal emperors continued to reign symbolically until 1858) and remained so until the establishment of an independent India and Pakistan in 1947.

The establishment of British colonial rule in India had significant consequences for both England and India. East India Company officials such as Sir William Jones (1746–1794) were the first Europeans to learn Sanskrit and to become serious scholars of ancient Indian culture. In beginning the translation of Indian classics such as the *Bhagavad Gita* into English and other European languages, Jones and his colleagues greatly enriched Western learning.

In India one of the important developments during the period of British rule was the emergence of a group of Indian thinkers, predominantly Hindus at first, who were fully conversant with both Indian and European culture. The earliest of these Indian intellectuals was Rammohun Roy (1772–1833). Born into a family of Bengali *brahmans,* Roy mastered ten languages and was broadly educated in Asian and European thought. For a time he worked for the East India Company. Roy believed that the British could benefit India by helping to abolish certain Hindu practices such as widow suicide (*sati*) and by bring European culture (science, technology, liberal po-

Selections 1 and 2 from *Sources of Indian Tradition,* 2nd ed., Vol. II, edited by Stephen Hay (New York: Columbia University Press, 1988), pp. 31–34; and *The Political Awakening in India,* edited by John R. McLane (Englewood Cliffs, N.J.: Prentice-Hall, 1970), pp. 28–30. Reprinted by permission of Simon & Schuster, Inc.

litical ideas, etc.) to the subcontinent. The two letters from Roy in the first selection illustrate some of his most important ideas.

In the second selection, written by Maulvi Syed Kutb Shah Sahib, we are taken into the heart of a major event in nineteenth-century India, the great popular uprising of 1857–1858, which used to be referred to as the Sepoy Mutiny. The upheaval did begin as a mutiny by Hindu and Muslim soldiers, known as sepoys, against their British officers. But modern scholars, many of whom are Indian, have established that the protests spread far beyond the army and were therefore much more than a military mutiny. In some ways the uprising resembled a popular war for Indian independence. However, religious and other differences between the rebels (issues which are addressed in the statement by Maulvi Syed Kutb Shah Sahib) prevented the development of a unified movement. In 1858 the British succeeded in restoring their authority, although it required massive military force to do so.

1. RAMMOHUN ROY

A. *Letter to the British Governor-General of India (1823)*

The establishment of a new Sangscrit School in Calcutta evinces the laudable desire of government to improve the Natives of India by Education—a blessing for which they must ever be grateful; and every well-wisher of the human race must be desirous that the efforts made to promote it should be guided by the most enlightened principles, so that the stream of intelligence may flow in the most useful channels.

When this Seminary of learning was proposed, we understood that the Government in England had ordered a considerable sum of money to be annually devoted to the instruction of its Indian Subjects. We were filled with sanguine hopes that this sum would be laid out in employing European Gentlemen of talent and education to instruct the Natives of India in Mathematics, Natural Philosophy, Chemistry, Anatomy, and other useful Sciences, which the Natives of Europe have carried to a degree of perfection that has raised them above the inhabitants of other parts of the world.

While we looked forward with pleasing hope to the dawn of knowledge thus promised to the rising generation, our hearts were filled with mingled feelings of delight and gratitude; we already offered up thanks to Providence for inspiring the most generous and enlightened Nations of the West with the glorious ambition of planting in Asia the Arts and Sciences of modern Europe.

We find that the Government are establishing a Sangscrit school under Hindoo pandits to impart such knowledge as is already current in India. This seminary (similar in character to those which existed in Europe before the time of Lord Bacon) can only be expected to load the minds of youth with grammatical niceties and metaphysical distinctions of little or no practicable use to the possessors or to society. The pupils will there acquire what was known two thousand years ago, with the addition of vain and empty subtleties since then produced by speculative men, such as is already commonly taught in all parts of India. . . .

In order to enable your Lordship to appreciate the utility of encouraging such imaginary learning as above characterised, I beg your Lordship will be pleased to compare the state of Science and Literature in Europe before the time of Lord Bacon with the progress of knowledge made since he wrote.

If it had been intended to keep the British nation in ignorance of real knowledge, the Baconian philosophy would not have been allowed to displace the system of the schoolmen, which was the best calculated to perpetuate ignorance. In the same manner the Sangscrit system of education would be best calculated to keep this country in darkness, if such had been the policy of the British Legislature. But as the improvement of the native population is the object of the Government, it will consequently promote a more liberal and enlightened system of instruction, embracing mathematics, natural philosophy, chemistry and anatomy, with other useful sciences, which may be accomplished with the sums proposed by employing a few gentlemen of talent and learning educated in Europe, and providing a college furnished with necessary books, instruments, and other apparatus.

In presenting this subject to your Lordship, I conceive myself discharging a solemn duty which I owe to my countrymen, and also to that enlightened Sovereign and Legislature which have extended their benevolent cares to this distant land, actuated by a desire to improve the inhabitants, and I therefore humbly trust you will excuse the liberty I have taken in thus expressing my sentiments to your Lordship.

B. Letter to an English Friend (1828)

Supposing that one hundred years hence the Native character becomes elevated from constant intercourse with Europeans and the acquirement of general and political knowledge as well as of modern arts and sciences, is it possible that they will not have the spirit as well as the inclination to resist effectually any unjust and oppressive measures serving to degrade them in the scale of society? It should not be lost sight of that the position of India is very different from that of Ireland, to any quarter of which an English fleet may suddenly convey a body of troops that may force its way in the requisite direction and succeed in suppressing every effort of refractory spirit. Were India to share one fourth of the knowledge and energy of that country, she would prove from her remote situation, her riches and her vast population, either useful and profitable as a willing province, an ally of the British Empire, or troublesome and annoying as a determined enemy.

In common with those who seem partial to the British rule from the expectation of future benefits, arising out of the connection, I necessarily feel extremely grieved in often witnessing Acts and Regulations passed by Government without consulting or seeming to understand the feelings of its Indian subjects and without considering that this people have had for more than half a century the advantage of being ruled by and associated with an enlightened nation, advocates of liberty and promoters of knowledge.

2. MAULVI SYED KUTB SHAH SAHIB CALLS FOR HINDU-MUSLIM UNITY (1857)

The English are people who overthrow all religions. You should understand well the object of destroying the religions of Hindustan; they have for a long time been causing books to be written and circulated throughout the country by the hands of their priests, and, exercising their authority, have brought out numbers of preachers to spread their own tenets: this has been learned from one of their own trusted agents. Consider, then, what systematic contrivances they have adopted to destroy our religions. For instance, first, when a woman became a widow they ordered her to make a second marriage. Secondly, the self-immolation of wives on the funeral pyres of their deceased husbands was an ancient religious custom; the English had it discontinued, and enacted their own regulations prohibiting it. Thirdly, they told people it was their wish that they (the people) should adopt their faith, promising that if they did so they would be respected by Government; and further required them to attend churches, and hear the tenets preached there. Moreover, they decided and told the rajahs [princes] that such only as were born of their wives would inherit the government and property, and that adopted heirs would not be allowed to succeed, although, according to your Scriptures, ten different sorts of heirs are allowed shares in the inheritance. By this contrivance they will rob you of your governments and possessions, as they have already done with Nagpur and Lucknow. Consider now another of their designing plans: they resolved on compelling prisoners, with the forcible exercise of their authority, to eat their bread. Numbers died of starvation, but did not eat it, others ate it, and sacrificed their faith. They now perceived that this expedient did not succeed well, and accordingly determined on having bones ground and mixed with flour and sugar, so that people might unsuspectingly eat them in this way. They had, moreover, bones and flesh broken small and mixed with rice, which they caused to be placed in the markets for sale, and tried, besides, every other possible plan to destroy our religions. At last some Bengali, after due reflection, said that if the troops would accede to the wishes of the English in this matter all the Bengalis would also conform to them. The English, hearing this approved of it, and said, "Certainly this is an excellent idea," never imagining they would be themselves exterminated. They accordingly now ordered the Brahmans and others of their army to bite cartridges, in the making up of which fat had been used. The Mussulman soldiers perceived that by this expedient the religion of the Brahmans and Hindus only was in danger, but nevertheless they also refused to bite them. On this the English now resolved on ruining the faith of both, and blew away from guns [by tying them to the mouths of cannons which were then fired] all those soldiers who persisted in their refusal. Seeing this excessive tyranny, the soldiery now, in self-preservation, began killing the English, and slew them wherever they were found, and are now considering means for slaying the few still alive here and there. It is now my firm conviction that if these English continued in Hindustan they will kill every one in the country, and will utterly overthrow our religions; but there are some of my countrymen who have joined the English, and are now fighting on their side. I have reflected well on their case also, and have come to the conclusion that the English will not leave your religion to both you and them. You should understand this well. Under these circumstances, I would ask, what course have you decided on to protect your lives and faith? Were your views and mine the same, we might destroy them entirely with a very little trouble; and if we do so, we shall protect our religions and save the country. And as these ideas have been cherished and considered merely from a concern for the protection of the religions and lives of all you Hindus and Mussulmans of this country, this letter is printed for your information. All you Hindus are hereby solemnly adjured, by your faith in Ganges, Tulsi, and Saligram; and all you Mussulmans, by your belief in God and the Koran, as these English are the common enemy of both, to unite in considering their slaughter extremely expedient, for by this alone will the lives and faith of both be saved. It is expedient, then, that you should coalesce and slay them. The slaughter of kine [cows] is regarded by the Hindus as a great insult to their religion. To prevent this a solemn compact and agreement has been entered into by all the Mahomedan chiefs of Hindustan, binding themselves, that if the Hindus will come forward to slay the English, the Mahomedans will from that very day put a stop to the slaughter of cows, and those of them who will not do so will be considered to have abjured the Koran, and such of them as will eat beef will be regarded as though they had eaten pork; but if the Hindus will not gird their loans to kill the English, but will try to save them, they will be as guilty in the sight of God as though they had committed the sins of killing cows and eating flesh. Perhaps the English may, for their own ends, try to assure the Hindus that as the Mussulmans have consented to give up killing cows from respect to the Hindu religion, they will solemnly engage to do the same, and will ask the Hindus to join them against the Mussulmans; but no sensible man will be gulled by such deceit, for the solemn promises and professions of the English are always deceitful and interested. Once their ends are gained they will infringe their engagements, for deception has ever been habitual with them, and the treachery they have always practised on the people of Hindustan is known to rich and poor. Do not therefore give heed to what they may say. Be well assured you will never have such an opportunity again. We all know that writing a letter is equivalent to an advance half way towards fellowship. I trust you will all write answers approving of what has been proposed herein. This letter has been printed under the direction of Moulavy Syed Kutb Shah Sahib, at the Bahaduri press, in the city of Bareilly.

STUDY QUESTIONS

1. Why did Roy object to the teaching of Sanskrit?
2. In these passages how does Roy reveal his understanding of European history and culture?
3. How does Roy envision the future of relations between India and the British?
4. What was Maulvi Syed Kutb Shah's objection to the English?
5. How does Maulvi Syed Kutb Shah's letter provide us with evidence of attempts by the British to introduced reforms in India? What is his attitude toward the reforms?
6. What evidence is there in this letter about the causes of the 1857–1858 uprising?
7. What seems to be the basis for conflict between the Hindus and the Muslims?
8. Were Roy and Maulvi Syed Kutb Shah nationalists?
9. What is the relationship between language, religion, and nationalism?
10. What do these documents suggest about changes that had occurred in India since the time of Babur? What had not changed? (See Chapter 5.)
11. How do the idea of these two Indian thinkers compare with those of their contemporaries in China and Japan? (See Chapter 17 and the Fukuzawa excerpt in Chapter 22.)

17

The Tanzimat Reforms
in the Ottoman Empire

By 1800 the power and wealth of the Ottoman Empire had declined considerably from its peak in the sixteenth century during the reign of Suleiman the Lawgiver. The Turkish army of the early nineteenth century was far from being the effective fighting force that had so impressed Ambassador Busbecq during his years in Constantinople (see Chapter 4). Corruption and ineffectiveness were rife in the Janissary corps, whose members were no longer recruited by means of the *devshirme* (the enslavement of non-Muslim children). The Turkish bureaucracy was also infected with corruption. In addition, the Ottoman economy had been greatly weakened by currency instability and by a policy of the sultans that gave special privileges to European merchants who resided in Turkish ports.

Ottoman weakness led to territorial losses. The Austrians pushed the Turks out of Hungary, and the Russians forced them to leave the region north of the Black Sea. Between 1798 and 1801 the French occupied Ottoman Egypt; when the French departed it was due to pressure from the British rather than from the Turks. In 1805 a revolt of the Janissaries in Serbia effectively ended Ottoman control of a key region in the Balkans. During the 1820s Greek rebels—who were assisted by France and Russia—succeeded in winning their independence from the Turks.

Jolted by the decline of their once-powerful and wealthy empire, Ottoman sultans promulgated a series of significant reforms during the first three quarters of the nineteenth century. Mahmud II (reigned 1808–1839) abolished the Janissary corps and introduced measures whose aim was to establish a clear distinction—unusual in an Islamic society—between religious and political authority. Under Mahmud's two sons and successors, Abdul Mejid (reigned 1839–1861) and Abdul Aziz (reigned 1861–1876), the Ottoman program of reform, known as the Tanzimat (meaning "restructuring" or "reorganization"), became still more far-reaching. New schools that embraced European learning were established, the army was reorganized, an imperial bank began operations, and taxes were equalized for Muslims and non-Muslims. Although the attempts by the Ottoman sultans and their advisors to stave off the collapse of the empire ultimately failed (see Chapter 29) the Tanzimat reforms were

Selections 1 and 2 from E. Hertslet, *The Map of Europe by Treaty*, 4 vols. (London: Butterworths, 1875–1891), Vol. II, pp. 1002–1005, 1243–1249.

nonetheless one of the most significant early efforts at modernization undertaken by a non-Western elite and invite comparison with similar attempts at reform in Russia, China, and Japan.

The basic principles of the Tanzimat reforms were laid down in two imperial rescripts issued by Sultan Abdul Mejid, the first in 1839 and the second in 1856. The selections follow.

1. IMPERIAL RESCRIPT OF NOVEMBER 3, 1839

All the world knows that in the first days of the Ottoman Monarchy, the glorious precepts of the Koran and the Laws of the Empire were always honoured. The Empire in consequence increased in strength and greatness, and all her Subjects, without exception, had risen in the highest degree to ease and prosperity. In the last 150 years a succession of accidents and divers causes have arisen which have brought about a disregard for the sacred code of Laws, and the Regulations flowing therefrom, and the former strength and prosperity have changed into weakness and poverty; an Empire in fact loses all its stability as soon as it ceases to observe its Laws.

The considerations are ever present to our mind, and, ever since the day of our advent to the Throne, the thought of the public weal, of the improvement of the state of the Provinces, and of relief of to the peoples, has not ceased to engage it. If, therefore, the geographical position of the Ottoman Provinces, the fertility of the soil, the aptitude and intelligence of the inhabitants are considered, the conviction will remain that, by striving to find efficacious means, the result, which by the help of God we hope to attain, can be obtained within a few years. Full of confidence, therefore, in the help of the Most High, assisted by the intercession of our Prophet, we deem it right to seek by new institutions to give to the Provinces composing the Ottoman Empire the benefit of a good Administration.

These institutions must be principally carried out under three heads, which are: 1. The guarantees insuring to our subjects perfect security for life, honour, and fortune. 2. A regular system of assessing and levying Taxes. 3. An equally regular system for the levy of Troops and the duration of their service. . . .

From henceforth, therefore, the cause of every accused person shall be publicly judged in accordance with our Divine Law, after enquiry and examination, and so long as a regular judgment shall not have been pronounced, no one can, secretly or publicly, put another to death by poison or in any other manner.

No one shall be allowed to attack the honour of any other person whatever.

Each one shall possess his Property of every kind, and shall dispose of it in all freedom, without let or hindrance from any person whatever; thus, for example, the innocent Heirs of a Criminal shall not be deprived of their legal rights, and the Property of the Criminal shall not be confiscated.

These Imperial concessions shall extend to all our subjects, of whatever Religion or sect they may be; they shall enjoy them without exceptions. We therefore grant perfect security to the inhabitants of our Empire, in their lives, their honour, and their fortunes, as they are secured to them by the sacred text of our Law. . . .

As all the Public Servants of the Empire receive a suitable salary, and that the salaries of those whose duties have not, up to the present time, been sufficiently remunerated, are to be fixed, a rigorous Law shall be passed against the traffic of favouritism and of appointments (*richvet*), which the Divine Law reprobates, and which is one of the principal causes of the decay of the Empire.

2. IMPERIAL RESCRIPT OF FEBRUARY 18, 1856

Let it be done as herein set forth.

To you, my Grand Vizier, Mehemed Emin Ali Pasha, decorated with my Imperial Order of the Medjidiyé of the first class, and with the Order of Personal Merit; may God grant to you greatness, and increase your power! . . .

It being now my desire to renew and enlarge still more the new Institutions ordained with the view of establishing a state of things conformable with the dignity of my Empire and— . . . by the kind and friendly assistance of the Great Powers, my noble Allies, . . . the guarantees promised on our part by the Hatti-Humaïoun of Gülhané, and in conformity with the Tanzimat, . . . are today confirmed and consolidated, and efficacious measures shall be taken in order that they may have their full and entire effect.

All the Privileges and Spiritual Immunities granted by my ancestors *ab antiquo,* and at subsequent dates, to all Christian communities or other non-Mussulman persuasions established in my Empire under my protection, shall be confirmed and maintained.

Every Christian or other non-Mussulman community shall be bound within a fixed period, and with the concurrence of a Commission composed *ad hoc* of members of its own body, to proceed with my high approbation and under the inspection of my Sublime Porte, to examine into its actual Immunities and Privileges, and to discuss and submit to my Sublime Porte the Reforms required by the progress of civilization and of the age. The powers conceded to the Christian Patriarchs and Bishops by the Sultan Mahomet II and his successors, shall be made to harmonize with the new position which my generous and beneficent intentions insure to these communities. . . . The principles of nominating the Patriarchs for life, after the revision of the rules of election now in force, shall be exactly carried out, conformably to the tenor of the Firmans of Investiture. . . . The ecclesiastical dues, of whatever sort or nature they be, shall be abolished and replaced by fixed revenues of the Patriarchs and heads of communities. . . . In the towns, small boroughs, and villages, where the whole population is of the same Religion, no obstacle shall be offered to the repair, according to their original plan, of buildings set apart for Religious Worship, for Schools, for Hospitals, and for Cemeteries. . . .

Every distinction or designation tending to make any class whatever of the subjects of my Empire inferior to another class, on account of their Religion, Language, or Race, shall be for ever effaced from the Administrative Protocol. The laws shall be put in force against the use of any injurious or offensive term, either among private individuals or on the part of the authorities.

As all forms of Religion are and shall be freely professed in my dominions, no subject of my Empire shall be hindered in the exercise of the Religion that he professes. . . . No one shall be compelled to change their Religion . . . and . . . all the subjects of my Empire, without distinction, nationality, shall be admissable to public employments. . . . All the subjects of my Empire, without distinction, shall be received into the Civil and Military Schools of the Government. . . . Moreover, every community is authorized to establish Public Schools of Science, Art, and Industry. . . .

All Commercial, Correctional, and Criminal Suits between Mussulmans and Christian or other non-Mussulman subjects, or between Christians or other non-Mussulmans of different sects, shall be referred to Mixed Tribunals. The proceedings of these Tribunals shall be public: the parties shall be confronted, and shall produce their witnesses, whose testimony shall be received, without distinction, upon oath taken according to the religious law of each sect. . . .

Penal, Correctional, and Commercial Laws, and Rules of Procedure for the Mixed Tribunals, shall be drawn up as soon as possible, and formed into a code. . . . Proceedings shall be taken, for the reform of the Penitentiary System. . . .

The organization of the Police . . . shall be revised in such a manner as to give to all the peaceable subjects of my Empire the strongest guarantees for the safety both of their persons and property. . . . Christian subjects, and those of other non-Mussulman sects, . . . shall, as well as Mussulmans, be subject to the obligations of the Law of Recruitment. The principle of obtaining substitutes, or of purchasing exemption, shall be admitted.

Proceedings shall be taken for a Reform in the Constitution of the Provincial and Communal Councils, in order to ensure fairness in the choice of the Deputies of the Mussulman, Christian, and other communities, and freedom of voting in the Councils. . . .

As the Laws regulating the purchase, sale, and disposal of Real Property are common to all the subjects of my Empire, it shall be lawful for Foreigners to possess Landed Property in my dominions. . . .

The Taxes are to be levied under the same denomination from all the subjects of my Empire, without distinction of class or of Religion. The most prompt and energetic means for remedying the abuses in collecting the Taxes, and especially the Tithes, shall be considered. The system of direct collection shall gradually, and as soon as possible, be substituted for the plan of Farming, in all the branches of the Revenues of the State.

A special Law having been already passed, which declared that the Budget of the Revenue and Expenditure of the State shall be drawn up and made known every year, the said law shall be most scrupulously observed. . . .

The heads of each Community and a Delegate, designated by my Sublime Porte, shall be summoned to take part in the deliberations of the Supreme Council of Justice on all occasions which might interest the generality of the subjects of my Empire. . . .

Steps shall be taken for the formation of Banks and other similar institutions, so as to effect a reform in the monetary and financial system, as well as to create Funds to be employed in augmenting the sources of the material wealth of my Empire.

Steps shall also be taken for the formation of Roads and Canals to increase the facilities of communication and increase the sources of the wealth of the country. Everything that can impede commerce or agriculture shall be abolished. . . .

Such being my wishes and my commands, you, who are my Grand Vizier, will, according to custom, cause this Imperial Firman to be published in my capital and in all parts of my Empire; and will watch attentively, and take all the necessary measures that all the orders which it contains be henceforth carried out with the most rigorous punctuality.

STUDY QUESTIONS

1. According to the Imperial Rescript of 1839, why, after so much early success, had the Ottoman Empire become weak and poor?
2. What remedies for Ottoman problems were proposed in the 1839 and 1856 rescripts?
3. Based on your reading of these two documents, what problems seem to have been most worrisome to the Ottoman authorities—political, economic, or religious?
4. What do the two rescripts say, or imply, about gender relations?
5. How might the two rescripts be thought of as a constitution? How did they fall short of being a constitution?
6. How did the timing, leadership, and nature of the Ottoman attempts at reform compare with similar movements in Russia, China, and Japan? What circumstances made the Ottoman situation unique? (See Chapters 3, 14, and 15 and the Fukuzawa excerpt in Chapter 22.)

18

Independence and Consolidation of New States (1810–1914)

Creoles, or American-born descendants of Spaniards and Portuguese, achieved independence from their former colonial masters between 1810 and 1825. Fifty years later, new political leaders, also from the creole class, overcame a long period of internal fighting and consolidated national governments in the last quarter of the nineteenth century.

Creoles were elitists, who considered themselves far superior to their mestizo, Indian, and black working classes. Owning the principal means of production and trade—that is, mines, haciendas, and merchant businesses—creoles employed and paternally controlled the racially different lower classes. By the end of the eighteenth century, creoles amounted to about 20 percent of the total population. Seeking freedom from colonial restrictions and a more autonomous role in government, creoles ridiculed the weaknesses of their mother country in Europe. When Napoleon invaded the Iberian Peninsula in 1808, the creoles in Latin America seized the initiative. After a number of military failures, creole armies in Spanish America gathered sufficient strength to expel Spain's expeditionary forces by 1825. In Brazil, where the king of Portugal resided after he escaped from Napoleon in 1808, the king's son, Pedro I, at the urging of the Brazilian creole elite, declared independence in 1822 after this father returned to Portugal in 1820.

Simón Bolivar, the liberator of northern South America, Peru, and Bolivia, came from this creole class. His political ideas clearly expressed the biases of his so-

Selection 1 from Simón Bolivar to the Congress of Angostura in 1819, in Vicente Lecuna and Harold A. Bierck, Jr., eds., *Selected Writings of Bolivar* (New York: Colonial Press, 1951), pp. 175–176, 183, 185–190. Selection 2 from Gabino Barreda's speech, September 16, 1867, in Carlos B. Gil, ed., *The Age of Porfirio Diaz: Selected Readings* (Albuquerque: University of New Mexico Press, 1977), pp. 35–36. Selection 3 from Porfirio Diaz interview, 1908, Carlos B. Gill, ed., *The Age of Porfirio Diaz: Selected Readings* (Albuquerque: University of New Mexico Press, 1977), pp. 78–81.

cial origins. He mistrusted the lower classes and advocated elite-run governments. In the first section these prejudices are clearly shown in Bolivar's advice to the legislators gathered at Angostura in 1819 to discuss the proposed constitution for the new state of Venezuela.

Once free, the creoles fought among themselves to determine control of an economy devastated by the wars of independence. A 50-year period of extreme political instability and civil war followed. Local *caudillos* (military leaders with a personal following) pillaged the treasury, ruled by extortion, and toppled one another in an endless succession of coups and countercoups. By the 1870s, new leaders from the creole class emerged. Well educated and wealthy (through exports of raw materials to the industrialized world), this new oligarchy ended caudillo rule.

In Mexico Porfirio Diaz ruled with an iron hand from 1876 to 1910. Although he was a rough mestizo military leader, Diaz enjoyed the support of the Mexican oligarchy and their articulate spokesmen. With the oligarchy's help, he ended 50 years of civil war. Through concessions to foreign investors, particularly in mining, railroads, and oil, Diaz presided over an impressive economic boom in exports to the United States. To maintain economic growth, the oligarchy sought stability, and Diaz provided it. In the second selection this call for order is expressed in a speech by Gabino Barreda, a Mexican intellectual who had just returned from France, where he studied under the positivist August Comte. Presented on September 16, 1867, the first Independence Day celebration after the French-installed European monarch, Maximilian, had been defeated by the Liberal General Benito Juarez, the speech called for an end to violent revolution and a new respect for order. The third selection is from an interview given by Porfirio Diaz in 1908 to the American reporter James Creelman. Diaz candidly revealed how he achieved order.

1. SIMÓN BOLIVAR'S ADVICE TO THE CONGRESS OF ANGOSTURA (1819)

We are not Europeans; we are not Indians; we are but a mixed species of aborigines and Spaniards. Americans by birth and Europeans by law, we find ourselves engaged in a dual conflict: we are disputing with the natives for titles of ownership, and at the same time we are struggling to maintain ourselves in the country that gave us birth against the opposition of the invaders.

Subject to the threefold yoke of ignorance, tyranny, and vice, the American people have been unable to acquire knowledge, power, or [civic] virtue. The lessons we received and the models we studied, as pupils of such pernicious teachers, were most destructive. We have been ruled more by deceit than by force, and we have been degraded more by vice than by superstition.

Venezuela had, has, and should have a republican government. Its principles should be the sovereignty of the people, division of powers, civil liberty, proscription of slavery, and the abolition of monarchy and privileges. We need equality to recast, so to speak, into a unified nation, the classes of men, political opinions, and public customs.

Like the North Americans, we have divided national representation into two chambers: that of Representatives and the Senate. The first is very wisely constituted. It enjoys all its proper functions, and it requires no essential revision, because the Constitution, in creating it, gave it the form and powers which the people

ATLANTIC OCEAN

San
Antonio

**MEXICO
1821**

*Gulf of
Mexico*

BAHAMA IS.
(Br.)

HAITI 1804

PUERTO RICO
(Sp.)

Mexico
City
Veracruz

CUBA
(Sp.)

**BR.
HONDURAS**

Caribbean Sea

TRINIDAD (Br.)

**UNITED PROVINCES OF
CENTRAL AMERICA
1823–1839**

Panama

Caracas

GUIANA

DUTCH GUIANA

**GRAN COLOMBIA
1819-1830**

FRENCH GUIANA

Bogotá

GALÁPAGOS IS.

Quito

Indefinite

Boundary

**EMPIRE
OF BRAZIL
1822**

Lima

**PERU
1821**

Bahia

**BOLIVIA
1825**

PACIFIC OCEAN

Sucre

**PARAGUAY
1811**

Rio de Janeiro

**CHILE
1817**

Asunción

Santiago

**UNITED
PROVINCES OF
LA PLATA
1826**

**URUGUAY
1828**

Montevideo

Buenos Aires

0   500   1000 Miles

0   1000 Kilometers

Latin America at Independence

deemed necessary in order that they might be legally and properly represented. If the Senate were hereditary rather than elective, it would, in my opinion, be the basis, the tie, the very soul of our republic. In political storms this body would arrest the thunderbolts of the government and would repel any violent popular reaction. Devoted to the government because of a natural interest in its own preservation, a hereditary senate would always oppose any attempt on the part of the people to infringe upon the jurisdiction and authority of their magistrates. It must be confessed that most men are unaware of their best interests and that they constantly endeavor to assail them in the hands of their custodians—the individual clashes with the mass, and the mass with authority. It is necessary, therefore, that in all governments there be a neutral body to protect the injured and disarm the offender. To be neutral, this body must not owe its origin to appointment by the government or to election by the people, if it is to enjoy a full measure of independence which neither fears nor expects anything from these two sources of authority. The hereditary senate, as a part of the people, shares its interests, its sentiments, and its spirit. For this reason it should not be presumed that a hereditary senate would ignore the interests of the people or forget its legislative duties. The senators in Rome and in the House of Lords in London have been the strongest pillars upon which the edifice of political and civil liberty has rested.

At the outset, these senators should be elected by Congress. The successors to this Senate must command the initial attention of the government, which should educate them in a *colegio* designed especially to train these guardians and future legislators of the nation. They ought to learn the arts, sciences, and letters that enrich the mind of a public figure. From childhood they should understand the career for which they have been destined by Providence, and from earliest youth they should prepare their minds for the dignity that awaits them.

The creation of a hereditary senate would in no way be a violation of political equality. I do not solicit the establishment of a nobility, for, as a celebrated republican has said, that would simultaneously destroy equality and liberty. What I propose is an office for which the candidates must prepare themselves, an office that demands great knowledge and the ability to acquire such knowledge. All should not be left to chance and the outcome of elections. The people are more easily deceived than is Nature perfected by art; and, although these senators, it is true, would not be bred in an environment that is all virtue, it is equally true that they would be raised in an atmosphere of enlightened education. Furthermore, the liberators of Venezuela are entitled to occupy forever a high rank in the Republic that they have brought into existence. I believe that posterity would view with regret the effacement of the illustrious names of its first benefactors. I say, moreover, that it is a matter of public interest and national honor, of gratitude on Venezuela's part, to honor gloriously, until the end of time, a race of virtuous, prudent, and persevering men who, overcoming every obstacle, have founded the Republic at the price of the most heroic sacrifices. And if the people of Venezuela do not applaud the elevation of their benefactors, then they are unworthy to be free, and they will never be free.

A hereditary senate, I repeat, will be the fundamental basis of the legislative power, and therefor the foundation of the entire government. It will also serve as a counterweight to both government and people; and as a neutral power it will weaken the mutual attacks of these two eternally rival powers. In all conflicts the calm reasoning of a third party will serve as the means of reconciliation. Thus the Venezuelan senate will give strength to this delicate political structure, so sensitive to violent repercussions; it will be the mediator that will lull the storms and it will maintain harmony between the head and the other parts of this political body.

No inducement could corrupt a legislative body invested with the highest honors, dependent only upon itself, having no fear of the people, independent of the government, and dedicated solely to the repression of all evil principles and to the advancement of every good principle—a legislative body that would be deeply concerned with the maintenance of a society, for it would share the consequences, be they honorable or disastrous. It has rightly been said that the upper house in England is invaluable to that nation because it provides a bulwark of liberty; and I would add that the Senate of Venezuela would be not only a bulwark of liberty but a bastion of defense, rendering the Republic eternal.

The British executive power possesses all the authority properly appertaining to a sovereign, but he is surrounded by a triple line of dams, barriers, and stockades. He is the head of the government, but his ministers and subordinates rely more upon law than upon his authority, as they are personally responsible, and not even decrees of royal authority can excempt them from this responsibility. The executive is commander in chief of the army and navy; he makes peace and declares war; but Parliament annually determines what sums are to be paid to these military forces. While the courts and judges are dependent on the executive power, the laws originate in and are made by Parliament. To neutralize the power of the King, his person is declared inviolable and sacred; but, while his head is left untouched, his hands are tied. The sovereign of England has three formidable rivals: his Cabinet, which is responsible to the people and to Parliament; the Senate [*sic*], which, representing the nobility of which it is composed, defends the interests of the people; and the House of Commons, which serves as the representative body of the British people and provides them with a place in which to express their opinions. Moreover, as the judges are responsible for the enforcement of the laws, they do not depart from them; and the administrations of the exchequer, being subject to prosecution not only for personal infractions but also for those of the government, take care to prevent any misuse of public funds. No matter how closely we study the composition of the English executive power, we can find nothing to prevent its being judged as the most perfect model for a kingdom, for an aristocracy, or for a democracy. Give Venezuela such an executive power in the person of a president chosen by the people or their representatives, and you will have taken a great step toward national happiness.

No matter what citizen occupies this office, he will be aided by the Constitution, and therein being authorized to do good, he can do no harm, because his ministers will coöperate with him only insofar as he abides by the law. If he attempts to infringe upon the law, his own ministers will desert him, thereby isolating him from the Republic, and they will even bring charges against him in the Senate. The ministers, being responsible for any transgressions committed, will actually govern, since they must account for their actions. The obligation which this system places upon the officials closest to the executive power, that is, to take a most interested and active part in the governmental deliberations and to regard this department as their own, is not the smallest advantage of the system. Should the president be a man of no great talent or virtue, yet, notwithstanding his lack of these essential qualities, he will be able to discharge his duties satisfactorily, for in such a case the ministry, managing everything by itself, will carry the burdens of the state.

Although the authority of the executive power in England may appear to be extreme, it would, perhaps, not be excessive in the Republic of Venezuela. Here the Congress has tied the hands and even the heads of its men of state. This deliberative assembly has assumed a part of the executive functions, contrary to the maxim of Montesquieu, to wit: A representative assembly should exercise no active function. It should only make laws and determine whether or not those laws are enforced. Nothing is as disturbing to harmony among the powers of government as their intermixture. Nothing is more dangerous with respect to the people than a weak executive; and if a kingdom has deemed it necessary to grant the executive so many powers, then in a republic these powers are infinitely more indispensable.

The people of Venezuela already enjoy the rights that they may legitimately and easily exercise. Let us now, therefore, restrain the growth of immoderate pretensions which, perhaps, a form of government unsuited to our people might excite. Let us abandon the federal forms of government unsuited to us; let us put aside the triumvirate which holds the executive power and center it in a president. We must grant him sufficient authority to enable him to continue the struggle against the obstacles inherent in our recent situation, our present state of war, and every variety of foe, foreign and domestic, whom we must battle for some time to come. Let the legislature relinquish the powers that rightly belong to the executive; let it acquire, however, a new consistency, a new influence in the balance of authority. Let the courts be strengthened by increasing the stability and independence of the judges and by the establishment of juries and civil and criminal codes dictated, not by antiquity nor by conquering kings, but by the voice of Nature, the cry of Justice, and the genius of Wisdom.

2. GABINO BARREDA'S SPEECH (SEPTEMBER 16, 1867)

Fellow citizens: we have taken giant strides in summarizing Mexico's emancipation; we have brought to mind all of the struggles and painful crises through which our country has traversed beginning with those that brought separation from Spain to the others that restored its emancipation from foreign tutelage under which it was subjected. We have seen that none of those struggles or crises have helped eliminate the harmful elements from our social constitution [i.e., the promonarchists and other conservatives]. We have likewise seen that, as a result of those painful but necessary crises, our full emancipation has gradually occurred too; that the assertion, made blindly or perversely by villainous politicians who deny to those conflicts signs of progress and incessant evolution, is wicked as it is irrational. Such politicians far too simply judge those conflicts as products of criminal aberrations or inexplicable delirium.

We have seen that two entire generations have sacrificed themselves to the present task of renovation and to the indispensable preparation of the materials necessary for reconstruction.

Moreover, the job is done; all the necessary elements for social reconstruction are gathered; all of the obstacles are razed; all of the moral, intellectual, or political forces that must offer their cooperation are at hand.

The foundation for the edifice is implanted. We have the Laws of the Reform which have placed us on the road to civilization farther ahead than any other people. We have a Constitution that has been a beacon which, amidst the tempestuous sea of invasion, everyone has sighted and taken as a source of consolation and as a guide, particularly for all the patriots who fought isolated and dispersed; it is a Constitution which, opening the gates to those innovations which experience may indicate as necessary, closes them to constitutional reform through revolution which is useless and imprudent, not to say criminal.

Now peace and order, maintained for an undefined period of time, will bring about everything that remains undone.

Fellow citizens: in the future let our motto be Liberty, Order, and Progress; Liberty as a means; Order as a base, and Progress as an end; it is a triple motto represented by the tricolor on our beautiful flag, that same flag which became in 1821 a blessed emblem of our independence in the hands of Guerrero and Iturbide; the emblem which, in the clutches of Zaragoza on May 5, 1862, assured the future of America and of the world by rescuing republican institutions.

In the future, may a complete freedom of conscience and an absolute freedom of expression permitting all ideas and inspirations, concede an enlightenment everywhere and make all disturbance not spiritual and all revolution which is not merely intellectual, unnecessary and impossible. May the physical order, conserved and maintained by all governors and respected by the governed, be a sure guarantor and the best way to walk forever along the florid path of progress and civilization.

3. INTERVIEW WITH PORFIRIO DIAZ (1908)

. . . I received this Government from the hands of a victorious army at a time when the people were divided and unprepared for the exercise of the extreme principles of democratic government. To have thrown upon the masses the whole responsibility of government at once would have produced conditions that might have discredited the cause of free government.

Yet, although I got power at first from the army, an election was held as soon as possible and then my authority came from the people. I have tried to leave the Presidency several times, but it has been pressed upon me and I remained in office for the sake of the nation which trusted me. The fact that the price of Mexican securities dropped eleven points when I was ill in Cuernavaca indicates the kind of evidence that persuaded me to overcome my personal inclination to retire from private life.

We preserved the republican and democratic form of government. We defended the theory and kept it intact. Yet we adopted a patriarchal policy in the administration of the nation's affairs, guiding the restraining popular tendencies, with full faith that an enforced peace would allow education, industry and commerce to develop elements of stability and unity in a naturally intelligent, gentle and affectionate people.

I have waited patiently for the day when the people of the Mexican Republic would be prepared to choose and change their government at every election without danger of armed revolutions and without injury to the national credit or interference with national progress. I believe the day has come.

· · ·

. . . The principles of democracy have not been planted very deeply in our people, I fear. But the nation has grown and it loves liberty. Our difficulty has been that the people do not concern themselves enough about public matters for a democracy. The individual Mexican as a rule thinks much about his own rights and is always ready to assert them. But he does not think so much about the rights of others. He thinks of his privileges, but not of his duties. Capacity for self-restraint is the basis of democratic government, and self-restraint is possible only to those who recognize the rights of their neighbors.

The Indians, who are more than half of our population, care little for politics. They are accustomed to looking to those in authority for leadership instead of thinking for themselves. That is a tendency they inherited from the Spanish, who taught them to refrain from meddling in public affairs and rely on the Government for guidance.

Yet I firmly believe that the principles of democracy have grown and will grow in Mexico.

· · ·

It is enough for me that I have seen Mexico rise among the peaceful and useful nations. I have no desire to continue in the Presidency. This nation is ready for her ultimate life of freedom. At the age of seventy-seven years I am satisfied with robust health. That is one thing which neither law nor force can create. I would not exchange it for all the millions of your American oil king.

· · ·

The railway has played a great part in the peace of Mexico. . . . When I became President at first there were only two small lines, one connecting the capital with Vera Cruz, the other connecting it with Querétaro. Now we have more than 19,000 miles of railways. Then we had a slow and costly mail service, carried on by stage coaches, and the mail coach between the capital and Puebla would be stopped by highwaymen two or three times in a trip, the last robbers to attack it generally finding nothing left to steal. Now we have a cheap, safe and fairly rapid mail service throughout the country with more than twenty-two hundred post offices. Telegraphing was a difficult thing in those times. Today we have more than forty-five thousand miles of telegraph wires in operation.

We began by making robbery punishable by death and compelling the execution of offenders within a few hours after they were caught and condemned. We ordered that wherever telegraph wires were cut and the chief officer of the district did not catch the criminal, *he should himself suffer**; and in the case the cutting oc-curred on a plantation *the proprietor* who failed *to prevent it should be hanged*† to the nearest telegraph pole. These were military orders, remember.

We were harsh. Sometimes we were harsh to the point of cruelty. But it was all necessary then to the life and progress of the nation. If there was cruelty, results have justified it.

. . .

It was better that a little blood should be shed that much blood should be saved. The blood that was shed was bad blood; the blood that was saved was good blood.

Peace was necessary, even an enforced peace, that the nation might have time to think and work. Education and industry have carried on the task begun by the army.

. . .

. . . I want to see education throughout the Republic carried on by the na-tional Government. I hope to see it before I die. It is important that all citizens of a republic should receive the same training, so that their ideals and methods may be harmonized and the national unity intensified. When men read alike and think alike they are more likely to act alike.

STUDY QUESTIONS

1. What is Bolivar's view of the common people of Venezuela?
2. What types of institutions does he recommend to rule these people? What type of legislature? What type of executive? Why are these types needed?
3. Who does Bolivar have in mind as the rightful rulers of Venezuela?
4. In Gabino Barreda's Independence Day speech he contrasts Mexico's past ex-periences and its future goals. How does he characterize Mexico's past? What are his goals for the future?
5. In what way did Porfirio Diaz, as ruler of Mexico, fulfill the ideas of Bolivar and Barreda? How did Diaz view the common people? What kind of government did he establish? How were his policies related to the economy? What was Diaz's goal for education?
6. Using these documents together: What were some of the key issues in Latin American politics in the nineteenth century?

*Editor's emphasis added.
†Editor's emphasis added.

19

Economy and Society of Latin America: "Slavery" on the Henequen Plantations of Yucatán

Hardly another area of Latin American exhibited such extreme economic dependency on the "industrial North" as did the henequen zone of Yucantán. First exported to the United States in the 1840s, henequen (a type of cactus plant) fibers supplied the raw material for rope cables used in outfitting clipper ships. But demand for henequen expanded greatly after the invention of a knotting mechanism for grain binders in 1878. Harvesting machine companies in the United States, particularly Cyrus McCormick's, imported hundreds of thousands of tons of henequen during the late nineteenth and early twentieth centuries. Exports from Yucatán increased from 40,000 bales in 1875 to 600,000 in 1910. In 1902, the same year that McCormick's company merged with other harvesting machine companies to form International Harvester, McCormick also negotiated secretly with the governor of Yucatán to lower prices of henequen in return for steady purchases from the governor's export companies. With that agreement, International Harvester established its "informal empire" in Yucatán. The company needed neither to own land in Yucatán nor to produce henequen directly. Production was left in the hands of a small group of local landowners and merchants, who became fabulously wealthy, and who also controlled the Yucatecan state government. But they were not independent. By controlling credit and the henequen market in the United States, Cyrus McCormick bound the Yucatecan oligarchy to the interests of International Harvester.

The expansion of henequen production also affected land tenure and labor relations in Yucatán. Prior to the great growth of exports, traditional haciendas, producing hides, corn, and small amounts of henequen, required little input from the Mayan rural laborers (*campesinos*) inhabiting the peninsula. The work regime on the traditional hacienda allowed the Mayan workers time enough to cultivate their own plots of corn (*milpas*). As well, in areas remote from the haciendas, Indian communities maintained a traditional agricultural lifestyle, free of hacienda obligations. But when henequen became king, new plantations absorbed Indian communal land and imposed on their workers a much stricter regime of work. The new, efficient

From Channing Arnold and Frederick J. Tabor Frost, *American Egypt: A Record of Travel in Yucatán* (London: Hutchinson and Co., 1909), pp. 324–325, 361, 365–367.

henequen plantation required constant attention, especially with regard to harvesting the leaves of the mature plants (after seven years) and weeding seedlings. No time was left for traditional agriculture. Because of labor shortages, plantation owners experimented with importation of captured Yaqui Indians from northern Mexico, and Puerto Rican and Korean workers. But most of all they relied on the local Mayan campesinos, whether they wanted to work on the plantation or not. The slavelike conditions on the henequen plantation are well revealed are the following selection, written by two visiting Englishmen in 1909.

The Yucatecans have a cruel proverb, "*Los Indios no oigan sino por las nalgas*" ("The Indians can hear only with their backs"). The Spanish half-breeds have taken a race once noble enough and broken them on the wheel of a tyranny so brutal that the heart of them is dead. The relations between the two peoples is ostensibly that of master and servant; but Yucatan is rotten with a foul slavery—the fouler and blacker because of its hypocrisy and pretence.

The peonage system of Spanish America, as specious and treacherous a plan as was ever devised for race-degradation, is that by which a farm labourer is legally bound to work for the land-owner, if in debt to him, until that debt is paid. Nothing could sound fairer: nothing could lend itself better to the blackest abuse. In Yucatan every Indian peon is in debt to his Yucatecan master. Why? Because every Indian is a spendthrift? Not at all; but because the master's interest is to get him and keep him in debt. This is done in two ways. The plantation-slave must buy the necessaries of his humble life at the plantation store, where care is taken to charge such prices as are beyond his humble earnings of sixpence a day. Thus he is always in debt to the farm; and if an Indian is discovered to be scraping together the few dollars he owes, the books of the hacienda are "cooked,"—yes, deliberately "cooked,"—and when he presents himself before the magistrate to pay his debt, say, of twenty dollars (£2) the haciendado can show scored against him a debt of fifty dollars. The Indian pleads that he does not owe it. The haciendado-court smiles. The word of an Indian cannot prevail against the Señor's books, it murmurs sweetly, and back to his slave-work the miserable peon must go, first to be cruelly flogged to teach him that freedom is not for such as he, and that struggle as he may he will never escape the cruel master who under law as at present administered in Yucatan has as complete a disposal of his body as of one of the pigs which root around in the hacienda yard.

Henequen (Spanish *jeniquen* or *geniquen*) is a fibre commercially known as Sisal hemp, from the fact that it is obtained from a species of cactus, the *Agave Sisalensis*, first cultivated around the tiny port of Sisal in Yucatan. The older Indian name for the plant is *Agave Ixtli*. From its fleshy leaves is crushed out a fine fibre which, from the fact that it resists damp better than ordinary hemp, is valuable for making ships' cables, but the real wealth-producing use of which is so bizarre that no one in a hundred guesses would hit on it. It is used in the myriad corn-binding machines of America and Canada. They cannot use wire, and cheap string is too easily broken. Henequen is at once strong enough and cheap enough. Hence the piles of money heaping up to the credit of Yucatecans in the banks of Merida. . . .

[At the mill] three or four Indians set to work to arrange the leaves so that their black-pointed ends are all in one direction. Next these thorny points are severed by a machete and in small bundles of six or eight the leaves are handed to men who are feeding a sliding belt-like platform about a yard wide, and on this they are conveyed to the machine. Before they enter its great blunt-toothed, gaping jaws, they are finally arranged, as the sliding belt goes its unending round, so that they do not enter more than one at a time. Woe betide the Indian who has the misfortune to get his fingers in these revolving jaws of the gigantic crusher, and many indeed are there fingerless, handless, and armless from this cause. . . .

For there is money for every one who touches the magic fibre except the miserable Indian, by whose never-ending labours the purse-proud monopolists of the Peninsula are enabled to be ever adding to their ill-gotten gold. There are in Yucantan to-day some 400 henequen plantations of from 25 to 20,000 acres, making the total acreage under cultivation some 140,000 acres. The cost of production, including shipping expenses, export duties, etc., is now about 7 pesos (14s.) per 100 kilogrammes. The average market price of henequen is 28 pesos per 100 kilogrammes, so the planter gets a return of 400 per cent. All this is obviously only possible as long as he can get slave-labour and the hideous truth about the exploitation of the Mayans is kept dark. The Indian gets a wage of 50 centavos for cutting a

A Panoramic View of the Palace of La Glorieta Outside of Sucre, Bolivia. Built by Francisco Argandona, an investor in Bolivia's silver boom in the 1870s and 1880s and a banker, the palace featured Italian-Moorish architecture. As much as their money would allow, the oligarchy of Latin America replicated the European life of leisure. (Blackwell Publishers Ltd., Oxford, UK.)

thousand leaves, and if he is to earn this in a day he must work ten hours. Near the big towns, 75 centavos are paid, but practically, on many haciendas, it is so managed that the labour is paid for by his bare keep.

STUDY QUESTIONS

1. What were the ties the bound the peon to the plantation?
2. In what ways were the plantation owners "dependent" on the industrial north?
3. Compare "informal imperialism" in Latin America during the late nineteenth century with "new imperialism" in Africa at the same time. What are the differences and similarities?
4. How much had labor conditions changed from the colonial period? (See Chapter 7.)

20

Literature and Cultural Values: "Civilization and Barbarism"

Latin American intellectuals in the middle of the nineteenth century despaired about their new nations' turmoil and lack of progress. Examining their traditions, inherited partly from Iberian and partly from native American sources, they concluded that their societies lagged far behind Europe. To catch up, they strove for rapid Europeanization of their population and culture. They sought not only immigrants from England, France, and Germany but also adoption of their political and economic forms.

An exaggerated example of this type of literature is *Life in the Argentine Republic in the Days of the Tyrants; or, Civilization and Barbarism* by Domingo F. Sarmiento. Published in 1868, the same year that Sarmiento became president of Argentina, the book describes the long struggle (1816–1862) between nativist, tyrannical forces, represented in the book by Facundo Quiroga, the caudillo of La Rioja province, and the liberal, urban politicians of Buenos Aires. Sarmiento belonged to the Europeanizers. He joined a liberal faction opposing another of the tyrants, Juan Manuel de Rosas, the caudillo of Buenos Aires province, who ruled the city and the province with extreme brutality from 1829 to 1852. Exiled to Chile in 1833, Sarmiento conspired with opponents of Rosas until he was overthrown in 1852. Ten years of civil war followed Rosas's fall. Bartolomé Mitre, the leader of a new army from Buenos Aires, allied with certain interior chieftains and finally defeated the worst of the old-style caudillos in 1862. In the 1860s Mitre and Sarmiento began the institutionalization of stable government, based on North American and European forms, and also opened Argentina to European immigrants.

Description of Lower Classes

In these long journeys, the lower classes of the Argentine population acquire the habit of living far from society, of struggling single-handed with nature, of disregarding privation, and of depending for protection against the dangers ever imminent upon no other resources than personal strength and skill.

From Domingo F. Sarmiento, *Life in the Argentine Republic in the Days of the Tyrants: or, Civilization and Barbarism,* (New York: Hafner Publishing Co., 1960), pp. 10–11, 112, 122–123, 126–127, 161–162, 250. Reprinted by permission of Simon and Schuster, Inc.

The people who inhabit these extensive districts, belong to two different races, the Spanish and the native; the combinations of which form a series of imperceptible gradations. The pure Spanish race predominates in the rural districts of Cordova and San Luis, where it is common to meet young shepherdesses fair and rosy, and as beautiful as the belles of a capital could wish to be. In Santiago del Estero, the bulk of the rural population still speaks the Quichua dialect, which plainly shows its Indian origin. The country people of Corrientes use a very pretty Spanish dialect. "Dame, general, una chiripà," said his soldiers to Lavalle. The Andalusian soldier may still be recognized in the rural districts of Buenos Ayres; and in the city foreign surnames are the most numerous. The negro race, by this time nearly extinct (except in Buenos Ayres), has left, in its zambos and mulattoes, a link which connects civilized man with the denizen of the woods. This race mostly inhabiting cities, has a tendency to become civilized, and possesses talent and the finest instincts of progress.

With these reservations, a homogeneous whole has resulted from the fusion of the three above-named families. It is characterized by love of idleness and incapacity for industry, except when education and the exigencies of a social position succeed in spurring it out of its customary pace. To a great extent, this unfortunate result is owing to the incorporation of the native tribes, effected by the process of colonization. The American aborigines live in idleness, and show themselves incapable, even under compulsion, of hard and protracted labor. This suggested the idea of introducing negroes into America, which has produced such fatal results. But the Spanish race has not shown itself more energetic than the aborigines, when it has been left to its own instincts in the wilds of America. Pity and shame are excited by the comparison of one of the German or Scotch colonies in the southern part of Buenos Ayres and some towns of the interior of the Argentine Republic; in the former the cottages are painted, the front-yards always neatly kept and adorned with flowers and pretty shrubs; the furniture simple but complete; copper or tin utensils always bright and clean; nicely curtained beds; and the occupants of the dwelling are always industriously at work. Some such families have retired to enjoy the conveniences of city life, with great fortunes gained by their previous labors in milking their cows, and making butter and cheese. The town inhabited by natives of the country, presents a picture entirely the reverse. There, dirty and ragged children live, with a menagerie of dogs; there, men lie about in utter idleness; neglect and poverty prevail everywhere; a table and some baskets are the only furniture of wretched huts remarkable for their general aspect of barbarism and carelessness.

On Buenos Aires

In 1777, Buenos Ayres had already become very conspicuous, so much so, indeed, that it was necessary to remould the administrative geography of the colonies, and to make Buenos Ayres the chief section. A viceroyal government was expressly created for it.

In 1806, the attention of English speculators was turned to South America, and especially attracted to Buenos Ayres by its river, and its probable future. In 1810, Buenos Ayres was filled with partisans of the revolution, bitterly hostile to anything originating in Spain or any part of Europe. A germ of progress, then, was still alive west of the La Plata. The Spanish colonies cared nothing for commerce or navigation. The Rio de la Plata was of small importance to them. The Spanish disdained it and its banks. As time went on, the river proved to have deposited its sediment of wealth upon those banks, but very little of Spanish spirit or Spanish modes of government. Commercial activity had brought thither the spirit and the general ideas of Europe; the vessels which frequented the waters of the port brought books from all quarters, and news of all the political events of the world. It is to be observed that Spain had no other commercial city upon the Atlantic coast. The war with England hastened the emancipation of men's minds and awakened among them a sense of their own importance as a state. Buenos Ayres was like a child, which, having conquered a giant, fondly deems itself a hero, and is ready to undertake greater adventures. The *Social Contract* flew from hand to hand. Mably and Raynal were the oracles of the press; Robespierre and the Convention the approved models. Buenos Ayres thought itself a continuation of Europe, and if it did not frankly confess that its spirit and tendencies were French and North American, it denied its Spanish origin on the ground that the Spanish Government had patronized it only after it was full grown. The revolution brought with it armies and glory, triumphs and reverses, revolts and seditions. But Buenos Ayres, amidst all these fluctuations, displayed the revolutionary energy with which it is endowed. . . .

Communication with all the European nations was ever, even from the outset, more complete here than in any other part of Spanish America; and now, in ten years' time (but only, be it understood, in Buenos Ayres), there comes to pass a radical replacement of the Spanish by the European spirit. We have only to take a list of the residents in and about Buenos Ayres to see how many natives of the country bear English, French, German, or Italian surnames.

Difference Between Bernadino Rivadavia, Liberal President of Argentina (1826–1827), and Juan Manuel de Rosas, dictator of Buenos Aires Province (1829–1852)

Thus elevated, and hitherto flattered by fortune, Buenos Ayres set about making a constitution for itself and the Republic, just as it had undertaken to liberate itself and all South America: that is, eagerly, uncompromisingly, and without regard to obstacles. Rivadavia was the personification of this poetical, utopian spirit which prevailed. He therefore continued the work of Las Heras upon the large scale necessary for a great American State—a republic. He brought over from Europe men of learning or the press and for the professor's chair, colonies for the deserts, ships for the rivers, freedom for all creeds, credit and the national bank to encourage trade, and all the great social theories of the day for the formation of his government. In a word, he brought a second Europe, which was to be established in America, and to accomplish in ten years what elsewhere had required centuries. Nor was this project altogether chimerical; all his administrative creations still exist, except those which the barbarism of Rosas found in its way. Freedom of conscience, advocated by the chief clergy of Buenos Ayres, has not been repressed; the European population is scattered on farms throughout the country, and takes arms of its own accord to resist the only obstacle in the way of the wealth offered by the soil. The rivers only need to be freed from governmental restrictions to become navigable, and the national bank, then firmly established, has saved the people from the poverty to which the tyrant would have brought them. And, above all, however fanciful and impracticable that great system of government may have been, it was at least easy and endurable for the people; and, notwithstanding the assertions of misinformed men, Rivadavia never shed a drop of blood, nor destroyed the property of any one; but voluntarily descended from the Presidency to poverty and exile. Rosas, by whom he was so calumniated, might easily have been drowned in the blood of his own victims; and the forty millions of dollars from the national treasury, with the fifty millions from private fortunes which were consumed in ten years of the long war provoked by his brutalities, would have been employed by the "*fool—*the *dreamer—*Rivadavia," in building canals, cities, and useful public buildings. Then let this man, who died for his country, have the glory of representing the highest aspirations of European civilization, and leave to his adversaries that of displaying South American barbarism in its most odious light. For Rosas and Rivadavia are the two extremes of the Argentine Republic, connecting it with savages through the pampas, and with Europe through the River La Plata.

Description of Tyrant Facundo Quiroga

Facundo is now in possession of La Rioja, its umpire and absolute master; no other voice is heard there, no other interest than his exists there. As there is no literature, there are no opposing opinions. La Rioja is a military machine. . . .

Facundo, ignorant, barbarous, for the greater part of his life an outlaw, and famous only for his acts of desperation; brave to rashness, endowed with herculean strength, always upon his horse, which he managed skillfully through terror and violence, knowing no other power than that of brute force, had no faith but in his horse, and depended for success upon bravery, the lance, and the terrible charges of his cavalry. In all the Argentine Republic there was not a more perfect specimen of the "*gaucho malo.*"

"When the Ignorant Rule"

Obscure men who rise to power through the chances of social revolutions, never fail to persecute in others the intelligence and knowledge which they have not themselves; when the ignorant rule, civilization is brought down to their own level, and woe to those who rise above it, be it ever so little. In France, in 1793, the sovereign people guillotined those who could read and write as aristocrats; in the Argentine Republic, men of culture were called *savages,* and had their throats cut, and though the name seems mere irony, it is something more when applied by the assassin, knife in hand. The Caudillos of the interior rid their provinces of all lawyers, doctors, and men of letters; and Rosas pursued them even within the walls of the university and private schools. Those who were allowed to remain were such persons as could be useful in getting up a repetition of the government of Philip II of Spain, and of the Inquisition.

STUDY QUESTIONS

1. What cultural values are expressed in Sarmiento's views of Argentina? What types of people are described positively? Negatively? What was Sarmiento's basis for judgment?

2. How might the twentieth-century novelist and 1982 Nobel prize winner, Gabriel García Márquez (see selection from "The Solitude of Latin America" in Chapter 39), view the tyrants and isolated lower classes described by Sarmiento? What might they signify to García Márquez?

3. Considering the cultural values expressed by Sarmiento, what might one conclude about the development of a Latin American civilization as distinct from other civilizations?

21

The Decades of Imperialism in Africa

The four selections in this chapter all date from the period 1880 to 1910. This was the great age of European imperialism in sub-Saharan Africa, when virtually all available territory was swept up by the British, French, Germans, or Belgians. African political and economic life was transformed by the inescapable European presence.

The first document comes from German southwest Africa. It is unusual in having been written, in Swahili, by an African trader. A prosaic account of theft on a trip to an inland tribal village, the statement shows how some Africans and their new rulers could interact to apparent mutual benefit.

The second document briefly describes the new work system the Europeans brought. It uses the derogatory term *kaffir,* taken from the Arab word for pagan, to describe labor in the British-controlled mines in South Africa, while at the same time it claims great benefits from the jobs. The vantage point is that of an owner and Westerner. What might the workers have thought of this system?

The third document, also from British-controlled southern Africa, describes a characteristic legal arrangement used to deprive African chiefs of their land. It was carried through by agents of Cecil Rhodes. By granting full powers to the concession holders, this land-use agreement made later incorporation into the British Empire possible.

Selection 1 from "The Uses of Colonial Government," in *Swahili Prose Texts: A Selection from the Material Collected by Carl Velten from 1893 to 1896,* edited and translated by Lyndon Harries (Oxford: Oxford University Press, 1965), pp. 243–244. Copyright © 1965 by Oxford University Press. Reprinted by permission. Selection 2 from John Noble, *Official Handbook: History, Production, and the Resources of the Cape of Good Hope,* 2nd ed. (Cape Town, 1886), pp. 194–195. Selection 3 from Sir Lewis Michell, *The Life of the Right Honourable Cecil John Rhodes,* Vol. I (London: 1910), pp. 244–245. Selection 4 from John D. Hargreaves, ed., *France and West Africa* (London: St. Martin's Press, Inc., 1969), pp. 198–199. Copyright © 1969 by St. Martin's Press, Inc. Reprinted by permission.

The fourth document, from French-held Mali in the region below the Sahara, was issued in 1890 by a French military commander who let no African stand in his way. The arrangement described was meant to regularize a local government, in part by playing different groups against each other, while disclaiming French power. What roles were reserved for the imperialist forces?

Collectively, the documents on the imperialist impact raise a number of basic questions. How did the Europeans view Africans at this point? How did imperialist penetration and controls compare with earlier colonial outposts described in Chapter 10? What accounts for the change? Finally, how would Africans perceive the new imperialism, and how might their reactions differ?

Imperialism is recent in African history. Understanding its impact, its limitations, and the responses it provoked is vital to a grasp of African patterns even after imperialism subsided.

1. AN AFRICAN ACCOUNT: THE USES OF COLONIAL GOVERNMENT

We consulted together, saying, "Brothers, hadn't we better get going? We talk, and this pagan does not hear. Perhaps he will change his mind and seek to kill us? Our property is lost, and shall not our souls be lost?" Some said, "Shall we not go to Karema and inform the European, because Chata has robbed us? Now when shall we get out of here? It is no good leaving in the daytime, for perhaps the tribesmen will follow us to get us on the way and kill us; we had better go to the Chief and tell him, We agree to what you say, keep our property safe, and we are going to look for Matumla."

We agreed and went to the Chief and told him what we intended, and he said, "Isn't that just what I wanted? Very well, take a hut and go to rest, do not be afraid; sleep until morning, let us take proper leave of one another, and I will give you food for the way (enough) until you arrive at your place (i.e. your destination)." And we sat disconsolately, being sorry for our property which was lost and for our brethren who were dead. It was without any proper reason.

In the morning we reached Karema, and we found the European still in bed. . . . So when the Bwana came, we told him, "Bwana, we have been attacked." And he asked, "Who has attacked you?" We replied, "Chata." And he said to us, "But haven't I said that all traders should first come to me! What did you go to do at the pagan's? But never mind, I will send soldiers to make enquiry why you traders have been robbed. And you provide one person from among you to go along with my soldier, so that he can listen to what my soldier says with Chata, and so that you yourselves may hear about it."

So they set off for Chata's place. The soldiers said to him, "You Chata, so now you have become a man who robs people of their property? Aren't you afraid of government rule?" And he said, "I did not attack them for nothing; I attacked them because of Matumla taking my property, twenty pieces of ivory." The soldiers told him, "Oh no, we don't agree, bring the traders' property, that is what the District Officer told us (you must do)." When he saw their superior strength he took out the stuff and gave it to the soldiers, and they brought it to Karema, all that was left of our goods.

When they reached Karema, the European called us (saying), "You traders, come here, come and look at your property, is this what Chata took?" We looked at it and told him, "Yes, Bwana, some more was lost in the fire." And he said, "Never mind, take this which is left."

2. AFRICAN WORK IN SOUTH AFRICA'S DIAMOND MINES

Kaffir labour is mainly employed in all the less responsible operations of the mines: in drilling holes for the dynamite cartridges, in picking and breaking up the ground in the claims and *trucking* it away from the depositing boxes and the margin on the mine and tipping it on the depositing floors, where it undergoes a variety of processes before it is ready for washing, and is again filled into trucks and driven to the machines. For every three truckloads of ground daily hauled out of the mine there is on an average one Kaffir labourer employed, and to every five Kaffirs there is one white overseer or artizan. In 1882 the number of native labourers at Kimberley mine was 4,000; but in 1884, owing to the serious stoppage of works, they had sunk to 1,500. These labourers are recruited from 16 or 20 different native tribes from various part of the Colony and the Interior, the proportion of the several tribes at any time on the Fields varying greatly according to the internal state, whether of peace or war, of the district whence they hail. Out of 20,000 natives arriving in search of work in the first half of 1882, 8,000 were Secocoeni's Basutos, 6,000 Shangaans, 1,500 British Basutos, and 1,000 Zulus, the balance consisting of representatives of no less than 16 other different tribes and races. The market afforded for the employment of native labour and the consequent development of native trade is not the least of the incidental benefits conferred on South Africa by the discovery of the Diamond Fields.

3. AN IMPERIALIST CONTRACT: AN ECONOMIC PACT WITH A REGIONAL KING

Know all men by these presents, that whereas Charles Dunell Rudd, of Kimberley; Rochfort Maguire, of London; and Francis Robert Thompson, of Kimberley, hereinafter called the grantees, have covenanted and agreed, and do hereby covenant and agree, to pay to me, my heirs and successors, the sum of one hundred pounds sterling, British currency, on the first day of every lunar month; and, further, to deliver at my royal kraal one thousand Martini-Henry breech-loading rifles, together with one hundred thousand rounds of suitable ball cartridge, five hundred of the said rifles and fifty thousand of the said cartridges to be ordered from England forthwith and delivered with reasonable dispatch, and the remainder of the said rifles and cartridges to be delivered as soon as the said grantees shall have commenced to work mining machinery within my territory; and further, to deliver on the Zambesi River a steamboat with guns suitable for defensive purposes upon the said river, or in lieu of the said steamboat, should I so elect to pay to me the sum of five hundred pounds sterling, British currency. On the execution of these presents, I, Lo Bengula, King of Matabeleland, Mashonaland, and other adjoining territories, in exercise of my council of indunas, do hereby grant and assign unto the said grantees, their heirs, representatives, and assigns, jointly and severally, the complete and exclusive charge over all metals and minerals situated and contained in my kingdoms, principalities, and dominions, together with full power to do all things that they may deem necessary to win and procure the same, and to hold, collect, and enjoy the profits and revenues, if any, derivable from the said metals and minerals, subject to the aforesaid payment; and whereas I have been much molested [of] late by diverse persons seeking and desiring to obtain grants and concessions of land and mining rights in my territories, I do hereby authorise the said grantees, their heirs, representatives, and assigns, to take all necessary and lawful steps to exclude from my kingdom, principalities, and dominions all persons seeking land, metals, minerals, or mining rights therein, and I do hereby undertake to render them all such needful assistance as they may from time to time require for the exclusion of such persons, and to grant no concessions of land or mining rights from and after this date without their consent and concurrence; provided that, if at any time the said monthly payment of one hundred pounds shall cease [the agreement's end dates from] the last-made payment.

4. THE FRENCH ARRANGE LOCAL GOVERNMENT

I have had you brought here to explain to you the French way of doing things. The French have not come to Ségou to take the country and govern it themselves, but with the intention of restoring it to the Bambaras, from whom it was stolen by the Tukolors. . . .

I am going to give Ségou to the son of your ancient kings. As from today your *Fama* will be Mari-Diara; but on certain conditions which will provide us with guarantees that the welfare of the country will be assured, that trade will be free, and that the Bambaras of the right bank will not be pillaged as were those of the left bank, where Mari-Diara was recently living.

To ensure this, the Commandant Supérieur will firstly station a white officer here, with troops. This Resident will reside in the *dionfoutou* of Ahmadu. Part of the fort will be demolished so that the Resident can have a private gate leading out of the village, and a view over the Niger.

The French Resident will not concern himself with administrative problems between the *Fama* and his villages. The *Fama* will exercise all his rights, will appoint or change chiefs as he thinks fit, but the Resident will have the right to be kept fully informed on all matters and to know everything that takes place.

He may help the *Fama* maintain order in the country by giving him military support, with his troops. . . . But the *Fama* will not have the right to make war or undertake negotiations in neighbouring countries without authorisation from the Resident. If such actions should be undertaken without the Resident's approval, the *Fama* would have to meet all the costs, and accept all the consequences. The Resident would not help him, but would report to the Commandant Supérieur, who is to decide whether the *Fama* has acted wisely or must be reprimanded. . . .

The Tukolors must leave the country within three days after the departure of the Commandant Supérieur; Major Colonna de Giovellina will protect their convoy. After that date the Bambaras may massacre those who remain behind.

STUDY QUESTIONS

1. What gains did Europeans think they were bringing to Africa through imperialism?
2. How did Europeans treat local rulers?
3. Why did Europeans find it appropriate to relegate Africans to low-level, dangerous, and low-paying jobs? What is the evidence on this subject in the Kimberley mines document?
4. What do these imperialist documents suggest about the effects of European conquest on Africa and Africans at the end of the nineteenth century?

Forces of Change

22

The Spread of Mass Education: Sources and Comparisons

One of the most striking developments in Western European and North American society in the nineteenth century was the unprecedented proliferation of education for the children of almost all social classes, both boys and girls. Education spread for several reasons: Enlightenment ideals, now influencing other political movements such as liberalism, argued that education would lead to progress, as children were open vessels that could be filled with knowledge. The advance of scientific discoveries led to a new belief in the importance of providing at least some groups with training in science and technology; the same held true, if a bit more vaguely, for the social sciences and history. Growing commitment to more democratic voting systems generated concern for training children to be good citizens; many people hoped that education would keep the lower classes away from dangerous doctrines such as socialism. The Industrial Revolution, although it actively involved child labor in its early stages, ultimately contributed to a redefinition of childhood: simpler work processes were increasingly accomplished by machines, making child labor less necessary, while humanitarian concerns also prompted movements to withdraw young children from the labor force. Schools, here, could serve as an alternative source of supervision for children.

Many countries began to expand school systems in the early decades of the nineteenth century. By the 1830s, some American states, such as Massachusetts, were making primary education obligatory, at least in principle. American schools

Selection 1 from Horace Mann, *On the Education of Free Men* (New York: Columbia University Press, 1987), pp. 49–59. Selection 2 from Noah Webster, *The American Spelling Book* (Lexington, Ky.: W.W. Worsley, 1831), pp. 53–57. Selection 3 from *The Autobiography of Yukichi Fukuzawa,* translated by Eūchi Kiyooka (New York: Columbia University Press, 1966), pp. 214–217. Selection 4 from *Sources of Japanese Tradition II,* edited by Ryusaku Tsunoda, W. T. de Bary, and Donald Keene (New York: Columbia University Press, 1958), pp. 139–140, 189–191.

had the additional function of teaching immigrant children "American ways" —including the English language. School attendance and literacy began to increase rapidly.

Western educational systems were an obvious exemplar for leaders in other societies who wanted to set the basis for industrial development and political change. Many Latin American liberals, for example, pushed for extensions of school systems by the later nineteenth century. One of the most important instances of educational change occurred in Japan. As the Japanese began to discuss the need for significant reform, in the wake of Western pressure to open Japan to international trade after 1853, education provided a key target. Japanese visitors to the West quickly seized on the importance of schools in providing the basis for new technical skills. Japan already had an extensive Confucian school system and considerable literacy, which helped highlight both the importance and the feasibility of further educational development. In 1872 the nation enacted a compulsory primary school system, and although it took almost 20 years to translate law into reality, educational expansion, and with it mass literacy, occurred very rapidly.

With all this, debates over the purposes of actual educational systems were intense and, often, inconsistent. The selections suggest the flavor of nineteenth-century discussions about education in the United States and Japan, during crucial decades in which mass primary schools were being established (1830s to 1840s in the United States, 1870s to 1890s in Japan). Discussions in each country revealed far more concern about using education as a means of controlling and indoctrinating children than might be imagined from resounding invocations of education for democracy or for the advance of scientific understanding.

Both Japanese and American educators sought to instill moral guidance, using schools to supplement or replace older sources of authority. Divisions occurred between reformers and more conservative moralists—although contradictions might emerge even within a reform statement. At the same time, Japanese and American debates were not identical. What Americans meant by moralization and control differed from what Japanese conservatives intended.

Two documents from each country follow. Horace Mann (1796–1859) was a reform leader in Massachusetts; the following passages are taken from reports he issued as head of the state Board of Education between 1839 and 1846. The second American document is a passage from Noah Webster's spelling book, in 1831. Yukichi Fukuzawa (1834–1904) was Japan's leading educational reformer, who traveled widely in the West beginning in 1860. His ideas had a profound effect on Japanese schools, and he describes his principles in his *Autobiography*, published in 1899. But reform currents and Western guidance provoked a reaction from conservatives in the government beginning in 1878; the second document reflects an anti-Western current, in the Imperial Rescript of 1890.

1. HORACE MANN, *THE GOALS OF EDUCATION*

The preservation of order, together with the proper despatch of business requires a mean, between the too much and the too little, in all the evolutions of the school, which it is difficult to hit. When classes leave their seats for the recitation-stand, and return to them again, or when the different sexes have a recess, or the hour of intermission arrives; —if there be not some order and succession of movement, the school will be temporarily converted into a promiscuous rabble, giving both the temptation and the opportunity for committing every species of indecorum and aggression. In order to prevent confusion, on the other hand, the operations of the school may be conducted with such military formality and procrastination: —the second scholar not being allowed to leave his seat, until the first has reached the door, or the place of recitation, and each being made to walk on tiptoe to secure silence, —that a substantial part of every school session will be wasted, in the wearisome pursuit of an object worth nothing when obtained.

When we reflect, how many things are to be done each half day, and how short a time is allotted for their performance, the necessity of system in regard to all the operations of the school, will be apparent. System compacts labor; and when the hand is to be turned to an almost endless variety of particulars, if system does not preside over the whole series of movements, the time allotted to each will be spent in getting ready to perform it. With lessons to set; with so many classes to hear; with difficulties to explain; with the studious to be assisted; the idle to be spurred; the transgressors to be admonished or corrected; with the goers and comers to observe; —with all these things to be done, no considerable progress can be made, if one part of the wheel is not coming up to the work, while another is going down. And if order do not pervade the school, as a whole, and in all its parts, all is lost; and this is a very difficult thing; —for it seems as though the school were only a point, rescued out of a chaos that still encompasses it, and is ready, on the first opportunity, to break in and reoccupy its ancient possession. As it is utterly impracticable for any committee to prepare a code of regulations coextensive with all the details, which belong to the management of a school, it must be left with the teacher; and hence the necessity of skill in this item of the long list of his qualifications.

The government and discipline of a school demands [sic] qualities still more rare, because the consequences of error, in these, are still more disastrous. What caution, wisdom, uprightness, and sometimes, even intrepidity, are necessary in the administration of punishment. After all other means have been tried, and tried in vain, the chastisement of pupils found to be otherwise incorrigible, is still upheld by law, and sanctioned by public opinion. . . . The discipline of former times was inexorably stern and severe, and even if it were wished, it is impossible now to return to it. The question is, what can be substituted, which, without its severity, shall have its efficiency.

In the contemplation of the law, the school committee are sentinels stationed at the door of every schoolhouse in the State, to see that no teacher ever crosses its threshold, who is not clothed, from the crown of his head to the sole of his foot, in garments of virtue; and they are the enemies of the human race, —not of contemporaries only, but of posterity, —who, from any private or sinister motive, strive to put these sentinels to sleep, in order that one, who is profane, or intemperate, or addicted to low associations, or branded with the stigma of any vice, may elude the vigilance of the watchmen, and be installed over the pure minds of the young, as their guide and exemplar. If none but teachers of pure tastes, of good manners, of exemplary morals, had ever gained admission into our schools, neither the school rooms, nor their appurtenances would have been polluted, as some of them now are, with such ribald inscriptions, and with the carvings of such obscene emblems, as would make a heathen blush. Every person, therefore, who endorses another's character, as one befitting a school teacher, stands before the public as his moral bondsman and sponsor, and should be held to a rigid accountability. . . .

One of the highest and most valuable objects, to which the influences of a school can be made conducive, consists in training our children to self-government. . . . So tremendous, too, are the evils of anarchy and lawlessness, that a government by mere force, however, arbitrary and cruel, has been held preferable to no-government. But self-government, self-control, a voluntary compliance with the laws of reason and duty, have been justly considered as the highest point of excellence attainable by a human being. No one, however, can consciously obey the laws of reason and duty, until he understands them. Hence the preliminary necessity of their being clearly explained, of their being made to stand out, broad, lofty, and as conspicuous as a mountain against a clear sky. There may be blind obedience without a knowledge of the law, but only of the will of the lawgiver; but the first step towards rational obedience is a knowledge of the rule to be obeyed, and of the reasons on which it is founded.

The above doctrine acquires extraordinary force, in view of our political institutions, —founded, as they are, upon the great idea of the capacity of man for self-government, —an idea so long denounced by the state as treasonable, and by the church as heretical. In order that men may be prepared for self-government, their apprenticeship must commence in childhood. The great moral attribute of self-government cannot be born and matured in a day; and if school children are not trained to it, we only prepare ourselves for disappointment, if we expect it from grown men. Everybody acknowledges the justness of the declaration, that a foreign people, born and bred and dwarfed under the despotisms of the Old World, cannot be transformed into the full stature of American citizens, merely by a voyage across the Atlantic, or by subscribing the oath of naturalization. If they retain the servility in which they have been trained, some self-appointed lord or priest, on this side of the water, will succeed to the authority of the master they have left behind them. If, on the other hand, they identify liberty with an absence from restraint, and an immunity from punishment, then they are liable to become intoxicated and delirious with the highly stimulating properties of the air of freedom; and thus, in either case, they remain unfitted, until they have been morally acclimated to our institutions, to exercise the rights of a freeman. But can it make any substantial difference, whether a man is suddenly translated into all the independence and prerogatives of an American citizen, from the bondage of an Irish lord or an English manufacturer, or from the equally rigorous bondage of a parent, guardian, or school teacher? He who has been a serf until the day before he is twenty-one years of age, cannot be an independent citizen the day after; and it makes no difference whether he has been a serf in Austria or in America. As the fitting apprenticeship for despotism consists in being trained to despotism, so the fitting apprenticeship for self-government consists in being trained to self-government; and liberty and self-imposed law are as appropriate a preparation for the subjects of an arbitrary power, as the law of force and authority is for developing and maturing those sentiments of self-respect, of honor, and of dignity, which belong to a truly republican citizen. . . . Now, for the high purpose of training an American child to become an

American citizen, —a constituent part of a self-governing people, —is it not obvious that, in all cases, the law by which he is to be bound should be made intelligible to him; and, as soon as his capacity will permit, that the reasons on which it is founded, should be made as intelligible as the law itself?

2. NOAH WEBSTER, *THE AMERICAN SPELLING BOOK*

Additional Lessons. Domestic Economy, Or, the History of Thrifty and Unthrifty

There is a great difference among men, in their ability to gain property; but a still greater difference in their power of using it to advantage. Two men may acquire the same amount of money, in a given time; yet one will prove to be a poor man, while the other becomes rich. A chief and essential difference in the management of property, is, that one man spends only the *interest* of his money, while another spends the *principal*. I know a farmer by the name of *Thrifty*, who manages his affairs in this manner: He rises early in the morning, looks to the condition of his house, barn, homelot, and stock—sees that his cattle, horses, and hogs are fed; examines the tools to see whether they are all in good order for the workmen—takes care that breakfast is ready in due season, and begins work in the cool of the day—When in the field, he keeps steadily at work, though not so violently as to fatigue and exhaust the body—nor does he stop to tell or hear long stories—When the labor of the day is past, he takes refreshment, and goes to rest at an early hour—In this manner he earns and gains money.

When *Thrifty* has acquired a little property, he does not spend it or let it slip from him, without use or benefit. He pays his taxes and debts when due or called for, so that he has not officers' fees to pay, nor expenses of court. He does not frequent the tavern, and drink up all his earnings in liquor that does him no good. He puts his money to use, that is, he buys more land, or stock, or lends his money at interest—in short, he makes his money produce some profit or income. These savings and profits, though small by themselves, amount in a year to a considerable sum, and in a few years they swell to an estate—*Thrifty* becomes a wealthy farmer, with several hundred acres of land, and a hundred head of cattle.

Very different is the management of UNTHRIFTY: He lies in bed till a late hour in the morning—then rises, and goes to the bottle for a dram, or to the tavern for a glass of bitters—Thus he spends six cents before breakfast late, when he ought to be at work. When he supposes he is ready to begin the work of the day, he finds he has not the necessary tools, or some of them are out of order,—the plow-share is to be sent half a mile to a blacksmith to be mended; a tooth or two in a rake or the handle of a hoe is broke; or a sythe or an ax is to be ground.—Now, he is in a great hurry, he bustles about to make preparation for work—and what is done in a hurry is ill done—he loses a part of the day in getting ready—and perhaps the time of his workmen. At ten or eleven o'clock, he is ready to go to work—then comes a boy and tells him, the sheep have escaped from the pasture—or the cows have got among his corn—or the hogs into the garden—He frets and storms, and runs to drive them out—a half hour or more time is lost in driving the cattle from mischief, and repairing a poor old broken fence—a fence that answers no purpose but to lull him into security, and teach his horses and cattle to be unruly—After all this bustle, the fatigue of which is worse than common labor, *Unthrifty* is ready to begin a day's work at twelve o'clock.—Thus half his time is lost in supplying defects, which proceed from want of foresight and good management. His small crops are damaged or destroyed by unruly cattle.—His barn is open and leaky, and what little he gathers, is injured by the rain and snow.—His house is in a like condition—the shingles and clapboards fall off and let in the water, which causes the timber, floors, and furniture to decay—and exposed to inclemencies of weather, his wife and children fall sick—their time is lost, and the mischief closes with a ruinous train of expenses for medicines and physicians.—After dragging out some years of disappointment, misery, and poverty, the lawyer and the sheriff sweep away the scanty remains of his estate. This is the history of UNTHRIFTY—his principal is spent—he has no interest.

Not unlike this, is the history of the Grog-drinker. This man wonders why he does not thrive in the world; he cannot see the reason why his neighbor *Temperance* should be more prosperous than himself—but in truth, he makes no calculations. Ten cents a day for grog is a small sum, he thinks, which can hurt no man! But let us make an estimate—arithmetic is very useful for a man who ventures to spend small sums every day. Ten cents a day amounts in a year to thirty-six dollars and a half—a sum sufficient to buy a good farm-horse! This surely is no small sum for a farmer or mechanic—But in ten years, this sum amounts to three hundred and sixty-five dollars, besides interest in the mean time! What an amount is this for drams and bitters in ten years! It is money enough to build a small house! But look at the amount in thirty years!—One thousand and ninety-five dollars!—What a vast sum to run down one man's throat. . . .

3. YUKICHI FUKUZAWA, *AUTOBIOGRAPHY*

In my interpretation of education, I try to be guided by the laws of nature and I try to co-ordinate all the physical actions of human beings by the very simple laws of "number and reason." In spiritual or moral training, I regard the human being as the most sacred and responsible of all orders, unable in reason to do anything base. Therefore, in self-respect, a man cannot change his sense of humanity, his justice, his loyalty, or anything belonging to his manhood even when driven by circumstances to do so. In short, my creed is that a man should find his faith in independence and self-respect.

From my own observations in both Occidental and Oriental civilizations, I find that each has certain strong points and weak points bound up in its moral teachings and scientific theories. But when I compare the two in a general way as to wealth, armament, and the greatest happiness for the greatest number, I have to put the Orient below the Occident. Granted that a nation's destiny depends upon the education of its people, there must be some fundamental differences in the education of Western and Eastern peoples.

In the education of the East, so often saturated with Confucian teaching, I find two things lacking; that is to say, a lack of studies in number and reason in material culture, and a lack of the idea of independence in spiritual culture. But in the West I think I see why their statesmen are successful in managing their national affairs, and the businessmen in theirs, and the people generally ardent in their patriotism and happy in their family circles.

I regret that in our country I have to acknowledge that people are not formed on these two principles, though I believe no one can escape the laws of number and reason, nor can anyone depend on anything but the doctrine of independence as long as nations are to exist and mankind is to thrive. Japan could not assert herself among the great nations of the world without full recognition and practice of these two principles. And I reasoned that Chinese philosophy as the root of education was responsible for our obvious shortcomings.

With this as the fundamental theory of education, I began and, though it was impossible to institute specialized courses because of lack of funds, I did what I could in organizing the instructions on the principles of number and reason. And I took every opportunity in public speech, in writing, and in casual conversations, to advocate my doctrine of independence. Also I tried in many ways to demonstrate the theory in my actual life. During my endeavor I came to believe less than ever in the old Chinese teachings. . . .

The true reason of my opposing the Chinese teaching with such vigor is my belief that in this age of transition, if this retrogressive doctrine remains at all in our young men's minds, the new civilization cannot give its full benefit to this country. In my determination to save our coming generation, I was prepared even to face single-handed the Chinese scholars of the country as a whole.

Gradually the new education was showing its results among the younger generation; yet men of middle age or past, who held responsible positions, were for the most part uninformed as to the true spirit of Western culture, and whenever they had to make decisions, they turned invariably to their Chinese sources for guidance. And so, again and again I had to rise up and denounce the all-important Chinese influence before this weighty opposition. It was not altogether a safe road for my reckless spirit to follow.

4. IMPERIAL RESCRIPT ON EDUCATION 1890

Know ye, Our subjects:

Our Imperial Ancestors have founded Our Empire on a basis broad and everlasting, and have deeply and firmly implanted virtue; Our subjects ever united in loyalty and filial piety have from generation to generation illustrated the beauty thereof. This is the glory of the fundamental character of Our Empire, and herein also lies the source of Our education. Ye, Our subjects, be filial to your parents, affectionate to your brothers and sisters; as husbands and wives be harmonious, as friends true; bear yourselves in modesty and moderation; extend your benevolence to all; pursue learning and cultivate arts, and thereby develop intellectual faculties and perfect moral powers; furthermore advance public good and promote common interests; always respect the Constitution and observe the laws; should emergency arise, offer yourselves courageously to the State; and thus guard and maintain the prosperity of Our Imperial Throne coeval with heaven and earth. So shall ye not only be Our good and faithful subjects, but render illustrious the best traditions of your forefathers.

From a Japanese Cartoon Series Entitled "Yokohama Prints to Acquaint People in the Far East with Western Civilization," late nineteenth century. The cartoon portrays Bernard Palissy, inventor of enameled pottery, viciously breaking a chair as fuel for his furnace, while a woman and child cower in fear. *What elements of the print were intended to shock Japanese viewers? What is the Western emphasis being lampooned?* (Corbis/Bettmann.)

The Way here set forth is indeed the teaching bequeathed by Our Imperial Ancestors, to be observed alike by Their Descendants and the subjects, infallible for all ages and true in all places. It is Our wish to lay it to heart in all reverence, in common with you, Our subjects, that we may all attain to the same virtue.

STUDY QUESTIONS

1. What did Horace Mann see as the primary purposes of education and the relationship between moral and intellectual training? Were there inconsistencies within his views about the best ways to raise free citizens—for example, in the relationship between discipline and individualism?

2. What kind of moralism did Noah Webster's reader seek to instill? How did it compare with Mann's approach?

3. Why did Fukuzawa attack Confucianism? What did he see as the main purposes of modern education?

4. How did the Imperial Rescript seek to modify Fukuzawa's approach?

5. How did Japanese and American views about moralism through education compare? What would a Japanese educational conservative think about Webster's moral principles? How did Fukuzawa and Mann compare as educational reformers?

6. Based on the documents, which pattern is more striking: the similarities in basic modern educational concerns and principles in the United States and Japan in the nineteenth century, or the ability to express different cultural goals through modern education?

7. Are nineteenth-century debates about the principles of education still reflected in Japanese and American school systems, and the differences between them?

23

Global Contacts: Nineteenth-Century Sports

One unexpected but powerful result of growing trade connections and cultural interchange in the nineteenth century was the beginning of a globalization of athletics—a process that has continued vigorously to the present day. The sports involved were Western in origin, soccer football heading the list. Their dissemination was a function of Western power and prestige. Western businessmen and diplomats played their familiar games on foreign soil—colonies and noncolonies alike—and gradually local residents sought to emulate what seemed to be part of a superior, or at least very attractive, way of life.

Sports history in nineteenth-century Western Europe and the United States was itself a vital development. At the beginning of the century few organized sports existed. Village games and individual athletic pastimes abounded, but overall patterns were haphazard. Industrialization spurred a set of changes in sports. First, many urban people began to see the need to exercise to make up for sedentary jobs, and they also valued the social contacts sports provided. Middle-class and working-class teams developed on this basis. Schools seized on sports as a diversion but also as building character: upper-class schools first trumpeted the horns of sports, but lower-class education soon followed their lead. In this context, by the 1850s and 1860s, entrepreneurs saw new ways to make money from sports. There was new equipment to sell, much of it based on the vulcanization of rubber. There were commercial teams to organize, to draw spectators into new stadiums (which would be reached by equally novel tramways). Initial professional teams emerged in English soccer and American baseball. All these developments gave sports an unprecedented importance in modern life. They also changed sports: athletics became more regulated, with standardized rules of play enforced by a new monitor, the official; consciousness of speed and recordkeeping increased; specialization affected sports, with different team members assigned distinct responsibilities.

The internationalization of sports brought some of the same qualities occurring in the West to a variety of other societies—starting with tremendous enthusiasm among young athletes and a wide range of spectators. Teams built by imitation and

Selection 1 from Pierre de Coubertin, "The Olympic Games of 1896," *The Century Magazine*, November 1896, pp. 35, 42, 46–48, 50, 53. Selection 2A. from *Buenos Aires Herald,* June 27, 1904; Selection 2B from Anstol Rosenfeld, "O futebol no Brasil," *Revista Argumento,* Vol. 4 (1979).

contact included a range of Latin American soccer groups, formed initially on the example of local British players. The first Buenos Aires football club, copied from British residents in the city, was founded in 1867, and a national network of teams had fanned out by the 1890s. Argentine soccer style was more exuberant and individualistic than the European version, showing a kind of cultural fusion even as imitation occurred. Japanese students began playing baseball by the 1890s and in 1896 proudly defeated a team of American sailors. At the same time, not all sports spread equally wide. The United States remained addicted to some parochial interests, like American football, not widely shared elsewhere. South Asians were interested in more individual sports, such as badminton and tennis, rather than team sports, with the exception of polo and cricket. Nevertheless, the rapid dissemination of sports as international currency constitutes a major development in world history.

The first selection picks up a formal aspect of sports internationalization: the revival of the Olympics in the 1890s, under the leadership of a French nobleman, Baron de Coubertin (1863–1937). An educational reformer, Coubertin had seen the importance of sports in American and British schools. He formed an International Olympic Congress in 1894 to push for a revival of the old Greek games, but now on an international basis: His hope was that sports would transcend national conflicts. On his death he ordered that his heart be sent to Greece and buried on Mt. Olympus. His comments in the document reflect on the first modern games, held in Athens in 1896. Obviously, the movement he launched has become a major reflection of and spur to sports internationalism, although some of the initial reliance on amateurism and avoidance of nationalistic rivalries has not proved durable. At the same time some of the limitations in Coubertin's vision have lifted as well: His statement reflects a transition in sports internationalism that hardly embraced most of the world directly. Progressively in the twentieth century, but particularly after World War II, the Olympics would do steadily better as a genuinely global assemblage.

The second selection—a pair of documents—conveys the initial atmosphere of the introduction of soccer into Latin America. One document describes the setting for one of the first matches in which Latin Americans were confident enough to invite a British team to play against them; elite Buenos Aires society turned out, including General Julio Roca, the president of the Republic (football had just been introduced into the Argentine army). The British team, Southampton, savaged the Argentine team and several others during their visit. The other document is from a poem by Ana Amélia (entitled "The Leap") to the goalie of the Brazilian team, Fluminense, around 1910, again suggesting the early days of Latin American soccer in which young men from good families displayed their masculine qualities to admiring young women of the same class. The subject of her poem, Marcos de Mendonça, played for the Brazilian national team in 1919 and also became a prominent banker and industrialist; he married Ana Amélia.

1. THE OLYMPICS

The Olympic games which recently took place in Athens were modern in character, not alone because of their programs, which substituted bicycle for chariot races, and fencing for the brutalities of pugilism, but because in their origin and regulations they were international and universal, and consequently adapted to the conditions in which athletics have developed at the present day. The ancient games had an exclusively Hellenic character; they were always held in the same place, and Greek blood was a necessary condition of admission to them. It is true that strangers were in time tolerated; but their presense at Olympia was rather a tribute paid to the superiority of Greek civilization than a right exercised in the name of racial equality. With the modern games it is quite otherwise. Their creation is the work of "barbarians." It is due to the delegates of the athletic associations of all countries assembled in congress at Paris in 1894. It was there agreed that every country should celebrate the Olympic games in turn. The first place belonged by right to Greece; it was accorded by unanimous vote; and in order to emphasize the permanence of the institution, its wide bearings, and its essentially cosmopolitan character, an international committee was appointed, the members of which were to represent the various nations, European and American, with whom athletics are held in honor. The presidency of this committee falls to the country in which the next games are to be held. A Greek, M. Bikelas, has presided for the last two years. A Frenchman now presides, and will continue to do so until 1900, since the next games are to take place at Paris during the Exposition. Where will those of 1904 take place? Perhaps at New York, perhaps at Berlin, or at Stockholm. The question is soon to be decided. . . .

While the Hellenic Committee . . . labored over the scenic requirements, the international committee and the national committees were occupied in recruiting competitors. The matter was not as easy as one might think. Not only had indifference and distrust to be overcome, but the revival of the Olympic games had aroused a certain hostility. Although the Paris Congress had been careful to decree that every form of physical exercise practised in the world should have its place on the program, the gymnasts took offense. They considered that they had not been given sufficient prominence. The greater part of the gymnastic associations of Germany, France, and Belgium are animated by a rigorously exclusive spirit; they are not inclined to tolerate the presence of those forms of athletics which they themselves do not practise; what they disdainfully designate as "English sports" have become, because of their popularity, especially odious to them. These associations were not satisfied with declining the invitation sent them to repair to Athens. The Belgian federation wrote to the other federations, suggesting a concerted stand against the work of the Paris Congress. These incidents confirmed the opinions of the pessimists who had been foretelling the failure of the fêtes, or their probable postponement. Athens is far away, the journey is expensive, and the Easter vacations are short. The contestants were not willing to undertake the voyage unless they could be sure that the occasion would be worth the effort. The different associations were not willing to send representatives unless they could be informed of the amount of interest which the contests would create. An unfortunate occurrence took place almost at the last moment. The German press, commenting on an article which had appeared in a Paris newspaper, declared that it was an exclusively Franco-Greek affair; that attempts were made to shut out other nations; and furthermore, that the German associations had been intentionally kept aloof from the Paris Congress of 1894. The assertion was acknowledged to be incorrect, and was powerless to check the efforts of the German committee under Dr. Gebhardt. M. Kémény in Hungary, Major Balck in Sweden, General de Boutonski in Russia, Professor W. M. Sloane in the United States, Lord Ampthill in England, Dr. Jiri Guth in Bohemia, were, meantime, doing their best to awaken interest in the event, and to reassure the doubt-

The Parade of the Winners at the First Modern Olympic Games, Athens, 1896. (The Granger Collection.)

ing. They did not always succeed. Many people took a sarcastic view, and the newspapers indulged in much pleasantry on the subject of the Olympic games. . . .

Needless to say that the various contests were held under amateur regulations. An exception was made for the fencing-matches, since in several countries professors of military fencing hold the rank of officers. For them a special contest was arranged. To all other branches of the athletic sports only amateurs were admitted. It is impossible to conceive the Olympic games with money prizes. But these rules, which seem simple enough, are a good deal complicated in their practical application by the fact that definitions of what constitutes an amateur differ from one country to another, sometimes even from one club to another. Several definitions are current in England; the Italians and the Dutch admit one which appears too rigid at one point, too loose at another. How conciliate these divergent or contradictory utterances? The Paris Congress made an attempt in that direction, but its decisions are not accepted everywhere as law, nor is its definition of amateurship everywhere adopted as the best. The rules and regulations, properly so called, are not any more uniform. This and that are forbidden in one country, authorized in another. All that one can do, until there shall be an Olympic code formulated in accordance with the ideas and the usages of the majority of athletes, is to choose among the codes now existing. It was decided, therefore, that the foot-races should be under the rules of the Union Française des Sports Athlétiques; jumping, putting the shot, etc., under those of the Amateur Athletic Association of England; the bicycle-races under those of the International Cyclists' Association, etc. This had appeared to us the best way out of the difficulty; but we should have had many disputes if the judges (to whom had been given the Greek name of ephors) had not been headed by Prince George, who acted as final referee. His presence gave weight and authority to the decisions of the ephors, among whom there were, naturally, representatives of different countries. The prince took his duties seriously, and fulfilled them conscientiously. He was always on the track, personally supervising every detail, an easily recognizable figure, owing to his height and athletic build. It will be remembered that Prince George, while traveling in Japan with his cousin, the czarevitch (now Emperor Nicholas II), felled with his fist the ruffian who had tried to assassinate the latter. During the weight-lifting in the Stadion, Price George lifted with ease an enormous dumb-bell, and tossed it out of the way. The audience broke into applause, as if it would have liked to make him the victor in the event. . . .

Many banquets were given. The mayor of Athens gave one at Cephissia, a little shaded village at the foot of Pentelicus. M. Bikelas, the retiring president of the international committee, gave another at Phalerum. The king himself entertained all the competitors, and the members of the committees, three hundred guests in all, at luncheon in the ball-room of the palace. The outside of this edifice, which was built by King Otho, is heavy and graceless; but the center of the interior is occupied by a suite of large rooms with very high ceilings, opening one into another through colonnades. The decorations are simple and imposing. The tables were set in the largest of these rooms. At the table of honor sat the king, the princes, and the ministers, and here also were the members of the committees. The competitors were seated at the other tables according to their nationality. The king, at dessert, thanked and congratulated his guests, first in French, afterward in Greek. The Americans cried "Hurrah!" the Germans, "*Hoch!*" the Hungarians, "*Eljen!*" the Greeks, "*Zito!*" the French, "*Vive le Roi!*" After the repast the king and his sons chatted long and amicably with the athletes. It was a really charming scene, the republican simplicity of which was a matter of wonderment particularly to the Austrians and the Russians, little used as they are to the spectacle of monarchy thus meeting democracy on an equal footing.

Then there were nocturnal festivities on the Acropolis, where the Partheon was illuminated with colored lights, and at the Piræus, where the vessels were hung with Japanese lanterns. Unluckily, the weather changed, and the sea was so high on the day appointed for the boat-races, which were to have taken place in the roadstead of Phalerum, that the project was abandoned. The distribution of prizes was likewise postponed for twenty-four hours. It came off with much solemnity, on the morning of April 15, in the Stadion. The sun shone again, and sparkled on the officers' uniforms. When the roll of the victors was called, it became evident, after all, that the international character of the institution was well guarded by the results of the contests. America had won nine prizes for athletic sports alone (flat races for

100 and 400 meters; 110-meter hurdle-race; high jump; broad jump; pole-vault; hop, step, and jump; putting the shot; throwing the discus), and two prizes for shooting (revolver, 25 and 30 meters); but France had the prizes for foil-fencing and for four bicycle-races; England scored highest in the one-handed weight-lifting contest, and in single lawn-tennis; Greece won the run from Marathon, two gymnastic contests (rings, climbing the smooth rope), three prizes for shooting (carbine, 200 and 300 meters; pistol, 25 meters), a prize for fencing with sabers, and a bicycle-race; Germany won in wrestling, in gymnastics (parallel bars, fixed bar, horse-leaping), and in double lawn-tennis; Australia, the 800-meter and 1500-meter foot-races on the flat; Hungary, swimming-matches of 100 and 1200 meters; Austria, the 500-meter swimming-match and the 12-hour bicycle-race; Switzerland, a gymnastic prize; Denmark, the two-handed weight-lifting contest. . . .

It is interesting to ask oneself what are likely to be the results of the Olympic games of 1896, as regards both Greece and the rest of the world. In the case of Greece, the games will be found to have had a double effect, one athletic, the other political. It is a well-known fact that the Greeks had lost completely, during their centuries of oppression, the taste for physical sports. There were good walkers among the mountaineers, and good swimmers in the scattered villages along the coast. It was a matter of pride with the young *palikar* to wrestle and to dance well, but that was because bravery and a gallant bearing were admired by those about him. Greek dances are far from athletic, and the wrestling-matches of peasants have none of the characteristics of true sports. The men of the towns had come to know no diversion beyond reading the newspapers, and violently discussing politics about the tables of the cafés. The Greek race, however, is free from the natural indolence of the Oriental, and it was manifest that the athletic habit would, if the opportunity offered, easily take root again among its men. Indeed, several gymnastic associations had been formed in recent years at Athens and Patras, and a rowing-club at Piræus, and the public was showing a growing interest in their feats. It was therefore a favorable moment to speak the words "Olympic games." No sooner had it been made clear that Athens was to aid in the revival of the Olympiads than a perfect fever of muscular activity broke out all over the kingdom. And this was nothing to what followed the games. I have seen, in little villages far from the capital, small boys, scarcely out of long clothes, throwing big stones, or jumping improvised hurdles, and two urchins never met in the streets of Athens without running races. . . .

When one realizes the influence that the practice of physical exercises may have on the future of a country, and on the force of a whole race, one is tempted to wonder whether Greece is not likely to date a new era from the year 1896. . . .

So much for Greece. On the world at large the Olympic games have, of course, exerted no influence as yet; but I am profoundly convinced that they will do so. May I be permitted to say that this was my reason for founding them? Modern athletics need to be *unified* and *purified*. Those who have followed the renaissance of physical sports in this century know that discord reigns supreme from one end of them to the other. Every country has its own rules; it is not possible even to come to an agreement as to who is an amateur, and who is not. All over the world there is one perpetual dispute, which is further fed by innumerable weekly, and even daily, newspapers. In this deplorable state of things professionalism tends to grow apace. Men give up their whole existence to one particular sport, grow rich by practising it, and thus deprive it of all nobility, and destroy the just equilibrium of man by making the muscles preponderate over the mind. It is my belief that no education, particularly in democratic times, can be good and complete without the aid of athletics; but athletics, in order to play their proper educational rôle, must be based on perfect disinterestedness and the sentiment of honor.

If we are to guard them against these threatening evils, we must put an end to the quarrels of amateurs, that they may be united among themselves, and willing to measure their skill in frequent international encounters. But what country is to impose its rules and its habits on the others? The Swedes will not yield to the Germans, nor the French to the English. Nothing better than the international Olympic games could therefore be devised. Each country will take its turn in organizing them. When they come to meet every four years in these contests, further ennobled by the memories of the past, athletes all over the world will learn to know one another better, to make mutual concessions, and to seek no other reward in the competition than the honor of the victory. One may be filled with desire to see the colors of one's club or college triumph in a national meeting; but how much stronger is the feeling when the colors of one's country are at stake! I am well assured that the victors in the Stadion at Athens wished for no other recompense when they heard the people cheer the flag of their country in honor of their achievement.

It was with these thoughts in mind that I sought to revive the Olympic games. I have succeeded after many efforts. Should the institution prosper,—as I am persuaded, all civilized nations aiding, that it will,—it may be a potent, if indirect, factor in securing universal peace. Wars break out because nations misunderstand each other. We shall not have peace until the prejudices which now separate the different races shall have been outlived. To attain this end, what better means than to bring the youth of all countries periodically together for amicable trials of muscular strength and agility? The Olympic games, with the ancients, controlled athletics and promoted peace. It is not visionary to look to them for similar benefactions in the future.

2. LATIN AMERICA TAKES ON FOOTBALL.

A. From the Buenos Aires Herald (1904)

The football field proper was fenced in with a strong and neat wire fence at the back of which was a space of about five yards in width, followed by a continuous row of stands on all sides of the field with the lowest row of benches well raised, so that their occupants could easily see over the heads of those using the standing room in front. Opposite the centre of the field on each side were the reserved seats, and on the south west side was a break in the stands, occupied by the box for the use of the President and the official guests. The seats to the north of the President's box being reserved for members of the Hippic club and their families. Long before 2 o'clock the seats were well filled, and at five minutes past two, the band of the 3rd Battalion of the line struck up 'Hail to the Chief' and the carriage of General Roca was seen to be approaching. . . . Great applause greeted his appearance, which he gracefully acknowledged.

· · ·

It is not clear why Southampton was chosen. It was, at the time, one of the leading professional teams in the Southern League and had twice been losing finalists in the FA Cup, in 1900 and 1902. The team swept through their five matches in Buenos

Aires and one in Montevideo like an irresistible force. The day after they got off the boat they beat Alumni 3–0. A team of Britishers was savaged 10–0, Belgrano destroyed 6–1: much was made of the first goal to be scored against 'foreigners' by Arthur Forester in that game. An Argentine eleven was then beaten 8–0 and a team representative of the league in Buenos Aires lost 5–3 to the triumphant visitors. On the way home a Uruguayan combination was similarly despatched 8–1 in Montevideo.

B. Ana W. Amélia

When I saw you today, executing your relaxed, daring and vigorous leap like a figure from the *Iliad* I trembled in the most intimate part of my being, swept by a frenetic impulse as if I was before a Greek, the hero of an Olympiad. Shaken like Dryad before Apollo, I measure his magnificent figure. Against the incomparable background of a pale twilight you threw yourself into space, tensed all your muscles, enrapt by the roar of the crowd's enthusiastic applause. Like an agile God that graciously came down from Olympus, you touched the ground, glorious, fervent, and fearless, perfect in the beauty of the classic Greek sculpture.

THE SPREAD OF FOOTBALL 1863–1985

Country	National Organization Set Up	Affiliation to FIFA*	National League	Professionalism Introduced	First International Match
England	1863	1905–20 1924–28 1946	1888	1885	v. Scotland 30 Nov 1872
Scotland	1873	1910–20 1924–28 1946	1890	1893	v. England
Denmark	1889	1904	1913	1978	v. France 19 Oct 1908
Argentina	1893	1912	1967	1931	v. Uruguay 16 May 1901
Switzerland	1895	1904	1934	1933	v. France 12 Feb 1905
Belgium	1895	1904	1896	1972	v. France 1 May 1904
Chile	1895	1912	1933	1933	v. Argentina 27 May 1910
Italy	1898	1905	1930	1929	v. France 13 May 1920
Netherlands	1899	1904	1957	1954	v. Belgium 30 April 1905
Germany	1900	1904–46 1950	1963 (WG†)		v. Switzerland 5 April 1908
Uruguay	1900	1923	1900	1932	v. Argentina 16 May 1901
Czechoslovakia (Bohemia pre-1918)	1901	1906	1925	1925	v. Hungary 5 April 1903
Hungary	1901	1906	1901	1926	v. Austria 12 Oct 1902
Norway	1902	1908	1961		v. Sweden 12 July 1908
Austria	1904	1905	1911	1924–38	v. Hungary 12 Oct 1902
Sweden	1904	1904	1925	1967	v. Norway 12 July 1908
Paraguay	1906	1921	1906	1935	v. Argentina 11 May 1919
Romania	1908	1930	1910		v. Yugoslavia 8 June 1922
Spain	1913	1904	1929	1929	v. Denmark 28 Aug 1920

*FIFA, International Federation of Football Associations.

†WG, West Germany.

THE SPREAD OF FOOTBALL 1863–1985 *(continued)*

Country	National Organization Set Up	Affiliation to FIFA*	National League	Professionalism Introduced	First International Match
United States	1913	1913	1967–84		v. Canada 28 Nov 1885
Brazil	1914	1923	1971	1933	v. Argentina 20 Sept 1914
Portugal	1914	1926	1935		v. Spain 18 Dec 1921
France	1918	1904	1932	1932	v. Belgium 1 May 1904
Yugoslavia	1919	1919	1923		v. Czechoslovakia 28 Aug 1920
Poland	1919	1923	1927		v. Hungary 18 Dec 1921
USSR (Soviet Union)	1922	1946	1936		v. Turkey 16 Nov 1924
Turkey	1923	1923	1959	1951	v. Romania 26 Oct 1923
Bulgaria	1923	1924	1949		v. Austria 21 May 1924
Greece	1926	1927	1960	1979	v. Sweden 28 Aug 1920
Colombia	1924	1936	1948	1948	v. Mexico 10 Feb 1938
Mexico	1927	1929	1948	1931	v. Spain 30 May 1928
Peru	1922	1924	1966	1931	v. Uruguay 1 Nov 1927
Egypt	1921	1923	1949		
New Zealand	1938	1963	1970		
Morocco	1955	1956	1916		
Tunisia	1956	1960	1921		
Algeria	1962	1963	1963		v. West Germany 1 Jan 1964
South Africa	1892	1952–76 (suspended 1964–76) 1992	1971		
Zaire	1919	1964	1958		
Zambia	1929	1964	1962		
Nigeria	1945	1959	1972		
Zimbabwe	1950	1965	1963		
Ghana	1957	1958	1957		
Côte d'Ivoire	1950	1960	1960		
Cameroon	1960	1962	1961		
Iran	1920	1948	1974		
Japan	1921	1929–45 1950	1993		
China	1924	1931–58 1979	1953		
South Korea	1928	1948	1983	1983	v. Mexico 2 Aug 1948
North Korea	1945	1958			
Iraq	1948	1951	1974		
Saudi Arabia	1959	1959	1979		
Australia	1961	1963	1977		

*FIFA, International Federation of Football Associations.

STUDY QUESTIONS

1. What was Coubertin's idea of internationalism? What problems did he encounter in trying to internationalize sports, and how did he handle them?
2. What "world" was represented at the first Olympics? Why might a European find the representation an impressive demonstration of internationalism, in the context of the 1890s?
3. How did Coubertin suggest a belief that sports might be a particularly European strength?
4. What did Coubertin think the results of international sports might be in Greece? What does his approach suggest about belief in the larger meaning of modern sports?
5. Why were British sports popular in Argentina? What kinds of Argentinians were first interested, and why? Are there any connections with the motivations involved in the revival of the Olympics?
6. Can the chronology of the international spread of football organizations be explained in terms of patterns of European influence?
7. Why have sports become such an important part of modern global culture?

SECTION THREE

The Twentieth Century

Growing challenges to Western world dominance, sparked by growing nationalism and by divisions within the West, produced new expressions of diversity in the major world civilizations. At the same time, international contacts increased in many ways. New technologies speeded exchange; so did heightened trade, new alliance systems and worldwide conflicts, and multinational companies spreading production and products literally around the globe. Much of twentieth-century world history involves oscillating tensions between new interchange and a growing desire and capacity to define separate systems and identities.

Within this general framework, a number of more specific changes occurred, also reflecting the twentieth century's role as a transition toward a new, but not fully defined, period of world history. Religion declined in some societies but was reasserted in others. Political structures varied from liberal-democratic to authoritarian to communist, as new nations or revolutions yielded different patterns in different parts of the globe. But amid renewed diversity, including widely varying levels of economic well-being, were some common themes. Many civilizations sought ways to modify earlier political traditions—very few regimes in place in 1914 still survived by the late 1990s. Changes in the outlook and conditions of women marked fundamental social and personal upheaval. Hardly uniform, the twentieth-century world also shared a need to come to terms with some basic forces of innovation in the areas of technology, ideas, and social forms.

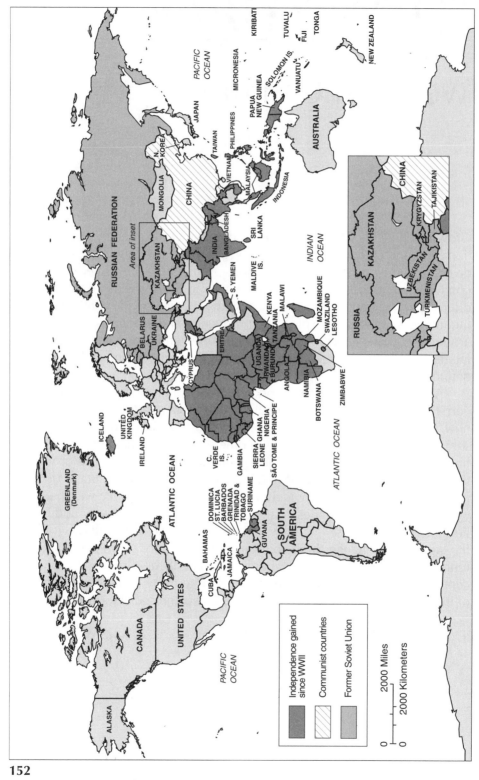

Global Relationships at the End of the 1990s

Legend:
- Independence gained since WWII
- Communist countries
- Former Soviet Union

2000 Miles
2000 Kilometers
0
0

Western Civilization

24

The Twentieth-Century Western State

One of the key new trends in Western society during the twentieth century has involved changes in the role of the state. Government powers expanded and contacts between state and ordinary citizens increased. Whether the form of government was democratic or not, voting was used to link individual and state. New ideologies and technologies alike expanded state activities. The growth of the Western state built on earlier trends, such as absolutism, and on the needs and capacities of industrial society. It was, nevertheless, a new creature.

The growth of this state power could take vitally different forms, however. Tensions in the Western political tradition, visible in the seventeenth and eighteenth centuries, emerged anew, focusing on the extent of government power as well as constitutional structure. Between the world wars, the most striking political development in the West was the rise of fascist or Nazi totalitarianism. The totalitarian state did not emerge everywhere in the West, but rather in nations where liberal traditions were relatively weak and the shocks of World War I particularly great. Hitler, the Nazi leader, defines the fascist worship of the state in his tract *Mein Kampf*, written in 1924.

The second main version of governmental growth was the welfare state, which became the common Western form after World War II. Britain, converting from liberal suspicion of government to a desire for new social responsibility, clearly illustrated welfare-state principles. The British welfare-state concept was sketched in a vital wartime planning document, the Beveridge Report, which was put into practice after 1945.

Selection 1 from *Mein Kampf* by Adolf Hitler, translated by Ralph Manheim, pp. 443, 449–451. Copyright 1943 and copyright © renewed 1971 by Houghton Mifflin Company. Reprinted by permission of Houghton Mifflin Company. Selection 2 from "Report by Sir William Beveridge," *Social Insurance and Allied Services* (Cmd 6404), London, Her Majesty's Stationery Office, 1942, pp. 6–8, 13, 158–159. British Crown copyright. Reproduced by the permission of the Controller of Her Britannic Majesty's Stationery Office.

Both the *Mein Kampf* and the Beveridge Report selections require some interpretation, for neither Hitler nor the Beveridge Commission spelled out a full definition of state functions in a tidy way. Hitler's writings were vague in most respects, featuring strong emotions more than careful programs. The Beveridge Report was a pragmatic planning exercise, not a statement of basic theory. A first task, then, is to figure out how state goals are defined and justified in each case—what Hitler means by state reliance on "personality"; what the welfare planners mean by state responsibility.

Nazi and welfare-state definitions obviously invite comparison. How did they differ in political ideals? How did each relate to earlier Western political standards? Why did the different state forms arise amid the crises conditions of world wars and economic depression in the West, and how would each affect ordinary citizens? But also, in what ways did Nazi and welfare states reflect some similar trends and principles?

The Nazi version of the state seems to have been confined, in the West, to the special conditions of the 1920s and 1930s. Might these reemerge? Is the welfare state a more durable Western form? If so, why? Compared with contemporary political structures elsewhere in the world, has the twentieth-century Western state remained particularly distinctive?

1. HITLER DEFINES THE STATE (1924)

Anyone who believes today that a folkish National Socialist state must distinguish itself from other states only in a purely mechanical sense, by a superior construction of its economic life—that is, by a better balance between rich and poor, or giving broad sections of the population more right to influence the economic process, or by fairer wages by elimination of excessive wage differentials—has not gone beyond the most superficial aspects of the matter and has not the faintest idea of what we call a philosophy. All the things we have just mentioned offer not the slightest guaranty of continued existence, far less of any claim to greatness. A people which did not go beyond these really superficial reforms would not obtain the least guaranty of victory in the general struggle of nations. A movement which finds the content of its mission only in such a general leveling, assuredly just as it may be, will truly bring about no great and profound, hence real, reform of existing conditions, since its entire activity does not, in the last analysis, go beyond externals, and does not give the people that inner armament which enables it, with almost inevitable certainty I might say, to overcome in the end those weaknesses from which we suffer today. . . .

The folkish state must care for the welfare of its citizens by recognizing in all and everything the importance of the value of personality, thus in all fields preparing the way for that highest measure of productive performance which grants to the individual the highest measure of participation.

And accordingly, the folkish state must free all leadership and especially the highest—that is, the political leadership—entirely from the parliamentary principle of majority rule—in other words, mass rule—and instead absolutely guarantee the right of the personality.

From this the following realization results:

The best state constitution and state form is that which, with the most unquestioned certainty, raises the best minds in the national community to leading position and leading influence.

But as, in economic life, the able men cannot be appointed from above, but must struggle through for themselves, and just as here the endless schooling, ranging from the smallest business to the largest enterprise, occurs spontaneously, with life alone giving the examinations, obviously political minds cannot be "discovered." Extraordinary geniuses permit of no consideration for normal mankind.

From the smallest community cell to the highest leadership of the entire Reich, the state must have the personality principle anchored in its organization.

There must be no majority decisions, but only responsible persons, and the word "council" must be restored to its original meaning. Surely every man will have advisers by his side, but *the decision will be made by one man.*

The principle which made the Prussian army in its time into the most wonderful instrument of the German people must some day, in a transferred sense, become the principle of the construction of our whole state conception: *authority of every leader downward and responsibility upward.*

Even then it will not be possible to dispense with those corporations which today we designate as parliaments. But their councillors will then actually give counsel; responsibility, however, can and may be borne only by *one* man, and therefore only he alone may possess the authority and right to command.

Parliaments as such are necessary, because in them, above all, personalities to which special responsible tasks can later be entrusted have an opportunity gradually to rise up.

This gives the following picture:

The folkish state, from the township up to the Reich leadership, has no representative body which decides anything by the majority, but only *advisory bodies* which stand at the side of the elected leader, receiving their share of work from him, and in turn if necessary assuming unlimited responsibility in certain fields, just as on a larger scale the leader or chairman of the various corporations himself possesses.

As a matter of principle, the folkish state does not tolerate asking advice or opinions in special matters—say, of an economic nature—of men who, on the basis of their education and activity, can understand nothing of the subject. It, therefore, divides its representative bodies from the start into *political and professional chambers.*

In order to guarantee a profitable cooperation between the two, a special *senate* of the élite always stands above them.

In no chamber and in no senate does a vote ever take place. They are working institutions and not voting machines. The individual member has an advisory, but never a determining, voice. The latter is the exclusive privilege of the responsible chairman.

This principle—absolute responsibility unconditionally combined with absolute authority—will gradually breed an élite of leaders such as today, in this era of irresponsible parliamentarianism, is utterly inconceivable.

Thus, the political form of the nation will be brought into agreement with that law to which it owes its greatness in the cultural and economic field.

· · ·

As regards the possibility of putting these ideas into practice, I beg you not to forget that the parliamentary principle of democratic majority rule has by no means always dominated mankind, but on the contrary is to be found only in brief periods of history, which are always epochs of the decay of peoples and states.

But it should not be believed that such a transformation can be accomplished by purely theoretical measures from above, since logically it may not even stop at the state constitution, but must permeate all other legislation, and indeed all civil life. Such a fundamental change can and will only take place through a movement which is itself constructed in the spirit of these ideas and hence bears the future state within itself.

Hence the National Socialist movement should today adapt itself entirely to these ideas and carry them to practical fruition within its own organization, so that some day it may not only show the state these same guiding principles, but can also place the completed body of its own state at its disposal.

2. GREAT BRITAIN PLANS THE WELFARE STATE (1942)

In proceeding from this first comprehensive survey of social insurance to the next task—of making recommendations—three guiding principles may be laid down at the outset.

The first principle is that any proposals for the future, while they should use to the full the experience gathered in the past, should not be restricted by consideration of sectional interests established in the obtaining of that experience. Now, when the war is abolishing landmarks of every kind, is the opportunity for using experience in a clear field. A revolutionary movement in the world's history is a time for revolutions, not for patching.

The second principle is that organisation of social insurance should be treated as one part only of a comprehensive policy of social progress. Social insurance fully developed may provide income security; it is an attack upon Want. But Want is one only of five giants on the road of reconstruction and in some ways the easiest to attack. The others are Disease, Ignorance, Squalor and Idleness.

The third principle is that social security must be achieved by co-operation between the State and the individual. The State should offer security for service and contribution. The State in organising security should not stifle incentive, opportunity, responsibility; in establishing a national minimum, it should leave room and encouragement for voluntary action by each individual to provide more than that minimum for himself and his family. . . .

Abolition of want requires, first, improvement of State insurance, that is to say provision against interruption and loss of earning power. All the principal causes of interruption or loss of earnings are now the subject of schemes of social insurance. If, in spite of these schemes, so many persons unemployed or sick or old or widowed are found to be without adequate income for subsistence according to the standards adopted in the social surveys, this means that the benefits amount to less than subsistence by those standards or do not last as long as the need, and that the assistance which supplements insurance is either insufficient in amount or available only on terms which make men unwilling to have recourse to it. None of the insurance benefits provided before the war were in fact designed with reference to the standards of the social surveys. Though unemployment benefit was not altogether out of relation to those standards, sickness and disablement benefit, old age pensions and widows' pensions were far below them, while workmen's compensation was below subsistence level for anyone who had family responsibilities or whose earnings in work were less than twice the amount needed for subsistence. To prevent interruption or destruction of earning power from leading to want, it is necessary to improve the present schemes of social insurance in three directions: by extension of scope to cover persons now excluded, by extension of purposes to cover risks now excluded, and by raising the rates of benefit.

Abolition of want requires, second, adjustment of incomes, in periods of earning as well as interruption of earning, to family needs, that is to say in one form or another it requires allowances for children. Without such allowances as part of benefit or added to it, to make provision for large families, no social insurance against interruption of earnings can be adequate. But if children's allowances are given only when earnings are interrupted and are not given during earning also, two evils are unavoidable. First, a substantial measure of acute want will remain among the lower paid workers as the accompaniment of large families. Second, in all such cases, income will be greater during unemployment or other interruptions of work than during work.

· · · ·

There is here an issue of principle and practice on which strong arguments can be advanced on each side by reasonable men. But the general tendency of public opinion seems clear. After trial of a different principle, it has been found to accord best with the sentiments of the British people that in insurance organised by the community by use of compulsory powers each individual should stand in on the same terms; none should claim to pay less because he is healthier or has more regular employment. In accord with that view, the proposals of the Report mark another step forward to the development of State insurance as a new type of human institution, differing both from the former methods of preventing or alleviating distress and from voluntary insurance. The term "social insurance" to describe this institution implies both that it is compulsory and that men stand together with their fellows. The term implies a pooling of risks except so far as separation of risks serves a social purpose. There may be reasons of social policy for adjusting premiums to risks, in order to give a stimulus for avoidance of danger, as in the case of industrial accident and disease. There is no longer an admitted claim of the individual citizen to share in national insurance and yet to stand outside it, keeping the advantage of his individual lower risk whether of unemployment or of disease or accident. . . .

A comprehensive national health service will ensure that for every citizen there is available whatever medical treatment he requires, in whatever form he requires it, domiciliary or institutional, general, specialist or consultant, and will ensure also the provision of dental, ophthalmic and surgical appliances, nursing and midwifery and rehabilitation after accidents. Whether or not payment towards the cost of the health service is included in the social insurance contribution, the service itself should

(i) be organized, not by the Ministry concerned with social insurance, but by Departments responsible for the health of the people and for positive and preventive as well as curative measures;

(ii) be provided where needed without contribution conditions in any individual case.

Restoration of a sick person to health is a duty of the State and the sick person, prior to any other consideration. The assumption made here is in accord with the definition of the objects of medical service as proposed in the Draft Interim Report of the Medical Planning Commission of the British Medical Association:

"(a) to provide a system of medical service directed towards the achievement of positive health, of the prevention of disease, and the relief of sickness;

(b) to render available to every individual all necessary medical services, both general and specialist, and both domiciliary and institutional."

STUDY QUESTIONS

1. What did Hitler mean by the personality principle?
2. What kind of state, with what purposes, did the Nazis seek?
3. What changes in state functions did the Beveridge Report advocate?
4. What were the main differences between Nazi and welfare-state political definitions?
5. Why did the twentieth century see a growth in state claims, albeit under various systems, in Western society?

25

The Feminist Revolt

The publication of *The Second Sex* in 1949 by the noted French intellectual Simone de Beauvoir marked the beginning of postwar feminism in Western society. It was followed by works such as Betty Friedan's *The Feminine Mystique* that frankly acknowledged their debt to de Beauvoir and by a number of powerful women's political movements in the United States and Western Europe. The following selection from de Beauvoir's manifesto calls for an assessment of what contemporary feminism is all about—what goals it has, what its grievances are.

This feminist statement is of course phrased in rather theoretical terms. But it corresponded to a rapid change in the actual roles and aspirations of women in the West, marked by a rise in educational levels, a new reduction of the birthrate (though only after 1962, following a "baby boom" period), and above all a real revolution in work roles, as adult women—including wives and mothers—poured into the formal labor force. Women's lives, and their position in society and the family, constituted one of the areas of great change in Western social history during the twentieth century. While part of the change followed from shifts in the economy such as the rise of service jobs, part also followed from new goals—which brings us back to the feminism of intellectual leaders like de Beauvoir. What was going on in Western society to spur such intense desire for fundamental upheaval in what many people, women as well as men, had viewed as biological destiny?

Feminist movements had existed before in the West, in the nineteenth and early twentieth centuries, that culminated in women's suffrage, granted in most Western countries between 1900 and 1920 and in some, such as France, after World War II. De Beauvoir's feminism argued that earlier gains were insufficient, that a more thoroughgoing attack on tradition, including nineteenth-century family ideals, was vital. An understanding of de Beauvoir's views as representative of contemporary intellectual feminism goes far toward creating an understanding of basic currents among twentieth-century Western women more generally.

In the context of world history, the rise of Western women—important in its own right—raises larger issues. Western feminism was not matched in other civilizations, and indeed many societies, such as Latin America and the Middle East, were

Feminism—An International Movement? American feminist leader Betty Friedan with Indian, Kenyan, and Egyptian representatives at the United Nations Conference on Women, 1984. (AP/Wide World Photos.)

wary of even lesser changes in women's status. What combination of values and problems spurred the distinctive Western movement? And is it likely that as industrialization and other "modern" forces advance elsewhere, comparable feminist drives will surface? Already, from Africa to Japan, women's rights advocates were stirring after World War II, although their movements lacked the sweep of those in the West. Will women's rights become part of an international agenda in new millennium? What general forces were prompting the new questions about what women were and what they should be doing?

The "feminine" woman in making herself prey tries to reduce man, also, to her carnal passivity; she occupies herself in catching him in her trap, in enchaining him by means of the desire she arouses in him in submissively making herself a thing. The emancipated woman, on the contrary, wants to be active, a taker, and refuses the passivity man means to impose on her. . . .

The innumerable conflicts that set men and women against one another come from the fact that neither is prepared to assume all the consequences of this situation which the one has offered and the other accepted. The doubtful concept of "equality in inequality," which the one uses to mask his despotism and the other to mask her cowardice, does not stand the test of experience: in their exchanges, woman appeals to the theoretical equality she has been guaranteed, and man the concrete inequality that exists. The result is that in every association an endless debate goes on concerning the ambiguous meaning of the words *give* and *take:* she complains of giving her all, he protests that she takes his all. Woman has to learn that exchanges—it is a fundamental law of political economy—are based on the value the merchandise offered has for the buyer, and not for the seller: she has been deceived in being persuaded that her worth is priceless. The truth is that for man she is an amusement, a pleasure, company, an inessential boon; he is for her the meaning, the justification of her existence. The exchange, therefore, is not of two items of equal value. . . .

But is it enough to change laws, institutions, customs, public opinion, and the whole social context, for men and women to become truly equal? "Women will always be women," say the skeptics. Other seers prophesy that in cutting off their femininity they will not succeed in changing themselves into men and they will become monsters. This would be to admit that the woman of today is a creation of nature; it must be repeated once more that in human society nothing is natural and that woman, like much else, is a product elaborated by civilization. The intervention of others in her destiny is fundamental: if this action took a different direction, it would produce a quite different result. Woman is determined not by her hormones or by mysterious instincts, but by the manner in which her body and her relation to the world are modified through the action of others than herself. The abyss that separates the adolescent boy and girl has been deliberately opened out between them since earliest childhood; later on, woman could not be other than what she *was made,* and that past was bound to shelter her for life. If we appreciate its influence, we see clearly that her destiny is not predetermined for all eternity.

We must not believe, certainly, that a change in woman's economic condition alone is enough to transform her, though this factor has been and remains the basic factor in her evolution; but until it has brought about the moral, social, cultural, and other consequences that it promises and requires, the new woman cannot appear. At this moment they have been realized nowhere, in Russia no more than in France or the United States; and this explains why the woman of today is torn between the past and the future. She appears most often as a "true woman" disguised as a man, and she feels herself as ill at ease in her flesh as in her masculine garb. She must shed her old skin and cut her own new clothes. This she could do only through a social solution. No single educator could fashion a *female human being* today who would be the exact homologue of the *male human being;* if she is raised like a boy, the young girl feels she is an oddity and thereby she is given a new kind of sex specification. Stendhal understood this when he said: "The forest must be planted all at once." But if we imagine, on the contrary, a society in which the equality of the sexes would be concretely realized, this equality would find new expression in each individual.

If the little girl were brought up from the first with the same demands and rewards, the same severity and the same freedom, as her brothers, taking part in the same studies, the same games, promised the same future, surrounded with women and men who seemed to her undoubted equals, the meanings of the castration complex and of the œdipus complex would be profoundly modified. Assuming on the same basis as the father the material and moral responsibility of the couple, the mother would enjoy the same lasting prestige; the child would perceive around her an androgynous world and not a masculine world. . . .

As a matter of fact, man, like woman, is flesh, therefore passive, the plaything of his hormones and of the species, the restless prey of his desires. And she, like him, in the midst of the carnal fever, is a consenting, a voluntary gift, an activity; they live out in their several fashions the strange ambiguity of existence made body. In those combats where they think they confront one another, it is really against the self that each one struggles, projecting into the partner that part of the self which is repudiated; instead of living out the ambiguities of their situation, each tries to make the other bear the abjection and tries to reserve the honor for the self. If, however, both should assume the ambiguity with a clear-sighted modesty, correlative of an authentic pride, they would see each other as equals and would live out their erotic drama in amity. The fact that we are human beings is infinitely more important than all the peculiarities that distinguish human beings from one another; it is never the given that confers superiorities: "virtue," as the ancients called it, is defined at the level of "that which depends on us." In both sexes is played out the same drama of the flesh and the spirit, of finitude and transcendence; both are gnawed away by time and laid in wait for by death, they have the same essential need for one another; and they can gain from their liberty the same glory. If they were to taste it, they would no longer be tempted to dispute fallacious privileges, and fraternity between them could then come into existence.

I shall be told that all this is utopian fancy, because woman cannot be "made over" unless society has first made her really the equal of man. Conservatives have never failed in such circumstances to refer to that vicious circle; history, however, does not revolve. If a caste is kept in a state of inferiority, no doubt it remains inferior; but liberty can break the circle. Let the Negroes vote and they become worthy of having the vote: let woman be given responsibilities and she is able to assume them. The fact is that oppressors cannot be expected to make a move of gratuitous generosity; but at one time the revolt of the oppressed, at another time even the very evolution of the privileged caste itself, creates new situations; thus men have been led, in their own interest, to give partial emancipation to woman: it remains only for women to continue their ascent, and the successes they are obtaining are an encouragement for them to do so. It seems almost certain that sooner or later they will arrive at a complete economic and social equality, which will bring about an inner metamorphosis.

However this may be, there will be some to object that if such a world is possible it is not desirable. When woman is "the same" as her male, life will lose its salt and spice. . . .

One can appreciate the beauty of flowers, the charm of women, and appreciate them at their true value; if these treasures cost blood or misery, they must be sacrificed.

But in truth this sacrifice seems to men a peculiarly heavy one; few of them really wish in their hearts for woman to succeed in making it; those among them who hold woman in contempt see in the sacrifice nothing for them to gain, those who cherish her see too much that they would lose. And it is true that the evolution now in progress threatens more than feminine charm alone: in beginning to exist for herself, woman will relinquish the function as double and mediator to which she owes her privileged place in the masculine universe; to man, caught between the silence of nature and the demanding presence of other free beings, a creature who is at once his like and a passive thing seems a great treasure. The guise in which he conceives his companion may be mythical, but the experiences for which she is the source or the pretext are none the less real: there are hardly any more precious, more intimate, more ardent. There is no denying that feminine dependence, inferiority, woe, give women their special character; assuredly woman's autonomy, if it spares men many troubles, will also deny them many conveniences; assuredly there are certain forms of the sexual adventure which will be lost in the world of tomorrow. But this does not mean that love, happiness, poetry, dream, will be banished from it.

Let us not forget that our lack of imagination always depopulates the future; for us it is only an abstraction; each one of us secretly deplores the absence there of the one who was himself. But the humanity of tomorrow will be living flesh and in its conscious liberty; that time will be its present and it will in turn prefer it. New relations of flesh and sentiment of which we have no conception will arise between the sexes; already, indeed, there have appeared between men and women friendships, rivalries, complicities, comradeships—chaste or sensual—which past centuries could not have conceived. To mention one point, nothing could seem to me more debatable than the opinion that dooms the new world to uniformity and hence to boredom. I fail to see that this present world is free from boredom or that liberty ever creates uniformity. . . .

It is nonsense to assert that revelry, vice, ecstasy, passion, would become impossible if man and woman were equal in concrete matters; the contradictions that put the flesh in opposition to the spirit, the instant to time, the swoon of immanence to the challenge of transcendence, the absolute of pleasure to the nothingness of forgetting, will never be resolved; in sexuality will always be materialized the tension, the anguish, the joy, the frustration, and the triumph of existence. To emancipate woman is to refuse to confine her to the relations she bears to man, not to deny them to her; let her have her independent existence and she will continue none the less to exist for him *also:* mutually recognizing each other as subject, each will yet remain for the other an *other.* The reciprocity of their relations will not do away with the miracles—desire, possession, love, dream, adventure—worked by the division of human beings into two separate categories; and the words that move us—giving, conquering, uniting—will not lose their meaning. On the contrary, when we abolish the slavery of half of humanity, together with the whole system of hypocrisy that it implies, then the "division" of humanity will reveal its genuine significance and the human couple will find its true form.

STUDY QUESTIONS

1. What did de Beauvoir see as the main problems for women in twentieth-century society? Did she believe that any fundamental changes had occurred?
2. What are the main changes de Beauvoir sought? How did she define the feminist agenda? How did her approach compare with earlier feminist campaigns that had focused on legal issues or the vote?
3. What kinds of losses does de Beauvoir refer to in a feminist society? Why does she view them as acceptable?
4. What has happened to de Beauvoir's basic ideas in the gender roles and women's movements in Western society in the final decades of the twentieth century?

Soviet Society

26

Lenin and the Russian Revolution

The year 1917 brought momentous change to Russia. Mass upheaval in the cities and the countryside, deriving in part from suffering associated with World War I, led to the destruction of key elements of the old order: The Romanov dynasty and the landlord class, each of which had deep roots in the Russian past, were swept away forever. These changes alone are important enough to place the Russian Revolution in the same category as the French Revolution. But the events of 1917 had an added significance, for the victorious Bolshevik revolutionaries did not seek to establish a Western-style middle-class society. Instead, they proclaimed socialism and communism as their goals.

If the meaning and legacy of the Russian Revolution have engendered much controversy, there is, nevertheless, widespread agreement on the central role played by Lenin (Valdimir Ilych Ulyanov, 1870–1924), the indefatigable leader of the Bolshevik party and the first head of the new Soviet regime. Lenin's leading role in the Russian Revolution is traceable to the force of his ideas and his organizing ability, illustrated in the following selections from his works. In reading the following excerpts from Lenin's writings, note the way in which his thought embraces various tensions. Do you see elements of realism as well as utopianism in Lenin? Does his commitment to class struggle mesh with his desire to modernize Russia? Can Lenin's desire for democracy be reconciled with his belief in the necessity of authoritarian rule?

Our Programme (1899)

We take our stand entirely on the Marxist theoretical position: Marxism was the first to transform socialism from a utopia into a science, to lay a firm foundation for

From The Lenin Anthology by Robert C. Tucker. Copyright © 1975 by W. W. Norton & Company, Inc. Reprinted by permission of W. W. Norton & Company, Inc.

this science, and to indicate the path that must be followed in further developing and elaborating it in all its parts. It disclosed the nature of modern capitalist economy by explaining how the hire of the labourer, the purchase of labour power, conceals the enslavement of millions of propertyless people by a handful of capitalists, the owners of the land, factories, mines, and so forth. It showed that all modern capitalist development displays the tendency of large-scale production to eliminate petty production and creates conditions that make a socialist system of society possible and necessary. It taught us how to discern, beneath the pall of rooted customs, political intrigues, abstruse laws, and intricate doctrines—the *class struggle,* the struggle between the propertied classes in all their variety and the propertyless mass, the *proletariat,* which is at the head of all the propertyless. It made clear the real task of a revolutionary socialist party: not to draw up plans for refashioning society, not to preach to the capitalists and their hangers-on about improving the lot of the workers, not to hatch conspiracies, *but to organise the class struggle of the proletariat and to lead this struggle, the ultimate aim of which is the conquest of political power by the proletariat and the organization of a socialist society.* . . . .

Leading a Revolutionary Movement (1902)

I assert that it is far more difficult to unearth a dozen wise men than a hundred fools. This position I will defend, no matter how much you instigate the masses against me for my "anti-democratic" views, etc. As I have stated repeatedly, by "wise men," in connection with organisation, I mean *professional revolutionaries,* irrespective of whether they have developed from among students or working men. I assert: (1) that no revolutionary movement can endure without a stable organisation of leaders maintaining continuity; (2) that the broader the popular mass drawn spontaneously into the struggle, which forms the basis of the movement and participates in it, the more urgent the need for such an organisation, and the more solid this organisation must be (for it is much easier for all sorts of demagogues to side-track the more backward sections of the masses); (3) that such an organisation must consist chiefly of people professionally engaged in revolutionary activity; (4) that in an autocratic state, the more we *confine* the membership of such an organisation to people who are professionally engaged in revolutionary activity and who have been professionally trained in the art of combating the political police, the more difficult will it be to unearth the organisation; and (5) the *greater* will be the number of people from the working class and from the other social classes who will be able to join the movement and perform active work in it. . . . .

Proclaiming the New Soviet Government (November 1917)

Comrades, the workers' and peasants' revolution, the need of which the Bolsheviks have emphasized many times, has come to pass.

What is the significance of this revolution? Its significance is, in the first place, that we shall have a soviet government, without the participation of bourgeoisie of any kind. The oppressed masses will of themselves form a government. The old state machinery will be smashed into bits and in its place will be created a new machinery of government by the soviet organizations. From now on there is a new page in the history of Russia, and the present, third Russian revolution shall in its final result lead to the victory of Socialism.

One of our immediate tasks is to put an end to the war at once. But in order to end the war, which is closely bound up with the present capitalistic system, it is necessary to overthrow capitalism itself. In this work we shall have the aid of the world labor movement, which has already begun to develop in Italy, England, and Germany.

A just and immediate offer of peace by us to the international democracy will find everywhere a warm response among the international proletariat masses. In order to secure the confidence of the proletariat, it is necessary to publish at once all secret treaties.

In the interior of Russia a very large part of the peasantry has said: Enough playing with the capitalists; we will go with the workers. We shall secure the confidence of the peasants by one decree, which will wipe out the private property of the landowners. The peasants will understand that their own salvation is in union with the workers.

We will establish a real labor control on production.

We have now learned to work together in a friendly manner, as is evident from this revolution. We have the force of mass organization which has conquered all and which will lead the proletariat to world revolution.

We should now occupy ourselves in Russia in building up a proletarian socialist state.

Long live the world-wide socialistic revolution.

Modernizing Russia (1920)

The essential feature of the present political situation is that we are now passing through a crucial period of transition, something of a zigzag transition from war to economic development. This has occurred before, but not on such a wide scale. This should constantly remind us of what the general political tasks of the Soviet government are, and what constitutes the particular feature of this transition. The dictatorship of the proletariat has been successful because it has been able to combine compulsion with persuasion. The dictatorship of the proletariat does not fear any resort to compulsion and to the most severe, decisive and ruthless forms of coercion by the state. The advanced class, the class most oppressed by capitalism, is entitled to use compulsion, because it is doing so in the interests of the working and exploited people, and because it possesses means of compulsion and persuasion such as no former classes ever possessed, although they had incomparably greater material facilities for propaganda and agitation than we have.

• • •

We have, no doubt, learnt politics; here we stand as firm as a rock. But things are bad as far as economic matters are concerned. Henceforth, less politics will be the best politics. Bring more engineers and agronomists to the fore, learn from them, keep an eye on their work, and turn our congresses and conferences, not into propaganda meetings but into bodies that will verify our economic achievements, bodies in which we can really learn the business of economic development.

• • •

While we live in a small-peasant country, there is a firmer economic basis for capitalism in Russia than for communism. That must be borne in mind. Anyone who has carefully observed life in the countryside, as compared with life in the cities, knows that we have not torn up the roots of capitalism and have not undermined the foundation, the basis, of the internal enemy. The latter depends on small-scale production, and there is only one way of undermining it, namely, to place the economy of the country, including agriculture, on a new technical basis, that of modern large-scale production. Only electricity provides that basis.

Communism is Soviet power plus the electrification of the whole country. Otherwise the country will remain a small-peasant country, and we must clearly realise that. We are weaker than capitalism, not only on the world scale, but also within the country. That is common knowledge. We have realised it, and we shall see to it that the economic basis is transformed from a small-peasant basis into a large-scale industrial basis. Only when the country has been electrified, and industry, agriculture and transport have been placed on the technical basis of modern large-scale industry, only then shall we be fully victorious. . . .

I recently had occasion to attend a peasant festival held in Volokolamsk Uyezd, a remote part of Moscow Gubernia, where the peasants have electric lighting. A meeting was arranged in the street, and one of the peasants came forward and began to make a speech welcoming this new event in the lives of the peasants. "We peasants were unenlightened," he said, "and now light has appeared among us, an 'unnatural light, which will light up our peasant darkness.' " For my part, these words did not surprise me. Of course, to the non-Party peasant masses electric light is an "unnatural" light; but what we consider unnatural is that the peasants and workers should have lived for hundreds and thousands of years in such backwardness, poverty and oppression under the yoke of the landowners and the capitalists. You cannot emerge from this darkness very rapidly. What we must now try is to convert every electric power station we build into a stronghold of enlightenment to be used to make the masses electricity-conscious, so to speak.

· · ·

We must see to it that every factory and every electric power station becomes a centre of enlightenment; if Russia is covered with a dense network of electric power stations and powerful technical installations, our communist economic development will become a model for a future socialist Europe and Asia.

Last Reflections (1923)

The general feature of our present life is the following: we have destroyed capitalist industry and have done our best to raze to the ground the medieval institutions and landed proprietorship, and thus created a very small peasantry, which is following the lead of the proletariat because it believes in the results of its revolutionary work. It is not easy for us, however, to keep going until the socialist revolution is victorious in more developed countries merely with the aid of this confidence, because economic necessity . . . keeps the productivity of labour of the small and very small peasants at an extremely low level. Moreover, the international situation, too, threw Russia back and, by and large, reduced the labour productivity of the people to a level considerably below pre-war. The West-European capitalist powers, partly deliberately and partly unconsciously, did everything they could to throw us back, to utilise the elements of the Civil War in Russia in order to spread as much ruin in the country as possible. It was precisely this way out of the imperialist war that seemed to have many advantages. They argued somewhat as follows: "If we fail to overthrow the revolutionary system in Russia, we shall, at all events, hinder its progress towards socialism." And from their point of view they could argue in no other way. In the end, their problem was half-solved. They failed to overthrow the new system created by the revolution, but they did prevent it from at once taking the step forward that would have justified the forecasts of the socialists, that would have enabled the latter to develop the productive forces with enormous speed, to develop all the potentialities which, taken together, would have produced socialism; socialists would thus have proved to all and sundry that socialism contains within itself gigantic forces and that mankind had now entered into a new stage of development of extraordinarily brilliant prospects. . . .

STUDY QUESTIONS

1. What were the main features of Marxism, according to Lenin? Why was it a potent revolutionary doctrine?
2. What were Lenin's organizational contributions to revolutionary Marxism?
3. What specific issues did Lenin face as leader of communist Russia? How did they relate to Marxist goals? How and why did Lenin approach the task of industrial and technological development?
4. What was Lenin's view of the place of Russia's revolution in the larger international context? What did he think needed to happen internationally to secure revolutionary gains?
5. Do these documents provide evidence about Lenin's individual qualities as a leader? Do they help explain why he played such a decisive role in Russian history?

27

Stalin and the Soviet Union During the 1930s: Progress and Terror

Lenin's death in 1924 left a huge void at the head of the Soviet government. Gradually, however, over the next several years Joseph V. Stalin (1879–1953) emerged as the dominant force in the revolutionary regime. By the late 1920s Stalin was firmly in charge. The result was a "second revolution" during the following decade.

The key to Stalin's "revolution from above" was the all-out drive to industrialize the economy and make agriculture a collective process. These policies were accompanied by a massive expansion of schools and health-care facilities. While the net effect of these policies was to move Soviet society rapidly along the road to modernization, the human cost was enormous. Living standards in the 1930s were quite low; several million peasants are thought to have died from starvation in 1932 and 1933. In addition, political repression reached an unparalleled peak. Between 1936 and 1938, 7 or 8 million Soviet citizens—many of them dedicated communists—were arrested and imprisoned or executed. Yet industrial growth advanced rapidly, an extraordinary achievement given the lack of outside assistance. Russia proudly avoided the economic depression that slowed the capitalist world at this time, and built a solid structure of factory industry undergirded if not by high living standards at least by various welfare benefits to workers.

The two selections illustrate important aspects of Stalin's policies and their consequences. The first document is from a speech that Stalin made in 1931 at a conference of Soviet business executives. What is his basic point? How do his ideas compare with Lenin's? How might the leader of a Third World country today react to this speech? The second excerpt comes from the autobiography of Yevgeny Yevtushenko, the most famous poet in the last decades of the Soviet Union. How does Yevtushenko help us understand Soviet attitudes toward Stalin and the 1930s?

Selection 1 from J. V. Stalin, *Works*, Vol. XIII (Moscow: Foreign Languages Publishing House, 1955), pp. 38–51, 43–44. Selection 2 from *A Precocious Autobiography* by Yevgeny Yevtushenko, translated by Andrew R. MacAndrew. Copyright © 1963 by Yevgeny Yevtushenko, renewed 1991 by Yevgeny Yevtushenko. Translation copyright © 1963 by E. P. Dutton, renewed 1991 by Penguin USA. Used by permission of Dutton, a division of Penguin Putnam Inc.

1. STALIN SPEAKS IN 1931

About ten years ago a slogan was issued: "Since Communists do not yet properly understand the technique of production, since they have yet to learn the art of management, let the old technicians and engineers—the experts—carry on production, and you, Communists, do not interfere with the technique of the business; but, while not interfering, study technique, study the art of management tirelessly, in order later, on, together with the experts who are loyal to us, to become true managers of production, true masters of the business." Such was the slogan. But what actually happened? The second part of this formula was cast aside, for it is harder to study than to sign papers; and the first part of the formula was vulgarised: non-interference was interpreted to mean refraining from studying the technique of production. The result has been nonsense, harmful and dangerous nonsense, which the sooner we discard the better. . . .

It is time, high time that we turned towards technique. It is time to discard the old slogan, the obsolete slogan of non-interference in technique, and ourselves become specialists, experts, complete masters of our economic affairs. . . .

This, of course, is no easy matter; but it can certainly be accomplished. Science, technical experience, knowledge, are all things that can be acquired. We may not have them today, but tomorrow we shall. The main thing is to have the passionate Bolshevik desire to master technique, to master the science of production. Everything can be achieved, everything can be overcome, if there is a passionate desire for it.

It is sometimes asked whether it is not possible to slow down the tempo somewhat, to put a check on the movement. No, comrades, it is not possible! The tempo must not be reduced! On the contrary, we must increase it as much as is within our powers and possibilities. . . .

To slacken the tempo would mean falling behind. And those who fall behind get beaten. But we do not want to be beaten. No, we refuse to be beaten! One feature of the history of old Russia was the continual beatings she suffered because of her backwardness. She was beaten by the Mongol khans. She was beaten by the Turkish beys. She was beaten by the Swedish feudal lords. She was beaten by the Polish and Lithuanian gentry. She was beaten by the British and French capitalists. She was beaten by the Japanese barons. All beat her—because of her backwardness, because of her military backwardness, cultural backwardness, political backwardness, industrial backwardness, agricultural backwardness. They beat her because to do so was profitable and could be done with impunity. You remember the words of the pre-revolutionary poet: "You are poor and abundant, mighty and impotent, Mother Russia." Those gentlemen were quite familiar with the verses of the old poet. They beat her, saying: "You are abundant," so one can enrich oneself at your expense. They beat her, saying: "You are poor and impotent," so you can be beaten and plundered with impunity. Such is the law of the exploiters—to beat the backward and the weak. It is the jungle law of capitalism. You are backward, you are weak—therefore you are wrong; hence you can be beaten and enslaved. You are mighty—therefore you are right; hence we must be wary of you.

That is why we must no longer lag behind.

In the past we had no fatherland, nor could we have had one. But now that we have overthrown capitalism and power is in our hands, in the hands of the people, we have a fatherland, and we will uphold its independence. Do you want our socialist fatherland to be beaten and to lose its independence? If you do not want this, you must put an end to its backwardness in the shortest possible time and develop a genuine Bolshevik tempo in building up its socialist economy. There is no other way. That is why Lenin said on the eve of the October Revolution: "Either perish, or overtake and outstrip the advanced capitalist countries."

We are fifty or a hundred years behind the advanced countries. We must make good this distance in ten years. Either we do it, or we shall go under. . . .

It is said that it is hard to master technique. That is not true! There are no fortresses that Bolsheviks cannot capture. We have solved a number of most difficult problems. We have overthrown capitalism. We have assumed power. We have built up a huge socialist industry. We have transferred the middle peasants on to the path of socialism. We have already accomplished what is most important from the point of view of construction. What remains to be done is not so much: to study technique, to master science. And when we have done that we shall develop a tempo of which we dare not even dream at present.

And we shall do it if we really want to.

2. YEVGENY YEVTUSHENKO REMEMBERS HIS CHILDHOOD

I was born on July 18, 1933, in Siberia, at Zima Junction, a small place near Lake Baikal. My surname, Yevtushenko, is Ukrainian.

Long ago, at the end of the last century, my great-grandfather, a peasant from the Zhitomir Province, was deported to Siberia for having "let out the red rooster" in his landlord's house. This is the Russian peasant way of saying that he had set fire to his house. That's probably the origin of my inclination to reach for that red rooster whenever I meet anyone with a landlord's mentality.

No one in our family uttered the word "Revolution" as if he were making a speech. It was uttered quietly, gently, a shade austerely. Revolution was the religion of our family.

My grandfather, Yermolay Yevtushenko, a soldier who could barely read, was one of the organizers of the peasant movement in the Urals and in eastern Siberia. Later, under the Soviet regime he studied at a military academy, became a brigade commander, and held the important post of deputy commander of artillery in the Russian Republican Army. But even in his commander's uniform he remained the peasant he had always been and kept his religious faith in Revolution.

I last saw him in 1938. I was five then. I remember our conversation very well.

My grandfather came into my room. I had already undressed and was lying in bed. He sat down on the edge of my bed. He had in his hands a box of liqueur-filled chocolates. His eyes, usually mischievous and smiling, that night looked at me from under his gray prickly crew-cut with a tired and sad expression. He offered me the box of chocolates and then pulled a bottle of vodka out of the pocket of his cavalry breeches.

"I want us to have a drink together," he said. "You have the candy and I'll have the vodka."

He slapped the bottom of the bottle with the flat of his hand and the cork shot out. I fished a chocolate out of the box.

"What shall we drink to?" I asked, trying hard to sound grown-up.

"To the Revolution," my grandfather said with grim simplicity.

We touched glasses—that is, my candy touched his bottle—and we drank.

"Now go to sleep," Grandfather said.

He switched off the light but remained sitting on my bed.

It was too dark for me to see his face but I felt that he was looking at me.

Then he began to sing softly. He sang the melancholy songs of the chain gangs, the songs of the strikers and the demonstrators, the songs of the Civil War.

And listening to them I went to sleep. . . .

I never saw my grandfather again. My mother told me had gone away for a long trip. I didn't know that on that very night he had been arrested on a charge of high treason. I didn't know that my mother stood night after night in that street with the beautiful name, Marine Silence Street, among thousands of other women who were also trying to find out whether their fathers, husbands, brothers, sons were still alive. I was to learn all this later.

Later I also found out what had happened to my other grandfather, who similarly had vanished. He was Rudolph Gangnus, a round-shouldered gray-bearded mathematician of Latvian origin, whose textbooks were used to teach geometry in Soviet schools. He was arrested on a charge of spying for Latvia.

But at this time I knew nothing.

I went with my father and mother to watch the holiday parades, organized workers' demonstrations, and I would beg my father to lift me up a little higher.

I wanted to catch sight of Stalin.

And as I waved my small red flag, riding high in my father's arms about that sea of heads, I had the feeling that Stalin was looking right at me.

I was filled with a terrible envy of those children my age lucky enough to be chosen to hand bouquets of flowers to Stalin and whom he gently patted on the head, smiling his famous smile into his famous moustache.

To explain away the cult of Stalin's personality by saying simply that it was imposed by force is, to say the least, rather naive. There is no doubt that Stalin exercised a sort of hypnotic charm.

Many genuine Bolsheviks who were arrested at that time utterly refused to believe that this had happened with his knowledge, still less on his personal instructions. Some of them, after being tortured, traced the words "Long live Stalin" in their own blood on the walls of their prison.

Did the Russian people understand what was really happening?

I think the broad masses did not. They sensed intuitively that something was wrong, but no one wanted to believe what he guessed at in his heart. It would have been too terrible.

The Russian people preferred to work rather than to think and to analyze. With a heroic, stubborn self-sacrifice unprecedented in history they built power station after power station, factory after factory. They worked in a furious desperation, drowning with the thunder of machines, tractors, and bulldozers the cries that might have reached them across the barbed wire of Siberian concentration camps.

STUDY QUESTIONS

1. What are Stalin's main goals? What do they have to do with Marxism? What other ideologies does he reflect?
2. How do Stalin's goals for a revolutionary Russia compare with Lenin's? What are the main similarities and differences?
3. Why was Stalin so insistent on communist mastery of technique and science? What problems was he addressing? What results did this approach have in the actual framework for Soviet industrialization and research?
4. What did Stalinism come to mean to Yevtushenko? How did this Stalinism compare with the approach outlined in Stalin's speech—were there any connections?
5. How does Yevtushenko explain the lack of resistance to political oppression?

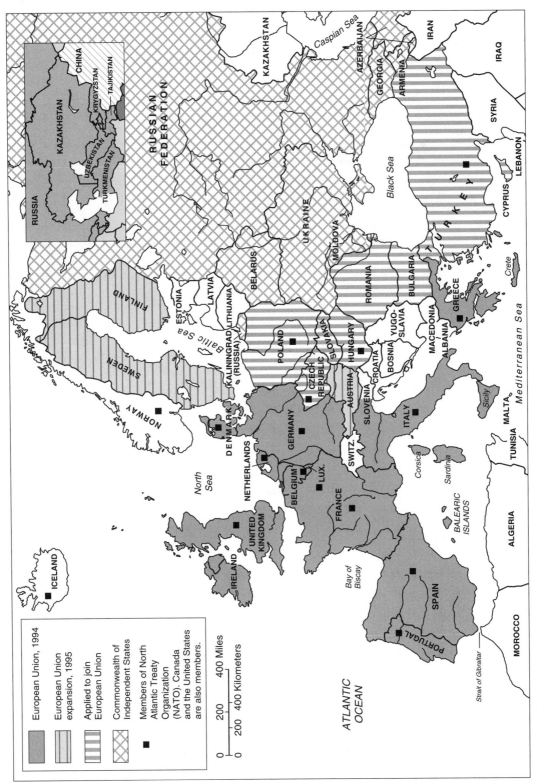

Present-Day Europe

28

The Collapse of the Soviet Union

Between 1985 and 1991, the Soviet system collapsed, and part of the even older Russian empire fell apart as well. This was one of the signal developments of the late twentieth century. It had repercussions that will almost surely persist for decades in terms of the future political and economic systems of Russia and other successor states and world diplomatic alignments given the end of Soviet–United States cold war rivalries.

Change began when Mikhail Gorbachev was named to the top leadership position in the Soviet Union, as first secretary of the Communist Party. Gorbachev was the first leader selected of his generation, and he had a different vantage point from older Bolsheviks. More important, he faced a number of crucial economic problems, after several post-World War II decades in which Soviet industrial growth had seemed quite strong. Workers' motivation was weakening, in part because of the absence of satisfactory consumer goods. Growing alcoholism and massive environmental problems were damaging health. Military expenditures, part of the cold war competition, were consuming up to a third of the total national product, limiting other kinds of investment and output. Gorbachev was firmly wedded to a socialist vision, but he argued that the Soviet version of this vision required massive transformation. Greater freedom for criticism and commentary was essential—what Gorbachev called *glasnost*—along with a restructuring of management to provide greater flexibility and motivation (*perestroika*), including more participation in the international economy.

Gorbachev's reforms unleashed a massive process of change, although political results accelerated more rapidly than economic shifts. New parties began to compete in elections. Eastern European countries in the Soviet empire began to insist on greater autonomy and then, by 1989, on abolition of the communist system. Hungary and Poland installed noncommunist governments in 1988, and other countries followed. Then in 1990 and 1991 regions within the Soviet Union began to press for independence, led by the three Baltic states—Latvia, Lithuania, and Estonia—which headed a parade that soon included key areas in Central Asia as well.

Many Soviet leaders were appalled at this process, and in August 1991, several organized a coup that imprisoned Gorbachev in his summer home. Led by a self-styled leader of democracy, Boris Yeltsin, the coup was thwarted; but Gorbachev re-

All selections from *The Soviet System: From Crisis to Collapse*, edited by Alexander Dallin and Gail W. Lapidus (Boulder, Colo.: Westview Press, 1994), pp. 284–287, 569–573, 644–646.

signed his position, now as president under a new constitution, at the end of the year. The process of change continued, both in Russia and in the newly independent nations. Market economies gained ground, although often with considerable disruption and hardship, against the old state-run operations. Efforts to revise international relations and internal political arrangements continued as well, with many uncertainties about ultimate outcomes.

The three selections illustrate key aspects of the Soviet crisis. In the first document, from 1986, Gorbachev explains his initial reform policies to a regional Communist Party meeting in the Asian city of Khabarovsk. In the second document, Vladimir Kryuchov, head of the KGB (the secret police), outlines pressing concerns about Soviet stability in a secret memo to Gorbachev in 1991, as the Soviet Union had already begun to break apart. Kryuchov was at this point a communist conservative, hoping to stem the tide of reform; he would later be a leader of the anti-Gorbachev coup and was arrested and expelled from the KGB after the plot failed. Finally, the third document stems from Gorbachev's resignation speech on December 25, 1991. Following his resignation the heads of the component Soviet Republics voted to dissolve the USSR and form the much looser Commonwealth of Independent States in its stead, and Boris Yeltsin assumed the leadership of the new Russian state.

The end of the Soviet system was as dramatic as its beginning in the 1917 revolution, and as significant in terms of larger world history. Seldom does a structure seemingly so well-established unravel so completely. Documents provide crucial insight into how reforms turned into collapse, and why the tide could not be turned back.

1. GORBACHEV AND REFORM (1986)

. . . None of us can continue living in the old way. This is obvious. In this sense, we can say that a definite step toward acceleration has been made.

However, there is a danger that the first step will be taken as success, that we will assume that the whole situation has been taken in hand. I said this in Vladivostok. I want to say it again in Khabarovsk. If we were to draw this conclusion, we would be making a big mistake, an error. What has been achieved cannot yet satisfy us in any way. In general, one should never flatter oneself with what has been accomplished. All of us must learn this well. Such are the lessons of the past decades—the last two, at least. And now this is especially dangerous.

No profound qualitative changes that would reinforce the trend toward accelerated growth have taken place as yet. In general, comrades, important and intensive work lies ahead of us. To put it bluntly, the main thing is still to come. Our country's Party, the entire Party, should understand this well. . . .

We should learn as we go along, accomplishing new tasks. And we must not be afraid of advancing boldly, of doing things on the march, in the course of the active accomplishment of economic and social tasks. . . .

Restructuring is a capacious word. I would equate the word restructuring with the word revolution. Our transformations, the reforms mapped out in the decisions of the April plenary session of the Party Central Committee and the 27th CPSU (Communist Party of the Soviet Union) Congress, are a genuine revolution in the entire system of relations in society, in the minds and hearts of people, in the psychology and understanding of the present period and, above all, in the tasks engendered by rapid scientific and technical progress.

There is a common understanding in the CPSU and in the country as a whole—we should look for answers to the questions raised by life not outside of socialism but within the framework of our system, disclosing the potential of a planned economy, socialist democracy and culture and the human factor, and relying on the people's vital creativity.

Some people in the West do not like this. There everyone lies in wait for something that would mean a deviation from socialism, for us to go hat in hand to capitalism, for us to borrow its methods. We are receiving a great deal of "advice" from abroad as to how and where we should proceed. Various kinds of provocative broadcasts are made, and articles are published, aimed at casting aspersions on the changes taking place in our country and at driving a wedge between the Party leadership and the people. Such improper attempts are doomed to failure. The interests of the Party and the people are inseparable, and our choice and political course are firm and unshakable. On this main point, the people and the Party are united.

But we also cannot allow ingrained dogmas to cloud our eyes, to impede our progress and keep us from creatively elaborating theory and applying it in practice, in the given, concrete historical stage through which our society is passing. We cannot allow this, either.

I am saying this also because among us there are still, of course, people who have difficulty in accepting the world "restructuring" [perestroika] and who even sometimes can pronounce it only with difficulty. In this process of renewal, they often see not what it in fact contains but all but a shaking of foundations, all but a renunciation of our principles. Our political line is aimed at fully disclosing the potential and advantages of the socialist system, removing all barriers and all obstructions to our progress, and creating scope for factors of social progress.

I want to say something else. The farther we advance into restructuring, the more the complexity of this task is revealed, and the more fully the enormous scale and volume of the forthcoming work is brought out. It is becoming clearer to what extent many notions about the economy and management, social questions, statehood and democracy, upbringing and education and moral demands still lag behind today's requirements and tasks, especially the tasks of further development.

We will have to remove layer by layer, the accumulated problems in all spheres of the life of society, freeing ourselves of what has outlived its time and boldly making creative decisions. . . .

Sometimes people ask: Well, just what is this odd business, restructuring? How do you understand it, "what do you eat it with," this restructuring? Yes, we're all for it, some say, but we don't know what to do. Many say this straight out. . . .

Restructuring proposes the creation of an atmosphere in society that will impel people to overcome accumulated inertia and indifference, to rid themselves, in work and in life, of everything that does not correspond to the principles of socialism, to our world views and way of life. Frankly, there is some work to be done here. But in this instance everyone must look first of all at himself, comrades—in the Politburo, in the primary Party organizations—and everyone must make a specific attempt to take himself in hand. In past years, we got used to some things in an atmosphere of insufficient criticism, openness and responsibility, things that do not all correspond to the principles of socialism. I apply this both to rank-and-file personnel and to officials. . . .

In general, comrades, we must change our style of work. It should be permeated with respect for the people and their opinions, with real, unfeigned closeness to them. We must actually go to people, listen to them, meet with them, inform them. And the more difficult things are, the more often we must meet with them and be with them when some task or other is being accomplished. In our country, people are responsive; they are a wonderful people, you can't find another people like them. Our people have the greatest endurance. Our people have the greatest political activeness. And now it is growing. This must be welcomed and encouraged in every way. Let us consider that we have come to an agreement on this in the Khabarovsk Party organization (*Applause.*)

In this connection, some words about public openness [glasnost]. It is sometimes said: Well, why has the Central Committee launched criticism, self-criticism and openness on such a broad scale? I can tell you that so far we have lost nothing, we have only gained. The people have felt an influx of energy; they have become bolder and more active, both at work and in public life. Furthermore, you know that all those who had been trying to circumvent our laws immediately began to quiet down. Because there is nothing stronger than the force of public opinion, when it can be put into effect. And it can be put into effect only in conditions of criticism, self-criticism and broad public openness. . . .

Incidentally, it looks as if many local newspapers in cities and provinces are keeping quiet. The central newspapers are speaking out in full voice, supporting everything good and criticizing blunders and shortcomings. But the local papers are silent. When a group of editors assembled in the Central Committee's offices, they said bluntly: "Well, you tell this to our secretaries in the city and district Party committees." And indeed, why shouldn't people know what is going on the district or the city? Why shouldn't they make a judgment on it and, if need be, express their opinion? This is what a socialism is, comrades. Are there any editors present? (*A voice:* Yes, we're here.)

I hope that the secretaries of the city and district Party committees will take our talk into account. They are the managers. These are their newspapers. We must not be afraid of openness, comrades. We are strong, and the people are in favor of socialism, the Party's policy, changes and restructuring. In general, it is impermissible to approach openness with the yardsticks of traditional short-term campaigns. Public openness is not a one-shot measure but a norm of present-day Soviet life, a continuous, uninterrupted process during which some tasks are accomplished and new tasks—as a rule, still more complicated ones—arise. (*Applause.*)

I could say the same thing about criticism and self-criticism. If we do not criticize and analyze ourselves, what will happen? For us, this is a direct requirement, a vital necessity for purposes of the normal functioning of the Party and of society. . . .

2. A SECRET POLICE REPORT (1991)

On the Political Situation in the Country

The acute political crisis which has enveloped our country threatens the fate of *perestroika*, the processes of democratization, the renewal of society. The possibility of the collapse of the unity of the USSR, the destruction of the sociopolitical and economic system has become real. Provoked by the decisions of a number of Union republics, the "war of sovereignties" has practically nullified efforts to stabilize the economy and has greatly complicated conditions for the signing of a new Union treaty. Under the influence of well-known decisions of the Congress of People's Deputies and the Supreme Soviet, the confrontations between the Center and the Union republics have received a powerful impetus. The head of the Russian parliament, together with certain forces, circles of shady business, have clearly declared their intention to create a "second Center" as a counterweight to the state political leadership of the USSR. Practically all opposition parties and movements have not failed to make use of it to strengthen their positions. National chauvinistic and separatist tendencies have increased in many regions of the country.

Events have confirmed our evaluation that the policy of appeasing the aggressive wing of the "democratic movement" is not able to forestall the spread of destructive processes and, in fact, allows the pseudo-democrats to realize unhindered their plans concerning the usurpation of power and changing the nature of the social system.

The danger of this tendency is further aggravated by the numerical growth and increasing power of illegal militarized formations. Today they have at their disposal state-of-the-art weapons, from automatic weapons and machine guns down to reactive shells. Taking into consideration this factor, social and national conflicts may assume a new character, turning into numerous hotbeds of civil war.

The outcome of the political battle in the coming months will depend on who wins the support of the bulk of the toiling population. In turn, active support of the leadership of the country, it would seem, hinges decisively on the extent of its success in averting a drastic decline in the living standard of the population. It is impossible not to take into account the fact that large social groups are poorly protected and are frequently impoverished. There exists no real possibility of improving their well-being at this time.

Taking into consideration the peculiarities of the economic structure of the USSR as well as the misapprehension by a significant portion of the population of even primitive forms of market relations, every step in the transition to a market economy demands circumspection, caution, and verification. The commitment to a forced introduction of market relations might turn out to exact an exorbitantly high price from the country. . . .

Public opinion reacts negatively to the way in which shady businessmen exploit the unfolding situation. The intensifying property stratification evokes an increase in social tensions. The process of enrichment, by its internal logic, draws shady business into the battle for political influence, so that within the framework of privatization it may further broaden the scope for property accumulation. That inevitably leads to the creation of a category of "new bourgeoisie" with all that it entails. . . .

The reality is such that the United States is working towards the collapse of the USSR as a superpower. In political circles of the United States the predominant opinion is that the weakening of the Soviet Union—down to the secession of a series of republics, above all the Baltics—is in the American national interest. The departure of Lithuania, for example, would in turn make the prospect of losing the Kaliningrad oblast quite real.

Taking into account this situation, we can scarcely count on significant financial and economic help from the United States. According to reliable information, the United States is putting pressure on Japan and Western Europe to limit the possible scale of their cooperation with the USSR. One should also be aware of the fact that even extensive help from the West would not, in itself, be sufficient to extricate this country from its economic crisis. . . .

The anticonstitutional forces, acting according to a scenario worked out with the participation of Western experts, view the present moment as favorable for the organization of a frontal attack on the existing governmental and social structures of the Soviet state. The leading role in this belongs to the organizationally formed block of opposition forces "Democratic Russia" (DR), whose political precepts the leadership of the Supreme Soviet of the [Russian Federation] [Boris Yeltsin] is trying to realize.

With the formation of the governing organs of DR, the task of "transforming the soviets on all levels into instruments of the opposition" has moved into the realm of practicality, as is the imminent winning to its side of the vast majority of the population. Measures are being taken for the creation of the cells of DR in industrial enterprises, in state institutions, and colleges. The attention "Democrats" pay to engineering and technical personnel, as well as to the working class as a whole, is growing, inasmuch as expectations of an "elite coup" by the humanitarian [cultural] intelligentsia have not been fulfilled. Opposition leaders have embarked on the formation of a party built on the foundation of DR that would be capable of pushing the CPSU out of the political area. It is assumed that it will be headed by the most prominent leaders among the "Democrats" and will become de facto the leading force in the alignment of political forces both in the Supreme Soviet of the RSFSR and in the soviets of a number of large republican centers. . . .

Supporters of the "Democrats" are taking persistent measures to extend their influence in the army, striving to neutralize it as one of the guarantors of the unity of the USSR and the integrity of the constitutional system. On the other hand, the recent events in the Baltic republics have had a very negative effect on the morale of the troops and have strengthened, especially among the officer corps, doubts about the ability of the country's leadership to keep the situation under control.

The escalation of the propaganda war that is being waged by the anticommunists against their own people, and the increased material means at their disposal (including the drawing in of shady capital), are devastating for the unity of the USSR and for Soviet society. The conquest of one propaganda organ after another is under way, and when that fails, they create new ones. Within just the last month in Russia, more specifically in Moscow, four substantial new publications have begun to appear and two radio stations have begun to broadcast. Western specialists are drawn into the activity in the sphere of psychological warfare (Radio Liberty, the NTS publishing company "Posev," etc.).

Official Soviet propaganda unjustifiably delays the unfolding of a powerful propaganda offensive. The question of preparing for the all-Union referendum on the preservation of the USSR reveals most graphically the imbalance in the propaganda war: While the "democratic press" decided to disparage the referendum as soon as it was announced, the central and party-controlled mass media have carried virtually no serious features on its behalf.

The interests of the Soviet constitutional system insistently dictate essential state control over the mass media and the inadmissibility of watering down its personnel, much less its transformation into a mouthpiece for antisocialist forces.

An analysis of the unfolding situation demands serious and critical comprehension of the extent to which the concepts of democratization and *glasnost* formulated six years ago have currently been implemented in practice. It is impossible not to see that antisocialist circles have, at a given stage, succeeded in replacing their contents, imposing upon society a vision of *perestroika,* not as the renewal of socialism but as the inexorable return into the "mainstream of world civilization"—capitalism. The thesis of the "illegality of the October Revolution" [of 1917] is being promoted. Democratization and *glasnost* come to be seen as the elimination of any limitations on political insinuations and unbridled slander under the flag of "freedom of speech." The cynical manipulation of public opinion shows with particular clarity in the firmly established "double standards," in accordance with which even the criminal actions of "democratic leaders" (down to the use of bloody coercion in Lithuania, Latvia, and Georgia) are unconditionally justified or hushed up, whereas the actions of the authorities in restoring order and constitutional norms are decried wholesale as illegal and dictatorial.

According to incoming information, an understanding of the dire consequences that the lingering crisis in the CPSU will have for the country is growing among the population. It is clear that the weakening of ideological work in defense of the socialist ideal cannot be made up by any other political force. Although the opposition is able to appeal to the personal interests of the average person, Party propaganda is still fumbling about for ways to conduct mass agitational work.

The failures of a series of recent provocative actions of the opposition—in the first place, the so-called all-Union political strike—demonstrate that it does not yet have enough reliable support among wide strata of the population. The political timidity of the "silent majority" preserves for the Party the possibility of using its indispensable advantages over the opposition, such as its extensive organizations, the propaganda apparatus, and its high intellectual potential.

With all its drama, the current situation can still be turned around, considering the unused arsenal of constructive measures. There is not a great deal of room in which to maneuver, but there is some. One must not fail to consider that, as is everywhere noted, people are tired of the hardships, stress, and social collisions and are losing their faith in the ability of the leadership to restore order. The danger arises that people will follow those who take it upon themselves to restore order.

The Supreme Soviet and the Congress of People's Deputies of the USSR, as the most constructive political institutions, can and must play an essential role in the search for a way out of the unfolding crisis. This requires protecting these organs of popular government from attacks and activating and strengthening their creative potential.

At the same time, considering the depth of the crisis and the probability of a dramatic worsening of circumstances, one cannot exclude the possibility of forming, at the appropriate moment, temporary bodies within the framework of extraordinary measures to be introduced by the President of the Supreme Soviet of the USSR.

Such a step would require powerful propaganda support, a direct address to the nation with an appeal to unity for the preservation of the USSR and the defense of the public order.

3. GORBACHEV'S RESIGNATION SPEECH (1991)

Dear compatriots! Fellow citizens! Due to the situation that has taken shape as a result of the formation of the Commonwealth of Independent States, I am ceasing my activity in the post of President of the USSR. I am making this decision out of considerations of principle.

I have firmly advocated the independence of peoples and the sovereignty of republics. But at the same time I have favored the preservation of the Union state and the integrity of the country.

Events have taken a different path. A policy line aimed at dismembering the country and disuniting the state has prevailed, something that I cannot agree with. . . .

Speaking to you for the last time as President of the USSR, I consider it necessary to express my assessment of the path traversed since 1985. Especially since there are a good many contradictory, superficial and unobjective opinions on this score.

Fate ordained that when I became head of state it was already clear that things were not going well in the country. We have a great deal of everything—land, petroleum, gas and other natural resources—and God has endowed us with intelligence and talent, too, but we live much worse than people in the developed countries do, and we are lagging further and further behind them.

The reason was evident—society was suffocating in the grip of the command-bureaucratic system. Doomed to serve ideology and to bear the terrible burden of the arms race, it had been pushed to the limit of what was possible.

All attempts at partial reforms—and there were a good many of them—failed, one after the other. The country had lost direction. It was impossible to go on living that way. Everything had to be changed fundamentally.

That is why I have never once regretted that I did not take advantage of the position of General Secretary just to "reign" for a few years. I would have considered that irresponsible and immoral.

I realized that to begin reforms on such a scale and in such a society as ours was an extremely difficult and even risky endeavor. But even today I am convinced of the historical correctness of the democratic reforms that were begun in the spring of 1985.

The process of renewing the country and of fundamental changes in the world community proved to be much more complex than could have been surmised. However, what has been accomplished should be appraised on its merits.

Society has received freedom and has been emancipated politically and spiritually. This is the most important gain, one that we have not yet become fully aware of, and for this reason we have not yet learned to make use of freedom.

Nevertheless, work of historic significance has been done:

—The totalitarian system, which for a long time deprived the country of the opportunity to become prosperous and flourishing, has been eliminated.

—A breakthrough has been achieved in the area of democratic transformations. Free elections, freedom of the press, religious freedoms, representative bodies of power and a multiparty system have become a reality. Human rights have been recognized as the highest principle.

—Movement toward a mixed economy has begun, and the equality of all forms of ownership is being established. Within the framework of a land reform, the peasantry has begun to revive, private farming has appeared, and millions of hectares of land are being given to rural and urban people. The economic freedom of the producer has been legalized, and entrepreneurship, the formation of joint-stock companies and privatization have begun to gather momentum.

—In turning the economy toward a market, it is important to remember that this is being done for the sake of human beings. In this difficult time, everything possible must be done for their social protection, and this applies especially to old people and children.

We are living in a new world:

—An end has been put to the cold war, and the arms race and the insane militarization of the country, which disfigured our economy and the public consciousness and morals, have been halted. The threat of a world war has been removed.

I want to emphasize once again that, for my part, during the transitional period I did everything I could to preserve reliable control over nuclear weapons.

—We opened up to the world and renounced interference in the affairs of others and the use of troops outside the country's borders. And in response we received trust, solidarity and respect.

—We have become one of the main bulwarks in the reorganization of present-day civilization on peaceful, democratic principles.

—Peoples and nations have received real freedom in choosing the path of their self-determination. Searches for democratic reforms in the multinational state led us to the threshold of concluding a new Union Treaty.

All these changes required enormous effort and took place in an acute struggle, with mounting resistance from old, obsolete and reactionary forces—both the former Party-state structures and the economic apparatus—and also from our habits, ideological prejudices, and a leveling and parasitic mentality. The changes ran up against our intolerance, low level of political sophistication and fear of change.

For this reason, we lost a great deal of time. The old system collapsed before a new one had time to start working. And the crisis in society became even more exacerbated.

I know about the dissatisfaction with the present grave situation and about the sharp criticism that is being made of the authorities at all levels, and of my personal activity. But I would like to emphasize once again: Fundamental changes in such an enormous country, and one with such a legacy, could not proceed painlessly or without difficulties and upheavals. . . .

It seems vitally important to me to preserve the democratic gains of the past few years. They were achieved through suffering throughout our history and our tragic experience. Under no circumstances and on no pretext can they be given up. Otherwise, all hopes for something better will be buried. . . .

I am grateful to state, political and public figures and the millions of people abroad who understood our plans, supported them, met us halfway, and embarked on sincere cooperation with us.

I am leaving my post with a feeling of anxiety. But also with hope and with faith in you, in your wisdom and strength of spirit. We are the heirs to a great civilization, and its rebirth into a new, up-to-date and fitting life now depends on each and every one of us.

I want to thank from the bottom of my heart those who during these years stood with me for a right and good cause. Certainly some mistakes could have been avoided, and many things could have been done better. But I am sure that sooner or later our common efforts will bear fruit and our peoples will live in a prosperous and democratic society.

I wish all of you the very best.

STUDY QUESTIONS

1. What kinds of reforms did Gorbachev envisage in 1986? What problems was he trying to address? What did he mean by "restructuring" and "public openness"?
2. What kinds of threats did the Secret Police highlight in 1991? How does the view of Soviet society implied here compare with Gorbachev's reform intentions? Does the report suggest the basis for Kryuchov's later attempted coup? What kind of state and society does Kryuchov seem to want?
3. What does Gorbachev say caused him to resign? What, by 1991, were his goals for Russian society, and how did they compare with the goals of 1986? How had his outlook toward the West changed?
4. From these documents, how much can be determined about the nature of and reasons for the collapse of the Soviet system? What kinds of disagreements persisted, into the 1990s, about the appropriate directions for Russian political and economic systems?

29

Ziya Gokalp: Turkish Nationalism and Western Civilization

In 1876 Sultan Abdul Hamid (reigned 1876–1909) issued the first constitution for the Ottoman Empire. The new constitution left great power in the hands of the sultan and declared that Islam was the state religion, but it also included many of the liberal provisions in European constitutions of the time—the promise of a free press and free education, equitable taxation, and elections for the lower house of a new bicameral legislature. The fondest dreams of the Tanzimat reformers (see Chapter 17) seemed to have been fulfilled.

However, the hopes of the Ottoman reformers that the sultans could lead the way toward the renewal of the Ottoman state were soon dashed. When the new parliament was convened, many of the delegates called for further changes. Becoming fearful that events would spin out of his control, the Sultan set aside the constitution, dismissed the parliament, and halted all efforts at further reform. The Tanzimat reform movement was dead.

The Ottoman state now lurched toward disintegration. As nationalism spread in the Balkans, the Turks were drawn into wars that they could neither afford nor win. The Balkan wars and a corrupt system of taxation drained the Ottoman treasury, forcing the Turks to borrow heavily from European banks. Ottoman foreign trade was by now almost entirely controlled by European merchants, a result of the sultans' long-standing policy of selling trade privileges to foreigners as a way of replenishing the depleted state treasury.

The downward spiral of the Ottoman state led, almost inevitably, to the rise of Turkish nationalism. During the 1890s groups of political activists who called themselves "Young Turks" began to explore what it meant to be a Turk (as opposed to an

From *Turkish Nationalism and Western Civilization: Selected Essays of Ziya Gokalp*, translated and edited by Niyazi Berkes (New York: Columbia University Press, 1959), pp. 259–262, 276–277, 310–311. Reprinted by permission.

Ottoman) and to discuss the relationship between "Turkism," Islam, and the West. In 1908 the Young Turks, aided by a military mutiny, succeeded in having the Constitution of 1876 restored. Turkish nationalists dominated the restored Ottoman parliament from 1908 to 1918.

As Turkish nationalists wrestled with the issue of national identity, the Ottoman state finally collapsed in the carnage of the First World War (which, because of fiercely contested territorial disputes with the Greeks, did not really end for the Turks until 1922). In 1923 Turkey was proclaimed a republic under the presidency of Mustapha Kemal Ataturk, the general who had led the postwar expulsion of Greeks from Anatolia.

Ataturk, who led Turkey until his death in 1938, was one of the most significant Westernizers of the early twentieth century. He was opposed to Western-style political democracy, but under Ataturk's leadership the *Shari'ya* (the traditional Muslim legal code) was replaced by a secular system of laws, a program of industrialization was launched, the Arabic alphabet was abandoned in favor of the Roman one, and political rights were extended to women. By the time Ataturk died the Republic of Turkey seemed well on its way to establishing itself as a successful model of modernity for the rest of the Middle East.

The selections that follow come from the writings of Ziya Gokalp (1876–1924), the most creative Turkish thinker of the late Ottoman–early republican period. Gokalp's ideas, especially his plea for the Westernization of Turkey, were widely discussed by his contemporaries and strongly influenced the shaping of public policy during the Ataturk years. The passages below come from essays written by Gokalp in 1923.

1. ON TURKISM

One of the fundamental principles of Turkism is the drive towards 'going to the people'. . . . What is meant by going to the people? Who are to go to these people?

The intellectuals and the thinkers of a nation constitute its élite. The members of the élite are separated from the masses by their higher education and learning. It is they who ought to go to the people. But why? Some would answer: in order to carry culture to the masses. But, as we have shown elsewhere, culture is something which is alive only among the people themselves. The élite are those who lack it. Then, how can the élite, lacking culture, carry culture to the common people who are a living embodiment of culture?

To answer the question, let us first answer the following questions: what do the élite and the people have? The élite are the carriers of civilization and the people the holders of culture. Therefore, the élite's approach to the people should only have the following two purposes: to receive a training in culture from the people and to carry civilization to them. Yes, it is only with these two purposes that the élite should go to the people. The élite will find culture only there and nowhere else. . . .

The élite do not acquire national culture through education from childhood. The schools in which they study are not the people's schools or national schools. Our élite get their education without acquiring national culture. Their education merely serves to denationalize them. They need to compensate the shortcoming by mixing with the people, by living with them, by learning their language, by observing the way they use their vernacular, by listening to their proverbs, their traditional wit and wisdom, by noting their mode of thinking and their style of feeling, by listening to their poetry and music, by seeing their plays and dances, by penetrating into their religiosity and morality, by tasting beauty in the simplicity of their clothes, their architecture, and their furniture. They should learn the folk-tales, anecdotes, epics, and beliefs, which are survivals from the ancient *töre*. . . . They should read their books, the books of the minstrels from Korkut Ata onwards, the hymns of mystics from Yunus Emre onwards, the people's humour from Nasreddin Hoca onwards, and discover the *karagöz* [shadow plays] and the *ortaoyunu* [open-air plays]. They have to find the old coffee-houses of the people where epics are being read, experience the nights of the holy month, the Friday communal feast gatherings, the religious holidays to which children look forward with so much enthusiasm. They have to build national museums in which works of art of the people will be exhibited.

It is only this way, only through such a contact with the national folk culture, and only by saturating their souls with the Turkish culture that the élite of the Turkish nation will nationalize themselves. It was through such a national education that Pushkin became the national poet of the Russians. Men like Dante, Petrarch, Rousseau, Goethe, Schiller, D'Annunzio became great creators of art and literature only because they had received their inspirations from the people.

As sociology has shown, genius is hidden in the people. An artist becomes a genius only because he becomes a manifestation of the aesthetic taste of the people. The reason why we lack great artists is that our men of art do not receive their aesthetic inspirations from the living museum of the people. No one, so far, has valued the art of the people. The old Ottoman élite scorned the peasant as 'stupid Turk'; the people of Anatolia were ridiculed as 'outsiders'; the title given to the people was 'vulgar.' The 'refined' were the Ottoman élite, who were the slaves of the court. As they had despised the people, nothing in language, poetry, literature, music, philosophy, ethics, politics, and economics has survived from the heritage of this ancient élite. The Turkish people have to start again from ABC. They did not even have a name as a nation until recently. The *Tanzimat*ists said to them: 'You are Ottomans. Don't claim a national existence distinct from other nations. If you do, you will cause the destruction of the Ottoman Empire.' The poor Turk, scared to lose his fatherland, had to say: 'By God, I am not a Turk, I am nothing but an Ottoman.'

But the Ottomanists could not see that in spite of whatever they did, foreign [non-Turkish] nations would do their best to secede from the Ottoman Commonwealth because such artificial commonwealths composed of several nations could no longer survive. Each nation would be independent and would have its own homogeneous, genuine, natural social life. This trend of social evolution, which had started in Western Europe five centuries earlier, certainly would start in Eastern Europe too. The downfall of the Austro-Hungarian, Russian, and Ottoman Empires after the [first] World War has shown that this is very near. What would be the fate of the Turks once they faced this catastrophe without a realization that they themselves were a nation, that they too had their own home and their rights in the Ottoman Empire? Were they to say: 'As the Ottoman Empire fell, we do not have national hope, or political aspiration any more?' When the Wilsonian points were known, certain conscientious Ottomanists, who until then had remained indifferent to Turkism, began to say: 'What would be our state today if Turkism had not taught many of us that we had a national home ethnographically drawn, a national existence independent of the Ottoman Empire, a national right to rule in this home in complete independence?' It was only one word, that sacred word Turk, which showed us the right path to be followed amidst anarchy.

Turkists not only taught the élite the name of the nation, but also the beautiful language of the nation. As the name they gave to the nation was taken from the people, this language also was taken from the people, because both had existed only among the people. The élite had been living the life of somnambulists until then. They, like somnambulists, had a dual personality. Their real personality was the Turk, but they thought themselves Ottomans under the delusions of their somnambulism. While their real language was Turkish, they talked an artificial language in their delirium. In poetry, they put aside their own metre and sang in artificial metres copied from the Persians.

Turkists, like a psychiatrist, tried to cure this split personality by making them believe that they were not Ottomans but Turks, that their language was Turkish, and that their poetry was the people's; they even demonstrated these scientifically. It was only then that the élite were cured from this abnormal state of somnambulism and began to think as normal men.

We must confess, however, that so far these men have taken only one step forward towards the people. To reach the people in a real sense, they must live amongst the people and get the national culture from the people. The only way to do this is for the nationalist youth to go to villages as schoolteachers. Those who are not young should at least go to the towns in inner Anatolia. The Ottoman élite will become a national élite only by completely assimilating the folk culture.

The second aim of going towards the people is to carry civilization to the people. The people lack civilization and the élite have its keys. But the civilization that they should carry to the people as a precious contribution will not be Oriental civilization or its offshoot, Ottoman civilization, but Western civilization, as we shall show below.

2. TOWARD WESTERN CIVILIZATION

There is only one road to salvation: To advance in order to reach—that is, in order to be equal to—Europeans in the sciences and industry as well as in military and judicial institutions. And there is only one means to achieve this: to adapt ourselves to Western civilization completely!

In the past, the makers of *Tanzimat* recognized this and set about to introduce European civilization. However, whatever they wanted to take from Europe, they always took not fully but by half. They created, for example, neither a real university nor a uniform judicial organization. Before they took measures to modernize national production, they wanted to change the habits of consuming, clothing, eating, building, and furniture. On the other hand, not even a nucleus of industry on European standards was built because the policy makers of *Tanzimat* attempted their reforms without studying conditions and without putting forth definite aims and plans. They were always taking only half-measures in whatever they attempted to do.

Another great mistake committed by the leaders of *Tanzimat* was their attempt to create a mental amalgam made up of a mixture of East and West. They failed to see that the two, with their diametrically opposed principles, could not be reconciled. The still existing dichotomy in our political structure, the dual court system, the two types of schools, the two systems of taxation, two budgets, the two sets of laws, are all products of this mistake. The dichotomies are almost endless. Religious and secular schools were not only two different institutions of education, but within each there was again the same dichotomy. Only in military and medical schools was education carried out exclusively along European lines. We owe to these institutions the generals and doctors who today save the life of the nation and the lives of the citizens. The training of specialists within these fields, in a way equal to their European colleagues, was made possible only because of the immunity of these two institutions from dichotomy. If the methods of warfare of the Janissaries or the medical practices of the old-fashioned surgeons were mixed into these modern institutions, we would not have our celebrated generals and doctors today. These two institutions of learning must be models for the educational revolution that has to materialize. Any attempt to reconcile East and West means carrying medieval conditions to the modern age and trying to keep them alive. Just as it was impossible to reconcile Janissary methods with a modern military system, just as it was futile to synchronize old-fashioned medicine with scientific medicine, so it is hopeless to carry the old and the new conceptions of law, the modern and the traditional conceptions of science, the old and the new standards of ethics, side by side. Unfortunately, only in the military arts and medicine was Janissary-ism abolished. It is still surviving in other professions as a ghost of medievalism. A few months ago, a new society was founded in Istanbul in order to bring Turkey into the League of Nations. What will be the use of it as long as Turkey does not enter definitely into European civilization? A nation condemned to every political interference by Capitulations is meant to be a nation outside of European civilization. Japan is accepted as a European power, but we are still regarded as an Asiatic nation. This is due to nothing but our non-acceptance of European civilization in a true sense. The Japanese have been able to take the Western civilization without losing their religion and national identity; they have been able to reach the level of Europeans in every respect. Did they lose their religion and national culture? Not at all! Why, then, should we still hesitate? Can't we accept Western civilization definitely and still be Turks and Muslims? . . .

3. ON THE NEED FOR A NATIONAL INDUSTRY

The modern state is based on large-scale industry. New Turkey, to be a modern state, must, above all, develop a national industry. What should we do to realize this?

The New Turkey, which has to introduce the latest and most developed techniques of Europe, cannot afford to wait for the spontaneous rise of the spirit of enterprise among individuals in order to industrialize. As we have done in the field of military techniques, we have to reach European levels in industry through a national effort. We have to start by utilizing the latest developments in European techniques, without necessarily following the stages of gradual evolution. The starting-point, for example, should be electrification. We must utilize the hydraulic power of the country and put it into an electric network. The people of Turkey, who have been able to adopt European military techniques in all their details, can learn and master the most modern industrial inventions and discoveries. Military techniques, however, were not introduced by the private initiative of individuals. This was accomplished through the state. Our medicine, which is equally advanced, was also initiated through state action. Therefore, only the state can achieve the task of introducing large-scale industry in every field. The Turkish state has the power to be an independent [national] state. Turks are temperamentally *étatists*. They expect the state to take the initiative in everything new and progressive. Even social changes are introduced through the state in Turkey, and it has been the state which has safeguarded social changes against the force of reaction.

In order that the state itself may become competent in economic enterprises, it must become an economic state. The statesmen and government employees should have economic experience and knowledge. The modern state, selecting its personnel with this point in view, is like a big business concern. . . . By following the same line, our state will, at the same time, perform a moral service because the rise of a new class of speculators will be prevented. The ambitions manifested in the Peace Conference clearly showed what a criminal people these capitalists, as they are called in Europe, are! Present-day European imperialism is based on private capitalism. If we accept the system of state capitalism, we will be able to prevent the rise of those insatiable and predatory capitalists in our country. . . .

STUDY QUESTIONS

1. According to Gokalp, what can the Turkish intellectuals learn from the Turkish people? What can the intellectuals teach the people?
2. How does Gokalp define Turkish culture?
3. What reasons does Gokalp give for his criticism of the old Ottoman elite?
4. Why does Gokalp think that the Turks must adapt themselves to Western civilization?
5. What is Gokalp's view of the Tanzimat reforms? (See Chapter 17.)
6. How do Gokalp's ideas compare with those of his contemporaries such as Lenin, Stalin, Sun Yat-sen, and Gandhi? (See Chapters 26, 27, 32 and 35.)
7. Must societies industrialize in order to achieve well-being?
8. What is a nation?
9. Why did Ataturk-type reforms become less attractive to the people of the Middle East during the late twentieth century? (See Chapter 31.)

30

Middle Eastern Dreams in Conflict: The Views of an Early Zionist and a Palestinian Refugee

The Arab-Israeli conflict that has so embittered the people of the Middle East for the past half century is rooted in two powerful and contradictory claims to the same "homeland," each side invoking history and love of the land in defense of its position. Beginning in the 1890s European Jews, responding to anti-Semitic prejudice, organized the Zionist movement in order to establish a "national home" in Palestine. At that time Palestine was a part of the Ottoman Empire and inhabited largely by Arabs. The proclamation of the state of Israel in 1948 was the realization of the Zionist dream.

Palestine, however, had been a part of the Arab and Muslim world since the seventh century. Palestinian Arabs resented the coming of the Zionists, and they opposed the founding of the new Jewish state. In 1948 and 1949, after the Israeli army defeated its Arab neighbors in the first Arab-Israeli War, hundreds of thousands of Palestinians went into exile. The vow of the Palestinians to return to their homeland constitutes a kind of Zionism in reverse.

The two selections help to illuminate the thinking of the founders of modern Israel and the Palestinian exiles. In the first document, Nahum Goldman, an early Zionist from Germany, discusses his first visit to Palestine. In the second document, Fawaz Turki remembers his family's flight from Palestine in 1948 and his childhood as an exile.

1. NAHUM GOLDMAN

As I have said, I was not a very diligent student and spent a lot of time during the academic year with my parents in Frankfurt and in excursions to the Odenwald or the Neckar Valley. All in all my relationship to the university was not very close, and

Selection 1 from Nahum Goldman, *The Autobiography of Nahum Goldman: Sixty Years of a Jewish Life* (New York: Holt, Rinehart and Winston, 1969), pp. 38–42, 44. Copyright © 1969 by Holt, Rinehart and Winston. Reprinted by permission. Selection 2 from Fawaz Turki, *The Disinherited: Journal of a Palestinian Exile* (New York: Monthly Review Press, 1972), pp. 43–45, 47–48, 54. Copyright © 1972 by Monthly Review Press. Reprinted by permission.

when the chance of going to Palestine was offered to me in 1913, I jumped at it. A group of students was going there on a visit organized and led by Theodor Zlocisti, one of the oldest German Zionists in Berlin, a physician by profession and a man of literary interests. I was asked if I would like to go along; my expenses would be paid by a wealthy friend of the family. The trip was supposed to last four weeks, but I stayed five months and skipped a whole semester at Heidelberg. . . .

I left the group, which was returning to Germany shortly in any case, and decided really to get to know the country. Although I have been in Palestine probably more than a hundred times since then, I have never again had the opportunity to discover it at such a leisurely yet intensive pace. Free of the group's daily hikes, receptions, and ceremonies and having decided to stay several months, I could dispose of my time as I pleased.

I spent several weeks in Tel Aviv, which then consisted of only a few streets, several more in Rishon le-Zion and Rehovot, and a week in Rosh Pina in Galilee. But most of the time I spent in Jerusalem, where I rented, in what was then the Russian apartment-house complex, a romantic attic with a balcony. I used to sleep on the balcony when the weather got warm.

A detailed account of [Jewish] colonization in those days is beyond the scope of this book, but it was all in quite a primitive stage, except for a few old-established settlements such as Petah Tiqva, Rishon le-Zion, and one or two others. I was especially impressed by kibbutzim, such as Deganyah and Kinneret, and by the type of young *halutz*, or pioneer, Zionists I encountered for the first time. In Jerusalem I tried to get to know the old *yishuv*, the pre-Zionist Orthodox Jewish community, as well as the new one and had some very impressive encounters with kabbalists and mystics in the Meah Sherim quarter of Jerusalem. . . .

I often used to take long moonlight rides with friends and once, on our way back, we were surrounded by a Bedouin band. They would certainly have robbed us and left us naked on the road if one of my companions, who was familiar with the country, had not advised us to act naturally, to sing and occasionally pat our hip pockets as if we were carrying guns. Apparently this produced the desired effect. After riding along with us for about ten minutes, the Bedouin suddenly scattered. Another time I found myself in a precarious situation when my Arab guide in Jericho arranged for me to be a hidden spectator at an Arab wedding and at the bride's dancing—something forbidden to foreigners under Bedouin law. I had already watched several dances, unforgettable in their wild passion, when my guide rushed up to me, pale with fear, and said that one of the bride's relatives had noticed something and was looking for me. We disappeared as fast as we could and got back to the hotel before it was too late. . . .

But even more than the people and the early achievements of Jewish colonization, the country itself impressed me. Never again was Palestine to have such an impact upon me. For one thing I was younger and more sensitive to such impressions and less distracted by other responsibilities than I was during later visits. The exceptional quality of this curious little territory, which has acquired a unique significance in human history not to be explained by its natural resources or geopolitical situation—what I would like to call its mystical meaning—was brought home to me then as never again. Later it became much more difficult to sense that special aura; one was too distracted by what was happening in and to the country. But at that time

Palestine was still untouched. You felt the presence of the mountains without having to think about the settlements that would be established on them. You rode across the plains unmarred by buildings and highways. You traveled very slowly; there were no cars and only a few trains; you usually rode on horseback or in a cart. It took two days to get from Haifa to Jerusalem. One saw the country clearly as if emerging from thousands of years of enchantment. The clearness of the air, the brilliance of the starry sky, the mystery of the austere mountains, made it seem as though its history had grown out of the landscape. In those days it was an extraordinarily peaceful, idealistic country, absorbed in a reverie of its own unique past. In the atmosphere lingered something of the prophets and the great Talmudists, of Jesus and the Apostles, of the Safed kabbalists, and the singers of bygone centuries. . . .

When I left Palestine my Zionism had been enriched by a momentous factor, the country itself. Until then Zionism had been an abstract idea to me, and I had no real conception of what the return of the Jews meant in any concrete sense. My visit gave me that feeling for the soil without which Zionism is bound to remain quite unsubstantial. From then on I began to understand what it means, not merely negatively in terms of leaving the Diaspora behind, but also positively, as a new beginning in a Jewish homeland.

2. FAWAZ TURKI

A breeze began to blow as we moved slowly along the coast road, heading to the Lebanese border—my mother and father, my two sisters, my brother and I. Behind us lay the city of Haifa, long the scene of bombing, sniper fire, ambushes, raids, and bitter fighting between Palestinians and Zionists. Before us lay the city of Sidon and indefinite exile. Around us the waters of the Mediterranean sparkled in the sun. Above us eternity moved on unconcerned, as if God in his heavens watched the agonies of men, as they walked on crutches, and smiled. And our world had burst, like a bubble, a bubble that had engulfed us within its warmth. From then on I would know only crazy sorrow and watch the glazed eyes of my fellow Palestinians burdened by loss and devastated by pain.

April 1948. And so it was the cruelest month of the year; but there were crueler months, then years. . . .

After a few months in Sidon, we moved again, a Palestinian family of six heading to a refugee camp in Beirut, impotent with hunger, frustration, and incomprehension. But there we encountered other families equally helpless, equally baffled, who like us never had enough to eat, never enough to offer books and education to their children, never enough to face an imminent winter. In later years, when we left the camp and found better housing and a better life outside and grew up into our early teens, we would complain about not having this or that and would be told by our mothers: "You are well off, boy! Think of those still living there in the camps. Just think of them and stop making demands." We would look out the window and see the rain falling and hear the thunder. And we would remember. We would understand. We would relent as we thought "of those still living there."

Man adapts. We adapted, the first few months, to life in a refugee camp. In the adaptation we were also reduced as men, as women, as children, as human beings. At times we dreamed. Reduced dreams. Distorted ambitions. One day, we hoped, our parents would succeed in buying two beds for me and my sister to save us the agonies of asthma, intensified from sleeping on blankets on the cold floor. One day, we hoped, there would be enough to buy a few pounds of pears or apples as we had done on those special occasions when we fought and sulked and complained because one of us was given a smaller piece of fruit than the others. One day soon, we hoped, it would be the end of the month when the UNRWA rations arrived and there was enough to eat for a week. One day soon, we argued, we would be back in our homeland.

The days stretched into months and those into a year and yet another. Kids would play in the mud of the winters and the dust of the summers, while "our problem" was debated at the UN and moths died around the kerosene lamps. A job had been found for me in a factory not far from the camp, where I worked for six months. I felt pride in the fact that I was a bread earner and was thus eligible to throw my weight around the house, legitimately demand an extra spoonful of sugar in my tea, and have my own money to spend on comic books and an occasional orange on the side. I had even started saving to buy my own bed, but I was fired soon after that.

A kid at work had called me a two-bit Palestinian and a fist fight ensued. The supervisor, an obese man with three chins and a green stubble that covered most of his face and reached under his eyes, came over to stop the fight. He decided I had started it all, slapped me hard twice, deducted three lira from my wages for causing trouble (I earned seven lira a week), paid me the rest, called me a two-bit Palestinian, and, pointing to my blond hair, suggested I had a whore mother and shoved me out the door.

I went to the river and sat on the grass to eat my lunch. I was shaken more by the two-bit Palestinian epithet than by the plight of being unemployed. At home and around the camp, we had unconsciously learned to be proud of where we came from and to continue remembering that we were Palestinians. If this was stigmatic outside, there it was an identity to be known, perpetuated, embraced. My father, reproaching us for an ignoble offense of some kind, would say: "You are a Palestinian." He would mean: as a Palestinian one is not expected to stoop that low and betray his tradition. If we came home affecting a Lebanese accent, our mother would say: "Hey, what's wrong with your own accent? You're too good for your own people or something? You want to sound like a foreigner when we return to Haifa? What's wrong with you, hey?"

· · ·

Our Palestinian consciousness, instead of dissipating, was enhanced and acquired a subtle nuance and a new dimension. It was buoyed by two concepts: the preservation of our memory of Palestine and our acquisition of education. We persisted in refusing the houses and monetary compensation offered by the UN to settle us in our host countries. We wanted nothing sort of returning to our homeland. And from Syria, Lebanon, and Jordan, we would see, a few miles, a few yards, across the border, a land where we had been born, where we had lived, and where we felt the earth. "This is my land," we would shout, or cry, or sing, or plead, or reason. And to that land a people had come, a foreign community of colonizers, aided by a Western world in a hurry to rid itself of guilt and shame, demanding independence from history, from heaven, and from us.

STUDY QUESTIONS

1. Why did Nahum Goldman decide to go to Palestine in 1913 and to remain there after his friends returned home to Germany?
2. What kinds of contacts did Goldman have with Palestinian Arabs?
3. What did Goldman's first visit to Palestine mean to him?
4. What does Fawaz Turki reveal about the standard of living in the Palestinian refugee camps?
5. What attitudes did Turki encounter among the Arabs in the host countries where the refugee camps were located?
6. According to Turki, what explains the growing strength of Palestinian nationalism? What do you think of his view that the Western world is partly responsible for the conflicts in the Middle East?
7. How do the conflicts between Israelis and Palestinians compare with the conflicts between Hindus and Muslims in south Asia? (See the passages from Maulvi Syed Kutb Shah Sahib in Chapter 16 and also Chapters 35 and 36.)
8. What is the relationship between Israeli and Palestinian nationalism and nationalism in other parts of the world? (See Chapter 29 on Turkey, Chapter 32 on China, Chapter 35 on India, Chapter 36 on Pakistan, Chapter 38 on Latin America, and Chapter 40 on Africa.)
9. What has been the trend since the beginning of the twentieth century regarding conflicts between people of different nationalities and religions? Have the conflicts increased, stayed the same, or decreased? How do you explain this?

31

The Resurgence of Islam

One of the most important developments in the world during recent decades has been the renewed vitality of Islam. The movement began in the original Islamic heartland of west Asia and North Africa, but it quickly spread in all directions, reaching countries such as Indonesia, Afghanistan, and Senegal, as well as numerous cities in Europe and the Americas.

The readings in this chapter concentrate on the Middle East, where the revitalization of Islam began and where it has had the biggest impact. In this region for the past several decades mosque attendance has been increasing, Islamic literature has proliferated, traditional Islamic dress for women has been in favor, and the popularity of Muslim student organizations in universities has risen sharply.

Islam has also made a dramatic imprint on the political life of the Middle East, most notably in Iran, where in 1979 Shiite Muslims took power and established an Islamic republic (a development that is illustrated in the second selection). In Egypt, Algeria, and Turkey—three key countries in the region with strong traditions of secular rule—powerful grassroots Islamic movements are bidding for political power. In addition, the Palestinian national movement, whose origins were more political than religious (see Chapter 30), has become increasingly influenced by Islam.

The first of the selections is by Hasan al-Banna (1906–1949), the Egyptian activist who founded the Muslim brotherhood, a secret organization that has had a major impact on the politics of the Middle East since the Second World War. The product of an earlier period, al-Banna's ideas nevertheless anticipate and underlie the thinking of many present-day Muslim intellectuals in the Middle East. In the second selection Ayatullah Murtada Mutahhari, a leader of the 1979 Iranian revolution, sheds light on the thinking of the revolution's leadership.

1. HASAN AL-BANNA (CA. 1949)

When we observe the evolution in the political, social, and moral spheres of the lives of nations and peoples, we note that the Islamic world—and, naturally, in the forefront, the Arab world—gives to its rebirth an Islamic flavor. This trend is ever-increasing. Until recently, writers, intellectuals, scholars, and governments glorified the principles of European civilization, gave themselves a Western tint, and adopted a European style and manner; today, on the contrary, the wind has changed, and reserve and distrust have taken their place. Voices are raised proclaiming the necessity for a return to the principles, teachings, and ways of Islam, and, taking into account the situation, for initiating the reconciliation of modern life with these principles, as a prelude to a final "Islamization."

This development worries a good number of governments and Arab powers, which, having lived during the past generations in a state of mind that had retained from Islam only lessons of fanaticism and inertia, regarded the Muslims only as weak drudges or as nations easily exploitable by colonialism. In trying to understand the new movement . . . these governments have produced all sorts of possible interpretations: "It is the result," said some, "of the growth of extremist organizations and fanatical groups." Others explained that it was a reaction to present-day political and economic pressures, of which the Islamic nations had become aware. Finally, others said, "It is only a means whereby those seeking government or other honors may achieve renown and position."

Now all these reasons are, in our opinion, as far as possible from the truth; for this new movement can only be the result of the following three factors, which we will now examine.

The first of the three is the failure of the social principles on which the civilization of the Western nations has been built. The Western way of life—bounded in effect on practical and technical knowledge, discovery, invention, and the flooding of world markets with mechanical products—has remained incapable of offering to men's minds a flicker of light, a ray of hope, a grain of faith, or of providing anxious persons the smallest path toward rest and tranquillity. Man is not simply an instrument among others. Naturally, he has become tired of purely materialistic conditions and desires some spiritual comfort. But the materialistic life of the West could only offer him as reassurance a new materialism of sin, passion, drink, women, noisy gatherings, and showy attractions which he had come to enjoy. Man's hunger grows from day to day: he wants to free his spirit, to destroy this materialist prison and find space to breathe the air of faith and consolation.

The second factor—the decisive factor in the circumstances—is the discovery by Islamic thinkers of the noble, honorable, moral, and perfect content of the principles and rules of this religion, which is infinitely more accomplished, more pure, more glorious, more complete, and more beautiful than all that has been discovered up till now by social theorists and reformers. For a long time, Muslims neglected all this, but once God had enlightened their thinkers and they had compared the social rules of their religion with what they had been told by the greatest sociologists and the cleverest leading theorists, they noted the wide gap and the great distance between a heritage of immense value on one side and the conditions experienced on the other. Then, Muslims could not but do justice to the spirit and the history of their people, proclaiming the value of this heritage and inviting all peoples—nonpracticing Muslims or non-Muslims—to follow the sacred path that God had traced for them and to hold to a straight course.

The third factor is the development of social conditions between the two murderous world wars (which involved all the world powers and monopolized the minds of regimes, nations, and individuals) which resulted in a set of principles of reform and social organization that certain powers, in deciding to put them into practice, have taken as an instructional basis. . . .

Thus, German Nazism and Italian Fascism rose to the fore; Mussolini and Hitler led their two peoples to unity, order, recovery, power, and glory. In record time, they ensured internal order at home and, through force, made themselves feared abroad. These regimes gave real hope, and also gave rise to thoughts of steadfastness and perseverance and the reuniting of different, divided men around the words "chief" and "order." In their resolutions and speeches, the Führer and the Duce began to frighten the world and to upset their epoch. . . .

The star of socialism and Communism, symbol of success and victory, shone with an increasing brilliance; Soviet Russia was at the head of the collectivist camp. She launched her message and, in the eyes of the world, demonstrated a system which had been modified several times in thirty years. The democratic powers—or, to use a more precise expression, the colonialist powers, the old ones worn out, the new ones full of greed—took up a position to stem the current. The struggle intensified, in some places openly, in others under cover, and nations and peoples, perplexed, hesitated at the crossroads, not knowing which was best; among them were the nations of Islam and the peoples of the Qur'ān; the future, whatever the circumstances, is in the hands of God, the decision with history, and immortality with the most worthy.

This social evolution and violent, hard struggle stirred the minds of Muslim thinkers; the parallels and the prescribed comparisons led to a healthy conclusion: to free themselves from the existing state of affairs, to allow the necessary return of the nations and peoples to Islam.

2. AYATULLAH MURTADA MUTAHHARI (1979)

Scholars and knowledgeable persons in contemporary history concede that in the second half of our century in almost all or at least in a large number of Islamic countries Islamic movements have been in ascent openly or secretly. These are practically directed against despotism, capitalist colonialism or materialist ideologies subscribing to colonialism in its new shape. Experts on political affairs acknowledge that after having passed through a period of mental crisis the Muslims are once again struggling to reestablish their "Islamic identity" against the challenges of the capitalist West and the communist East. But in no Islamic country has this type of movement gained as much of depth and extent as in Iran since the year 1960. Nor is there a parallel to the proportions which the Iranian movement has obtained. It, therefore, becomes necessary to analyze this remarkably significant event of history.

Like all natural occurrences, social and political events also tend to differ from one another in their behaviours. All historical movements cannot be considered identical in their nature. The nature of the Islamic movement is in no case similar to the French revolution or to the great October revolution of Russia.

The current Iranian movement is not restricted to any particular class or trade union. It is not only a labour, an agrarian, a student, an intellectual or a bourgeois movement. Within its scope fall one and all in Iran, the rich and the poor, the man and the woman, the school boy and the scholar, the warehouse man and the factory labourer, the artisan and the peasant, the clergy and the teacher, the literate and the illiterate, one and all. An announcement made by the preceptor of the highest station guiding the movement is received in the length and breadth of the country with equal enthusiasm by all classes of the people. . . .

This movement is one of the glaring historical proofs which falsifies the concept of materialistic interpretation of history and that of the dialectics of materialism according to which economy is recognised as the cornerstone of social structure and a social movement is considered a reflection of class struggle. . . .

The awakened Islamic conscience of our society has induced it to search for Islamic values. This is the conscience of the cumulative enthusiasms of all classes of people, including perhaps some of the heretofore dissident groups, which has galvanized them into one concerted upsurge.

The roots of this movement shall have to be traced in the events that occurred during the last half century in our country [during the reign of the Pahlavi shahs, 1925–1979] and the way these events came into conflict with the Islamic spirit of our society.

It is evident that during the last half century, there have been events which adopted a diametrically opposite direction as far as the nobler objectives of Islam were concerned and which aimed at nullifying the aspirations of the well-meaning reformers for the last century. This state of affairs could not continue for long without reaction.

What happened in Iran during the last half century may be summed up as under:

1. Absolute and barbaric despotism.
2. Denial of freedom of every kind.
3. A new type of colonialism meaning an invisible and dangerous colonialism embracing political, economic and cultural aspects of life.
4. Maintaining distance between religion and politics. Rather, divorcing politics from religion.
5. An attempt at leading Iran back to the age of ignorance of pre-Islamic days. . . .
6. Effecting a change and corrupting the rich Islamic culture and replacing it with the ambiguous Iranian culture.
7. Gruesome killing of Iranian Muslims, imprisonment and torture of the alleged political prisoners.
8. Ever increasing discrimination and cleavage among the classes of society despite so-called reforms.
9. Domination of non-Muslim elements over the Muslim elements in the government and other institutions.
10. Flagrant violation of Islamic laws either directly or by perpetrating corruption in the cultural and social life of the people.
11. Propaganda against Persian literature (which has always been the protector and upholder of Islamic spirit) under the pretext of purifying the Persian language of foreign terminology.
12. Severing relations with Islamic countries and flirting with non-Islamic and obviously with anti-Islamic countries like Israel.

· · ·

What is the objective pursued by the movement and what does it want? Does it aim at democracy? Does it want to liquidate colonialism from our country? Does it rise to defend what is called in modern terminology human rights? Does it want to do away with discrimination, inequality? Does it want to uproot oppression? Does it want to undo materialism and so forth and so on?

In view of the nature of the movement and its roots as already brought under consideration and also in view of the statements and announcements given out by the leaders of the movement, what one may gather as an answer to these questions is "Yes" as well as "No."

"Yes" because all the objectives mentioned above form the very crux of it. And "No" because the movement is not limited to only these or any one of these objectives. An Islamic movement cannot, from the point of its objective, remain a restricted affair, because Islam, in its very nature, is "an indivisible whole" and with the realization of any of the objectives set before it, its role does not cease to be.

· · ·

No movement can be led successfully without leadership. But who should be the leader or the group of leaders when the movement is an Islamic one in its nature and when its objective is exclusively Islam?

Evidently the leadership should, in the first place, fulfill the general conditions of the task before it. Then the leaders must be deeply Islamic, fully conversant with the ethical, social, political and spiritual philosophy of Islam. They must have the knowledge of Islam's universal vision, its insight about empirical matters like the creation, the origin, the creator of the universe, the need for creation of the universe, etc. They must have the deep knowledge of Islam's views and stipulations on man and his society. It is of great importance that the leaders must have a clear picture of the Islamic ideology of man's relations with his society; his manner and method of framing the social order; his abilities of defending and pursuing certain things and resisting others; his ultimate objectives and the means of attaining those objectives, etc.

It is obvious that only such persons can lead as have been brought up under the pure Islamic culture having perfectly mastered the branches of religious learning and Islamic sciences, the Qur'ān, tradition, jurisprudence, etc. It is, therefore, only ecclesiastics who qualify for the leadership of such a movement.

STUDY QUESTIONS

1. How does Hasan al-Banna explain the resurgence of Islam? What is his criticism of the Western way of life? What does he see as the strengths of Islam? What is Hasan al-Banna's view of Nazism, Fascism, and Communism?

2. According to Ayatullah Murtada Mutahhari, how was the Iranian revolution of 1979 different from earlier revolutions elsewhere?

3. How does Ayatullah Murtada Mutahhari explain the causes of the Iranian revolution? Does he see the causes as basically political, economic, or religious? How does he describe the revolution's goals?

4. How do the ideas of Hasan al-Banna and Ayatullah Murtada Mutahhari compare with those of Ziya Gokalp? (See Chapter 29.) How do you explain the differences?

5. How do you explain the renewed appeal of Islam during the past several decades? Are there similar tendencies in other world religions such as Christianity and Hinduism? What are the advantages and disadvantages of separating political authority from religious authority?

6. How do you think the 1979 revolution in Iran compares with eighteenth-century revolutions such as the American Revolution and the French Revolution? How does the revolution in Iran compare with other revolutions in the twentieth century? (See Chapter 26 on Russia, Chapter 32 on China, and Chapter 38 on Latin America.) In your view, which of the twentieth-century revolutions seems to have been most important for world history?

32

Chinese Revolutionaries: Sun Yat-sen and Mao Zedong

The twentieth century was one of the most tumultuous in the history of China. Buffeted by the shocks from Western and Japanese imperialism and unable to deal effectively with China's many internal problems, the Ch'ing dynasty finally collapsed in 1912. A republic was immediately declared, but a protracted period of instability and confusion ensued. For more than a decade warlords fought for control of the country. During this period Sun Yat-sen (1866–1925) emerged as the leading advocate of a Western-style republic in China. Sun, who had been born near Hong Kong and educated in Western schools, founded China's first real political party, the Guomindang (Nationalist party) and became enormously popular as its leader. But at the time of Sun's death China's crisis was far from resolved.

In 1927 Chiang Kai-shek, Sun's successor as head of the Guomindang, was able to impose a kind of unity on China from his capital in Nanking. Chiang was the nominal head of state in China until 1949, but his regime, while strongly nationalistic in rhetoric and gesture, was corrupt and ineffective. When Japan invaded eastern China in 1937 Chiang's government was unable to muster much of a defense. He moved his capital deep into the interior of the country and became increasingly dependent on aid from the British and the United States.

In contrast to Chiang's ineffectiveness, China's rural-based Communist party, led by Mao Zedong (1891–1976), organized a strong and popular resistance movement against the Japanese. By the end of World War II in 1945 the Chinese Communist party claimed millions of members, had its own large and battle-tested army, and governed much of northern China. Attempts to reconcile the communists

Selection 1 from *Sources of Chinese Tradition*, Vol. II, edited by Theodore de Bary, Wing-tsit Chan, and Burton Watson (New York: Columbia University Press, 1960), pp. 768–771; Selection 2 from *The People's Republic of China: A Documentary History of Revolutionary Change*, edited by Mark Selden (New York: Monthly Review Press, 1979), pp. 176–178.

and the nationalists in 1945 and 1946 quickly broke down. The result was full-scale civil war. In 1949 the communists swept to power—moving from the countryside to the cities and from north to south—and they have governed the country ever since.

The first selection is a series of passages taken from lectures that Sun Yat-sen gave to Nationalist party members in 1924. The second selection comes from a speech given by Mao Zedong in the summer of 1949. In the speech Mao discusses the policies that would guide the soon-to-be-founded People's Republic of China.

1. SUN YAT-SEN (1924)

[*China as a Heap of Loose Sand*]. For the most part the four hundred million people of China can be spoken of as completely Han Chinese. With common customs and habits, we are completely of one race. But in the world today what position do we occupy? Compared to the other peoples of the world we have the greatest population and our civilization is four thousand years old; we should therefore be advancing in the front rank with the nations of Europe and America. But the Chinese people have only family and clan solidarity; they do not have national spirit. Therefore even though we have four hundred million people gathered together in one China, in reality they are just a heap of loose sand. Today we are the poorest and weakest nation in the world, and occupy the lowest position in international affairs. Other men are the carving knife and serving dish; we are the fish and the meat. Our position at this time is most perilous. If we do not earnestly espouse nationalism and weld together our four hundred million people into a strong nation, there is danger of China's being lost and our people being destroyed. If we wish to avert this catastrophe, we must espouse nationalism and bring this national spirit to the salvation of the country. . . .

[*China as a "Hypo-Colony"*]. Since the Chinese Revolution [of 1911], the foreign powers have found that it was much less easy to use political force in carving up China. A people who had experienced Manchu oppression and learned to overthrow it, would now, if the powers used political force to oppress it, be certain to resist, and thus make things difficult for them. For this reason they are letting up in their efforts to control China by political force and instead are using economic pressure to keep us down. . . . As regards political oppression people are readily aware of their suffering, but when it comes to economic oppression most often they are hardly conscious of it. China has already experienced several decades of economic oppression by the foreign powers, and so far the nation has for the most part shown no sense of irritation. As a consequence China is being transformed everywhere into a colony of the foreign powers.

Our people keep thinking that China is only a "semi-colony"—a term by which they seek to comfort themselves. Yet in reality the economic oppression we have endured is not just that of a "semi-colony" but greater even than that of a full colony. . . . Of what nation then is China a colony? It is the colony of every nation with which it has concluded treaties; each of them is China's master. Therefore China is not just the colony of one country; it is the colony of many countries. We are not just the slaves of one country, but the slaves of many countries. In the event of natural disasters like flood and drought, a nation which is sole master appropriates funds for relief and distributes them, thinking this its own duty; and the people who are its slaves regard this relief work as something to which their masters are obligated. But when North China suffered drought several years ago, the foreign powers did not regard it as their responsibility to appropriate funds and distribute relief; only those foreigners resident in China raised funds for the drought victims, whereupon Chinese observers remarked on the great generosity of the foreigners who bore no responsibility to help. . . .

From this we can see that China is not so well off as Annam [under the French] and Korea [under the Japanese]. Being the slaves of one country represents a far higher status than being the slaves of many, and is far more advantageous. Therefore, to call China a "semi-colony" is quite incorrect. If I may coin a phrase, we should be called a "hypo-colony." This is a term that comes from chemistry, as in "hypo-phosphite." Among chemicals there are some belonging to the class of phosphorous compounds but of lower grade, which are called phosphites. Still another grade lower, and they are called hypo-phosphites. . . . The Chinese people, believing they were a semi-colony, thought it shame enough; they did not realize that they were lower even than Annam or Korea. Therefore we cannot call ourselves a "semi-colony" but only a "hypo-colony." . . .

[*Nationalism and Traditional Morality*]. If today we want to restore the standing of our people, we must first restore our national spirit. . . . If in the past our people have survived despite the fall of the state [to foreign conquerors], and not only survived themselves but been able to assimilate these foreign conquerors, it is because of the high level of our traditional morality. Therefore, if we go to the root of the matter, besides arousing a sense of national solidarity uniting all our people, we must recover and restore our characteristic, traditional morality. Only thus can we hope to attain again the distinctive position of our people.

This characteristic morality the Chinese people today have still not forgotten. First comes loyalty and filial piety, then humanity and love, faithfulness and duty, harmony and peace. Of these traditional virtues, the Chinese people still speak, but now, under foreign oppression, we have been invaded by a new culture, the force of which is felt all across the nation. Men wholly intoxicated by this new culture have thus begun to attack the traditional morality, saying that with the adoption of the new culture, we no longer have need of the old morality. . . . They say that when we formerly spoke of loyalty, it was loyalty to princes, but now in our democracy there are no princes, so loyalty is unnecessary and can be dispensed with. This kind of reasoning is certainly mistaken. In our country princes can be dispensed with, but not loyalty. If they say loyalty can be dispensed with, then I ask: "Do we, or do we not, have a nation? Can we, or can we not, make loyalty serve the nation? If indeed we can no longer speak of loyalty to princes, can we not, however, speak of loyalty to our people?"

2. MAO ZEDONG (1949)

Twenty-four years have passed since Sun Yat-sen's death, and the Chinese Revolution, led by the Communist Party of China, has made tremendous advances both in theory and practice and has radically changed the face of China. Up to now the principal and fundamental experience the Chinese people have gained is twofold:

1. Internally, arouse the masses of the people. That is, unite the working class, the peasantry, the urban petty bourgeoisie and the national bourgeoisie, form a domestic united front under the leadership of the working class, and advance from this to the establishment of a state which is a people's democratic dictatorship under the leadership of the working class and based on the alliance of workers and peasants.

2. Externally, unite in a common struggle with those nations of the world which treat us as equals and with the peoples of all countries. That is, ally ourselves with the Soviet Union, with the people's democracies, and with the proletariat and the broad masses of the people in all other countries, and form an international united front.

"You are leaning to one side." Exactly. The forty years' experience of Sun Yat-sen and the twenty-eight years' experience of the Communist Party have taught us to lean to one side, and we are firmly convinced that in order to win victory and consolidate it we must lean to one side. In the light of the experiences accumulated in these forty years and these twenty-eight years, all Chinese without exception must lean either to the side of imperialism or to the side of socialism. Sitting on the fence will not do, nor is there a third road. . . .

"We want to do business." Quite right, business will be done. We are against no one except the domestic and foreign reactionaries who hinder us from doing business. Everybody should know that it is none other than the imperialists and their running dogs, the Chiang Kai-shek reactionaries, who hinder us from doing business and also from establishing diplomatic relations with foreign countries. When we have beaten the internal and external reactionaries by uniting all domestic and international forces, we shall be able to do business and establish diplomatic relations with all foreign countries on the basis of equality, mutual benefit, and mutual respect for territorial integrity and sovereignty.

"Victory is possible even without international help." This is a mistaken idea. In the epoch in which imperialism exists, it is impossible for a genuine people's revolution to win victory in any country without various forms of help from the international revolutionary forces, and even if victory were won, it could not be consolidated. This was the case with the victory and consolidation of the great October Revolution, as Stalin told us long ago. This was also the case with the overthrow of the three imperialist powers in World War II and the establishment of the people's democracies. And this is also the case with the present and the future of People's China. . . .

"You are dictatorial." My dear sirs, you are right, that is just what we are. All the experience the Chinese people have accumulated through several decades teaches us to enforce the People's Democratic Dictatorship, that is, to deprive the reactionaries of the right to speak and let the people alone have that right.

Who are the people? At the present stage in China, they are the working class, the peasantry, the urban petty bourgeoisie, and the national bourgeoisie. These classes, led by the working class and the Communist Party, unite to form their own state and elect their own government; they enforce their dictatorship over the running dogs of imperialism—the landlord class and bureaucrat-bourgeoisie, as well as the representatives of those classes, the Kuomintang reactionaries and their accomplices—suppress them, allow them only to behave themselves and not to be unruly in word or deed. If they speak or act in an unruly way, they will be promptly stopped and punished. Democracy is practiced within the ranks of the people, who enjoy the rights of freedom of speech, assembly, association and so on. The right to vote belongs only to the people, not to the reactionaries. The combination of these two aspects, democracy for the people and dictatorship over the reactionaries, is the People's Democratic Dictatorship. . . .

The serious problem is the education of the peasantry. The peasant economy is scattered, and the socialization of agriculture, judging by the Soviet Union's experience, will require a long time and painstaking work. Without socialization of agriculture, there can be no complete, consolidated socialism. The steps to socialize agriculture must be coordinated with the development of a powerful industry having state enterprise as its backbone. The state of the People's Democratic Dictatorship must systematically solve the problems of industrialization. . . .

The People's Democratic Dictatorship is based on the alliance of the working class, the peasantry and the urban petty bourgeoisie, and mainly on the alliance of the workers and the peasants, because these two classes comprise 80 to 90 percent of China's population. These two classes are the main force in overthrowing imperialism and the Kuomintang reactionaries. The transition from new democracy to socialism also depends mainly upon their alliance.

During much of the 1930s and 1940s, Mao Zedong and the other leaders of the Chinese Communist Party lived in the caves at Yenan, depicted here in 1991. (Stephen S. Gosch.)

The People's Democratic Dictatorship needs the leadership of the working class. For it is only the working class that is most farsighted, most selfless and most thoroughly revolutionary. . . .

To sum up our experience and concentrate it into one point, it is: the People's Democratic Dictatorship under the leadership of the working class (through the Communist Party) and based upon the alliance of workers and peasants. This dictatorship must unite as one with the international revolutionary forces. This is our formula, our principal experience, and our main program.

STUDY QUESTIONS

1. Why did Sun Yat-sen think that the Chinese people must "espouse nationalism"?
2. According to Sun, how had China become stronger since the revolution of 1911?
3. What did Sun mean by the term "hypo-colony"?
4. What was the Sun's attitude toward China's traditional Confucian culture?
5. According to Mao Zedong in 1949, what important changes had taken place in China since the death of Sun Yat-sen?
6. What did Mao mean by "leaning to one side"?
7. How did Mao define "People's Democratic Dictatorship"?
8. What view of China's traditional Confucian culture was implied in Mao's address?
9. What similarities and differences do you see in the ideas of Sun Yat-sen and Mao Zedong? In what sense were Sun and Mao ambivalent toward the West? How did their views compare with the ideas in the "self-strengthening" movement in nineteenth-century China? (See Chapter 15.)
10. Compare the ideas of Mao with those of Lenin and Stalin. (See Chapters 26 and 27.) What similarities and differences do you see?

33

A Chinese Peasant Maps His Road to Wealth

When the Ch'ing dynasty collapsed in 1912 the vast majority of the people of China—perhaps 80 percent of the population—lived in the countryside, producing wheat if they lived in the north or rice if they lived in the south. Most of China's peasants were poor. Farms were quite small by Western standards, averaging from three to five acres in size (compared with about 150 acres in the United States). In addition, many Chinese farms were composed of noncontiguous plots, adding to the difficulty of farm labor. Perhaps a third of the rural population was landless; peasants without their own land were forced to rent plots from prosperous landowners, usually at very high rates. Many other peasants owned plots that were too small for them to survive on; they too were compelled to rent land.

During the 1930s and 1940s conditions worsened for Chinese peasants in significant ways. The worldwide Great Depression of the 1930s hit the Chinese economy hard and drove living standards down sharply for both urban and rural dwellers. The 1937 Japan invasion of China led to bitter fighting, much of it in the Chinese countryside, which lasted until 1945. During the war against the Japanese much of the rural economy was devastated; most of the ten million Chinese who died in the fighting were peasants. In the civil war of 1946 to 1949 between the communists and the nationalists the farming economy was battered once again, bringing the suffering of the peasants to a new low.

How have Chinese peasants fared under communist rule? The selection, from the memoir of Wang Xin, a Chinese peasant who was born in the countryside near Beijing in 1941, helps us to answer this question. Readers should note that Wang Xin's account of his life appeared in the *Beijing Review,* an official publication of the Chinese government. Not surprisingly, Wang underplays the hardships experienced by many Chinese peasants during the period of the Great Leap Forward (1958–1960), when Mao's policies to collectivize land and industrialize immediately resulted in massive famine and economic chaos. Nonetheless, Wang's recollections are valuable for the light they shed on how life changed for hundreds of millions of Chinese peasants during the Mao period (1949–1976), and then changed

From Wang Xin with Yang Xiaobing, "A Peasant Maps His Road to Wealth," *Beijing Review,* 27 (12 November 1984), pp. 28–30. Reprinted by permission.

again as a result of policies introduced by Mao's successor, Deng Xiaoping (1904–1997), during the 1980s.

There is a long story behind my family's prosperity. My family's history is closely linked with the history of the Chinese society. So let me start my story with the rise and fall of the country.

In 1941, I was born to a poor peasant family in Pinggu County. At the time, my family had 10 members from three generations, but we had no farmland at all. My grandpa and his brother had to work for the landlord. My father and his brother wove at home and traded their coarse cloth at the market for some food. While peddling their handmade cloth, they had to be alert and evasive to avoid being forced to bribe the police.

One winter day, my grandpa's brother had two fingers bit off while feeding cattle for the landlord. The landlord simply dismissed him when he saw he was no longer useful. This made our lives even worse. My grandma had no other way to earn money but to pick wild jujubes in the mountains, which were ground up and mixed with wild herbs to make something like a bun.

At the time, my grandparents and parents wanted to work hard and get rich. Their desire, however, was merely a dream.

Bright Dawn

In 1949 New China was founded and we peasants became masters of the country. Land reform was carried out, with feudalist land ownership abolished and farmland returned to the tillers. All the 300 peasant families in my village got shares of farmland, averaging 0.2 hectare per person [approximately one-half acre]. For us peasants, this really meant something to live on.

During the land reform, the landlords' surplus rooms were confiscated and the extra rooms were distributed among the poor. My family moved from a three-room thatched house into a tile-roofed house with seven rooms. Though only a small child at the time, I clearly remember how happy the peasants were.

In 1951 the agricultural collectivization movement got underway in my village. We first got organized into mutual-aid production teams and then into elementary agricultural co-operatives, pooling our land and sharing the dividends. In 1956 we switched to the advanced agricultural co-operatives and put our farmland into public ownership. The principle of "to each according to his work" was followed. The removal of land boundary stakes made it possible to develop a unified farming plan on a larger scale and created favourable conditions for water conservation projects and agricultural mechanization.

With the land under public ownership, all the villagers met to discuss how to use their farmland and how to distribute the income. This was completely different from preliberation days when we had no land at all.

During those years, since everyone worked hard and the government provided the co-operative with preferential loans and farm tools, production grew rapidly. The grain output, for instance, grew from 2,250 kg per hectare before 1949 to 4,225 kg in 1956. I remember my family got more than enough wheat that year. We lived quite well during those years.

In July of 1957, our village was hit by a hailstorm. With crops ruined, old people worried that they would have to go begging as they had in the past when natural disasters struck. But when the government heard about our problems, it exempted us from agricultural taxes for that whole year, shipped in grain seeds and potato seedlings and urged us to tide over the difficulty while developing production. By relying on the collective strength of the village and everybody's hard work, no one ran short of food.

In 1957 something important happened to me. I was enrolled in the county's middle school after I graduated from the primary school in my village. Before me, for generations all my family had been illiterate.

Twists and Turns

In 1958 we got organized into the people's commune, which brought about some desirable changes, but also resulted in some baffling developments.

A people's commune usually consisted of several villages (a village was usually an advanced co-operative). To see many people working on a vast expanse of land was really a spectacular view. Soon after the founding of the people's commune, a tractor station was set up to oversee ploughing and sowing.

The year of 1959, however, was chaotic. Some people said we had arrived at real communism. All the people in my village ate at the same canteen, free of charge. We produced hundreds of thousands of kilogrammes of sweet potatoes. But nobody wanted them. The result was that all the potatoes rotted in the field. Some people were prone to boasting and exaggeration. There was a 0.13 hectare plot of farmland by my middle school. About 2,500 kg of wheat seeds were sown and people said it would yield 100,000 kg. But, in reality, it produced only 250 kg (because far too many seeds were sown). Though the Central Committee of the Chinese Communist Part later criticized this mistake of being boastful and exaggerating, much of wealth had already been wasted. The negative impacts of such actions were felt for years.

The people's commune authorities also gave some arbitrary and impractical orders. Our village had a piece of land which should have been planted with soybeans. Some cadres of the people's commune, however, ordered us to grow carrots. Another piece of land which had already been planted with sweet potatoes was designated for soybeans. All these illogical orders resulted in sizable losses.

It now becomes clear that the inclination to boast and give arbitrary orders came from "Leftist" thinking.

Of course, the people's commune did some good. The most visible improvements were the water conservation projects. I myself took part in building several big projects.

In 1960 I came back home after graduation from junior middle school. My family of 10 members was then broken up into several small ones. I moved in with my uncle and his wife. Peasants from surrounding villages were then building the Haizi Reservoir, which would irrigate almost 10,000 hectares, one-third of the county's total farmland. The builders, in addition to getting subsidies from the state, were paid in cash by the people's commune and received food rations. This made it attractive work and made it possible for the people's commune to mobilize enough people to build the big projects. The water conservation projects on which I worked are still benefiting the people.

I got married in 1962 and later had two sons and one daughter. More mouths need more money. I managed to increase the income for my family. The next year, I spent my spare time collecting firewood in the winter and growing melons on my family's private plot in the summer. The extra work brought in more than 400 yuan. Our life was pretty good.

In 1966, the chaotic "cultural revolution" began. I could no longer collect firewood or grow melons because these were seen as capitalist undertakings. We peasants, unlike workers who have regular wages, had to work in the fields or we would have had nothing to eat. So our agricultural production continued as usual.

In retrospect, my life improved steadily after I began working. But I always thought I could have done much better. I was held back. In 1969, I was elected deputy leader of the brigade in charge of sideline production. One day I bought some eggs from a state chicken farm in order to hatch chickens for the brigade. I sold some the surplus eggs and made 100 yuan for the brigade. I was shocked when I was criticized for selling the eggs. I was labelled a capitalist speculator.

Affluence Begins

It is only in recent years that I have been able to work hard and grow prosperous without restrictions.

In 1979 I learnt from newspapers and broadcasts that the Party had adopted flexible policies in the countryside. The contract responsibility system, which guaranteed more pay for more work, became popular in my village. The new policies allowed us peasants to become the real masters of agriculture and set us free to work hard and make more money. I wondered what I could do to get wealthy.

In 1981, I chose to raise chickens. I spent 380 yuan to buy 500 chicks. I was then a Communist Party member and the brigade's deputy leader. What I did raised some eyebrows in the village, but it didn't affect my job. The policy supported me. I got rich by working hard. Nothing wrong. I earned 850 yuan that year.

I then expanded the scope of my chicken business. The state credit co-operative offered me loans and encouraged me to forge ahead. I read books and studied to learn how to raise chickens scientifically. I also learnt how to treat chicken diseases such as diarrhoea and typhoid fever. In 1982, I sold the state 6,000 chickens for 9,000 yuan. With my income from the brigade and other household sidelines, I earned a total of more than 10,000 yuan, a figure larger than my combined income for the previous 10 years. The county recognized my achievements and rewarded me.

The Party policy is to bring into full play everyone's enthusiasm for production. It creates more wealth for the country and provides a good life for the peasants. Being among the first in my county to get rich, I'd like to lead others to prosperity.

Wang Shuchen has eight family members, but only two are able men. They have had a hard time. I explained the Party's policy to him and asked if he would like to raise chickens, too. I lent him 580 yuan, saying, "Please use this money to raise chickens. If the chickens die, I won't ask for the money back." Because he was less experienced in raising chickens, I went to his home several times every day to help him write observation notes, make plans for buying chicken feed, keep balance sheets and cure chicken diseases. Last year Wang earned more than 5,000 yuan from his chicken business alone.

So far, I have encouraged 80 families to raise chickens. Last year alone, I lent the families 5,800 yuan free of interest. In addition, I took time to help them treat chicken diseases and teach them how to raise chickens. I was always available whenever I was asked.

My family's life has improved very much in recent years. However, I spent only 400 yuan buying a radio cassette recorder for my daughter to study a foreign language for her college examinations. Other than that, I have spent not a single penny for other electric appliances for my family. I'd rather spend my money expanding production. I bought a walking tractor that cost more than 3,000 yuan.

Not long ago, I was elected secretary of the village Party branch. Since the Party job took much of my time, my chicken business suffered. But it is worth it, because we are helping more people become prosperous.

I am now wondering how to boost enthusiasm even more so that we can turn our village into a village which specializes in chicken raising. We also want to develop other sideline business and to raise other livestock in order to make our village more competitive in commodity production. Our village cadres have decided that whoever comes up with a practical plan to make more than 10,000 yuan next year will be the first to get material assistance from the village.

STUDY QUESTIONS

1. How did Wang Xin and his family benefit from policies introduced by the communists after they took power in 1949?
2. What evidence is there in Wang's memoir of problems in China after 1949?
3. How did Chinese agricultural policies of the 1980s differ from those of the early period?
4. Do you see hints in Wang Xin's account of his life of the continuing importance of Confucian values in China?
5. Is Wang Xin a communist or a capitalist?
6. Which label would better describe Chinese realities in the 1990s, "communism with Chinese characteristics" or "capitalism with Chinese characteristics"?
7. How successful have China's communists been in their attempts to solve the problems pointed to by Sun Yat-sen? (See Chapter 32.) Is China still a "heap of loose sand"?
8. Why did communism collapse in Russia but not in China? (See Chapter 28.)

34

Changing Gender Relations in Modern Japan

Japan's emergence as a modern industrial society was one of the most important developments in world history during the second half of the twentieth century. At the end of World War II the country lay in ruins. However, postwar economic growth—the Japanese "miracle"—quickly overcame both the cost of the war and the destruction from U.S. air raids in 1944 and 1945. By 1965 the Japanese economy was nearly four times as productive as it had been in the 1930s. In the late 1990s the Japanese gross national product was one of the largest in the world and Japanese living standards were also among the highest worldwide.

The dynamic growth of Japanese industry and agriculture was accompanied by the rapid urbanization of the country; these long-term processes had major implications for gender relations. The extended family of the countryside was replaced by the urban nuclear family. Life expectancy for both men and women went up significantly (making for much longer marriages), while the number of children born to the average woman fell sharply. New educational and occupational opportunities opened up for both men and women.

There were also major political and legal reforms during the postwar period that affected gender relations. During the period of the U.S. occupation (1945 to 1952) a new constitution and a series of additional legal reforms extended full political rights to women and established the principle of equality before the law for men and women.

Despite the foregoing changes, in Japan, as elsewhere, many men (and women) held fast to the view that women should be subordinate to men. Japanese women who sought careers in business, government, and academia faced obstacles more formidable than those faced by their Western counterparts.

The selection is from an article written in the 1980s by the feminist and social critic Heichi Keiko; it illustrates many of the changes in Japanese gender relations that have been under way since World War II.

"The Age of Women"—so ran the catch-phrase adorning a Japanese newspaper advertisement on New Year's Day 1979, the eve of the 80s. The ad went on in part to

From Higuchi Keiko, "Japanese Women in Transition," *Japan Quarterly*, 29 (July-September 1982), p. 311, 313–318.

say: "Dazzling—simply dazzling, the women of today. Mothers and daughters taking off suddenly on trips abroad, or giving up their diets and going in for yoga instead. Expressing themselves freely, without fear or hesitation, these are women who know the art of enjoying life to the full. . . . Today's women are off the sidelines to stay."

The slogan notwithstanding, this message is probably best understood as a gift of flattery from male salesmen to female buyers. Beginning with this advertisement, the decade of the 80s has come with increasing frequency to be called "the age of women." And yet one has the distinct sense that before yielding any substantial results, the term was quickly taken over by the advertising industry as a piece of "fashion." In any case, the emergence of language such as this in newspaper advertising is surely a sign of change in the situation of Japanese women. . . .

The consciousness of Japanese women is now in a state of transition. Their attitude toward the idea that "men should work outside the home, women inside" has changed greatly in the last 10 years. In a 1972 survey of attitudes on women's issues undertaken by the Prime Minister's Office, over 80 percent of women respondents agreed with the idea as stated above. But in a similar survey conducted in 1976, the year after International Women's Year, those concurring that "men work, and women stay home" were 49 percent, while 40 percent disagreed and 11 percent were undecided. The wording of the question as well as the range of possible answers vary, making simple comparisons difficult, but it would seem clear at any rate that doubts regarding the traditional idea of sex-differentiated work roles are rapidly growing. In 1979 the Prime Minister's Office conducted another survey posing the same questions as in 1976, but this time, in response to the assertion that "men work and women stay home," pollees were evenly divided among "agree," "disagree" and "don't know," with each answer drawing a response in the 30th percentile. When the question pertains to "men" and "women," people are somewhat likely to go against the traditional view, but when the words "husbands" and "wives" are substituted, resistance declines. Acceptance of sex-differentiated work roles is still deep-rooted in Japan.

Among the younger generation, however, there is possibility for more rapid change. In the 1979 survey by the Prime Minister's Office, the assertion by 25 percent of unmarried women that they had "no wish to marry" attracted wide notice. Japanese have a high marriage rate, so much so that they have been called a people "fond of marrying": by age 50, 97 percent of both men and women have been married at least once. The Prime Minister's Office asked the same question in 1972, but at that time only 14 percent of women declared themselves uninterested in marrying. In the 1979 survey, a mere 12 percent of men selected the same response, thus revealing a gap in attitudes toward marriage between the sexes. Moreover, women responding that "a woman's happiness lies in marriage" went down from 40 percent to 32 percent.

Yearly surveys by Nippon Recruit Center, an employment agency, on "attitudes of female university students toward employment" shows that until the late 70s, even among graduates of four-year colleges, those desiring to work "until retirement age" amounted to scarcely 20 percent. In the 1981 survey, however, 41 percent of respondents (19 percent for junior college graduates) gave that answer. The most frequently given answer was to work "until a child is born, then again after the child is older" (58.7 percent). Significantly, those who said simply "until marrying" or "until a child is born" —thus relegating work to a brief period early in their lifetimes—were in the minority for the first time at 25.3 percent or one quarter of the sample. For Japan, where women are held to be at a particular disadvantage in combining marriage and a career, and where long-term female employment is much rarer than in Europe and America, such a shift in attitudes is truly remarkable. . . .

In the Tokyo residential area where I live, around 10 every morning housewives clad in short, above-the-knee outfits get on their bikes, tennis rackets in baskets, and pedal off in a row for the local tennis court. A conspicuous change in the last 10 years has been the phenomenal growth in large cities nationwide of housewives' hobby and culture centers, sponsored by newspapers, broadcasting companies, department stores and even big businesses. Women in their 30s and 40s, freed from the burden of caring for small children, flock to tennis courts and culture centers out of a desire to be with others like themselves—a hunger, perhaps, for companionship—as they seek the pattern for the latter half of their lives. In the past, Japanese women were referred to by their husbands as *kanai,* meaning literally "inside the house"—and that is exactly where they stayed. Today, as women step out more and more in search of entertainment, education and a wide variety of activities, one sometimes hears a man say of his wife, "She's no *kanai;* she's my *kagai* ('outside the house')."

But housewives commuting to tennis courts and cultural enrichment centers are, after all, outnumbered by those commuting to work. The number of female employees is steadily increasing, and at present nearly 70 percent are married. In addition, more than half of all unemployed housewives aged 40 and above "would like to work." By far their biggest motivation is to bring the family budget out of the red. Although real earnings of household heads have declined in the last few years, the standard of living has held its own, thanks largely to increases in wives' earnings.

Not long ago, when I was in a department store, two clerks called out to me one after the other. They told me they had heard me speak at a lecture meeting sponsored by a grade-school PTA. Both of them are active as PTA members while holding down part-time jobs in a department store. The day of the lecture meeting, they said, they had taken off work to attend. I could not help feeling struck by this clear example of change. It wasn't many years ago that at PTA meetings one frequently heard the complaint that "so many women have jobs nowadays, there's nobody to work for the PTA." Some ladies even went so far as to take part-time jobs only when officers' elections came around, then plead work as an excuse to decline. Now many women manage successfully to juggle work outside the home with active participation in community affairs. Working housewives have become so commonplace that it can no longer be said that "PTA is for mothers who don't work."

Toward the end of April 1982, the Ministry of Labor published results of a "Basic survey on Wage Structure in 1981." According to these results, although until recently male workers attained their top earning power in their 50s, now male wages have begun to peak earlier, in the 45–50 age bracket. "My husband's earnings will peak when he's in his 40s—so I'd better go to work to help out the budget." This sort of determination appears to be spreading rapidly among Japanese women.

Women in Japan are stepping out of the house in ever-swelling numbers. Yet men persist in clinging to the notion that "women's work is in the home." Those most critical of sex-differentiated labor roles are not men, but women. It appears inevitable, therefore, that discord will arise between the sexes.

Conflict between husband and wife is apt to arise from the work overload of working wives. The belief that household affairs are the wife's exclusive responsibility is deeply ingrained in Japanese society, and many women would in fact regard their husband's entrance into the kitchen as an unwelcome intrusion. According to a 1976 research survey by the Prime Minister's Office on "Lifestyles in Society," unemployed housewives spend an average of five hours and 54 minutes each day on housework and childcare, compared to three hours and 29 minutes for those with outside jobs. Husbands of unemployed wives, for their part, contribute an average of seven minutes daily to the same tasks, while for husbands of working women the figure is an astounding six minutes. Thus, utterly betraying the expectation that "it is only natural for the husband to help around the house if the wife works too," Japanese married men reign as *shujin* ("husband"; literally, "master") in their homes, and whether or not the wife has an outside job they do virtually no housework.

The husband expects his wife to look after the home, and in the home he seeks a place of recreation and relaxation in which to garner strength for the coming day's work. This is the view of the wife's role, and of the function of the home, given often in Japanese textbooks for the lower, compulsory levels of school. The husband, behaving exactly as the textbooks predict he will, hands over his pay envelope to his wife without even looking inside. Most big corporations nowadays transfer paychecks directly to employees' bank accounts, but the wife remains firmly in charge of home finances. The husband sees the act of turning over his entire salary to his wife simultaneously as an expression of love and a fulfillment of obligation. The wife, however, has begun to entertain misgivings about an existence spent for the most part waiting passively at home for her husband's return.

The profound changes in the lifestyles of Japanese women surely have few precedents anywhere in the world. It is well known that Japanese women expend more love and energy on their children than on their husbands. But the children who are objects of so much maternal devotion have decreased drastically in number per family while average life expectancies have continued to rise. In 1940, a woman whose youngest child had just entered school had only 7.6 years of life remaining; in 1978, the number of years she could count on had jumped to 44. After the youngest child marries, moreover, she and her husband can still look forward to nearly a score of years of married life. . . .

The new women's liberation movement which spread to Japan in the early 70s brought pressure for change in the lives of both men and women. And the U.N.'s Decade for Women forced the Japanese government to face up to many of the issues involved. At the same time, the extremely rapid aging of Japanese society—a phenomenon without precedent or equal in the world—is forcing upon us, willy-nilly, a reevaluation of relationships between the sexes, married and unmarried alike.

Aged people (those 65 years old and above) now comprise a mere 9 percent of the population of Japan, but in the coming 30 to 40 years it is anticipated that their numbers will swell to more than 23 percent. No advanced nation has yet experienced a society in which one out of every four people is elderly.

The life span of Japanese women is approaching 80 years. The question of how middle-aged Japanese women are to spend the latter half of this extended lifetime is one that must be asked. With marriage as the single-minded goal of their youth, followed by harried years of caring for husband and children, they have had little time for self-reflection; now, realizing after their children are grown or their husband retires that without a personal goal they will be unable to face the loneliness of widowhood, these women are full of consternation. Among Japanese aged 65 and over, those whose spouse is living account for 80 percent of the men, but only one in three of the women. Soon there will be one million old people living alone in Japan, 80 percent of them female. Their income, moreover, is less than half that of men. And of those looking after elderly invalids in their own homes, as many as 90 percent are women. Lately the idea that "the problems of old age are women's problems" is voiced more and more often at women's gatherings. . . .

The traditional life-patterns for Japanese men and women—until very recently thought natural and common-sensical—are now, under the pressures of a highly developed, rapidly aging industrial society, in a period of transition, as people seek to put them in a new frame of reference.

STUDY QUESTIONS

1. How did attitudes toward gender relations and work begin to change in Japan during the 1970s? How did differences in attitudes vary by age and sex?
2. How are leisure-time activities and employment patterns changing for Japanese women?
3. What do you learn from the article about family life in Japan? What hints about the continuing influence of Confucian values on the Japanese family does the article contain? What changes seem to be under way?
4. How do demographic changes in Japan since the 1940s help to explain the recent changes in gender relationships?
5. Compare the ideas of Higuchi Keiko with those of Simone de Beauvoir and Madhu Kishwar. (See Chapters 25 and 37.) What similarities and differences do you see?
6. Does the process of industrialization inevitably move societies in the direction of gender equality?

35

Gandhi and Modern India

No individual has been more important to the history of modern India than Mohandas K. Gandhi (1869–1948). Descended from a prosperous Hindu family of merchants and public officials in western India, Gandhi studied law in London during the late 1880s. He then spent 20 years in South Africa, where he led the Indian minority community in a struggle against discrimination by the British and the Boers. Returning to India in 1915. Gandhi plunged into the nationalist movement. From the end of World War I to his assassination three decades later Gandhi was the most popular and most effective leader of the Indian struggle for freedom from British colonial rule.

Gandhi's legacy is both rich and ambiguous. For many Indian patriots Gandhi's greatest achievement was his leadership in transforming the leading nationalist organization, the Indian National Congress, into a genuine mass movement. There is general agreement among scholars that it was the Mahatma (Great Soul) who won the peasants of Indian to the national cause after World War I and that this development was decisive in compelling the British to withdraw from India following World War II. In addition, many of his contemporaries in India and around the world admired Gandhi's commitment to *satyagraya* (nonviolent resistance) as well as his vigorous efforts on behalf of India's untouchables and his desire for harmony between Hindus and Muslims (called "communal unity" in India). On the other hand, some Hindus—including Gandhi's assassin—and most Muslims saw him as too favorable to their religious adversaries. Other critics of Gandhi think that his opposition to both modern technology and the kind of mass insurrection that the communists led in China contributed to the survival of poverty and inequality in independent India.

From *The Moral and Political Writings of Mahatma Gandhi*, Vol. III, *Non-Violent Resistance and Social Transformation*, edited by Raghaven Iyer (Oxford: Clarendon Press, 1987), pp. 370–374.

The following selection comes from a speech given by Gandhi in 1936.

. . . I am going to say nothing new today. The cult of the spinning-wheel is 18 years old. I said in 1918 that we could win *swaraj* through the spinning-wheel. My faith in the ability of the spinning-wheel is as bright today as when I first declared it in 1918. It has become richer for the experience and experiment of all these years.

But you should know the implications of the wheel or *khadi* [hand-spun cloth], its product. It is not enough that one wears *khadi* on ceremonial occasions or even wears it to the exclusion of all other cloth if he surrounds himself with *videshi* [foreign goods] in everything else. *Khadi* means the truest *swadeshi* [self-reliant] spirit, identification with the starving millions.

Let there be no mistake about my conception of *swaraj*. It is complete independence of alien control and complete economic independence. So at one end you have political independence, at the other the economic. It has two other ends. One of them is moral and social, the corresponding end is *dharma*, i.e., religion in the highest sense of the term. It includes Hinduism, Islam, Christianity, etc., but is superior to them all. You may recognize it by the name of Truth, not the honesty of expedience but the living Truth that pervades everything and will survive all destruction and all transformation. Moral and social uplift may be recognized by the term we are used to, i.e., non-violence. Let us call this the square of *swaraj*, which will be out of shape if any of its angles is untrue. In the language of the Congress we cannot achieve this political and economic freedom without truth and non-violence, in concrete terms without a living faith in God and hence moral and social elevation.

By political independence I do not mean an imitation of the British House of Commons, or the Soviet rule of Russia or the Fascist rule of Italy or the Nazi rule of Germany. They have systems suited to their genius. We must have ours suited to ours. What that can be is more than I can tell. I have described it as *Ramarajya*, i.e., sovereignty of the people based on pure moral authority. The Congress constitutions of Nagpur and Bombay for which I am mainly responsible are an attempt to achieve this type of *swaraj*.

Then take economic independence. It is not a product of industrialization of the modern or the Western type. Indian economic independence means to me the economic uplift of every individual, male and female, by his or her own conscious effort. Under that system all men and women will have enough clothing—not the mere loin-cloth, but what we understand by the term necessary articles of clothing and enough food including milk and butter which are today denied to millions.

This brings me to socialism. Real socialism has been handed down to us by our ancestors who taught: 'All land belongs to Gopal, where then is the boundary line? Man is the maker of the line and he can therefore unmake it.' Gopal literally means shepherd; it also means God. In modern language it means the State, i.e., the people. That the land today does not belong to the people is too true. But the fault is not in the teaching. It is in us who have not lived up to it.

I have no doubt that we can make as good an approach to it as is possible for any nation, not including Russia, and that without violence. The most effective substitute for violent dispossession is the wheel with all its implications. Land and all property is his who will work it. Unfortunately the workers are or have been kept ignorant of this simple fact.

Let us now see how India came to be utterly impoverished. History tells us that the East India Company ruined the cotton manufacture and by all kinds of means made her dependent upon Lancashire for her cloth, the next great necessity of man. It is still the largest item of import. It thus created a huge army of partially unemployed men and women counted in millions and gave them no other employment in return. With the destruction of hand-ginning, carding, spinning and weaving to a certain extent, perished the other industries of India's villages. Continuous unemployment has induced in the people a kind of laziness which is most depressing. Thus whilst the alien rule is undoubtedly responsible for the growing pauperism of the people, we are more responsible for it. If the middle-class people, who betrayed their trust and bartered away the economic independence of India for a mess of pottage, would now realize their error and take the message of the wheel to the villagers and induce them to shed their laziness and work at the wheel, we can ameliorate the condition of the people to a great extent. It would be a terrible thing if laziness replaces industry and despair triumphs over hope.

The parliamentary programme is in the air. It has come to stay and rightly. But it cannot bring us independence. Its function is strictly limited though quite necessary. Its success will prevent the Government from claiming that Ordinance rule or any measure restricting our progress to the goal was sanctioned by popular representatives. Hence the necessity for voters voting for the Congress candidates who dare not vote for unpopular measures without being liable to Congress discipline. The success of that programme may also bring some relief in individual cases such as the release of Shri Subhas Bose or the detenus. But that is not independence, political or economic.

Then look at it in another way. Only a limited number of men and women can become members of legislatures, say 1,500. How many from this audience can become legislators? And just now no more than $3\frac{1}{2}$ crores [upper income groups, about 35 million people] can vote for these 1,500 members. What about the remaining $31\frac{1}{2}$ crores? In our conception of *swaraj* they are the real masters and the $3\frac{1}{2}$ crores are the former's servants who in their turn are masters of the 1,500. Thus the latter are doubly servants, if they will be true to their trust.

But the $31\frac{1}{2}$ crores have also a trust to discharge towards themselves and the nation of which they as individuals are but tiny parts. And if they remain lazy, know nothing of *swaraj* and how to win it, they will themselves become slaves of the 1,500 legislators. For my argument the $3\frac{1}{2}$ crores of voters here belong to the same category as the $31\frac{1}{2}$ crores. For if they do not become industrious and wise, they will be so many pawns in the hands of 1,500 players, it is of little consequence whether they are Congressmen or otherwise. If the voters wake up only to register their votes every three years or more and then go off to sleep, their servants will become their masters.

The only way I know to prevent such a catastrophe is for the 35 crores to be industrious and wise. This they can only be if they will take up the spinning-wheel and the other village industries. They will not take to them unintelligently. I can tell you from experience that the effort means adult education of the correct type and requires possession of patience, moral fibre and a scientific and practical knowledge of the industry the worker seeks to introduce in the village of his choice.

In such a scheme the spinning-wheel becomes its centre. If you call it the solar system, the wheel becomes the golden disc and the industries the planets revolving round it in obedience to the inviolable law of the system. When the sun lost its illuminating power by the action of the East India Company, the planets lost their power and became invisible or almost so. The sun is being reinstated in his past status now and the planets are regaining their motion in exact proportion to the strength of the sun.

Now perhaps you will understand the meaning and the message of the *charkha* [spinning wheel]. I said in 1920 that if the Congress truly and successfully worked the programme laid down in 1920 including the fourfold Constructive Programme of *khadi*, communal unity, prohibition of intoxicants and removal by Hindus of untouchability, the attainment of *swaraj* within a year was a certainty. I am neither sorry for nor ashamed of having made that declaration. I would like to repeat that declaration before you today. Whenever the fourfold programme is achieved in its fulness, you can have *swaraj* for the asking. For you will then have attained the power to take it. Just think for a moment where the *charkha* stands today in your faith or action. Is the mutual secret assassination of Bombay a sign of communal unity? Where is total prohibition? Have the Hindus rid themselves of untouchability root and branch? One swallow does not make a summer. Travancore's great Proclamation [ending certain kinds of discrimination against untouchables] may be the beginning of the end, but it is not the end. If we remove the untouchability of *Harijans* [literally, "children of God," Gandhi's name for the untouchables], but treat Mussalmans or others as such, we have not removed the blot. 'All land belongs to God' has a deeper meaning. Like the earth we, of it, also belong to God, and hence we must all feel like one and not erect boundary walls and issue prohibition decrees against one another.

This is the non-violent way in action. If we could fulfil this programme, there would be no need to offer disobedience, there would certainly be no need to do violence. Thirty-five crores of people conscious of their numerical strength as one man would be ashamed of doing violence to 70,000 white men in India, no matter how capable they are of dealing destruction and administering poison gas to millions in a moment. The *charkha* understood intelligently can spin not only economic salvation but can also revolutionize our minds and hearts and demonstrate to us that the non-violent approach to *swaraj* is the safest and the easiest. Though the progress may seem slow, it will prove quickest in the long run.

Believe me if Jawaharlal [Nehru, independent India's first Prime Minister, 1947–1964] is not in jail today, it is not because he is afraid of it. He is quite capable of walking into prison doors as of mounting the gallows with a smile on his lips. I do not think I have lost the power or faith in the efficacy of such suffering. But there is no issue for it today as far as I can see. But what I feel is that all that suffering can be avoided if by united faith and will we achieve the Constructive Programme. If we can, I promise that we won't need to struggle with or against the British nation, but Lord Linlithgow will come to us and own that he was mistaken in his disbelief of our nonviolence and truth and will undertake on behalf of his nation to abide by our decisions. Whether he does or not, I am working towards that and no other. 'All belong to God.'

STUDY QUESTIONS

1. What did Gandhi mean by the "square of *swaraj*"?
2. What was Gandhi's attitude toward Western-style capitalist industrialization?
3. Was Gandhi a socialist?
4. According to Gandhi, how had British rule harmed India? How would the use of the spinning wheel help to counteract the problems created by the British?
5. What was Gandhi's attitude toward parliamentary government?
6. What was Gandhi's "Constructive Programme" of 1920?
7. Was Gandhi opposed to modernization?
8. In what ways was this speech an attempt by Gandhi to shift his listeners' sense of identify from caste, region, and religion to a sense of membership in the Indian nation? Does he include everyone?
9. Compare Gandhi's ideas with those of Rammohun Roy. (See Chapter 16.)
10. Gandhi, Ziya Gokalp (see Chapter 29), and Sun Yat-sen (See Chapter 32) were all born within a few years of 1870. What similarities and differences do you see in their ideas? What sets Gandhi apart from the others?

36

Jinnah and the Founding of Pakistan

The end of the Mughal dynasty in 1858 was a traumatic development for the 25 percent of the Indian population that was Muslim. For more than 300 years the rulers of India, the descendants of Babur (reigned 1526–1530), had been Muslims. Now, in the aftermath of the suppression of the uprising of 1857 and 1858, India became a formal part of the British Empire.

The emergence of the Indian National Congress around the turn of the twentieth century as the leading organization in the struggle against the British led to further disquiet among many Indian Muslims who saw the Congress as the voice of the Hindu majority community. Gandhi worked hard on behalf of Hindu-Muslim unity from the 1920s until his assassination in 1948. However, despite Gandhi's efforts many Indian Muslims continued to fear that if the British left India in the hands of the Congress, the result would be Hindu rule over—and discrimination against—the Muslim minority community.

Muhammad Ali Jinnah (1876–1948) was the most important leader of Indian Muslims during the first half of the twentieth century. Jinnah was born into a prosperous family of merchants in Karachi. Like Gandhi, Jinnah studied law in London but then, unlike Gandhi, he became a successful and wealthy attorney in Bombay. As a young lawyer Jinnah joined both the Congress and the leading organization of Indian Muslims, the Muslim League. Until 1920 Jinnah was active in both organizations and was known to many Congress activists as the "ambassador of Hindu-Muslim unity." However, Gandhi's success in mobilizing the Hindu peasants and urban poor, a development that led to many violent confrontations between Hindus and Muslims, convinced Jinnah that the Muslim minority population would never be safe in an independent India under the leadership of the Congress. Gradually, as the leader of the Muslim League during the 1920s and 1930s, Jinnah moved toward the view, expressed in the speech excerpted in the selection, that Indian Muslims were a separate nation and should have their own sovereign state.

Hindu Indians and many Muslims were strongly opposed to the establishment of a separate Muslim state. However, in 1947, seeing no possibility of compromise on this issue, the British reluctantly agreed with Jinnah and decided to partition India. On August 15, 1947, British rule in India ended and two new states came into being, predominantly Hindu India and overwhelmingly Muslim Pakistan.

From *Sources of Indian Tradition*, 2nd ed., Vol. 2, edited by Stephen Hay (New York: Columbia University Press, 1988), pp. 228–231.

The passages that follow come from one of Jinnah's most important speeches. It was given at the 1940 annual meeting of the Muslim League.

The British government and Parliament, and more so the British nation, have been for many decades past brought up and nurtured with settled notions about India's future, based on developments in their own country which has built up the British constitution, functioning now through the Houses of Parliament and the system of cabinet. Their concept of party government functioning on political planes has become the ideal with them as the best form of government for every country, and the one-sided and powerful propaganda, which naturally appeals to the British, has led them into a serious blunder, in producing the constitution envisaged in the Government of India Act of 1935. We find that the most leading statesmen of Great Britain, saturated with these notions, have in their pronouncements seriously asserted and expressed a hope that the passage of time will harmonize the inconsistent elements of India.

A leading journal like the London *Times,* commenting on the Government of India Act of 1935, wrote: "Undoubtedly the differences between the Hindus and Muslims are not of religion in the strict sense of the word but also of law and culture, that they may be said, indeed, to represent two entirely distinct and separate civilizations. However, in the course of time, the superstition will die out and India will be molded into a single nation." So, according to the London *Times,* the only difficulties are superstitions. These fundamental and deep-rooted differences, spiritual, economic, cultural, social, and political, have been euphemized as mere "superstitions." But surely it is a flagrant disregard of the past history of the subcontinent of India as well as the fundamental Islamic conception of society vis-à-vis that of Hinduism to characterize them as mere "superstitions." Notwithstanding a thousand years of close contact, nationalities, which are as divergent today as ever, cannot at any time be expected to transform themselves into one nation merely by means of subjecting them to a democratic constitution and holding them forcibly together by unnatural and artificial methods of British parliamentary statute. What the unitary government of India for one hundred fifty years had failed to achieve cannot be realized by the imposition of a central federal government. It is inconceivable that the fiat or the writ of a government so constituted can ever command a willing and loyal obedience throughout the subcontinent by various nationalities except by means of armed force behind it.

The problem in India is not of an intercommunal character but manifestly of an international one, and it must be treated as such. So long as this basic and fundamental truth is not realized, any constitution that may be built will result in disaster and will prove destructive and harmful not only to the Mussalmans but to the British and Hindus also. If the British government are really in earnest and sincere to secure [the] peace and happiness of the people of this subcontinent, the only course open to us all is to allow the major nations separate homelands by dividing India into "autonomous national states." There is no reason why these states should be antagonistic to each other. On the other hand, the rivalry and the natural desire and efforts on the part of one to dominate the social order and establish political supremacy over the other in the government of the country will disappear. It will lead more towards natural good will by international pacts between them, and they can live in complete harmony with their neighbors. This will lead further to a friendly settlement all the more easily with regard to minorities by reciprocal arrangements and adjustments between Muslim India and Hindu India, which will far more adequately and effectively safeguard the rights and interests of Muslims and various other minorities.

It is extremely difficult to appreciate why our Hindu friends fail to understand the real nature of Islam and Hinduism. They are not religions in the strict sense of the word, but are, in fact, different and distinct social orders, and it is a dream that the Hindus and Muslims can ever evolve a common nationality, and this misconception of one Indian nation has gone far beyond the limits and is the cause of most of your troubles and will lead India to destruction if we fail to revise our notions in time. The Hindus and Muslims belong to two different religious philosophies, social customs, literatures. They neither intermarry nor interdine together and, indeed, they belong to two different civilizations which are based mainly on conflicting ideas and conceptions. Their aspects on life and of life are different. It is quite clear that Hindus and Mussalmans derive their inspiration from different sources of history. They have different epics, different heroes, and different episodes. Very often the hero of one is a foe of the other and, likewise, their victories and defeats overlap. To yoke together two such nations under a single state, one as a numerical minority and the other as a majority, must lead to growing discontent and final destruction of any fabric that may be so built up for the government of such a state.

. . . History has also shown us many geographical tracts, much smaller than the subcontinent of India, which otherwise might have been called one country, but which have been divided into as many states as there are nations inhabiting them. [The] Balkan Peninsula comprises as many as seven or eight sovereign states. Likewise, the Portuguese and the Spanish stand divided in the Iberian Peninsula. Whereas under the plea of the unity of India and one nation, which does not exist, it is sought to pursue here the line of one central government, we know that the history of the last twelve hundred years has failed to achieve unity and has witnessed, during the ages, India always divided into Hindu India and Muslim India. The present artificial unity of India dates back only to the British conquest and is maintained by the British bayonet, but termination of the British regime, which is implicit in the recent declaration of His Majesty's government, will be the herald of the entire break-up with worse disaster than has ever taken place during the last one thousand years under Muslims. Surely that is not the legacy which Britain would bequeath to India after one hundred fifty years of her rule, nor would Hindu and Muslim India risk such a sure catastrophe.

Muslim India cannot accept any constitution which must necessarily result in a Hindu majority government. Hindus and Muslims brought together under a democratic system forced upon the minorities can only mean Hindu raj [rule]. Democracy of the kind with which the Congress High Command is enamored would mean the complete destruction of what is most precious in Islam. We have had ample experience of the working of the provincial constitutions during the last two and a half years and any repetition of such a government must lead to civil war and raising of private armies as recommended by Mr. Gandhi to [the] Hindus of Sukkur when he said that they must defend themselves violently or nonviolently, blow for blow, and if they could not, they must emigate.

Mussalmans are not a minority as it is commonly known and understood. One has only got to look round. Even today, according to the British map of India, four out of eleven provinces, where the Muslims dominate more or less, are functioning notwithstanding the decision of the Hindu Congress High Command to noncooperate and prepare for civil disobedience. Mussalmans are a nation according to any definition of a nation, and they must have their homelands, their territory, and their state. We wish to live in peace and harmony with our neighbors as a free and independent people. We wish our people to develop to the fullest our spiritual, cultural, economic, social, and political life in a way that we think best and in consonance with our own ideals and according to the genius of our people. Honesty demands and the vital interests of millions of our people impose a sacred duty upon us to find an honorable and peaceful solution, which would be just and fair to all. But at the same time we cannot be moved or diverted from our purpose and objective by threats or intimidations. We must be prepared to face all difficulties and consequences, make all the sacrifices that may be required of us to achieve the goal we have set in front of us.

STUDY QUESTIONS

1. Why did Jinnah think that Muslims and Hindus were two nations rather than simply two religious communities within the Indian nation? How was Jinnah's view different from the one expressed by the writer in the London *Times*? How was his view similar to that of the *Times* writer?
2. How did Jinnah use his knowledge of comparative world history to strengthen his argument?
3. Why did Jinnah think that Muslim Indians could not accept Hindu majority rule?
4. Compare the goals of Jinnah and Gandhi. (See Chapter 35.) What similarities and differences do you see?
5. How do Jinnah's ideas compare with those of Maulvi Syed Kutb Shah Sahib? (See Chapter 16.) How do you explain the differences?
6. Compare Jinnah's ideas to those of Ziya Gokalp (Chapter 29) and the Ayatullah Murtada Mutahhari (Chapter 31) on the issue of Islam and the nation. Do you see a trend? How do you explain it?

37

Love and Marriage in Modern India

The establishment of Indian independence in 1947 led to important legal reforms regarding gender relations. Voting rights were extended to women by the Constitution of 1950, which also outlawed discrimination by sex. Laws adopted somewhat later provided for divorce by mutual consent, banned polygamy (except among Indian Muslims), and established the right of women to have abortions.

The new laws benefited upper-class, well-educated women who took advantage of increased opportunities for careers in politics, business, and education. However, as elsewhere, career women in India, regardless of the law and their abilities, were often unable to win acceptance as equals by their male colleagues and associates. Circumstances were far worse for the hundreds of millions of poor women, most of whom lived in India's 560,000 rural villages. For these women issues such as access to the most minimal level of education, obtaining adequate nutrition and basic health care (especially relating to childbirth), and opportunities for paid work of any kind remained major concerns.

The continuing obstacles faced by Indian women led in the 1970s to the emergence of a feminist movement. As their counterparts did in other countries. Indian feminists founded organizations and journals, conducted major research on gender issues, lobbied governmental officials, became active in the labor movement, ran for public office, and organized protest demonstrations. The striking achievements in recent decades of Indian woman writers such as Anita Desai, Ruth Prawer Jhabvala, Gita Mehta, and Arundhati Roy gave literary expression to the new feminist activism.

Indian feminists have had to face more difficult challenges compared with those confronted by feminists in the West. The tradition of *purdah* (the physical exclusion of women) continues to be significant in India's rural villages. In addition, owing to widespread poverty and the social pressure on families to provide dowries for their daughters, female infanticide in some rural regions is a serious problem. Finally, there is widespread prejudice in India against widows, a lingering legacy of the once-significant practice of widow-suicide (*sati*).

As the product of Indian realities (as well as contacts with feminists in the West and elsewhere), the views of Indian feminists have their own distinctiveness. The selection by Madhu Kishwar, one of India's leading feminists, provides us with an in-

From Madhu Kishwar, "Love and Marriage," *Manushi*, 80 (1994): 11–14, 17–19.

teresting illustration of this point. Kishwar's essay, which appeared in the journal *Manushi* (woman), argues in favor of what she calls "family-arranged" marriage (which is still the way most marriages come about in India), as opposed to Western-style "self-arranged" marriage. The article led to much debate in the pages of *Manushi* and should not be understood as *the* authoritative view of India's feminists on the issue of marriage. It is, nonetheless, an important statement and is included here because of the window it opens on important aspects of Indian society and culture in the late twentieth century.

Feminists, socialists and other radicals often project the system of arranged marriages as one of the key factors leading to women's oppression in India. This view derives from the West, which recognises two supposedly polar opposite forms of marriage—"love marriage" versus arranged marriage. "Love marriages" are assumed to be superior because they are supposedly based on romance, understanding, and mutual love—they are said to facilitate compatibility. In "love marriages" the persons concerned are supposed to have married out of idealistic considerations while arranged marriages are assumed to be based on materialistic considerations, where parents and family dominate and deny individual choice to the young people. Consequently, family arranged marriages are believed to be lacklustre and loveless. It is assumed that in arranged marriages compatibility rarely exists because the couple are denied the opportunity to discover areas of common interests and base their life together on mutual understanding. Moving away from family arranged marriages towards love marriages is seen as an essential step towards building a better life for women. To it the social reformers add another favourite *mantra*—dowryless marriages as proof that money and status considerations play no role in determining the choice of one's life partner. The two together—that is, a dowryless love marriage—[are] projected as the route to a happy married life.

Does experience bear this out? From what I have seen of them, "love marriages" compel me to conclude that most of them are not based on love and often end up being as big a bore or fiasco as many arranged marriages. Among the numerous cases I know I have found that often there is nothing more than a fleeting sexual attraction which does not last beyond the honeymoon period. And then the marriage is as loveless or even worse than a bad arranged marriage. Nor have I found any evidence that material considerations do not play as important a role in people's choice when they decide to "fall in love" with someone with a view to matrimony. . . .

My colleague Giri Deshingkar tells me an amusing story of the time he worked as a pool typist in England. Like most Indian men, he never wore a wedding ring. Mistaking him as an eligible bachelor, his female colleagues showered him with attention and competed with each other in wooing him. However, as soon as they got to know through a chance remark that he was already married, they dropped him like a hot brick. No more teas and coffees and other gestures of attention. Suddenly he became invisible for them. They would not hesitate to discuss their boyfriends and love affairs in his presence. He found them absolutely cynical in their calculation of who they were going to select as a target for loving attention. The experience cured him of all naive notions about love and romance.

This does not surprise me because I have seen these calculations at work at close quarters. For instance, during my university days, I found most of my fellow Mirandians from an English speaking elite background determined to "fall in love" with a Stephanian and would not "stoop" to have a relationship with a man from Khalsa or Rao Tula Ram College, because those were considered low status institutions, where people from ordinary middle class backgrounds went to study. The additional qualification they looked for was that the man's family own a house in one of South Delhi's posh colonies. Thus men from colonies such as Jor Bagh, Golf Links or Sundar Nagar were much sought after. Likewise, sons of senior bureaucrats, ambassadors, and top industrialists could have the choicest pick among the beauties and cuties of Miranda House. But a man whose father was a small shopkeeper in Kamla Nagar or a clerk in a government office stood no chance, no matter how bright or decent he might be. I witnessed several instances of my fellow students ditching a man they had been having an affair with for years as soon as someone from a wealthier background appeared on the scene. Often they would not even bother to hide the crassness of their calculations; a friend conveniently "fell out of love" with her boyfriend who owned a motorbike in favour of someone who had a car to take her out on dates.

While many of my friends would have scoffed at the idea of their parents "arranging" for them to meet a man with a view to matrimony, they were only too eager to go to parties arranged by Stephanians so that they could pick girl friends. In western campuses young people eagerly read notices of "Mixers" in order to find future mates.

Men do precisely what women do about "falling in love." They take family status, who among her family are "green card" holders, and other such material considerations into account before they take the plunge.

While men and women may be somewhat more adventurous when choosing someone for a mere sexual affair, the same people tend to become far more "rational" in their calculations when "falling in love" is meant to be a prelude to marriage.

In the 1950s a study which is considered a classic on factors that determine love and marriage in America showed that it was easy to statistically predict the characteristics of the person a man or a woman is likely to fall in love with and marry. Three major factors that have a great influence on who a person falls in love with are: proximity, opportunity, and similarity. Thus it is no coincidence that most whites marry whites and rich people marry among themselves even in a "free" society like America where marriages are self contracted. Why then are we surprised if most Brahmins marry within the Brahmin fold or Jats and Mahars do likewise in family contracted marriages?

Whatever the form of marriage, the motivations and calculations that go into it are fairly simple. Desire for regular sex, economic security, enhancement of one's social status and the desire to have children all play a role in both kinds of marriages. Therefore, instead of describing them as "love" marriages, it is more appropriate to call them self arranged marriages. Love, in the sense of caring for another person, may even be altogether absent in these marriages. Therefore, I feel the term love marriage needs to be restricted to those marriages where people actually have a loving respect for each other and where there is continuing satisfaction in togetherness.

Self Arranged Marriages

Critics of the family arranged marriage system in India have rightly focused on how prospective brides are humiliated by being endlessly displayed for approval when marriages are being negotiated by families. The ritual of *ladki dikhana,* with the in-evitable rejections women (now even men) often undergo before being selected, does indeed make the whole process extremely stressful.

However, women do not really escape the pressures of displaying and parading themselves in cultures where they are expected to have self arranged marriages. Witness the amount of effort a young woman in western societies has to put in to look attractive enough to hook eligible young men. One gets the feeling they are on constant self display as opposed to the periodic displays in family arranged marriages. Western women have to diet to stay trim since it is not fashionable nowadays to be fat, get artificial padding for their breasts (1.5 million American women are reported to have gone through silicon surgery to get their breasts reshaped or enlarged), try to get their complexion to glow, if not with real health, at least with a cosmetic blush. They must also learn how to be viewed as "attractive" and seductive to men, how to be a witty conversationalist as well as an ego booster—in short, to become the kind of appendage a man would feel proud to have around him. Needless to say, not all women manage to do all the above, though most drive themselves crazy trying. Western women have to compete hard with each other in order to hook a partner. And once having found him, they have to be alert to prevent other women from snatching him. So fierce is the pressure to keep off other grabbing females that in many cases if a woman is divorced or single she is unlikely to be invited over to a married friend's house at a gathering of couples lest she try to grab someone else's husband.

The humiliations western women have to go through, having first to grab a man, and then to devise strategies to keep other women off him, is in many ways much worse than what a woman in parent arranged marriages has to go through. She does not have to chase and hook men all by herself. Her father, her brother, her uncles and aunts and the entire *kunba* join together to hunt for a man. In that sense the woman concerned does not have to carry the burden of finding a husband all alone. And given the relative stability of marriage among communities where families take a lot of interest in keeping the marriage going, a woman is not so paranoid about her husband abandoning her in favour of a more attractive woman. Consequently, Indian women are not as desperate as their western counterparts to look for ever youthful, trim and sexually attractive marriage partners. . . .

Family Pressures

My impression is that it takes much more than two people to make a good marriage. Overbearing parents on either side can indeed make married life difficult for a young couple and often women have to put up with a great deal of maltreatment at the hands of their in-laws. But more solidly enduring and happy marriages are almost always those where the families on both sides genuinely join together to celebrate their coming together and invest a lot of effort and emotion in making the marriage work. Very few people have the emotional and other resources required to make a happy marriage all on their own. Two people locked up with each other in a nuclear family having to meet with varied expectations inevitably generate too much heat and soon tend to suffocate each other. The proximity of other family members takes a lot of the load off. They can act as a glue, especially during times of crisis. In cultures where marriage is considered an internal affair of the couple with no responsibility taken by families on either side for the continuation and well being of the marriage, breakdown in marriages is more frequent.

There is also the negative side. In communities where families consider it their responsibility to prevent divorce as far as possible women do very often get to be victims of vicious pressures against breaking out of abusive marriages. Among several communities in India a divorced woman is viewed with contempt and parents often force their daughters to keep their marriages going no matter what the cost. Consequently, many end up committing suicide or getting murdered because they are unable to walk out of abusive marriages. Many more have to learn to live a life of humiliation and even suffer routine beatings and other forms of torture. However, in such cultures, divorced men get to be viewed with some suspicion and are somewhat stigmatised. . . .

In family arranged marriages, few parents are interested in marrying their young daughter to a divorced man, unless he is willing to marry a woman from a much poorer family (so that the family escapes having to pay dowry) or marry a divorced woman or widow. In India, relatively few men resort to divorce even when they are unhappy in marriage. The sigma attached to divorce for men, if not as great as for women, is at least substantial enough to get them to try somewhat to control themselves. They know that they cannot get away with having a series of divorces, as they do in the West, and yet find a young, beautiful bride 30 years their junior. But this is only true for marriage within tight knit communities where the two families have effective ways of checking on each other's background. There is no dearth of instances nowadays in which parents fail to investigate the groom's background and end up marrying their daughters to men who have beaten or even murdered the first wife. My impression is that this is happening more among groups who are marrying beyond their kinship groups through matrimonial advertisement or professional marriage brokers.

Inter Community Marriages

Hollywood, Bollywood propaganda tells us that passionate romance is the foundation of a real marriage; according to these myth makers marriage is and ought to be an affair between two individuals. Marriages between people who defy caste, class, community and other prevalent norms are seen as demonstrating thereby their true love for each other and are glorified. This is not only over simplistic but highly erroneous.

Our crusades against social inequality and communal prejudices [are] one thing. The ingredients that make for a good marriage are quite another. A married couple is more likely to have a stable marriage if the spouses can take 90 per cent of things for granted and have to work at adjustment in no more than 10 per cent of the areas of mutual living. The film *Ek Duje ke Liye* type of situation is very likely to spell disaster in real life. The hero and the heroine come from very different regional and linguistic groups. They don't even understand each other's languages and communicate mostly through sign or body language—yet are shown as willing to die for each other. In real life this may make for a brief sexual affair, but not a good marriage. The latter depends more on how well people understand and appreciate each other's language, culture, food habits, personal nuances and quirks, and get along [with] and win respect from each other's family. If the income gap is too large and the standards of living of the two families are dramatically different, the couple are likely to find it much harder to adjust to each other.

The willing participation of the groom's family is very often crucial to the well being of a marriage especially if the couple lives in a joint family with the groom's parents. But even if the couple is to live in a nuclear family after marriage, the support of her in-laws will help a woman keep her husband disciplined and domesticated. Most of my friends who have happy and secure marriages get along with their in-laws so well that they are confident that if their husbands were to behave irresponsibly or start extra marital affairs, their in-laws would not only side with the daughter in-law but go as far as to ask the son to quit the house.

Safety Measures for Women

I am not against self arranged marriages but I feel they have a poor track record despite pompous claims about their superiority. A self arranged marriage cannot arrogate to itself the nomenclature of a love marriage unless it endures with love. My own experience of the world tells me that marriages in which the two people concerned genuinely love and respect each other, marriages which slowly grow in the direction of mutual understanding, are very rare even among groups and cultures who believe in the superiority of self arranged marriages.

The outcome of marriage depends on how realistic the calculations have been. For instance, a family may arrange the marriage of their daughter with a man settled in the USA in the hope of providing better life opportunities to the daughter. But if they have not been responsible enough to inquire carefully into the family, personal and professional history of the man, they could end up seriously jeopardising their daughter's well being. He may have boasted of being a computer scientist but could turn out to be a low paid cab driver or a guard in New York. He could well be living with or married to an American woman and take the Indian wife to be no more than a domestic servant or a camouflage to please his parents. He could in addition be a drunkard given to violent bouts of temper. His being so far away from India would isolate the young wife from all sources of support and thus make her far more vulnerable than if she were married in the same city as her parents.

Another case at the other end of the spectrum could end up just as disastrously if the woman concerned makes wrong calculations. Let's say a young student in an American University decides to arrange her marriage with a fellow student setting out to be a doctor. Through the years that her husband is studying to become a doctor, she works hard at a low or moderately paying job to support the family. When he becomes a doctor she decides to leave her job and have a baby. In a few years he becomes successful whereas she has become economically dependent on him. At this point he finds a lot of young and attractive women willing to fall at his feet and he decides to "fall in love" with one of them, divorces his wife and remarries a much younger woman. The wife is left at a time when she needs a marriage partner most. All she can hope to do is to get some kind of a financial settlement after lengthy legal proceedings. But that is not a substitute for a secure family.

The factors that decide the fate of women in marriage are:

- Whether the woman has independent means of survival. If she is absolutely dependent on her husband's goodwill for survival, she is more likely to have to lead a submissive life than if she is economically self sufficient.

- Whether or not her husband is willing and equipped to take on the responsibility that goes with having a family.
- Whether or not a woman's in-laws welcome her coming into the family and how eager they are to make it work.
- How well the two families get along with and respect each other.
- Whether or not there are social restraints through family and community control on men's behaviour. In societies where men can get away with beating wives or abandoning them in favour of younger women, women tend to live in insecurity. However, in communities where a man who treats his wife badly is looked down upon and finds it harder to find another wife because of social stigma, men are more likely to behave with a measure of responsibility.
- The ready availability of other women even after a man is known to have maltreated his wife tilts the balance against women. If men can easily find younger women as they grow older while women cannot as readily find marriage partners when they are older or divorced, the balance will inevitably tilt in favour of men irrespective of whether marriages in that culture are self arranged or parent arranged.
- Whether or not her parents are willing to support her emotionally and financially if she is facing an abusive marriage. Most important of all is whether her parents are willing to give her the share due to her in their property and in the parental home. In communities where parents' expectation concerning a daughter is that only her *arthi* (funeral pyre) should come out of her husband's house, family pressure can prove really disastrous.

Undoubtedly, there are numerous situations whereby family elders do take an altogether unreasonable position; defiance of their tyranny then becomes inevitable, even desirable. Parents can often go wrong in their judgments. Parents must take into account their children's best interests and preferences if they are to play a positive role.

We have to devise ways to tilt family support more in favour of women rather than seeking "freedom" by alienating oneself from this crucial source of support over romanticising self arranged marriages and insisting on individual choice in marriage as an end in itself rather than as one means to more stable, dignified and egalitarian marriages.

STUDY QUESTIONS

1. According to Madhu Kishwar, what is wrong with the idea of "love marriage"? Why does she believe that "self-arranged" marriage is more useful term than "love marriage"?
2. What advantages does Kishwar see in "family-arranged" marriages? What problems does she acknowledge in "family-arranged" marriages?
3. Is there a contradiction between "family-arranged" marriages and love between spouses?
4. What does this article suggest about the emotional life of Indian married couples? About the importance of individualism in India?
5. Is Kishwar's portrait of marriage in the West accurate?
6. How do the views of Madhu Kishwar compare with those of Simone de Beauvoir in Chapter 25, Higuchi Keiko in Chapter 34, and the African women in Chapter 41?

38

Twentieth-Century Latin American Politics: The Revolutionary Challenge

Since their independence from Spain and Portugal (1810–1825), Latin American republics have experienced periods of severe political instability. From the 1830s to the 1860s *caudillos,* local military leaders left over from the wars of independence, often seized national office, pillaged the treasury, and were in turn deposed by others. During the late nineteenth century, when Latin America began exporting raw materials (metals, fertilizers) and food (sugar, coffee, wheat, bananas), oligarchical elites closely linked to the export economy consolidated stable political regimes. This stability was purchased by limiting the exercise of political power to a narrow few and excluding commoners through voting restrictions. At the beginning of the twentieth century, population growth plus immigration from Europe greatly swelled the ranks of laborers, professionals, clerical people, and the urban poor. Most remained apolitical, but key groups such as railroad workers, dockworkers, and meatpackers formed unions, while professionals, small property owners, and clerical people formed middle-class political parties.

Social unrest along with often inflexible political regimes has led to a series of revolutions and other upheavals in twentieth-century Latin America. The following selections deal with three of the major episodes. All express some of the basic social grievances that have created unrest, thus suggesting answers to the question of why Latin America has been so productive of political turmoil in our century.

Selection 1 from Emiliano Zapata, *The Plan of Ayala* (29 November 1911), translated by Erick D. Langer. Reprinted by permission. Selection 2 from Angel Perelman, *Como Hicimo el 17 d Octobre* (Buenos Aires: Editorial Coyoacan, 1961), pp. 44–46, translated in *Why Peron Came to Power. The Background to Peronism in Argentine,* edited by Joseph R. Barager (New York: Alfred A. Knopf, 1968), pp. 200–202. Copyright © 1968, Alfred A. Knopf. Reprinted by permission. Selection 3 from Fidel Castro, *History Will Absolve Me. Moncada Trial Defence Speech Santiago de Cuba, October, 16, 1956* (London: Jonathan Cape, 1958), pp. 40–45. First published in Cuba in 1967, and published in Great Britain in 1968 by Jonathan Cape Limited. Reprinted by permission.

The first selection comes from the Mexican Revolution of 1910. It was issued by the most radical peasant leader, Emiliano Zapata. Zapata never sized control of the Mexican Revolution, but the radical economic demands of his Plan of Ayala influenced the course of Mexican social development for the next 30 years.

The second selection reflects a new kind of strongman rule that characterized several major Latin states during the twentieth century. Juan Perón, in Argentina, resembled revolutionaries in seeking to avoid foreign (in this case almost entirely economic) domination. Perón, a middle-class military man, appealed to working people neglected by earlier civilian governments. The passage shows how union leaders—in this case the head of the metalworkers' union—had become disenchanted with communist control and preferred a military ruler who could get things done for the workers. This decision resulted in state control of unions after Perón became president, from 1946 to 1955, and an enduring attachment of many Argentine workers to an authoritarian, but populist, government.

A new round of revolutionary activity emerged during the 1950s, building on social and economic problems similar to those in Mexico earlier on. The lone successful change came in 1959, with Fidel Castro in Cuba, but his example then spurred other guerrilla movements which, particularly in Central America, have continued to the present day; later on it also helped inspire outright revolution in Nicaragua.

Although he became a symbol of communist insurrection, Castro viewed his revolution as authentically Cuban. Looking back into Cuba's past, Castro saw a deformed nation. At each moment when a true nationalist sought political power, either he was blocked by foreign intervention, or he betrayed the cause. José Marti, the intellectual spirit of the Cuban independence movement against Spain in 1895, was an authentic Cuban hero. Yet his political program was never realized because of the intervention of the United States during the Spanish-American War of 1898. From that year until Castro seized power in 1959, the United States dominated Cuba politically and economically, despite Cuba's nominal independence. Presidents of Cuba, such as Batista (1940–1944, 1952–1958), talked of reform but used their office to become wealthy, especially by diverting U.S. loans into their own pockets. Meanwhile, the majority of the Cuban people—the poor—were neglected. For Cuba to take control of its destiny, Castro saw the necessity of revolution. After the failure of his first military operation on July 26, 1953, Castro—while in jail—described what the revolution was being fought for and what he would do once in power. In Selection 3, one can see that the spirit that animates his program is the same spirit that guides revolutionaries in other parts of Latin America.

1. THE PLAN OF AYALA

The liberating Plan of the sons of the State of Morelos, affiliated with the Insurgent Army which defends the fulfillment of the Plan of San Luis Potosí, with the reforms which they have believed necessary to add for the benefit of the Mexican Fatherland.

We, the subscribers [to this Plan], constituted in a Revolutionary Council . . . declare solemnly before the countenance of the civilized world which judges us and before the Nation to which we belong and love, the principles which we have formulated to terminate the tyranny which oppresses us and redeem the Fatherland from the dictatorships which are imposed on us, which are determined in the following Plan:

1. [Accuses Francisco I. Madero, the leader of the 1910 revolution and President of Mexico, of betraying the Revolution and allying himself with the oppressive old guard in the State of Morelos.]

2. Francisco I. Madero is disavowed as Chief of the Revolution and as President of the Republic, for the above reasons, [and we will] endeavor to overthrow this official.

3. The illustrious General Pascual Orozco, second of the *caudillo* Don Francisco I. Madero, is recognized as Chief of the Liberating Revolution, and in case he does not accept this delicate post, General Emiliano Zapata is recognized as Chief of the Revolution.

4. The Revolutionary Junta of the State of Morelos manifests the following formal points . . . and will make itself the defender of the principles that it will defend until victory or death.

5. The Revolutionary Junta of the State of Morelos will not admit transactions or political compromises until the overthrow of the dictatorial elements of Porfirio Díaz and Francisco I. Madero, since the Nation is tired of false men and traitors who make promises as liberators but once in power, forget them and become tyrants.

6. As an additional part of the Plan which we invoke, we assert that: the fields, woodland, and water which the haciendados [landlords], *científicos* or bosses in the shadow of tyranny and venal justice have usurped, will revert to the possession of the towns or citizens who have their corresponding titles to these properties. [These properties] have been usurped through the bad faith of our oppressors, who maintained all along with arms in hand the above mentioned possession. The usurpers who feel they have the right [to ownership], will demonstrate this before special tribunals which will be established when the Revolution triumphs.

7. In virtue of the fact that the immense majority of the towns and Mexican citizens are not masters of the soil they step upon, suffering horrors of misery without being able to better their social condition at all nor dedicate themselves to industry or agriculture because of the monopoly in a few hands of the land, woodlands, and waters, for this reason [the lands] will be expropriated, with indemnity of the third part of these monopolies to their powerful owners, so that the towns and citizens of Mexico can obtain common lands (*ejidos*), colonies, and legitimate resources for towns or agricultural fields and that above all the lack of prosperity and wellbeing of the Mexican people is improved.

8. The haciendados, *científicos* or bosses who oppose directly or indirectly the present plan, will have their possessions nationalized and two thirds of what they own will be destined for war indemnities, [and] pensions for the widows and orphans of the victims who succumb in the fight for this Plan.

9. To regulate the procedures in regard to the items mentioned above, the laws of disentailment and nationalization will be applied as is appropriate. [The laws] put into effect by the immortal Juarez regarding Church lands will serve as a guide and example, which set a severe example to the

despots and conservatives who at all times have tried to impose the igno-
minious yoke of oppression and backwardness.

10. The insurgent military chiefs of the Republic, who rose up in armed re-
    volt at the behest of Francisco I. Madero to defend the Plan of San Luis
    Potosí and who now oppose by force the present Plan, are to be judged
    traitors to the cause they defended and to the Fatherland, given the fact
    that in actuality many of them to please the tyrants for a handful of coins,
    or for bribes, are spilling the blood of their brethren who demand the
    fulfillment of the promises which don Francisco I. Madero made to the
    Nation.

[11–14. Details the payment of the expenses of war, the administration of the
    country after the Plan's success, and bids Madero to step down voluntar-
    ily.]

15. Mexicans: Consider that the cleverness and the bad faith of one man is
    spilling blood in a scandalous manner because of his inability to govern;
    consider that his system of government is putting the Fatherland in
    chains and by brute force of bayonets trampling under foot our institu-
    tions; and as we raised our arms to elevate him to power, today we turn
    them against him for having gone back on his agreements with the Mexi-
    can people and having betrayed the Revolution he initiated; we are not
    personalists, we are believers in principles, not in men.

People of Mexico: Support with your arms in hand this Plan and you will create prosperity and happiness for the Fatherland.

Justicia y ley.
Ayala, 28 of November, 1911.

2. PERONISM

Once the resistance of the [Communist] directors was overcome, we arranged with
the Secretariat of Labor to convoke a meeting at which Perón would speak to the
metal workers. The date fixed, we calculated that we could fill the assembly hall of
the Deliberating Council, where the Secretariat of Labor and Social Welfare was located.

We had no resources for publicizing this meeting. Until noon of the day of
the gathering, we were still sticking together some posters announcing the convo-
cation. It was a great surprise when, by the time of the meeting, the meeting hall
was completely filled, and an enormous multitude of nearly 20,000 metal workers
was concentrated outside in the Diagonal Roca. The shops they came from were
identified by improvised placards and reflected the enormous repercussion the
growth of industry was having on the working class at that time. . . .

Colonel Perón, in one of the salient parts of his discourse, told us that he was
gratified to see the metal workers enter the house of the workers and that he had
assumed that, since they were one of the last unions to come together there, they
must be very well paid. But he added that, as a result of the remarks of the comrade
who had preceded him on the platform, it appeared that this was not so, and con-

sequently he was urging the metal workers to form a powerful union to defend their rights and the country's sovereignty. At this moment a metal worker interrupted to shout: "Thus speaks a *criollo!*" [true Argentine] Banners and posters fluttered approval of the metal worker's remark. We went out of that meeting with the conviction that the metal workers' union would soon be transformed into a very powerful labor organization. And in effect it was; from a membership of 1,500 we transformed that union "of form" into the present Union of Metal Workers (UOM) with 300,000 workers in the fold. So profound was the need for the country to defend its political independence and economic sovereignty, and for the working class to organize at last its unions on a grade scale, that, faced by the treason of the parties of the left, this need had to be embodied in a military man who had come from the ranks of the Army.

And we came to constitute then that ideological tendency known by many people as the "national left." In our union activities at the end of 1944 we witnessed unbelievable happenings: labor laws neglected in another era were being carried out; one did not need recourse to the courts for the granting of vacations; such other labor dispensations as the recognition of factory delegates, guarantees against being discharged, etc., were immediately and rigorously enforced. The nature of internal relations between the owners and the workers in the factories was completely changed. The internal democratization imposed by the metal workers' union resulted in factory delegates constituting the axis of the entire organization and in the direct expression of the will of the workers in each establishment. The owners were as disconcerted as the workers were astounded and happy. The Secretariat of Labor and Social Welfare was converted into an agency for the organization, development, and support of the workers. It did not function as a state regulator for the top level of the unions; it acted as a state ally of the working class. Such were the practical results that constituted the basis for the political shift of the Argentine masses and that were manifested in the streets on October 17, 1945. [Date when a massive demonstration took place that secured Perón's release from prison.]

3. CASTRO'S PROGRAM

When we speak of the people we do not mean the comfortable ones, the conservative elements of the nation, who welcome any regime of oppression, any dictatorship, any despotism, prostrating themselves before the master of the moment until they grind their foreheads into the ground. When we speak of struggle, the people means the vast unredeemed masses to whom all make promises and whom all deceive; we mean the people who yearn for a better, more dignified and more just nation; who are moved by ancestral aspirations of justice, for they have suffered injustice and mockery generation after generation; who long for great and wise changes in all aspects of their life; people who, to attain the changes, are ready to give even the very last breath of their lives, when they believe in something or in someone, especially when they believe in themselves. . . . The people we counted on in our struggle were these:

Seven hundred thousand Cubans without work, who desire to earn their daily bread honestly without having to emigrate in search of a livelihood.

Five hundred thousand farm labourers inhabiting miserable shacks (*bohíos*), who work four months of the year and starve during the rest, sharing their misery with their children; who have not an inch of land to till, and whose existence would move any heart not made of stone.

Four hundred thousand industrial labourers and stevedores whose retirement funds have been embezzled, whose benefits are being taken away, whose homes are wretched quarters, whose salaries pass from the hands of the boss to those of the money-lender (*garrotero*), whose future is a pay reduction and dismissal, whose life is eternal work and whose only rest is in the tomb.

One hundred thousand small farmers who live and die working on land that is not theirs, looking at it with sadness as Moses looked at the promised land, to die without ever owning it; who, like feudal serfs, have to pay for the use of their parcel of land by giving up a portion of its products: who cannot love it, improve it, beautify it, nor plant a lemon or an orange tree on it, because they never know when a sheriff will come with the rural guard to evict them from it.

Thirty thousand teachers and professors who are so devoted, dedicated and necessary to the better destiny of future generations and who are so badly treated and paid.

Twenty thousand small business men, weighted down by debts, ruined by the crisis and harangued by a plague of grafting and venal officials.

Ten thousand young professionals: doctors, engineers, lawyers, veterinarians, school teachers, dentists, pharmacists, newspapermen, painters, sculptors, etc., who come forth from school with their degrees, anxious to work and full of hope, only to find themselves at a dead end with all doors closed, and where no ear hears their clamour or supplication.

These are the people, the ones who know misfortune and, therefore, are capable of fighting with limitless courage!

To the people whose desperate roads through life have been paved with the bricks of betrayals and false promises, we were not going to say: "We will eventually give you what you need," but rather—"Here you have it, fight for it with all your might, so that liberty and happiness may be yours!"

In the brief of this case, the five revolutionary laws that would have been proclaimed immediately after the capture of the Moncada Barracks and would have been broadcasted to the nation by radio should be recorded. It is possible that Colonel Chaviano may deliberately have destroyed these documents, but even if he has done so I remember them.

The First Revolutionary Law would have returned power to the people and proclaimed the Constitution of 1940 the supreme Law of the State, until such time as the people should decide to modify or change it. And, in order to effect its implementation and punish those who had violated it, there being no organization for holding elections to accomplish this, the revolutionary movement, as the momentous incarnation of this sovereignty, the only source of legitimate power, would have assumed all the faculties inherent in it, except that of modifying the Constitution itself: in other words, it would have assumed the legislative, executive and judicial powers. . . .

The Second Revolutionary Law would have granted property, non-mortgageable and non-transferable, to all planters, non-quota planters, lessees, share-croppers, and squatters who hold parcels of five *caballerías* of land or less, and the State would indemnify the former owners on the basis of the rental which they would have received for these parcels over a period of ten years.

The Third Revolutionary Law would have granted workers and employees the right to share thirty per cent of the profits of all the large industrial, mercantile and mining enterprises, including the sugar mills. The strictly agricultural enterprises would be exempt in consideration of other agrarian laws which would be implemented.

The Fourth Revolutionary Law would have granted all planters the right to share fifty-five per cent of the sugar production and a minimum quota of forty thousand *arrobas* for all small planters who have been established for three or more years.

The Fifth Revolutionary Law would have ordered the confiscation of all holdings and ill-gotten gains of those who had committed frauds during previous regimes, as well as the holdings and ill-gotten gains of all their legatees and heirs. To implement this, special courts with full powers would gain access to all records of all corporations registered or operating in this country, in order to investigate concealed funds of illegal origin, and to request that foreign governments extradite persons and attach holdings rightfully belonging to the Cuban people. Half of the property recovered would be used to subsidize retirement funds for workers and the other half would be used for hospitals, asylums and charitable organizations.

STUDY QUESTIONS

1. The documents offer a comparison with earlier grievances, when Latin American nations struggled for political independence (see Chapter 18). What has changed among the goals and actors on center stage?
2. How do the goals of Peronist workers resemble as well as differ from more explicitly revolutionary currents in Latin America?
3. How radical were Castro's goals? What were the political implications of implementing them? Who would have been harmed by their implementation? Who would have benefited? How do they compare with Zapata's goals?

39

Searching for the Soul
of the Latin American Experience

Essayists and novelists have struggled to capture the uniqueness of Latin America. Although their descriptions are set in specific countries and locations, they tend toward common themes. For example, the Mexican essayist Octavio Paz, in search of his identity as well as that of his nation, wrote about the "labyrinth of solitude." The Colombian novelist Gabriel García Márquez examined the experiences of a family and a town through "one hundred years of solitude." The common theme of solitude becomes for these two men the chief vehicle for understanding Latin American civilization.

Gabriel García Márquez was awarded the Nobel Prize for literature in 1982. In his acceptance speech, "The Solitude of Latin America," he explained the source of that solitude. To García Márquez, Latin Americans lacked a conventional means of believing their past. Rather, they lived in a world of illusion that produced separation and solitude. Neither was this "fantasy reality" understood by outsiders, equipped only with their own cultural tools. Europeans, for example, accepted Latin American literature. They, however, ridiculed the Latin Americans' attempts at social change. Latin Americans were accepted not as a distinct whole, but as an incomplete Western form. García Márquez asserts that Latin America is distinct. Latin Americans will invent their own solutions and utopias. They will affirm their own reality, illusory or not.

The concern about identity in Latin America reflects an important facet of Latin American culture, but this is not unique. Other twentieth-century civilizations worry about identity issues; these Latin American reflections can thus be compared with the issues of identity in societies such as sub-Saharan Africa.

Antonio Pigafetta, a Florentine navigator who went with Magellan on the first voyage around the world, wrote, upon his passage through our southern lands of America, a strictly accurate account that nonetheless resembles a venture into fantasy. In it he recorded that he had seen hogs with navels on their haunches, clawless birds whose hens laid eggs on the backs of their mates, and others still, resembling tongueless pelicans, with beaks like spoons. He wrote of having seen a misbegotten

From Gabriel García Márquez, "The Solitude of Latin America" (Nobel Lecture, 1982), translated from the Spanish by Mariana Castaneda in Julio Ortega, *Gabriel García Márquez and the Powers of Fiction* (Austin: University of Texas Press, 1988), pp. 87–91. Reprinted by permission of The Nobel Foundation.

creature with the head and ears of a mule, a camel's body, the legs of a deer and the whinny of a horse. He described how the first native encountered in Patagonia was confronted with a mirror, whereupon that impassioned giant lost his senses to the terror of his own image.

This short and fascinating book, which even then contained the seeds of our present-day novels, is by no means the most staggering account of our reality in that age. The Chroniclers of the Indies left us countless others. Eldorado, our so avidly sought and illusory land, appeared on numerous maps for many a long year, shifting its place and form to suit the fantasy of cartographers. In his search for the fountain of eternal youth, the mythical Alvar Núñez Cabeza de Vaca explored the north of Mexico for eight years, in a deluded expedition whose members devoured each other and only five of whom returned, of the six hundred who had undertaken it. One of the many unfathomed mysteries of that age is that of the eleven thousand mules, each loaded with one hundred pounds of gold, that left Cuzco one day to pay the ransom of Atahualpa and never reached their destination. Subsequently, in colonial times, hens were sold in Cartagena de Indias, that had been raised on alluvial land and whose gizzards contained tiny lumps of gold. The founders' lust for gold beset us until recently. As late as the last century, a German mission appointed to study the construction of an interoceanic railroad across the Isthmus of Panama concluded that the project was feasible on one condition: that the rails not be made of iron, which was scarce in the region, but of gold.

Our independence from Spanish domination did not put us beyond the reach of madness. General Antonio López de Santa Anna, three times dictator of Mexico, held a magnificent funeral for the right leg he had lost in the so-called Pastry War. General Gabriel García Moreno ruled Ecuador for sixteen years as an absolute monarch; at his wake, the corpse was seated on the presidential chair, decked out in full-dress uniform and a protective layer of medals. General Maximiliano Hernández Martínez, the theosophical despot of El Salvador who had thirty thousand peasants slaughtered in a savage massacre, invented a pendulum to detect poison in his food, and had street lamps draped in red paper to defeat an epidemic of scarlet fever. The statue to General Francisco Morazán erected in the main square of Tegucigalpa is actually one of Marshal Ney, purchased at a Paris warehouse of second-hand sculptures.

Eleven years ago, the Chilean Pablo Neruda, one of the outstanding poets of our time, enlightened the audience with his word. Since then, the Europeans of good will—and sometimes those of bad, as well—have been struck, with ever greater force, by the unearthly tidings of Latin America, that boundless realm of haunted men and historic women, whose unending obstinacy blurs into legend. We have not had a moment's rest. A promethean president, entrenched in his burning palace, died fighting an entire army, alone; and two suspicious airplane accidents, yet to be explained, cut short the life of another great-hearted president and that of a democratic soldier who had revived the dignity of his people. There have been five wars and seventeen military coups; there emerged a diabolic dictator who is carrying out, in God's name, the first Latin American ethnocide of our time. In the meantime, twenty million Latin American children died before the age of one—more than have been born in Europe since 1970. Those missing because of repression number nearly one hundred and twenty thousand, which is as if no one could account for all the inhabitants of Upsala. Numerous women arrested while pregnant have given birth in Argentina prisons, yet nobody knows the whereabouts and identity of their children, who were furtively adopted or sent to an orphanage by order of the military authorities. Because they tried to change this state of things, nearly two hundred thousand men and women have died throughout the continent, and over one hundred thousand have lost their lives in three small and ill-fated countries of Central America: Nicaragua, El Salvador, and Guatemala. If this had happened in the United States, the corresponding figure would be that of one million six hundred thousand violent deaths in four years.

One million people have fled Chile, a country with a tradition of hospitality— that is, ten percent of its population. Uruguay, a tiny nation of two and a half million inhabitants which considered itself the continent's most civilized country, has lost to exile one out of every five citizens. Since 1979, the civil war in El Salvador has produced almost one refugee every twenty minutes. The country that could be formed of all the exiles and forced emigrants of Latin America would have a population larger than that of Norway.

I dare to think that it is this outsized reality, and not just its literary expression, that has deserved the attention of the Swedish Academy of Letters. A reality not of paper, but one that lives within us and determines each instant of our countless daily deaths, and that nourishes a source of insatiable creativity, full of sorrow and beauty, of which this roving and nostalgic Colombian is but one cipher more, singled out by fortune. Poets and beggars, musicians and prophets, warriors and scoundrels, all creatures of that unbridled reality, we have had to ask but little of imagination, for our crucial problem has been a lack of conventional means to render our lives believable. This, my friends, is the crux of our solitude.

And if these difficulties, whose essence we share, hinder us, it is understandable that the rational talents on this side of the world, exalted in the contemplation of their own cultures, should have found themselves without a valid means to interpret us. It is only natural that they insist on measuring us with the yardstick that they use for themselves, forgetting that the ravages of life are not the same for all, and that the quest of our own identity is just as arduous and bloody for us as it was for them. The interpretation of our reality through patterns not our own serves only to make us ever more unknown, ever less free, ever more solitary. Venerable Europe would perhaps be more perceptive if it tried to see us in its own past. If only it recalled that London took three hundred years to build its first city wall, and three hundred years more to acquire a bishop; that Rome labored in a gloom of uncertainty for twenty centuries, until an Etruscan king anchored it in history; and that the peaceful Swiss of today, who feast us with their mild cheeses and apathetic watches, bloodied Europe as soldiers of fortune, as late as the sixteenth century. Even at the height of the Renaissance, twelve thousand lansquenets in the pay of the imperial armies sacked and devastated Rome and put eight thousand of its inhabitants to the sword.

I do not mean to embody the illusions of Tonio Krüger, whose dreams of uniting a chaste north to a passionate south were exalted here, fifty-three years ago, by Thomas Mann. But I do believe that those clear-sighted Europeans who struggle, here as well, for a more just and humane homeland, could help us far better if they reconsidered their way of seeing us. Solidarity with our dreams will not make us feel less alone, as long as it is not translated into concrete acts of legitimate support for all the peoples that assume the illusion of having a life of their own in the distribution of the world.

Latin America neither wants, nor has any reason, to be a pawn without a will of its own; nor is it merely wishful thinking that its quest for independence and originality should become a Western aspiration. However, the navigational advances that have narrowed such distances between our Americas and Europe seem, conversely, to have accentuated our cultural remoteness. Why is the originality so readily granted us in literature so mistrustfully denied us in our difficult attempts at social change? Why think that the social justice sought by progressive Europeans for their own countries cannot also be a goal for Latin America, with different methods for dissimilar conditions? No: the immeasurable violence and pain of our history are the result of age-old inequities and untold bitterness, and not a conspiracy plotted three thousand leagues from our home. But many European leaders and thinkers have thought so, with the childishness of old-timers who have forgotten the fruitful excesses of their youth as if it were impossible to find another destiny than to live at the mercy of the two great masters of the world. This, my friends, is the very scale of our solitude.

In spite of this, to oppression, plundering, and abandonment, we respond with life. Neither floods nor plagues, famines nor cataclysms, not even the eternal wars of century upon century have been able to subdue the persistent advantage of life over death. An advantage that grows and quickens: every year, there are seventy-four million more births than deaths, a sufficient number of new lives to multiply, each year, the population of New York sevenfold. Most of these births occur in the countries of least resources—including, of course, those of Latin America. Conversely, the most prosperous countries have succeeded in accumulating powers of destruction such as to annihilate, a hundred times over, not only all the human beings that have existed to this day, but also the totality of all living beings that have ever drawn breath on this planet of misfortune.

On a day like today, my master William Faulker said, "I decline to accept the end of man." I would feel unworthy of standing in this place that was his, if I were not fully aware that the colossal tragedy he refused to recognize thirty-two years ago is now, for the first time since the beginning of humanity, nothing more than a simple scientific possibility. Faced with this awesome reality that must have seemed a mere utopia through all of human time, we, the inventors of tales, who will believe anything, feel entitled to believe that it is not yet too late to engage in the creation of the opposite utopia. A new and sweeping utopia of life, where no one will be able to decide for others how they die, where love will prove true and happiness be possible, and where the races condemned to one hundred years of solitude will have, at last and forever, a second opportunity on earth.

STUDY QUESTIONS

1. What occurrences in Latin American history led García Márquez to conclude that the reality of Latin America was "unearthly," "outsized," and "unbridled?"
2. What is the source of "solitude" in Latin America?

3. In what ways should Europeans view Latin America, according to García Márquez?

4. Compare the cultural values expressed in this selection with the cultural values expressed in Sarmiento's "Civilization and Barbarism" in Chapter 20.

5. Just like the Latin Americans, sub-Saharan Africans also worry about identity issues. Why does the theme of defining identity echo in both African and Latin American civilizations? Is it in effect the same theme?

40

African Nationalism

Nationalism was one of the crucial, though unintended, products of European imperialism. Local leaders—particularly aspiring newcomers often exposed to European education—saw the importance of nationalism in Western society and used it as a vehicle for protesting colonial controls and demanding independence. Nationalism could also be used to elicit loyalty to a newly free state, especially when appeals to tradition could not suffice because the nation combined different cultural groups. Thus nationalism had the merit of appealing both to past values and to the idea of progress, although the combination could sometimes be uncomfortable.

Nationalism began to blossom in Africa between the world wars. It had several facets, as indicated in the three selections that follow. One nationalist source stemmed from black leaders in the United States and West Indies sincerely concerned about Africa but also eager for the liberation of their own people. Marcus Garvey's black nationalist movement won loyalty on both sides of the Atlantic in the 1920s and helped define a positive African spirit. Jomo Kenyatta, a British-educated Kenyan—ultimately the first president of Kenya after many jail terms as a nationalist agitator under the colonial government—represents African nationalism directly. Writing in 1938, Kenyatta used traditional kinds of allegory to blast European greed and also defined a special African agenda of combining tradition with change plus very selective borrowing from the West.

The final selection is postcolonial and invites comparison with the earlier nationalist expression: How was nationalism maintained once independence had been achieved, and what changes resulted in tone and purpose? Written by Kwame

Selection 1 from Marcus Garvey, "Redeeming the African Motherland," in *Philosophy and Opinions of Marcus Garvey,* Vol. 1, edited by Amy Jacques Garvey (New York: University Publishing House, 1923), pp. 71–74. Reprinted with the permission of Scribner, a Division of Simon & Schuster Inc. Copyright 1923, 1925 by Amy Jacques-Garvey. Selection 2 from Jomo Kenyatta, *Facing Mt. Kenya* (New York: Random House, Inc., 1962). Copyright © 1962 by Random House, Inc. Reprinted by permission. Selection 3 from Kwame Nkrumah, *Revolutionary Path* (London: Panaf Books Limited, 1973). Copyright © 1973 Panaf Books Limited. Reprinted by permission of Zed Books Ltd.

Nkrumah, an American-educated leader and the first president of Ghana, this nationalist statement reflects a turn away from Africa-in-general to a specific new nation. It also shows some shifts in goals. Once independence was achieved, what targets did African nationalists have? Nkrumah's own career illustrates some of the nationalist dilemma. A brilliant agitator, he proved less successful in running an independent Ghana. The economic problems he defined as next on the nationalist agenda proved more elusive than earlier goals of independence. Yet nationalism remained a factor in Africa, a guide to policy and a popular rallying point in the new nations. These three selections, from different decades as well as different inspirations, give a flavor of African nationalism and some indication of its power. They also permit comparison of African with Indian or Arab nationalism. Is nationalism always the same movement?

1. MARCUS GARVEY PREACHES AFRICAN REVOLUTION

George Washington was not God Almighty. He was a man like any Negro in this building, and if he and his associates were able to make a free America, we too can make a free Africa. Hampden, Gladstone, Pitt and Disraeli were not the representatives of God in the person of Jesus Christ. They were but men, but in their time they worked for the expansion of the British Empire, and today they boast of a British Empire upon which "the sun never sets." As Pitt and Gladstone were able to work for the expansion of the British Empire, so you and I can work for the expansion of a great African Empire. Voltaire and Mirabeau were not Jesus Christs, they were but men like ourselves. They worked and overturned the French Monarchy. They worked for the Democracy which France now enjoys, and if they were able to do that, we are able to work for a democracy in Africa. Lenin and Trotsky were not Jesus Christs, but they were able to overthrow the despotism of Russia, and today they have given to the world a Social Republic, the first of its kind. If Lenin and Trotsky were able to do that for Russia, you and I can do that for Africa. Therefore, let not man, let no power on earth, turn you from this sacred cause of liberty. I prefer to die at this moment rather than not to work for the freedom of Africa. If liberty is good for certain sets of humanity it is good for all. Black men, Colored men, Negroes have as much right to be free as any other race that God Almighty ever created, and we desire freedom that is unfettered, freedom that is unlimited, freedom that will give us a chance and opportunity to rise to the fullest of our ambition and that we cannot get in countries where other men rule and dominate.

We have reached the time when every minute, every second must count for something done, something achieved in the cause of Africa. We need the freedom of Africa now, therefore, we desire the kind of leadership that will give it to us as quickly as possible. You will realize that not only individuals, but governments are using their influence against us. But what do we care about the unrighteous influence of any government? Our cause is based upon righteousness. And anything that is not righteous we have no respect for, because God Almighty is our leader and Jesus Christ our standard bearer. We rely on them for that kind of leadership that will make us free, for it is the same God who inspired the Psalmist to write "Princes shall come out of Egypt and Ethiopia shall stretch out her hands unto God." At this moment methinks I see Ethiopia stretching forth her hands unto God and methinks I see the Angel of God taking up the standard of the Red, the Black and the Green, and saying "Men of the Negro Race, Men of Ethiopia, follow me." Tonight we are following. We are following 400,000,000 strong. We are following with a determination that we must be free before the wreck of matter, before the crash of worlds.

It falls to our lot to tear off the shackles that bind Mother Africa. Can you do it? You did it in the Revolutionary War. You did it in the Civil War; You did it at the Battles of the Marne and Verdun; You did it in Mesopotamia. You can do it marching up the battle heights of Africa. Let the world know that 400,000,000 Negroes are prepared to die or live as free men. Despise us as much as you care. Ignore us as much as you care. We are coming 400,000,000 strong. We are coming with our woes behind us, with the memory of suffering behind us—woes and suffering of three hundred years—they shall be our inspiration. My bulwark of strength in the conflict of freedom in Africa, will be the three hundred years of persecution and hardship left behind in this Western Hemisphere. The more I remember the suffering of my fore-fathers, the more I remember the lynchings and burnings in the Southern States of America, the more I will fight on even though the battle seems doubtful. Tell me that I must turn back, and I laugh you to scorn. Go on! Go on! Climb ye the heights of liberty and cease not in well doing until you have planted the banner of the Red, the Black and the Green on the hilltops of Africa.

2. JOMO KENYATTA DEFINES AMERICAN NATIONALISM

Once upon a time an elephant made a friendship with a man. One day a heavy thunderstorm broke out, the elephant went to his friend, who had a little hut at the edge of the forest, and said to him: "My dear good man, will you please let me put my trunk inside your hut to keep it out of this torrential rain?" The man, seeing what situation his friend was in, replied: "My dear good elephant, my hut is very small, but there is room for your trunk and myself. Please put your trunk in gently." The elephant thanked his friend, saying: "You have done me a good deed and one day I shall return your kindness." But what followed? As soon as the elephant put his trunk inside the hut, slowly he pushed his head inside, and finally flung the man out in the rain, and then lay down comfortably inside his friend's hut, saying: "My dear good friend, your skin is harder than mine, and as there is not enough room for both of us, you can afford to remain in the rain while I am protecting my delicate skin from the hailstorm."

The man, seeing what his friend had done to him, started to grumble; the animals in the nearby forest heard the noise and came to see what was the matter. All stood around listening to the heated argument between the man and his friend the elephant. In this turmoil the lion came along roaring, and said in a loud voice: "Don't you know that I am the King of the Jungle! How dare anyone disturb the peace of my kingdom?" On hearing this the elephant, who was one of the high ministers in the jungle kingdom, replied in a soothing voice, and said: "My Lord, there is no disturbance of the peace in your kingdom. I have only been having a little discussion with my friend here as to the possession of this little hut which your lordship sees me occupying." The lion, who wanted to have "peace and tranquillity" in his kingdom, replied in a noble voice, saying: "I command my ministers to appoint a Commission of Enquiry to go thoroughly into this matter and report accordingly." He then turned to the man and said: "You have done well by establishing friendship with my people, especially with the elephant who is one of my honourable ministers of state. Do not grumble any more, your hut is not lost to you. Wait until the sitting of my Imperial Commission, and there you will be given plenty of opportunity to state your case. I am sure that you will be pleased with the findings of the Commission." The man was very pleased by these sweet words from the King of the Jungle, and innocently waited for his opportunity, in the belief that naturally the hut would be returned to him.

The elephant, obeying the command of his master, got busy with other ministers to appoint the Commission of Enquiry. The following elders of the jungle were appointed to sit in the Commission: (1) Mr. Rhinoceros; (2) Mr. Buffalo; (3) Mr. Alligator; (4) The Rt. Hon. Mr. Fox to act as chairman; and (5) Mr. Leopard to act as Secretary to the Commission. On seeing the personnel, the man protested and asked if it was not necessary to include in this Commission a member from his side. But he was told that it was impossible, since no one from his side was well enough educated to understand the intricacy of jungle law. Further, that there was nothing to fear, for the members of the Commission were all men of repute for their impartiality in justice, and as they were gentlemen chosen by God to look after the interest of races less adequately endowed with teeth and claws, he might rest assured that they would investigate the matter with the greatest care and report impartially. . . .

Then the man decided that he must adopt an effective method of protection, since Commissions of Enquiry did not seem to be of any use to him. He sat down and said: "Ng'enda thi ndeagaga motegi," which literally means, "there is nothing that treads on the earth that cannot be trapped," or in other words, you can fool people for a time, but not forever.

Early one morning, when the huts already occupied by the jungle lords were all beginning to decay and fall to pieces, he went out and built a bigger and better hut a little distance away. No sooner had Mr. Rhinoceros seen it than he came rushing in, only to find that Mr. Elephant was already inside, sound asleep. Mr. Leopard next came in at the window, Mr. Lion, Mr. Fox, and Mr. Buffalo entered the doors, while Mr. Hyena howled for a place in the shade and Mr. Alligator basked on the roof. Presently they all began disputing about their rights of penetration, and from disputing they came to fighting, and while they were embroiled together the man set the hut on fire and burnt it to the ground, jungle lords and all. Then he went home, saying "Peace is costly, but it's worth the expense," and lived happily ever after. . . .

There certainly are some progressive ideas among the Europeans. They include the ideas of material prosperity, of medicine, and hygiene, and literacy which enables people to take part in world culture. But so far the Europeans who visit Africa have not been conspicuously zealous in imparting these parts of their inheritance to the Africans, and seem to think that the only way to do it is by police discipline and armed force. They speak as if it was somehow beneficial to an African to work for them instead of for himself, and to make sure that he will receive this benefit they do their best to take away his land and leave him with no alternative. Along with his land they rob him of his government, condemn his religious ideas, and ignore his fundamental conceptions of justice and morals, all in the name of civilisation and progress.

If Africans were left in peace on their own lands, Europeans would have to offer them the benefits of white civilisation in real earnest before they could obtain the African labour which they want so much. They would have to offer the African a way of life which was really superior to the one his fathers lived before him, and a share in the prosperity given them by their command of science. They would have to let the African choose what parts of European culture could be beneficially transplanted, and how they could be adapted. He would probably not choose the gas bomb or the armed police force, but he might ask for some other things of which he does not get so much today. As it is, by driving him off his ancestral lands, the Europeans have robbed him of the material foundations of his culture, and reduced him to a state of serfdom incompatible with human happiness. The African is conditioned, by the cultural and social institutions of centuries, to a freedom of which Europe has little conception, and it is not in his nature to accept serfdom for ever. He realises that he must fight unceasingly for his own complete emancipation; for without this he is doomed to remain the prey of rival imperialisms, which in every successive year will drive their fangs more deeply into his vitality and strength.

3. ECONOMIC NATIONALISM: KWAME NKRUMAH

Organization presupposes planning, and planning demands a programme for its basis. The Government proposes to launch a Seven-Year Development Plan in January, 1963. The Party, therefore, has a pressing obligation to provide a programme upon which this plan could be formulated.

We must develop Ghana economically, socially, culturally, spiritually, educationally, technologically and otherwise, and produce it as a finished product of a fully integrated life, both exemplary and inspiring.

This programme, which we call a programme for "Work and Happiness," has been drawn up in regard to all our circumstances and conditions, our hopes and aspirations, our advantages and disadvantages and our opportunities or lack of them. Indeed, the programme is drawn up with an eye on reality and provides the building ground for our immediate scientific, technical and industrial progress.

We have embarked upon an intensive socialist reconstruction of our country. Ghana inherited a colonial economy and similar disabilities in most other directions. We cannot rest content until we have demolished this miserable structure and raised in its place an edifice of economic stability, thus creating for ourselves a veritable paradise of abundance and satisfaction. Despite the ideological bankruptcy and moral collapse of a civilization in despair, we must go forward with our preparations for planned economic growth to supplant the poverty, ignorance, disease, illiteracy and degradation left in their wake by discredited colonialism and decaying imperialism.

In the programme which I am today introducing to the country through this broadcast, the Party has put forward many proposals. I want all of you to get copies of this programme, to read and discuss it and to send us any observations or suggestions you may have about it.

Tomorrow, the National Executive Committee of the Party will meet to discuss the Party programme and officially present it to the nation. I feel sure that it will decide in favour of an immediate release of this programme to the people. The Party, however, will take no action on the programme until the masses of the people have had the fullest opportunity of reviewing it.

This programme for "Work and Happiness" is an expression of the evidence of the nation's creative ability, the certainty of the correctness of our Party line and action and the greatest single piece of testimony [to] our national confidence in the future.

Ghana is our country which we must all help to build. This programme gives us the opportunity to make our contributions towards the fulfillment of our national purposes.

As I look at the content of the programme and the matters it covers, such as Tax Reform, Animal Husbandry and Poultry Production, Forest Husbandry, Industrialization, Handicrafts, Banking and Insurance, Foreign Enterprise, Culture and Leisure, I am convinced beyond all doubt that Ghana and Ghanians will travel full steam ahead, conscious of their great responsibilities and fully aware that the materialization of this bright picture of the future is entirely dependent on their active and energetic industry. Remember that it is at the moment merely a draft programme and only your approval will finalize it.

At this present moment, all over Africa, dark clouds of neocolonialism are fast gathering. African States are becoming debtor-nations and client States day in and day out, owing to their adoption of unreal attitudes to world problems, saying "no" when they should have said "yes," and "yes" when they should have said "no." They are seeking economic shelter under colonialist wings, instead of accepting the truth—that their survival lies in the political unification of Africa.

Countrymen, we must draw up a programme of action and later plan details of this programme for the benefit of the whole people. Such a programme is the one that the Party now brings to you, the people of Ghana, in the hope that you will approve it critically and help to make it a success.

We have a rich heritage. Our natural resources are abundant and varied. We have mineral and agricultural wealth and, above all, we have the will to find the means whereby these possessions can be put to the greatest use and advantage. The Party's programme for work and happiness is a pointer to the way ahead, the way leading to a healthier, happier and more prosperous life for us all. When you have examined and accepted this programme, the Government and the people will base on it and initiate our Seven-Year Development Plan, which will guide our action to prosperity.

STUDY QUESTIONS

1. What are Marcus Garvey's goals for Africa? How does he justify them? Does he identify crucial African values? Does he suggest what Africa will be once it is free?

2. How does Kenyatta describe European imperialism—and is it a fair characterization (see Chapter 21)? What does he see as the goals of African nationalism? What methods does he suggest?

3. What is Kenyatta's attitude to Western achievements? What aspects of African tradition does he seek to protect or restore?

4. How do Nkrumah's concerns as a nationalist compare with those of preindependence leaders like Kenyatta? What problems is he referring to under the heading of neocolonialism? What are his main solutions? Do they fit under the heading of nationalism?

5. What are the similarities and differences between African and Turkish nationalism? (See Chapter 29.) Between African and Gandhi's Indian nationalism? (See Chapter 35.)

41

Changes in African Culture and Society

New forces continued to have an impact on the traditional culture of sub-Saharan Africa throughout the twentieth century. Conversions both to Islam and to Christianity gained ground, although a polytheist minority remained. Whereas in 1900 80 percent of all sub-Saharan Africans adhered to traditional religions, by 1990 80 percent were either Muslim or Christian. Conversion brought more than new beliefs about the deity; it also attacked family traditions (such as polygamy, for Christians) and traditional ideas of harmony with nature. Some African conservatives blamed the new religions for Africans' willingness to attack animals and forests with a new vigor that threatened ecological balance, for the monotheistic religions held humans to be above nature. Education spread, and with it not only literacy but, often, knowledge of a European language—another force for change.

The selections that follow deal with missionary activity, urbanization, and changes in family roles as sources of change and tension in twentieth-century African society. European missionary activity, both Catholic and Protestant, increased rapidly from 1890 onward, as various Western teachers and medical personnel worked hard to modify or undermine traditional African religious values, property concepts, and family practices. African reactions to missionary efforts ranged from stark rejection to a combination effort to outright acceptance. (It is important to remember that Islam was also spreading rapidly in the nineteenth and twentieth centuries; Christians were not the only missionaries, and Muslims might be preferred precisely because they were not European.)

Urban growth was another framework for cultural change. African cities, once small, grew rapidly both under colonial administration and with independence. About a quarter of all sub-Saharan Africans lived in cities by the 1970s, and the rate increases steadily. Urban Africans, though often poor, were more often educated than their rural counterparts, and they enjoyed the excitement of city life. But they were also confusingly torn from traditional community customs.

Selection 1 from Chinua Acheba, *Things Fall Apart* (London: William Heinemann Ltd., 1959), pp. 138–141, 162, 163, 166–167, 186–188. Copyright © 1959 by Chinua Achebe. Reprinted by permission of William Heinemann Limited. Selection 2 from Chinua Achebe, *No Longer At Ease* (London: William Heinemann, Ltd., 1960), pp. 19–22, 149–150. Copyright © 1960 by Chinua Achebe. Reprinted by permission of William Heinemann Limited. Selection 3 from Perdita Huston, *Third World Women Speak Out* (New York: Praeger Publishers, 1979), pp. 21, 22–23, 42–43. Copyright © 1979 by Praeger Publishers. Reprinted by permission. Selection 4 from Ifi Amadiume, *Male Daughters, Female Husbands: Gender and Sex in an African Society* (London: Zed Books, 1987), pp. 3–4, 15, 89–90, 91, 132, 141. Reprinted by permission of the publisher.

The selections in this chapter are divided into two parts: the first two selections deal with successive waves of cultural change affecting parts of Nigeria; they are drawn from the work of a perceptive Nigerian novelist who chronicled what he saw as major and in some ways tragic cultural disruption. The third and fourth selections involve reactions of African women, drawn to change themselves but with various specific qualifications and hesitations.

The first selection, by Chinua Achebe, reflects deep awareness of the complex balance of gain and loss brought by changes away from tradition. Discussing British missionary activity around 1900, Achebe conveys the different types of Africans and different kinds of motives involved in at least partial religious conversion, and at the same time the reasons for resistance (and its failure). The selection is fictional and written after the fact, but it conveys ongoing intellectual issues in Africa. The passage ends with a resistance meeting, centered on the strong traditionalist figure of Okonkwo (whose son had converted) and the arrival and death of a messenger sent by the British colonial administration to prevent disorder.

The second selection comes from another Achebe novel, this one involving Okonkwo's grandson, now an urbanite, after World War II but before independence. Obi Okonkwo is the first village member to receive higher education in British-run schools. He goes to Lagos, the growing Nigerian capital, to take a civil-service job. He finds the glitter of city life there, but also a consumerist culture and a pleasure-seeking sexual ethic both influenced by Western standards. These at first shock and then beguile him so that he cannot respond to village customs in the old way, for example, a tragedy such as his mother's death. The combination of stimulation and confusion gives this Achebe novel its title, *No Longer at Ease.*

The third selection focuses less on confusion, more on new aspirations and opportunities. Many African women found new roles as they moved to cities and gained education. Even rural women had new power when their men left to take urban jobs; willy-nilly, they had to run their families and often support themselves. Thus African family bonds, which once gave women security while holding them subordinate, loosened rapidly. The passages come from a series of interviews by a Western anthropologist with women in Kenya, including one group organized in a cooperative to try to compensate for new uncertainties about family ties and support from men.

Cultural change, including some expressions striking for their resemblance to modern Western movements such as feminism, is clearly a major factor in contemporary Africa. In the fourth selection, the African feminist Ifi Amadiume discusses gender relations between African men and women, although in terms that challenge Western feminism as well as current African realities.

All these cultural changes and reactions express Africa's growing international contacts, but also new uncertainties as older institutions unravel; as in the West in previous periods, greater individualism can be both exhilarating and damaging. Africans themselves disagree over whether new opportunity or the erosion of vital traditions should receive the main emphasis. Not surprisingly, important traditional emphases, such as family solidarity, persist as well, as Africans create their own cultural amalgams.

1. THINGS FALL APART

The missionaries spent their first four or five nights in the marketplace, and went into the village in the morning to preach the gospel. They asked me who the king of the village was, but the villagers told them that there was no king. "We have men of high title and the chief priests and the elders," they said.

It was not very easy getting the men of high title and the elders together after the excitement of the first day. But the missionaries persevered, and in the end they were received by the rulers of Mbanta. They asked for a plot of land to build their church.

Every clan and village had its "evil forest." In it were buried all those who died of the really evil diseases, like leprosy and smallpox. It was also the dumping ground for the potent fetishes of great medicine men when they died. An "evil forest" was, therefore, alive with sinister forces and powers of darkness. It was such a forest that the rulers of Mbanta gave to the missionaries. They did not really want them in their clan, and so they made them that offer which nobody in his right senses would accept.

"They want a piece of land to build their shrine," said Uchendu to his peers when they consulted among themselves. "We shall give them a piece of land." He paused, and there was a murmur of surprise and disagreement. "Let us give them a portion of the Evil Forest. They boast about victory over death. Let us give them a real battlefield in which to show their victory." They laughed and agreed, and sent for the missionaries, whom they had asked to leave them for a while so that they might "whisper together." They offered them as much [of] the Evil Forest as they cared to take. And to their greatest amazement the missionaries thanked them and burst into song.

"They do not understand," said some of the elders. "But they will understand when they go to their plot of land tomorrow morning." And they dispersed.

The next morning the crazy men actually began to clear a part of the forest and to build their house. The inhabitants of Mbanta expected them all to be dead within four days. The first day passed and the second and third and fourth, and none of them died. Everyone was puzzled. And then it became known that the white man's fetish had unbelievable power. It was said that he wore glasses on his eyes so that he could see and talk to evil spirits. Not long after, he won his first three converts.

Although Nwoye had been attracted to the new faith from the very first day, he kept it secret. He dared not go too near the missionaries for fear of his father. But whenever they came to preach in the open marketplace or the village playground, Nwoye was there. And he was already beginning to know some of the simple stories they told.

"We have now built a church," said Mr. Kiaga, the interpreter, who was now in charge of the infant congregation. The white man had gone back to Umuofia, where he built his headquarters and from where he paid regular visits to Mr. Kiaga's congregation at Mbanta.

"We have now built a church," said Mr. Kiaga, "and we want you all to come in every seventh day to worship the true God."

On the following Sunday, Nwoye passed and repassed the little red-earth and thatch building without summoning enough courage to enter. He heard the voice of singing and although it came from a handful of men it was loud and confident. Their church stood on a circular clearing that looked like the open mouth of the Evil Forest. Was it waiting to snap its teeth together? After passing and re-passing by the church, Nwoye returned home.

It was well known among the people of Mbanta that their gods and ancestors were sometimes long-suffering and would deliberately allow a man to go on defying them. But even in such cases they set their limit at seven market weeks or twenty-eight days. Beyond that limit no man was suffered to go. And so excitement mounted in the village as the seventh week approached since the impudent missionaries built their church in the Evil Forest. The villagers were so certain about the doom that awaited these men that one or two converts thought it wise to suspend their allegiance to the new faith.

At last the day came by which all the missionaries should have died. But they were still alive, building a new red-earth and thatch house for their teacher, Mr. Kiaga. That week they won a handful more converts. And for the first time they had a woman. Her name was Nneka, the wife of Amadi, who was a prosperous farmer. She was very heavy with child.

Nneka had had four previous pregnancies and childbirths. But each time she had borne twins, and they had been immediately thrown away. Her husband and his family were already becoming highly critical of such a woman and were not unduly perturbed when they found she had fled to join the Christians. It was a good riddance. . . .

"Does the white man understand our custom about land?"

"How can he when he does not even speak our tongue? But he says that our customs are bad; and our own brothers who have taken up his religion also say that our customs are bad. How do you think we can fight when our own brothers have turned against us? The white man is very clever. He came quietly and peaceably with his religion. We were amused at his foolishness and allowed him to stay. Now he has won our brothers, and our clan can no longer act like one. He has put a knife on the things that held us together and we have fallen apart." . . .

There were many men and women in Umuofia who did not feel as strongly as Okonkwo about the new dispensation. The white man had indeed brought a lunatic religion, but he had also built a trading store and for the first time palm-oil and kernel became things of great price, and much money flowed into Umuofia. . . .

Mr. Brown [the missionary to the Ibo village] learned a good deal about the religion of the clan and he came to the conclusion that a frontal attack on it would not succeed. And so he built a school and a little hospital in Umuofia. He went from family to family begging people to send their children to his school. But at first they only sent their slaves or sometimes their lazy children. Mr. Brown begged and argued and prophesied. He said that the leaders of the land in the future would be men and women who had learned to read and write. If Umuofia failed to send her children to the school, strangers would come from other places to rule them. They could already see that happening in the Native Court, where the D.C.

was surrounded by strangers who spoke his tongue. Most of these strangers came from the distant town of Umuru on the bank of the Great River where the white man first went.

In the end Mr. Brown's arguments began to have an effect. More people came to learn in his school, and he encouraged them with gifts of singlets and towels. They were not all young, these people who came to learn. Some of them were thirty years old or more. They worked on their farms in the morning and went to school in the afternoon. And it was not long before the people began to say that the white man's medicine was quick in working. Mr. Brown's school produced quick results. A few months in it were enough to make one a court messenger or even a court clerk. Those who stayed longer became teachers; and from Umuofia laborers went forth into the Lord's vineyard. New churches were established in the surrounding villages and a few schools with them. From the very beginning religion and education went hand in hand. . . .

"You all know why we are here, when we ought to be building our barns or mending our huts, when we should be putting our compounds in order. My father used to say to me: 'Whenever you see a toad jumping in broad daylight, then you know that something is after its life.' When I saw you all pouring into this meeting from all the quarters of our clan so early in the morning, I knew that something was after our life." He paused for a brief moment and then began again:

"All our gods are weeping. Idemili is weeping, Ogwugwu is weeping, Agbala is weeping, and all the others. Our dead fathers are weeping because of the shameful sacrilege they are suffering and the abomination we have all seen with our eyes." He stopped again to steady his trembling voice.

"This is a great gathering. No clan can boast of greater numbers or greater valor. But are we all here? I ask you: Are all the sons of Umuofia with us here?" A deep murmur swept through the crowd.

"They are not," he said "They have broken the clan and gone their several ways. We who are here this morning have remained true to our fathers, but our brothers have deserted us and joined a stranger to soil their fatherland. If we fight the stranger we shall hit our brothers and perhaps shed the blood of a clansman. But we must do it. Our fathers never dreamed of such a thing, they never killed their brothers. But a white man never came to them. So we must do what our fathers would never have done. Eneke the bird was asked why he was always on the wing and he replied: 'Men have learned to shoot without missing their mark and I have learned to fly without perching on a twig.' We must root out this evil. And if our brothers take the side of evil we must root them out too. And we must do it *now*. We must bale this water now that it is only ankle-deep. . . ."

At this point there was a sudden stir in the crowd and every eye was turned in one direction. There was a sharp bend in the road that led from the marketplace to the white man's court, and to the stream beyond it. And so no one had seen the approach of the five court messengers until they had come round the bend, a few paces from the edge of the crowd. Okonkwo was sitting at the edge. . . .

"What do you want here?"

"The white man whose power you know too well has ordered this meeting to stop."

In a flash Okonkwo drew his machete. The messenger crouched to avoid the blow. It was useless. Okonkwo's machete descended twice and the man's head lay beside his uniformed body.

The waiting backcloth jumped into tumultuous life and the meeting was stopped. Okonkwo stood looking at the dead man. He knew that Umuofia would not go to war. He knew because they had let the other messengers escape. They had broken into tumult instead of action. He discerned fright in that tumult. He heard voices asking: "Why did he do it?"

He wiped his machete on the sand and went away.

2. NO LONGER AT EASE

As a boy in the village of Umuofia he had heard his first stories about Lagos from a soldier home on leave from the war. Those soldiers were heroes who had seen the great world. They spoke of Abyssinia, Egypt, Palestine, Burma and so on. Some of them had been village ne'er-do-wells, but now they were heroes. They had bags and bags of money, and the villagers sat at their feet to listen to their stories. One of them went regularly to a market in the neighboring village and helped himself to whatever he liked. He went in full uniform, breaking the earth with his boots, and no one dared touch him. It was said that if you touched a soldier, Government would deal with you. Besides, soldiers were as strong as lions because of the injections they were given in the army. It was from one of these soldiers that Obi had his first picture of Lagos.

"There is no darkness there," he told his admiring listeners, "because at night the electric shines like the sun, and people are always walking about, that is, those who want to walk. If you don't want to walk you only have to wave your hand and a pleasure car stops for you." His audience made sounds of wonderment. Then by way of digression he said: "If you see a white man, take off your hat for him. The only thing he cannot do is mold a human being."

For many years afterwards, Lagos was always associated with electric lights and motorcars in Obi's mind. Even after he had at last visited the city and spent a few days there before flying to the United Kingdom his views did not change very much. Of course, he did not really see much of Lagos then. His mind was, as it were, on higher things. He spent the few days with his "countryman," Joseph Okeke, a clerk in the Survey Department. Obi and Joseph had been classmates at the Umuofia C.M.S. Central School. But Joseph had not gone on to a secondary school because he was too old and his parents were poor. He had joined the Education Corps of the 82nd Division and, when the war ended, the clerical service of the Nigerian Government.

Joseph was at Lagos Motor Park to meet his lucky friend who was passing through Lagos to the United Kingdom. He took him to his lodgings in Obalende. It was only one room. A curtain of light-blue cloth ran the full breadth of the room separating the Holy of Holies (as he called his double spring bed) from the sitting area. His cooking utensils, boxes, and other personal effects were hidden away under the Holy of Holies. The sitting area was taken up with two armchairs, a settee (otherwise called "me and my girl"), and a round table on which he displayed his photo album. At night, his houseboy moved away the round table and spread his mat on the floor.

Joseph had so much to tell Obi on his first night in Lagos that it was past three when they slept. He told him about the cinema and the dance halls and about political meetings.

"Dancing is very important nowadays. No girl will look at you if you can't dance. I first met Joy at the dancing school." "Who is Joy?" asked Obi, who was fascinated by what he was learning of this strange and sinful new world. "She was my girl friend for—let's see . . . "—he counted off his fingers— ". . . March, April, May, June, July—for five months. She made these pillowcases for me."

Obi raised himself instinctively to look at the pillow he was lying on. He had taken particular notice of it earlier in the day. It had the strange word *osculate* sewn on it, each letter in a different color.

"She was a nice girl but sometimes very foolish. Sometimes, though, I wish we hadn't broken up. She was simply mad about me; and she was a virgin when I met her, which is very rare here."

Joseph talked and talked and finally became less and less coherent. Then without any pause at all his talk was transformed into a deep snore, which continued until the morning.

The very next day Obi found himself taking a compulsory walk down Lewis Street. Joseph had brought a woman home and it was quite clear that Obi's presence in the room was not desirable; so he went out to have a look round. The girl was one of Joseph's new finds, as he told him later. She was dark and tall with an enormous pneumatic bosom under a tight-fitting red and yellow dress. Her lips and long fingernails were a brilliant red, and her eyebrows were fine black lines. She looked not unlike those wooden masks made in Ikot Ekpene. Altogether she left a nasty taste in Obi's mouth, like the multicolored word *osculate* on the pillowcase. . . .

On top of it all came his mother's death. He sent all he could find for her funeral, but it was already being said to his eternal shame that a woman who had borne so many children, one of whom was in a European post, deserved a better funeral than she got. One Umuofia man who had been on leave at home when she died brought the news to Lagos to the meeting of the Umuofia Progressive Union.

"It was a thing of shame," he said. Someone else wanted to know, by the way, why that beast (meaning Obi) had not obtained permission to go home. "That is what Lagos can do to a young man. He runs after sweet things, dances breast to breast with women and forgets his home and his people. Do you know what medicine that *osu* woman may have put into his soup to turn his eyes and ears away from his people?" . . .

"Everything you have said is true. But there is one thing I want you to learn. Whatever happens in this world has a meaning. As our people say: 'Wherever something stands, another things stands beside it.' You see this thing called blood. There is nothing like it. That is why when you plant a yam it produces another yam, and if you plant an orange it bears oranges. I have seen many things in my life, but I have never yet seen a banana tree yield a coco yam. Why do I say this? You young men here, I want you to listen because it is from listening to old men that you learn wisdom. I know that when I return to Umuofia I cannot claim to be an old man. But here in this Lagos I am an old man to the rest of you." He paused for effect. "This boy that we are all talking about, what has he done? He was told that his mother died and he did not care. It is a strange and surprising thing."

3. KENYAN WOMEN SPEAK OUT

What we need in this village is teachers to teach women handicrafts and sewing and agricultural skills. We have organized a women's group. I am one of the leaders. We are saving up for a building to meet in. All women are trying to earn money, and we want to have a building for our meetings. It will be called the "adult education building" —with rooms for handicrafts, literacy, and other things.

We also want our children to be educated—so we can have good leaders to keep our country good. I think now it is best to have only four children—so you can take care of them.

It is better to educate a girl than a boy, although one should educate both. Girls are better. They help a lot. See this house? My daughters built it for me. If you don't have any daughters, who will build for you? The boys will marry and take care of their wives—that's all. They don't care about mothers. For example, if my son gets married, the daughter-in-law will say, "Let's take our mothers to live with us." The son will say, "No, we will just have our own family and do our own things." So you are left alone. What do you do? . . .

My mother has eleven children. She is my father's only wife. She works in the fields and grows the food we eat. She plants cabbage, spinach, and corn. She works very hard, but with so many children it is difficult to get enough food or money. All of my sisters and brothers go to school. One is already a teacher, and that is why I am trying to learn a profession. If I can get enough schooling, I can serve the country and my own family. I can also manage to have a life for myself. That is why I came to this school. We have a big family, and I have to help.

My life is very different from my mother's. She just stayed in the family until she married. Life is much more difficult now because everybody is dependent on money. Long ago, money was unheard of. No one needed money. But now you can't even get food without cash. Times are very difficult. That is why the towns are creating day-care centers—so women can work and have their own lives. I have to work, for without it I will not have enough money for today's life.

These are the problems I face and try to think about. How shall I manage to pick up this life so that I can live a better one? You know, we people of Kenya like to serve our parents when they are still alive—to help the family. But first, women have to get an education. Then if you get a large family and don't know how to feed it—if you don't have enough money for food—you can find work and get some cash. That's what I will teach my children: "Get an education first."

If I had a chance to go to the university, I would learn more about health education. I could help women that way. If I were in a position of authority, I would really try to educate women. Right now, girls are left behind in education. It costs money, and parents think it is more important to educate boys. But I think that if people are intelligent, there is no difference. Girls and boys should be educated the same. I would make rules and teach women who are not educated and who have never been to school. They, too, much understand what today's problems are.

If I have any spare time, I want to learn new things. I would like to learn how to manage my life, my future life, and have enough say in things so that my husband and I could understand each other and share life with our family. And I would change the laws so that men would understand women and their needs and not beat them as they do.

I only hope that I will have a mature husband who will understand and discuss things with me. . . .

Most women don't rely on their husbands now. If they get some money, well and good; and if they don't, they just try to get money for themselves—selling vegetables or making and selling handicrafts.

Life is very difficult these days, and men are paying less attention to their wives. You see, men have wrongly just taken advantage of having more money. Instead of using money properly, to improve the lives of their families, they spend it on all the "facilities" available at hotels. Instead of spending nights in their own homes, they fight at home and seek women outside—in the hotels. Many men cheat on their wives now because they are employed and have money. A husband can say, "I have been sent as a driver to Nairobi" (or elsewhere), when he actually spends the money on girls.

So women are fed up. They think now that relying on a man can be a problem. They say, "We should try to do something ourselves. Then, whether we get something from our men or not, we still will be able to raise our children properly." The problem that many women face is that they must become self-supporting. They either have no support from their husbands at all, or very little. And there is no law to protect them.

But women *are* trying to do something for themselves, and if they had the capital they could establish businesses to help them make money. The main problem here is the money problem. Many women are alone. They need to earn for their families.

Women feel very hurt because they think their men don't recognize them as human brings. They are unhappy because of this inequality. I am lucky; my husband is good. He never took another wife. We are still together. . . . My wish would be that men and women could live as two equal people.

4. IFI AMADIUME

When the 1960s and 1970s female academics and Western feminists began to attack social anthropology, riding on the crest of the new wave of women's studies, the issues they took on were androcentrism and sexism. . . . The methods they adopted indicated to Black women that White feminists were no less racist than the patriarchs of social anthropology whom they were busy condemning for male bias. They fantasized a measure of superiority over African and other Third World women. Black women's critique could not therefore be restricted to the male bias of social anthropology and not challenge White women. Drawing their data from the Third World, especially Africa, works on women produced in Europe and America have shown White women's unquestioning acceptance of anthropology's racist division of the world. In the debates in the West, the Third World supplied the 'raw data' for random sampling, citation and illustration of points. It baffles African women

African Women's Work. From Kenya, in the late 1990s. *What does this type of work say about women's conditions in contemporary Africa?* (Betty Press/Woodfin Camp & Associates.)

that Western academics and feminists feel no apprehension or disrespectful trivialization in taking on all of Africa or, indeed, all the Third World in one book. It is revealing that most such works have not been written by women from Third World nations; they, instead, tend to write about their particular ethnic group, their country or surrounding region. . . .

Igbo women were clearly unlike European women. . . . In their system, male attributes and male status referred to the biologically male sex—man—as female attributes and female status referred to the biologically female sex—woman. To break this rigid gender construction carried a stigma. Consequently, it was not usual to separate sex from gender, as there was no status ambiguity in relation to gender.

The flexibility of Igbo gender construction meant that gender was separate from biological sex. Daughters could become sons and consequently male. Daughters and women in general could be husbands to wives and consequently males in relation to their wives, etc. . . .

An insight into this remarkable gender system is crucial to the understanding and appreciation of the political status women had in traditional Igbo societies and the political choices open to them. . . .

It can, therefore, be claimed that the Igbo language, in comparison with English for example, has not built up rigid associations between certain adjectives or attributes and gender subjects, nor certain objects and gender possessive pronouns. The genderless word *mmadu,* humankind, applies to both sexes. There is no usage, as there is in English, of the word 'man' to represent both sexes, neither is there the cumbersome option of saying 'he or she,' 'his or her,' 'him or her.' In Igbo, *O* stands for he, she and even it, *a* stands for the impersonal one, and *nya* for the imperative, let him or her.

This linguistic system of few gender distinctions makes it possible to conceptualize certain social roles as separate from sex and gender, hence the possibility for either sex to fill the role. This, of course, does not rule out competition between the sexes, and situations in which a particular sex tends to monopolize roles and positions, and generates and stresses anti–opposite sex gender ideologies in order to maintain its own interests.

The two examples of situations in which women played roles ideally or normally occupied by men—what I have called male roles—in indigenous Nnobi society . . . were as 'male daughters' and 'female husbands'; in either role, women acted as family head. The Igbo word for family head is the genderless expression *di-bu-no*. The genderless *di* is a prefix word which means specialist in, or expert at, or master of something. Therefore, *di-bu-no* means one in a master relationship to a family and household, and a person, woman or man, in this position is simply referred to as *di-bu-no*. In indigenous Nnobi society and culture, there was one head or master of a family at a time, and 'male daughters' and 'female husbands' were called by the same term, which translated into English would be 'master.' Some women were therefore masters to other people, both men and women.

The reverse applied to those in a wife relationship to others. The Igbo word for wife, *onye be,* is a genderless expression meaning a person who belongs to the home of the master of the home. The other words for wife, *nwunye* or *nwanyi,* female or woman, also denote one in a subordinate, service or domestic relationship to one in a master position. It was therefore possible for some men to be addressed by the term 'wife,' as they were in service or domestic relationship to a master. . . . There is a series of contradictions here; . . . there were, for example, women in master or husband roles and men in wifely or domestic roles. . . .

The use of these weapons of war must be understood in the context of polygynous marriage and compound structure. Of course it was possible for a man to turn to another wife when one wife refused to have sexual relations with him. The important point here is that women lived separately. The fact that a wife did not spend the night with her husband made it possible for her to use sexual refusal as a weapon of war without running the risk of marital rape. This is not the case for women in monogamous marriages who cling to the Christian idea of the sanctity and sexual exclusiveness of their matrimonial beds. Western feminists are still finding it difficult to have rape in marriage recognized as a legal offence.

Refusal of sexual compliance by a wife still proved effective even when a man had sexual access to other wives. Such refusal implied defiance and denial of rights, and was ultimately a challenge to a husband's authority over his wife. The customary solution was not for the man to take the law into his own hands; he had the option of calling in other members of the family or appealing to the formal patrilineage organizations. . . . Obviously the weapon of sexual denial was most effective when used collectively, either by all the wives of a man, all the wives of a patrilineage, or better still, all the women of Nnobi.

Indeed the earliest recorded mass protest movement by Igbo women was the Nwaobiala—the dancing women's movement of 1925. The basic demand of the movement, which was dominated by elderly women, was the rejection of Christianity and a return to traditional customs. Nnobi is mentioned as one of the three towns where a military escort was sent to restore order, as women there burnt the market, blocked the main road and piled refuse in the court house. Children were withdrawn from school and the market was boycotted. . . .

This resistance to conversion has been sustained by a few people in Nnobi. Eze Agba, the present priest of Idemili, does not go to church, nor does Nwajiuba, the 'male daughter,' who is head of the first and most senior *obi* in Nnobi. Together with a few other elderly people, they practise the indigenous religion—the worship of the goddess. The Christians refer to them as 'pagans' or 'heathens,' but they call themselves *ndi odinani*, the custodians of the indigenous culture. The youngest of them are middle-aged. All their children and grandchildren are Christians. Ironically, a new resistance against Christianity now springs from the Western-educated élite, who were in fact brought up in the church and educated in mission schools. They are now strong supporters and admirers of the indigenous religionists and preach the doctrine of cultural revival while condemning aspects of Western culture and dominance. . . .

Overwhelming evidence shows that women in Nnobi and in Igboland in general were neither more comfortable nor more advantaged from an economic point of view under colonialism. They had lost their grip on the control of liquid cash; men had invaded the general market, and women were becoming helpless in their personal relations with husbands. But, most important of all, pro-female institutions were being eroded both by the church and the colonial administration. . . .

. . . [W]omen's centrality in the production and sale of palm-oil and kernels in traditional Nnobi society gave them a considerable advantage over their husbands. The introduction of pioneer oil mills mechanized the whole process of extracting the palm-oil and cracking the kernels. This, of course, meant a much higher oil yield which necessitated bulk buying by the agents of the mills and the channelling of most of the village's palm fruit to the mills. The main centre of production was therefore shifted from the family to the mills. At the same time, wives lost the near monopoly they enjoyed in the traditional method of production and the independent income they derived from it. . . . Instead of wives selling the palm-oil and keeping some of the profits, husbands now sold direct to the oil mills or their agents, and collected the money.

STUDY QUESTIONS

1. What were the main disputes over Christianity in the Nigerian region Achebe describes? What kinds of people were most drawn to this religion? Why? What kinds of people most resisted?
2. Given the novel's title, *Things Fall Apart*, does Achebe suggest that it would be best to go back to the traditional values?

3. What are the value dilemmas in the excerpt from *No Longer at Ease*? What are the dominant features of the urban culture of Lagos? How do they relate to traditional culture?

4. What are the main aspirations of the Kenyan women interviewed in the third selection? What is new about them? In what ways do they clearly seek to defend older cultural and social traditions?

5. What problems of interpretation do novels raise in trying to get at historical conditions? What kinds of problems do interviews raise, conducted by even a skilled Western scholar?

6. On what bases does Ifi Amadiume criticize the evaluations of African women by Western feminists and anthropologists?

7. What, in her view, were the three main strengths, for women, of traditional Igbo language, family structure, and economy? By implication, what goals should modern Igbo women have?

8. Would the Kenyan women interviewed in the third selection agree or disagree with Amadiume's prescriptions, in the main? Are they reacting to changes in ways Amadiume would approve of?

9. Do Achebe and Amadiume agree on the nature of African gender traditions? Do they agree on what combination of change and tradition is desirable for contemporary Africa?

10. How do the cultural changes discussed in this chapter compare with African nationalist goals and reactions? Would nationalism help deal with some of the cultural issues raised by Achebe, Amadiume, and the Kenyan women?

42

The Environment in the Twentieth Century: A Disaster Story

One of the key issues of twentieth-century world history involves changes in and anxieties about the natural environment. Human impact on the environment goes far back in world history, and the precedents are important. Agriculture, both in its settled and its slash-and-burn varieties, early involved deforestation and impacts on riverways. Several agricultural societies markedly altered their environments, and some may have perished as a result. Excessive grain growing reduced soil quality in part of the Middle East and North Africa, in some cases expanding desert conditions.

Modern environmental history adds three new factors to the old story of human impact and its frequent heedlessness. The first factor involves the massive increase in population. Handling human wastes, long a problem for some cities, takes on more general proportions. Efforts to expand the food supply, which so far, against some dire expectations, have been largely successful, involve use of chemical fertilizers and additional deforestation. The second new factor is the intensification and expansion of modern industry. Chemical pollutants jeopardize air as well as water quality, affecting rivers, lakes, and soils in many areas. Societies that have pressed for rapid industrialization as a means of catching up with the West have sometimes suffered particular problems, although the United States remains the world pollution leader. By the 1990s one quarter of Russia was judged environmentally degraded; China, with its growing manufacturing as well as its vast population, was moving into the number two spot in generating air pollutants that cause global warming.

The third novel factor involves the international scale, as well as the extent, of environmental problems. Industry in the American Midwest affects trees in Canada,

From Grigorii Medvedev, *The Truth About Chernobyl*, translated by Evelyn Rossiter (New York: Basic Books, 1991), pp. 86–87, 238–242.

thanks to high smokestacks that spread chemical pollutants; the Ruhr mining and metallurgical center in western Germany has a similar impact on Scandinavia. International oil shipments recurrently generate ocean spills that affect many shorelines. The general increase in the international production of hydrocarbons is widely seen as raising temperatures worldwide, while global markets for certain minerals and agricultural products, inducing clearance of tropical rain forests, eliminate certain animal and vegetable species while reducing the production of oxygen. By the 1970s, international conferences began to take the global dimensions of the environment into account, and many countries pledged controls. But the tension between local economic expansion and more amorphous environmental criteria promised a long struggle to achieve effective implementation.

The following document deals with the most famous among several disastrous environmental "events" of the late twentieth century: the explosions that on April 25, 1986, destroyed a nuclear reactor at the Chernobyl power plant in the Soviet Union (in the region that is now part of Ukraine). The result was an unprecedented meltdown that spread radiation over the whole region, with measurable increases also in nations to the west and north. Twenty-six people died immediately; many others were injured and probably still more genetically damaged. Some who died from the explosion had to be buried in lead coffins, lest irradiated bodies further contaminate the soil. The account comes from Grigorii Medvedev, a nuclear expert who had held a high position at Chernobyl in the 1970s. He was assigned to report, and later wrote a book about, the whole catastrophe. In the first passage, he sketches some eyewitness accounts, and in the second he describes his own visit, with a driver, Volodya, two weeks after the explosions.

It is important to note that this is only one of many examples of environmental "events." An American chemical company operating in Bhopal, India, suffered an explosion that killed and injured far more people. A Japanese village experienced a series of deaths in the 1970s from chemical poisoning. An obvious question is: What general conclusions can be drawn from these recurrent if scattered events?

1. EYEWITNESS

On hearing the explosions and seeing the fire, most of the people out fishing stayed there until morning, while others, vaguely alarmed by these events, returned to Pripyat, with dry throats and smarting eyes. The booming that normally accompanied the opening of relief valves sounded just like an explosion, so people had grown accustomed to ignoring such loud noises. As for the fire, someone would doubtless extinguish it. It was really nothing! Hadn't there been fires at the Armyanskaya and Byeloyarsk nuclear power stations?

At the time of the explosion, there were two more fishermen sitting on the bank of the feeder channel, trying to catch young fish, 260 yards (240 m) directly across from the turbine hall. Serious fishermen dream about catching fry like this. And without fry as bait it's better not to try for perch. Here the fry, especially in spring, manage to come closer and closer to the reactor unit, straight for the pump station, where they mass in great numbers. One of the two fishermen, by the name of Pustovoit, had no particular occupation. The second, Protasov, was a maintenance man who had been brought in from Kharkov. He thought very highly of Chernobyl; it had such clean air and wonderful fishing. He had even thought of taking up residence there permanently—if it could be arranged. It was, after all, in the Kiev region, where residence permits were hard to come by; it would be no easy matter moving there. He was catching plenty of fish fry that night and was in a good mood. It was a warm, starry Ukrainian night. It was hard to believe that it was still April, as it felt more like July. No. 4 reactor unit, a handsome snowy-white building, lay straight ahead. The unexpected combination of magnificent, dazzling nuclear power and the tender young fish wriggling in the net was a most pleasant surprise.

First they heard two dull explosions within the unit, which sounded as if they had come from underground. The fishermen could feel the ground shake. Then came a powerful steam explosion; and only after that did the reactor explode, with a blinding flash of flame and a firework display consisting of fragments of red-hot fuel and graphite. Pieces of reinforced concrete and steel beams went cascading through the air, blasted in all directions.

The fishermen's figures were, unknown to them, illuminated by nuclear light. Thinking that something had burst inside the plant, perhaps a gasoline tank, the two men went on fishing, not suspecting that they, just like the fry they hoped to catch, had themselves been caught in the powerful trap of a nuclear disaster. They watched with some curiosity as events unfolded. They could see with their own eyes as Pravik and Kibenok deployed their teams of firefighters, who then climbed up nearly 100 feet and attacked the fire.

"See that? One of them has got up on top of V block, more than 200 feet up! He's taken his helmet off! Fantastic! He's a real hero! You can see how hot it is over there."

A few hours later, as dawn approached, the two fishermen, each of whom had received a dose of 400 roentgens, became severely nauseated and both felt extremely ill. They had a burning sensation inside their chests, their eyelids smarted, and their heads felt as if they had just been on a wild drinking spree. And nonstop vomiting left them totally exhausted. By morning their skin had turned black, as if they had been roasting in the sun at Sochi, on the Black Sea coast, for a month. They now had a nuclear tan, but still had not the faintest idea what was happening to them.

At daybreak they noticed that the men who had been up on the roof seemed also extremely sluggish and disoriented. That made them feel slightly better, as they were clearly not the only ones. But what had hit them all of a sudden? What could it be?

They made their way somehow to the medical center, and eventually were sent to the Moscow clinic.

Much later, one of them tried to make light of it, saying: "If you're ignorant, being curious can only get you into trouble, especially if your sense of responsibility is atrophied."

In the summer of 1986, Pustovoit, the man with no particular occupation, appeared on the cover of a foreign magazine and became famous in Europe. Misfortune can befall any living creature, but nuclear misfortune is all the more profound in that it runs counter to life itself.

Even next morning, on 26 April, more and more fishermen arrived at the same spot. The fact that they did shows how ignorant and careless people can be, how they had come to take emergencies for granted throughout all the years when news of such events was suppressed, and when those responsible were never punished. . . .

2. THE LATER REPORT

A Moskvich drove up from the direction of Pripyat and was stopped. The wheels and underside of the car, and the top of the trunk, were checked with a sensor. The passengers and driver were asked to get out; then the car was washed with desorbent solutions. The soldiers were wearing respirators, and tight cloth hoods covered their head and ears, with a large flap descending over their shoulders.

One of the soldiers, with a radiometer on his chest and a long stick-sensor, waved to us to stop. He checked our pass, which Volodya had stuck on the windscreen, and found it in order. The sensor, when passed over our Niva, showed background levels.

"You can go," he said. "But remember, your car will get contaminated where you're going. That Moskvich over there has 3 roentgens per hour, and washing won't get it off. Take pity on your car!"

"We have a radiometer," said I, pointing to the instrument. "And we'll be careful."

The soldier stared at me with his piercing blue eyes and seemed to be shaking his head uncertainly, as if doubting my word. He then slammed the door and waved us on.

Volodya accelerated, and the car shot forward with a whistling noise. I looked at the asphalt roadway bordered by pink concrete shoulders, and thought that we had rejoiced too soon, back in the days when the concrete had just been added, at not having to repair cracked asphalt any more. Now everything—including the asphalt and the concrete—was severely contaminated.

Thinking it might be interesting to see how fast the radioactivity increased as we approached Pripyat, I rolled down the window and held the sensor outside. On the right and straight ahead, beyond the radioactive vegetation flashing past, I could see the buildings of the Chernobyl nuclear power station, a bright white in the May sunlight, and the latticework structures of the high tension power masts of the 330- and 750-kilovolt switching stations.

I already knew that the explosion had ejected fragments of fuel onto the ground around the 750-kilovolt switching stations, where they continued to emit large amounts of radiation.

The pile of blackened wreckage visible outside No. 4 unit made a stark, painful contrast with all that elegant whiteness and latticework.

To begin with, the needle on the radiometer showed 100 milliroentgens per hour, and then steadily crept to the right—200, 300, 500 milliroentgens per hour. Suddenly it shot off the scale. I switched through the ranges. What could that mean? Probably a nuclear gust from the damaged reactor building. A mile or so farther on, the needle dropped again, this time to 700 milliroentgens per hour.

The familiar old sign was now plainly visible in the distance: "Lenin Nuclear Power Station, Chernobyl" with a concrete torch. Beyond that, a concrete sign: "Pripyat, 1970."

**Helicopter taking radiation measurements over the ruins of the
Chernobyl nuclear plant, April 1986.** (Corbis/Bettmann.)

We turned right, past the construction offices and the cement plant, toward
the reactor unit straight ahead and then slightly to the left, in the direction indicated by the concrete arrow, the bridge over the railroad, with Yanov station on the
left, and then into the town of Pripyat, where only recently 50,000 people used to
live. But now . . .

"Volodya, let's go into Pripyat first."

He veered off to the left, accelerated, and soon we were crossing the bridge.
Soon the snow-white town came into view, in the bright sunlight. As the needle on
the radiometer had swung right on the bridge, I began to switch through the
ranges.

"Let's get out of here—fast," I said. "The radioactive cloud passed this way
and did some real damage. Faster!"

We shot over the hump of the bridge and raced into the streets of the dead town. A painful sight met our eyes immediately: the bodies of cats and dogs, everywhere, on the roads, in the yards, on the squares—white, brown, black, and spotted corpses of shot animals.

These sinister sights reminded us that this was an empty, abandoned town, to which normal times would never return. I wondered, nonetheless, why someone did not clean up. After all . . .

"Drive along Lenin Street," I said to Volodya. "It's easier to go by the house where I lived when I worked here."

It was number 9, I remembered.

Down the middle of Lenin Street there were young poplars, already quite tall, and on either side of the street, paths with benches and thick bushes. The imposing building of the Party Committee of Pripyat could be seen at the end of the street. To the right of that was the ten-story Pripyat Hotel, and farther to the right, the jetty on the Pripyat River. Beyond that was a restaurant, and the road to the Lastochka Hotel, where visiting high officials used to stay.

The town looked really strange, as if it was quite early in the morning; but, in fact, it was bright daylight, with the sun high in the sky. Everything was in a deep sleep, from which it could not be awakened. There were household objects and laundry on the balconies and wilted flowers on the window sills. The sun's reflections in some of the windows had an unreal quality; one window had been left open, its curtain hanging out like a dead man's tongue.

"Stop, Volodya. Here, on the right. Slow down."

The needle of the radiometer crept in either direction, from 1 roentgen per hour to 700 milliroentgens per hour.

"Go slow," I asked. "There's my house. That's where I lived, on the second floor. Look how high that mountain ash has grown. Its blossom is all radioactive now. When I was here, it hadn't reached the second floor, but now it's up to the fourth."

The place was empty. The windows were all shuttered, but you could sense that there was no life behind the shutters. They were painfully still. There were some bicycles on the balcony, some boxes, an old refrigerator, skis with red poles. And no sign of life anywhere.

The body of a large black Great Dane with white spots lay across the narrow concrete path across the yard. I asked Volodya to stop nearby so that I could check the radiation level on its coat. He turned so that the left wheels went over a flower bed and stopped. Radiation had darkened the green leaves and made the flowers wilt. The ground and the concrete on the road measured 60 roentgens per hour.

"Look!" said Volodya, pointing to the three-story school building and the large windows of the gymnasium. "My son went there. I remember going to the school hall for special occasions, and all the kids and teachers looking so happy."

Two large but emaciated pigs were running toward us along a narrow path from the school, along the wall of a five-story building. They rushed toward the car and, whimpering, rubbed their snouts against the wheels and the radiator. They had a plaintive, hunted look in their bloodshot eyes, and their movements were shaky and ill coordinated. They were obviously extremely weak.

I held my sensor close to the side of one of the pigs—50 roentgens per hour; and then to the body of the Great Dane—110 roentgens per hour. The pig tried to catch the sensor in its teeth, but I pulled it away in time. The radioactive pigs started to devour the Great Dane. They easily tore off chunks of the partially decomposed flesh, shaking the body and dragging it along the concrete. A swarm of alarmed blue flies flew out of the open mouth and the decaying eyes.

"Just look at those flies! Aren't they something? Radiation has no effect on them! Let's go back, Volodya."

"Where to?"

"To the bridge and then on to the damaged reactor building."

"What if we stall?" said Volodya a second time, with a sly smile.

"If it stalls, you'll start it again," I said, with exactly the same tone. "Let's go."

Once we had turned onto Lenin Street, Volodya asked, "Shall we go in the wrong lane. Or what? We should be over there. Shall we drive round the square?"

"There's no need."

"It feels really funny. People get tickets for things like that."

"See any traffic anywhere?"

Volodya smiled grimly, and we drove quickly past the corpses of cats and dogs, on the wrong side of the road, toward the damaged reactor building. We went really fast over the railroad bridge. The radiometer reading was suddenly very high and then fell again.

We drove along the old road which runs past the power station construction offices, the residential construction plant, the Lisova Peniya restaurant, and the cement works.

On the right we could see the horrendous destruction that had occurred at the No. 4 reactor building. The smashed masonry and the pile of rubble were all severely charred. Streams of gas ionized by radiation were surging upward above the floor of what had once been the central hall, where the reactor was located. Amid the blackened wreckage, the drum-separators, which had been wrenched from their moorings and lifted sideways, looked curiously new and sinister as they reflected the bright rays of the sun.

STUDY QUESTIONS

1. What happened at Chernobyl? What were the immediate environmental consequences?
2. Why were initial reactions often casual?
3. How does an event like Chernobyl fit into twentieth-century Soviet history? How does it fit into world history?
4. Did the Soviet government seem to react vigorously to the disaster? Can and should governments be responsible for preventing such crises?

43

Global Contacts: The Emergence of Multinational Companies

Commercial companies with international activities have been a factor in world history for many centuries. In the postclassical period, Arab merchants knew how to use banks to transfer money from one region of trade to another, and they also used local representatives in their extensive shipping operations. In the early modern period, European companies established representatives in many regions, again to facilitate trade. Thus English merchants might have "factors" stationed in Russia or the Ottoman Empire or India to arrange the transfer of goods and funds. Industrialization added new dimensions to international companies. With more goods to trade, and larger ships to send them in, international commercial ventures proliferated. But many factory centers also found it profitable to set up branch production operations abroad, using their special techniques and know-how to earn profits in several national markets. Even some middle-sized textile firms in northern France, for example, set up operations in Rhode Island and in South America in 1850. Branch operations proliferated after 1870, in industries such as chemicals, agricultural equipment and, soon, automobiles; by this point, United States companies were becoming aggressive, along with British, German, Belgian, and other European ventures, in setting up international trade and production branches.

The post–World War II multinational company was an outgrowth of this historical context, but it had some additional features. In the first place, Japanese and Pacific Rim companies, as well as European and American concerns, were now actively in the game, adding to the complexity of international contacts. In the second place, international connections now meant even more than commercial representation and branch production: they meant relatively easy acquisitions of established companies across national boundaries and setting up specialized manufacturing centers wherever labor conditions and laws provided a particular advantage. Increasingly, products like automobiles were composed of parts made in nine or ten different countries, each division located for best advantage. And these develop-

Selection 1 from "Sony and CBS Records: What a Romance!" *The New York Times*, September 18, 1988, pp. 35–36, 38, 40, 42, 44, 46–47. Selection 2 from Norma Prieto, *Beautiful Flowers of the Maquiladora: Life Histories of Women Workers in Tijuana*. translated by Michael Stone and Gabriella Winkler (Austin: University of Texas Press, 1997), pp. 2–3, 4–5, 11, 16–17, 19–20, 48, 52–53, 91, 95. Reprinted by permission.

ments meant, finally that multinational companies now wielded huge power, often greater than that of many national governments. Their capacity to influence labor conditions, the environment, and even politics grew immensely.

The first of the two selections in this chapter, from a journalistic account, outlines how multinational companies like Japan-based Sony now operate in the international arena. It shows how setbacks in one region—in this case, a "Black Friday" stock market collapse in the United States—can work to the advantage of alert multinationals elsewhere. It shows how easily huge international deals can be made, thanks to modern technology and a clearly international business culture. And it shows how multinationals affect culture as well as the economy.

The second selection involves the other side of the multinational company phenomenon: the worker's side. The passages come from interviews with women Mexican workers, by a Mexican social scientist whose work was first published in 1985. Her focus was on the type of work situation fostered by United States- and Japanese-based multinationals, as they spread operations to Mexico from the 1970s onward.

Multinationals deliberately seek cheap labor (and sometimes limitations on trade unions and lax environmental laws) to manufacture parts for products that may be assembled elsewhere and certainly will be sold in various markets, including those of industrial societies like the United States. The results bring lower prices for consumers and/or larger profits for the companies. They also bring into factory work large numbers of Mexicans, Chinese, Filipinos, and others in societies where manufacturing has advanced but remains less fully developed than in the multinationals' home base. In this passage, dealing with what is called the *maquiladora* industry sponsored by foreign, mainly United States, multinationals (the term *maquiladora* is often not translated, but it has come to mean border factory), Mexican women workers in Tijuana (just south of San Diego, and convenient for reshipping back to the United States) describe their conditions. What is the impact of multinationals on them? Debate rages over precisely this interpretive issue, with some arguing that experience and regular (if low) wages will help places like Mexico set a basis for further development, others arguing that sheer exploitation only holds the society back. Workers themselves report important pluses and minuses and find it difficult to protest, as the passage from the end of the interview suggests. Debate rages also over the resultant impact on places like the United States: Are maquiladora workers taking jobs away from Americans, or do lower prices and greater purchasing power enhance the United States' opportunities?

Finally, the two sides of the multinationals—the tycoon side and the worker side—need to be combined into a judgment about what multinationals are and what impact they have on all societies concerned.

1. SONY AND CBS RECORDS

On the morning of last Oct. 20, Laurence A. Tisch, the president and chief executive officer of CBS, Inc., sat in his office on the 35th floor of Black Rock thinking pessimistic thoughts. In the background, a single television set was tuned to the Financial News Network, which was airing a Wall Street report. Tisch was meeting with a business associate that morning, and their conversation was the conversation that businessmen across the country were having that day, the day after Black Monday, when the stock market collapsed: What could it mean?

Mr. Tisch believed he knew its meaning, and it was bleak. It meant a whole new ball game, he said: investors' attitudes would be changed forever. "Business in the United States," Tisch darkly concluded, "will never be the same again."

Six thousand miles away, in a corporate office in Tokyo, where it was late evening, a starkly different mood prevailed. At the headquarters of Sony, the giant international electronics firm, there was an air of excitement and anticipation, and for Sony executives, a feeling approaching triumph. To them, as a senior Sony official later put it, "Black Monday was a very fortunate day." After 13 months of frustration, Sony's quest to acquire CBS Records, the largest record company in the world, was near fruition. Sony's man in America was on the phone, telling them that Tisch had decided, finally and firmly, to sell.

For more than a month, Sony's latest offer to meet Tisch's price—a staggering $2 billion, fattened from an original bid of $1.25 billion—had sat on the table, sniffed over and pondered by a CBS board of directors that was reluctant to part with a cherished piece of CBS's legacy nearly as old as the company itself. The hesitancy largely reflected the ambivalence of William S. Paley, the CBS founder who bought Columbia Records, the flagship label of what became CBS Records, in 1938, and had spoken of it, even half a century later, as "my baby." But this was business, and $2 billion was a rich price. Tisch, the tough-minded investor who was running CBS now, wanted the deal; Black Monday was the convincer.

And so, the deal was done, and CBS Records—pioneer of the LP, repository of the great Broadway musical recordings from "My Fair Lady" to "A Chorus Line," recording home of Michael Jackson and Billy Joel, Barbra Streisand and Bruce Springsteen and Cyndi Lauper—passed into Japanese hands. It was the first Japanese jumbo acquisition of an American company, and the transaction made headlines. But the story of Sony's acquisition of CBS Records is much more than that.

It is a story of Larry Tisch's drastic transformation of Bill Paley's CBS, and of a bitter personality clash, between the colorful, free-wheeling head of CBS Records, Walter R. Yetnikoff, and Tisch, the cost-conscious corporate president. And, in the end, it is a story of two profoundly different business and cultural philosophies— the investor orientation of Tisch, with its focus on stock price and earnings (familiar thinking in American business culture in the 1980's), and the longer-term strategy of Sony, which hoped for a deal that history, if not Wall Street, would admire. Tisch was selling off pieces of CBS, and building a pile of cash; Sony wanted a marriage of hardware and software that would still be paying off in the next century. Stock management on one side, company management on the other.

A year later, both sides are delighted with the deal. Tisch is happy because the sale brought CBS "increased earnings per share, and at the same time removed the risk in a business that is both cyclical and can be hazardous." Akio Morita, the 67-year-old co-founder and chairman of Sony, on the other hand, looks past the short-term risks and stock values to the day that Sony's ownership of the world's biggest record company will give its hardware innovations an irresistible edge in the marketplace. "Twenty years from now," Morita says, "history will prove us right." . . .

[In November 1986], Michael P. Schulhof, vice chairman of Sony's American operations and a pilot, landed the Sony jet at Teterboro Airport in New Jersey after a flight from California. At the airport, he telephoned his office for messages and was told that he'd received an urgent call from Walter Yetnikoff. He called Yetnikoff, and the record executive told him that he'd been authorized by Tisch to find a buyer for CBS Records. Yetnikoff said that he'd tried to work out a leveraged buyout on his own and was ready to give up on that. Would Sony be interested? "The deal is $1.25 billion for CBS Records," Yetnikoff told Schulhof, plus a side deal that would keep Yetnikoff and his management team in place. As Yetnikoff put it that day: "Fifty million dollars for me and the *mishpocheh*"—the family. There was some urgency, Yetnikoff said; the CBS board was meeting in two days.

The phone call didn't totally surprise Schulhof. He'd known Yetnikoff for several years and had heard him complain about Tisch's style of management—that no one on the corporate side of CBS cared about the records division, that CBS in the Tisch era was obsessed with costs and indifferent to "managing creative talent," as Yetnikoff put it. Yetnikoff wanted out from under his new boss, and if his own leveraged buyout wasn't workable, then Sony was the natural buyer; the electronics giant could easily come up with the cash, and besides, it had the inside track on CBS Records. For 20 years, CBS/Sony, a joint venture between the two companies, had operated in Tokyo. Walter Yetnikoff, then a young CBS lawyer, had drafted that deal in 1967. He knew the Sony people and liked them, and the sentiment appeared to be mutual.

Schulhof recalls standing at the Teterboro Airport and thinking, "This is a once-in-a-lifetime opportunity, and we ought to make a quick decision, which is not something the Japanese companies are known for. . . . " He was certain, however, that Sony wanted the deal. For one thing, there was the joint venture, which was far more than just a corporate backwater to Sony. Beginning in 1968 with $1 million from each company, it had, without any further capital investment, grown to produce sales of $730 million and more than $100 million in pretax profits last year. The value of the property owned by CBS/Sony in land-squeezed Tokyo was incalculable. If CBS Records were going to get a new corporate parent, Sony had more than a passing interest.

But more compellingly, there was Sony's dream for the future: the marriage of software—the records, tapes and compact disks that are the business of CBS Records—and hardware—the equipment that consumers play them on, which is Sony's core business. Sony had learned a hard lesson in the 1970's with Betamax, its videotape player, which lost its war with the "other" format, VCR. Although Beta was widely deemed a superior product, it turned out that consumers didn't much care; the VCR, marketed by a group of other companies, was cheaper, and viewers were interested in seeing programs, not technology. Had Sony owned a movie studio, it could have fed the marketplace movies in the Beta format exclusively, and the result might have been different. (With an eye toward future technologies, Sony is, in fact, reportedly contemplating a studio purchase).

In the consumer electronics business, the fundamental imperative is to keep coming up with new technology—the Sony "Walkman" portable stereo, for example. Now, with several other companies, Sony is developing the digital audio tape recorder. The D.A.T., as it is called, is a computerized recording system capable of rendering near-perfect sound. In late 1986, Sony began to envision how much easier it would be to sell the new system if it were linked to the catalogue of music belonging to the world's largest record company. "Software and hardware," says Norio Ohga, Sony's president and C.E.O., "are two wheels of the same cart."

So Sony was definitely interested, but Schulhof would have to act quickly. Still at Teterboro Airport, where it was 7 P.M., Schulhof called Tokyo, where the work day was beginning, and told Morita and Ohga of the development. Twenty minutes later, he called Yetnikoff back: CBS had a deal if it wanted it.

Sony, innocent in the ways of big-time mergers and acquisitions, knew that it would need help. Schulhof called on a new "boutique" merchant banking firm, The Blackstone Group, headed by a former co-C.E.O. of the Lehman Brothers investment banking firm and United States Secretary of Commerce, Peter G. Peterson, and Stephan A. Schwarzman, an acquaintance of Schulhof's. The next morning, the two dealmakers met with Schulhof and Sony's lawyer, Paul Burak, at the Mayfair Regent hotel on Park Avenue. They discussed the ramifications of the acquisition, and concluded that the first order of business was to make a deal with Yetnikoff. It was by then 9:30 A.M., but Schulhof knew that Yetnikoff, a late riser, would still be at home, so the four men got in their cars and were driven the few blocks to Yetnikoff's home on East 56th Street. After an hour, they had their deal with management.

It was all new and strange for Sony, both because of the size of the transaction and the haste that it required. Even Yetnikoff was startled by how fast things were moving—"I thought maybe I didn't ask for enough money," he later joked. But what happened next seemed little short of bizarre. The management deal set, Yetnikoff, still in his bathrobe, called Tisch. The others in the room watched as a look of concern came over his face; something was clearly wrong. Peterson, who knew Tisch, asked to speak with him, but it was too late; Tisch had hung up. Yetnikoff then broke the bad news. Tisch had spoken to board members, but was hesitant to say anything until the board met formally the next day.

The following afternoon, Tisch called Morita, who by pure coincidence was in New York City at the time. Tisch wanted the deal, but Paley didn't; some on the board had been shocked when Tisch presented the idea in an informal meeting the night before.

The Sony brass was dumb founded. Was this the way Americans did big deals? "I was so surprised," says Norio Ohga. "The head of the company said they would sell to us. Then we start to negotiate, and the board of the company said, 'No-no-no, this is just Mr. Tisch's idea.' It was a very unusual circumstance. We have never seen such a thing. The president wanted to sell, but not the board. . . . Such a headache!" . . .

In the meantime, Sony remained patient. In New York, Schulhof, with Tisch's approval, quietly went to work on Paley, arranging a series of private meetings. . . . Tisch was once again ready to push for a sale.

Schulhof got Tisch's call on a Monday morning, as he was preparing to fly to Tokyo for routine Sony meetings. Tisch said it was important, so Schulhof found Peter Peterson and went to see Tisch, who told the two that he'd decided on a new price. "If you're willing to offer $2 billion for this company, I'll sell it to you," Schulhof quotes Tisch as saying. Schulhof says that he expressed reservations about Paley's willingness, and Tisch answered, "Don't worry, I'll talk to Bill. I'll convince him this is in the interest of the shareholders." The CBS financial officer, Fred Meyer, came up with the record division's profits and loss statements and projections, and Schulhof had them sent to Japan by satellite facsimile, then boarded a plane for Tokyo. Again, haste was of the essence; the CBS board was to meet two days later.

When Schulhof arrived in Tokyo, it was the evening of the next day, a holiday in Japan. Still, he found Morita, Ohga and several members of the board awaiting him at Sony headquarters. Yetnikoff, who was in Japan for Michael Jackson's tour, also stopped by. They discussed Tisch's new price, a hefty jump from Sony's last offer. Yetnikoff thought it was too much money. But the yen was by then worth significantly more dollars, and Morita, sensing that Tisch's price was not negotiable, finally gave the approval. Schulhof telephoned Tisch in New York, where it was by now the morning of the CBS board meeting, and said, "O.K., we'll meet your price."

This time, the Japanese were confident that they had a deal. Still, Schulhof suggested it would be a good idea for Morita to make a personal call to Paley, one pioneer to another. Morita made the call, telling his old acquaintance that he understood how hard this must be for him, but that Sony was in the best position to care for the company Paley had nurtured. Morita offered Paley a place in the new company, as honorary chairman, and he said that Sony would make a contribution in Paley's name to his pet project, the Museum of Broadcasting. Then, the Sony group retired for the night.

The next morning, they reassembled, eager to hear the results of the CBS board meeting. Yetnikoff was designated to make the call to Tisch.

Again, Sony was in for a shock. Tisch said the board hadn't made up its mind on a sale, and what's more, it wanted to commission an outside consulting firm to assess the future of the record business. The decision had been postponed for at least another month. . . .

Then, five days after the CBS board had for the third time refused Sony's offer, Sony got lucky: the stock market crashed. Suddenly, Tisch's spinoff idea didn't look very good; who would buy the stock? For that matter, it occurred to him that maybe Sony would no longer be willing to pay the $2 billion. . . .

In Tokyo, Morita made the decision to go ahead with the deal. While Black Monday may have been significant to Tisch, the investor, Morita was unmoved. "If it was worth $2 billion to us a week ago," he told his associates, "it is worth $2 billion now."

The deal was done.

With the announcement of Sony's purchase of CBS Records, some in the record industry lamented the selling of a part of American culture to the Japanese. "We're obviously very disappointed that a great American record company with a very strong history in the business has been sold to a foreign company," a Warner's executive told The Wall Street Journal. One columnist wrote of the Japanese, "They make good cars, TV sets, tractors. But will they, or the executives they hire, know another Duke Ellington when they hear one?"

Some inside CBS feared a dramatic culture change at the company, an invasion of Japanese executives sent from the home base. But so far, there has been virtually no change at CBS Records. The only Japanese have been Sony accountants, acquainting themselves with the record company's accounting system.

Indeed, by most accounts, life at CBS Records has improved under Sony's hand. For example, now that the company is a tenant in the CBS building, the floors are cleaned regularly (the janitorial staff had been pared on one of Tisch's cutbacks, but if you lease, you get special services). As for Yetnikoff, he is the happiest of all, and understandably so. One of his first acts under Sony was to replace the president of CBS Records, Alvin N. Teller, with one of his old pals, Tommy Mottola, who had headed a successful management office. Mottola and three other new senior executives were given a rich deal that Yetnikoff insists wouldn't have been possible under Tisch.

What's more, Yetnikoff is now personally secure. He has a multiyear deal with Sony that will pay him $20 million. Earlier this year, he went to a Jaguar dealership and ordered a 1988 Vanden Plas, the top of the line. When the salesman asked what options Yetnikoff wanted, he replied, "All of them." And, there is a new toy in his office—a model of the corporate jet, a Falcon 900, that Sony has agreed to buy for Yetnikoff.

On the other hand, there looms an issue that may bring the beneficence of Sony's stewardship into question: the matter of digital audio tape. Sony helped create the new, advanced sound system, but its marketing in the United States has been passionately opposed by record companies—with CBS Records leading the opposition. They argue that the near-perfect reproduction capability of D.A.T. will encourage pirating of tapes and disks, costing the industry (and recording artists) millions in lost royalties. Yetnikoff insists that he is not worried, and that now that Sony owns a record company, it would not do anything to hurt its interests.

But it is clear that Sony intends for D.A.T. to have its day. Morita, the engineer who built the giant hardware company, becomes nearly dreamy when discussing the new technology. "Digital sound," he says, "is the first innovation since Edison invented the phonograph." Schulhof, too, suggests its inevitability: "Eventually, there will be a digital replacement for compact cassettes."

Even Yetnikoff allows that there is a conflict between his view that Sony will protect CBS Records from the evils of D.A.T. and Sony's expressed strategy of teaming hardware with software. "Yes, it is somewhat inconsistent, yes, I acknowledge that," he says. "On the other hand, since they have spent a lot of money on this company, they're not going to do something to screw it up. Because we are so close, maybe we can find a common solution. I can use them to talk to the hardware people and they can use me to talk to the software people."

In the matter of D.A.T., as with the CBS Records deal itself, Sony seems prepared to wait for the proper moment. "I'm not in a rush," Morita says. "You know, sometimes American people are rushing. Always they say, 'We have no time.' But business has to continue a long, long time. So, it doesn't have to be this year. I'm very patient."

2. MAQUILADORA WORKERS

Angela, on Managers

Angelita paused for a breath: "Really, thank God he switched us back, because it was a killer to work all night and get home just in time to make breakfast and clean the house, before trying to get some sleep with all the daytime racket."

Ángela was grateful to the manager. She associated the North Americans with the good and the humane. At various times she has commented to me that they should replace all the Mexican supervisors with North Americans, because the latter are much better. Many female factory workers shared this notion. In their opinion, the Mexicans were tyrants, good-for-nothings. The women concurred in viewing the North Americans as more responsible, more considerate, and, above all, more appreciative and considerate of women. As one observed, "We have never had North American supervisors, but I know that they're better because those who have been to the factory, the engineers and the coordinators, are very nice people."

The workers at Ángela's plant once proposed to the manager that he replace all the Mexican supervisors with North Americans. He smiled at the flattery of his North American pride. "Let's see what we can do," he responded, but nothing changed. Clearly, the firm has no interest in changing supervisors. It is necessary to maintain the reputation of the considerate North American, but the supervisor, as an intermediary representing the owners' interests, can rarely afford to be considerate. Besides, a North American supervisor would earn a very high salary, paid in dollars. . . .

Angela, on Work and Pay

I lasted seven years assembling cassettes, and I was doing the same thing for hours, days, and years. I got so tired that I asked for a transfer. I was so exhausted that I felt like my lungs were collapsing. At times I arrived home crying from the pain. I went to a private doctor and he told me I was very tired, that the best thing would be to rest a bit, although he knew that I couldn't stop working. He said that if I continued working, my lungs were going to collapse. They ignored my complaints at Social Security. They said there was nothing wrong with me, and then sent me back home without doing anything. They never even took an X ray to see what was going on with me. . . .

In the factory's good times we were sixteen hundred women making cassettes. There was a lot of competition among us, and none of us wanted to let up. We ate in ten minutes instead of the fifty minutes the company allowed, because we were interested in making more cassettes than our counterparts. I had a very good record; they took all the women on our line out to eat a number of times as a prize for having been the most productive group. During that period I never felt any aches and pains, and I didn't feel exhausted. Initially, I earned $18.99 a week, then $26.50, $36.00, and $56.00. Then, after the devaluation, we began to be paid in pesos. We were all very angry because we preferred to be paid in dollars, but the company said it was not convenient.

Gabriela, on Health Conditions

The room still lacks good fans, and the ones they have often don't work at all. I don't know how the *muchachas* keep working there, because neither the general conditions nor the safety measures have been improved in the least. Surely, they are going to suffer the same problems that I did. That work with acids is very exacting and dangerous, because if you don't mix the chemicals properly, they can explode. Everything has to be done by the book, using precise measures. Despite the hazardous nature of the work, and the fact that you must be specially trained to do it, they pay the same as for any other job, and they fail to recognize its critical importance.

One time there was an explosion and two co-workers were burned. Fortunately, their clothing was stripped off right away and they were washed down, which kept them from being badly burned. If the chemicals had gotten on them, even one drop in the eyes, they would have been blinded. One of the safety measures that we did have was goggles, but we rarely used them because they made us so hot, as the room has no ventilation. . . .

Alma, on Pay and Product

I had been working for six years in a textile maquiladora, where I nearly destroyed my kidneys and my eyes. I never earned a fixed salary. They paid me by the job, on a piecework basis, as they also call it. In this maquiladora here, we work quite differently from the way they do in other textile plants. . . .

The dresses we make are beautiful, for very fashionable women. They're incredibly expensive! They sell them in the best stores in the United States and they cost $200 or $300. And what do we get? We make 45 pesos [about U.S. $1.00] per dress. Incredible, don't you think? We spend ten hours a day in front of a sewing machine to make a man rich and we don't even know him. And the worst of it is that we continue doing it, some not even making the minimum wage, without complaining, asleep at the wheel, watching time go by, years in front of the sewing machine. I recognize the glares, I know how we protest on the inside because we don't dare say anything to the bosses. We wait for the quitting bell to ring so we can hit the street, believing that it's all a bad dream, and that it's going to change. It's like we put these thoughts aside for a moment and go back to work, without doing anything more about it. At times we forget why the devil we're working, just waiting for a little bit of money so our kids can survive.

You get used to it all, or at least we pretend to. At times we let ourselves be carried away by the noise or the music of the radios we all carry. It helps us forget the fatigue and the back pain we all have working in front of the sewing machine. The moment came when I just couldn't take any more and I quit, knowing that the money my husband makes, together with what our oldest daughter gives us, wasn't going to be enough.

Elena and Gabriela, on Conditions

I was very apprehensive about going to work in a maquiladora. I preferred to find work as a domestic. I always thought that the plants could easily catch fire, because they're full of electric wires, machines, and other things. Still, I decided to go to work there because I needed the money.

At first when I arrived in Tijuana, the girls I knew told me about the maquiladoras and they urged me to go to work with them. They told me, "Here they pay you every week, you get health benefits, and you know lots of people; it's not like domestic work!" I had never been inside a factory, but I had an idea of what they were like, because I had seen some in the movies and on television.

The picture I had about the maquiladoras was pretty close to reality. When I went inside, I saw that the place was pretty old. It was like a refurbished warehouse with a tin roof. Oh, the dreams I have of that cursed tin roof. It's wretched! Here in Tijuana the climate is very extreme, so in winter the factory is freezing, and in summer it's an inferno. . . .

The plants don't have any windows. It's just walls on all sides, so the lights and ventilation are artificial. In winter it gets dark very early, so we enter and leave work in darkness; we go for days without seeing the sun. It's like another world. I know that working for so many hours under artificial light is bad for the eyes, most of all because the lights are so poor. At times everything looks yellow because the light is so low. It really irritates me! What would it cost them to put in some more lights? I don't get it. In the factory where my sister works everything is very clean and well lit. It's a new factory, really big, with a very nice atmosphere. What we would give to have such a nice place to work. If one is obliged to work, at least it could be nice and clean, with the best conditions.

Where I work, there's only one fan for the entire department of sixty workers. The environment is oppressive from bad ventilation; the air is full of gas from arsenic and other chemicals whose names I don't know, because we just distinguish them by the color keys they come marked with. . . .

Maria Luisa, on Urban Life

I didn't know anything about Tijuana. I had never been in a city. I had never left the village, and the village wasn't very big! So it was quite an experience to go to Mazatlán and take the train. Everything seemed beautiful to me.

I got to Tijuana and I couldn't pronounce a lot of words. I couldn't pronounce "carpet," or "linoleum," or "newspaper." I didn't even know these things existed. The old lady's niece told me, "You don't say it like that! You say it this way." She taught me how to pronounce the words correctly. I was really taken with TV because I had never seen it. I had seen movies, because there was a man who brought them to show in the village. I had only seen movies, that was it. But I had never imagined there could be this little box, you turn it on, and there are people talking. I really liked TV. It's very entertaining! . . .

Angela, on Factory Life Compared with Village Work and the Domination of an Abusive Husband

It might seem like I exaggerate, but it gave me a great sense of happiness to start working at the maquiladora; I thought I had overcome my past. It was the moment in which God heard my prayers and changed my life. I could forget what was behind me. That part of my life was so very difficult that on one occasion I threw myself in front of a car, and on another I took a bunch of pills. What I wanted was to die.

Obdulia, on Hopes

I hope that my son is successful in his studies and becomes a doctor. He's been at it for a year and a half, and I'm going to help him so he can continue. Being a doctor must be an excellent career; anyway it's better to work on your own account than to be under a supervisor's thumb all day long.

Gabriela, on a Plant Strike

We workers were affected by the devaluation, but for the owners it was a great deal. Here in Tijuana, and generally along the entire border, we have to buy a lot of American products—basic necessities—with prices marked in dollars. Every time there is a devaluation we buy fewer products; every time we poor people become poorer, and the rich become richer.

During the strike the manager tried to bribe the union membership, offering money and better salaries on the condition the people leave the union. After ten days of striking, the Board of Conciliation and Arbitration [Junta de Conciliación y Arbitraje] declared the strike null and void.

The first day of February 1983 they closed the plant permanently. They fooled us good. We were all demoralized: the state government, the American owners, and the Mexican manager had united to do us in. They stopped at nothing to destroy the union. We pressured the Board of Conciliation and Arbitration to secure compensation, and after fighting around the clock, they gave us only 70 percent of what we were owed.

STUDY QUESTIONS

1. Why did it make sense for a major Japanese company to buy CBS Records? Why did Sony think it needed an American, rather than another Japanese, company?
2. What were the potential bonds between the industry giants Morita and Paley? Why did the U.S. government help facilitate this deal?
3. How was a company like Sony able to be so adept in dealing with American concerns—in CBS, in the U.S. government—as part of its purchase campaign?
4. How do modern technologies facilitate deals like the Sony–CBS Records deal? How do modern cultural contacts, between countries like the United States and Japan, also facilitate deals in culturally dependent businesses like the record industry?
5. Were there any particular international impediments in the way of this deal? Was the deal much different from a major business purchase deal within a single country?
6. How do maquiladora workers and their conditions compare with those of workers in industrialized societies? Why do multinationals locate facilities in places like Tijuana?
7. What are the main advantages and disadvantages of working for a multinational in Mexico? Are most workers basically contented or discontented, and why?
8. What is the Mexican government's policy toward multinationals in Tijuana?
9. Are multinational business operations good, bad, or indifferent for individual nations such as the United States, Japan, and Mexico? Is the answer basically the same for each country? How might the answer vary, depending on the social group involved *within* each nation?